BALZAC CRITICISM
IN FRANCE
1850–1900

BALZAC CRITICISM
IN FRANCE
1850–1900

The Making of a Reputation

by

DAVID BELLOS

CLARENDON PRESS · OXFORD
1976

Oxford University Press, Ely House, London W.1

GLASGOW NEW YORK TORONTO MELBOURNE WELLINGTON
CAPE TOWN IBADAN NAIROBI DAR ES SALAAM LUSAKA ADDIS ABABA
DELHI BOMBAY CALCUTTA MADRAS KARACHI LAHORE DACCA
KUALA LUMPUR SINGAPORE HONG KONG TOKYO

ISBN 0 19 815530 1

© *Oxford University Press 1976*

*Printed in Great Britain by
Butler & Tanner Ltd, Frome and London*

'... we should realise that in the realm of the mind, as in every other, there is no such thing as an iron necessity for affairs to follow a certain course ...'

Levin L. Schücking, *The Sociology of Literary Taste*

Acknowledgements

THE research on which this book is based was originally done for a thesis supervised by Dr. Bruce Tolley, whose erudition and intelligent guidance were of invaluable help. I should like to thank the President and Fellows of Magdalen College, Oxford and the Board of Trustees of the Heath Harrison Scholarship for their support and assistance.

The present book was written at the University of Edinburgh, and I should like to thank the Travel and Research Committee and the Postgraduate Studies Committee for the help they have given me.

It is impossible to mention all those who have contributed in one way or another to whatever qualities this book may have: but M. Roger Pierrot, of the Bibliothèque nationale, Dr. Alan Raitt, and Dr. Robert Shackleton have my especial gratitude for their suggestions, corrections, and criticisms.

Edinburgh
December 1974

DAVID BELLOS

Contents

Abbreviations

AB	*L'Année balzacienne.*
ALUB	*Annales littéraires de l'Université de Besançon.*
BN	Bibliothèque nationale.
Éd. déf.	H. de Balzac, *Œuvres complètes,* édition définitive (Calmann-Lévy, 1869–71).
HOB	Charles Spœlberch de Lovenjoul, *Histoire des Œuvres de Balzac,* 3rd edition (Calmann-Lévy, 1886).
Lov.	Bibliothèque Spœlberch de Lovenjoul, Chantilly.
MLR	*Modern Language Review.*
n.d.	no date given.
n.t.	no title.
Pl.	H. de Balzac, *La Comédie humaine* (Biliothèque de la Pléiade, 1951–64).
RDM	*La Revue des deux mondes.*
RDP	*La Revue de Paris.*
repr.	Reprinted.
RHLF	*La Revue d'histoire littéraire de la France.*
RSH	*La Revue des sciences humaines.*

Note on Place of Publication

The place of publication of books and journals referred to in the footnotes and appendices is Paris, unless otherwise stated.

Introduction

I GENERAL INTRODUCTION

THIS book describes the ways in which the critical reputation of
Honoré de Balzac changed in the fifty years that followed his death
in 1850. At the start of this period he was a notorious novelist of the
second rank; by the end of it, he was a classic, firmly established in the
canon of great writers alongside Molière and Shakespeare. Since one
may not simply assume that the real value of his *Comédie humaine* only
became apparent as the century grew older and wiser, we have to find
some way of accounting for the radically different evaluations made
of the same unchanging texts over these decades. Consequently, although much of this book is historical and descriptive, it is also concerned with the general nature of novel-criticism in nineteenth-century
France, and with the elaboration of methods appropriate to the study
of reputations as dynamic elements in the history of literary phenomena.

Balzac's literary activity spanned three decades, from 1820 to 1850,
but it was not until the publication of *La Peau de chagrin* in 1831 that
he made any stir in the world of letters. He became a literary celebrity
almost overnight, rather like Lucien de Rubempré, the hero of *Illusions
perdues* (1837–43), whose eye-catching review of *L'Alcade dans
l'embarras*[1] is a pastiche of the opening paragraph of Jules Janin's review of *La Peau de chagrin*.[2] Yet what Balzac acquired, like Lucien
in the novel, was not a solid reputation but a fickle notoriety. The injustice of contemporary critics and journalists towards the *Comédie
humaine* has been deplored many times,[3] and has been ascribed in
large measure to motives of a personal nature. The vindictiveness of
many of the reviews written in the 1830s and 1840s is indeed rather
shocking: many of the attacks on Balzac's personal foibles were almost
libellous. The early course of Balzac's reputation is none the less
relevant to its later development. Unjust and libellous criticism cannot
be dismissed simply because it now appears wrong. On the other

---

[1] *Pl.* IV. 729–30.   [2] *L'Artiste,* 14 Aug. 1831.

[3] By Asseline, Baudelaire, Zola, Bourget in the last century; by nearly every biographer
in this century.

hand, it would be unwise to base any generalizations about novel-criticism on this sort of material, for changes in evaluations and in the detail of argument were closely related to changes in the personal relationship between critic and author. Jules Janin and Philarète Chasles, for example, were friends of the novelist in 1831 but personal enemies ten years later; and their critical views fully reflect this personal change. A full study of Balzac's reputation in the 1830s and 1840s would be a mostly biographical narrative, charting the novelist's friendships and enmities, critics' loyalties and obligations, and the editorial policies of different newspapers and journals. Such a story would be entertaining and instructive, but it would contribute only a little to the real aim of this book—to describe and understand how Balzac's lasting reputation as a classic was made.

When Balzac died in August 1850, personal animosities and friendships did not die with him. Indeed, for some critics, particularly Sainte-Beuve and Barbey d'Aurevilly, they became deeper and more entrenched. However, the vitiating element of biography is necessarily absent after 1850, and no changes of argument or evaluation can be ascribed to changes in personal relationships. A host of other incidental and non-literary factors continue to weigh upon the content of what was written about Balzac, of course, but reasons must be found either within what the novelist had written or within what had been written about him to account for the applicability of these factors. Many of these external factors—such as political changes, developments in secondary and higher education, and the beginnings of literary scholarship—had a bearing on criticism as a whole, and not on Balzac's reputation alone. Thus the reason for making the obituary notices that appeared in August 1850 the notional starting-point for this study of Balzac's reputation is very simple. His posthumous life is a richer, more important, and more interesting subject than an unravelling of his relationships with critics during his own lifetime.

Much of this book is taken up with the evidence of who said what and when. Some of the material is new, and some of it has been presented before, mostly by Bernard Weinberg in one chapter of his thesis on *French Realism: The Critical Reaction, 1830–70.*[4] Unlike Weinberg, however, I have not set out to find 'periods' in Balzac's reputation, nor to link these with changes in 'taste'. It seems un-

---

[4] New York, 1937. See also Michel Raimond, 'Balzac vu par les romanciers français de Zola à Proust', unpublished thesis (1966), Sorbonne Library, Paris.

reasonable to invoke a change in 'period' or in 'public taste' as an *explanation* for changes in critical arguments and evaluations, when these arguments and evaluations themselves constitute the principal evidence that a change of period or taste has taken place.

The general hypothesis which underlies the argument of this book might be termed a global one. The assumption is made that no expressed opinion of a literary work is completely 'unprimed' or naïve. Individual genius, originality, and insight are qualities in criticism that can only be grasped by the historian against the context of other, more standard appreciations; moreover, these qualities only exist in relationship to other criticism written both before and after. Any reading of Balzac, and *a fortiori* any expressed opinion of his works, however original, is primed by all or part of what had been written about him up to that point (and by what was said, if we could only know it). Therefore one can conceive an underlying system consisting of all the statements made at any given point in time in connection with our author. Some of these statements contradict others: thus rules can be imagined which would account for the ways in which the statements had actually been combined in different appreciations of the novelist and his works; a table could be constructed to indicate which combinations occurred with a favourable interpretation, and which with a hostile view. The underlying system is an abstraction of Balzac criticism; the actual content of the statements which constitute it are the 'themes' of Balzac criticism. The evidence shows that these themes were few in number and, perhaps surprisingly, increased only slightly in the fifty years of critical writing between 1850 and 1900. What also becomes readily apparent is that any given theme of criticism possesses no particular valency in itself. That is to say, no concrete statement about the *Comédie humaine* can be said to represent on its own a favourable or an unfavourable assessment of the work. For example, the minuteness of apparently observed detail in Balzac's descriptions of people and places is a theme of hostile and favourable criticism alike from the 1830s to the 1890s, as is the contradictory statement that his descriptions are gross and bold exaggerations of the real world. Value-judgements are associated with combinations of this, or any other, theme with a second one—for example, that Balzac makes no moral judgement of his fictional characters. The combination of the latter theme with the statement that Balzac was accurately observant of physical detail has a favourable valency in the later 1850s and after; combined with the view that the novelist's descriptions are exaggerated, it is typical of unfavourable assessments from the 1840s to the 1860s. 'Change' in Balzac criticism does not then mean a change in 'public taste' or a movement from one ill-defined 'period' to another. It comes to mean a change in the possible combinations of existing themes; or a change in the valency of existing combinations. More rarely, it may mean the addition of an entirely new theme to the stock of possible statements about Balzac, such as those created by the publication of the novels of Flaubert and Zola.

The general framework sketched out here is argued more fully in Chapter 3. It is an approach that has grown out of the very specific material dealt with in this book, but it has a number of wider applications. It would appear to offer an escape from the circular argument of most descriptions of change in the history of cultural ideas; moreover, it is an approach that need not be restricted to studies of the reputations of individual writers, nor indeed to the nineteenth century. Just as the underlying system of Balzac criticism could be thought of as made up of a number of overlapping, partial Balzac criticisms, so it could be seen in its turn as an overlapping part of a novel-criticism and indeed of a similarly hypothetical literary criticism of the same era. This method opens up the possibility of a coherent, non-circular, and global description of the development of ideas about literature.

One objection to a global approach is that it relies on knowledge that is not global. Although the Bibliography lists over one thousand books and articles on Balzac that appeared (mostly in Paris) in the period in question, it would be rash to claim that it is complete. The material on which this account is based can only be considered a sample, and it cannot be known what the relationship of size is between the sample and what a statistician would call the 'total universe' of actual Balzac criticism. The details of the method used in compiling the material can be found in the Foreword to Appendix III on page 201. It is unlikely that any new material to be found would alter the arguments of this book to any very great extent, but even more unlikely that there is no further material to be found at all.

One further disadvantage of the approach used in this book is that it is more or less inapplicable to a small body of material, such as Balzac criticism in 1830 or even 1835. Only historical hindsight allows us to perceive patterns of significance in the early reviews of the novels that were to be included in the *Comédie humaine*, but this material must none the less be looked at in order to build up a picture of the critical themes present in 1850. Consequently, a fairly traditional and chronological method of exposition will be used in the following pages, which give introductory, but necessary, background information on Balzac criticism before 1850.

II   THE MAIN TRENDS OF BALZAC CRITICISM
BEFORE 1850

In the 1820s Balzac published several novels under different pseudonyms, but virtually no critical attention was paid to them. Later on, in 1834, Sainte-Beuve and others commented on these *œuvres de jeunesse*, but almost certainly without knowledge of the few reviews that had appeared originally.[1]

Le Dernier Chouan appeared in 1829 under Balzac's own name, and received a few rather insignificant reviews. In an article that appeared the following year, however, Anselme Petetin distinguished himself from these lukewarm commentators by describing this romantic tale of political intrigue as 'une œuvre très-supérieure à toute la littérature marchande dont nous sommes inondés'.[2] Since the novel was a historical fiction, set in the year 1800 amidst the local colour of Brittany, the militantly Romantic *Mercure de France au XIXe siècle* used *Le Dernier Chouan* as another prop for its own polemics, and it was to this, rather than to Balzac's work, that opponents of the new school were reacting.[3]

The following year saw the publication of the first *Scènes de la vie privée*, a collection of five short stories about marriage in a contemporary setting. For one critic, Balzac was at the same time 'un auteur de la littérature nouvelle', and guilty of overlong expositions and of 'trop de longueurs dans les scènes qui ne sont pas directement liées à l'action'.[4] The book was attacked by *Le Corsaire* out of factional hostility,[5] but the criticism made in *Le Globe*—that the stories lacked an overall message, or 'idée mère'—derived from the Saint-Simonian ideology for which that newspaper spoke.[6]

The fanfare of laudatory reviews that greeted the appearance of *La Peau de chagrin* in 1831 had been prepared to some extent at least by Balzac himself. Through his journalistic activity in the preceding

---

[1] See P. Barbéris, *Aux Sources de Balzac* (Les Bibliophiles de l'Originale, 1965) for an account of the reception of the early works.

[2] *La Revue encyclopédique*, Mar. 1830, p. 727.

[3] See P. Barbéris, 'L'Accueil critique aux premières grandes œuvres de Balzac', *AB* (1967), 51–72 and (1968), 165–95.

[4] *Le Sylphe*, 29 Apr. 1830.   [5] Issue of 8 May 1830.

[6] Issue of 25 June 1830.

two years, he had acquired a number of friends and contacts among the fashionable reviewers of the day and had become a minor celebrity on the fringes of the literary world. Whatever the reasons for this favourable reception were, however, *La Peau de chagrin* made Balzac's name well known, and he was treated subsequently as a writer of some stature.

Two critics who were close friends of the novelist in 1831, Jules Janin and Philarète Chasles, made much of the modernity of *La Peau de chagrin*, and saw its hero, Raphaël de Valentin, as a character of social significance.[7] For Émile Deschamps, the modernity of the novel lay in what he called its 'rhythm'.[8] The more staid reviewers in the major newspapers of both left and right also read the novel as a criticism of modern society, but they censured it for not providing any positive remedies.[9] Similarly, the religious thinker Montalembert, who devoted a long and sympathetic article to Balzac's novel, saw it as evidence of the need for 'un pain nouveau'—a spiritual solution to social and political problems.[10]

Balzac brought out a number of major works in the following three years: *Louis Lambert* (1832), *Les Contes drolatiques* (1832, 1833), *Le Médecin de campagne* (1833), *Eugénie Grandet* (1833). They attracted a considerable amount of attention, which remained predominantly favourable. In 1834, Balzac became worthy of a full-length article by the acknowledged authority on literary taste, Charles-Augustin Sainte-Beuve. For a new writer whose reputation was barely three years old, this marked a particularly rapid rise to a certain kind of eminence.

Sainte-Beuve's study, in its original form,[11] gives a general impression of detached benevolence. Of course, the critic made many amendments in later years which changed the whole tone of the article,[12] but there is no suggestion that he was not trying to be impartial in 1834.

Balzac's use of language is here criticized in detail for the first time.

[7] *Le Messager des Chambres*, 6 Aug. 1831 (Chasles); and *L'Artiste*, 14 Aug. 1831. A. Levin, in the only book in English on Chasles (*The Legacy of Philarète Chasles*, N. Carolina, 1957) claims erroneously that Chasles was the only critic to review *La Peau*.

[8] *RDM* 1 Nov. 1831.

[9] e.g. *La Quotidienne*, 28 Aug.; *Le National*, 8 Sept.; and *Le Constitutionnel*, 28 Oct. 1831.

[10] *L'Avenir*, 6 Nov. 1831.

[11] 'Poètes et romanciers modernes de la France. XIV. M. de Balzac. *La Recherche de l'Absolu*', *RDM* 15 Nov. 1834.

[12] See below, pp. 69–75.

However, in his extensive practical suggestions and in the general plea that the novelist should rewrite his texts less frenetically, Sainte-Beuve seems to be offering sensible and well-intentioned advice.

The critic's major objection to Balzac's work in general and to *La Recherche de l'absolu* in particular is that his descriptions are overdone, that his details are exaggerated, and that the whole is infused with disproportionate passion. These became standard themes of Balzac criticism in later years. For Sainte-Beuve, it seems, the only justification for Balzac's techniques of exposition and description would have been to portray reality 'as it was', and thus to abandon any imaginative sources of creation. Balzac may well have been disappointed or angered by this view, which now seems a total misunderstanding of the novelist's methods and aims, particularly in *La Recherche de l'absolu*. He is said to have declared, upon reading the article, 'Il me payera cela. Je lui passerai ma plume au travers du corps', and to have written *Le Lys dans la vallée* in order to outdo Sainte-Beuve's own novel, *Volupté*. It must be pointed out that the entire story originates with Sainte-Beuve himself, who characteristically ascribed its source to Jules Sandeau.[13] Neither Sainte-Beuve nor Sandeau can be considered reliable sources of information on Balzac, and there is little reason to regard the story as more than apocryphal.

Although Sainte-Beuve's original piece was not in any real sense hostile, it foreshadowed by a few months the introduction of personal vindictiveness into Balzac criticism. Over the next ten years, the viciousness and number of outright personal attacks rose and fell in response to a number of events: a spate occurred towards the end of 1835 and throughout 1836, fanned by the opposing faction in the protracted court-case between Balzac and the powerful François Buloz over the rights to *Le Lys dans la vallée*; another outburst greeted the criticism of journalists in the second part of *Illusions perdues* (1839); the fiasco of Balzac's first play, *Vautrin* (1840), and the even greater scandal over the staging of *Les Ressources de Quinola* three years later brought new onslaughts. At no point between 1835 and 1845 was the element of vindictive fault-finding entirely absent from Balzac criticism.

Characteristic of 'anti-Balzacian' criticism was the association of the

[13] *Portraits contemporains* (Michel Lévy, 1869), II. 357. Sainte-Beuve had previously noted this story, together with a number of other (mostly offensive) phrases about Balzac, in his *Cahier vert*. See C. A. Sainte-Beuve, *Cahiers, ed.* Raphaël Molho (Gallimard, 1973), I. 81.

man and his works. Alleged personal foibles—vanity and eccentricities, for example—were used to invalidate his literary achievements; and, vice versa, the fictions of his novels were used as evidence in attacks on his personal 'immorality'. Balzac's vanity was the most frequent reproach, and its originates as a theme of criticism in the very first of the unambiguously hostile articles—Muret's scurrilous piece for the aptly named and equally scurrilous *Voleur* in January 1835.[14] The novelist's literary failings, Muret claimed, derived from his over-production; and he wrote too much simply in order to earn vast sums so as to indulge his 'besoin de luxe' and 'vanité folle'.

In the satirical *Charivari*, Balzac's mannerisms and eccentricities were derided by frequent short space-fillers throughout 1836 and 1837. The novelist's aristocratic pretensions, political ambitions, and use of neologisms provided the bulk of the material.[15] Even his living-quarters (presumably the rue Cassini flat) became the butt of ridicule: one journalist described them as resembling the home of some 'joueur subitement enrichi par un coup inespéré de bourse'.[16]

Le Père Goriot (1835) represents for many modern critics the full flowering of Balzac's technique as a novelist. It is also the first novel to use systematically the device of the 'reappearing characters', who provide the links between the wide diversity of subjects treated in the different stories and groupings of the *Comédie humaine*. According to his sister, Laure Surville, Balzac thought that the invention of the reappearing characters made him a genius:[17] and the device was certainly presented in these terms in the prefaces that Félix Davin wrote for various novels in 1835.[18] Few critics agreed with this assessment of the reappearing characters. In the view of most, it was a device that simply allowed Balzac to publish unfinished novels. Clémence Robert, for example, disliked the lack of a true dénouement in *Le Père Goriot*: 'Tout cesse et ne finit pas,' she complained.[19] Joël Cherbuliez thought that Balzac would soon lose his popularity with the reading public if he continued to produce 'half-works',[20] and similar criticisms

---

[14] According to Weinberg, op. cit., p. 215, this article first appeared in *La Mode*.
[15] See issues of 29 Oct. 1836, 23 June and 20 Aug. 1837.
[16] *Le Mercure de France*, 15 July 1835.
[17] Cf. A. Maurois, *Prométhée ou la vie de Balzac* (Hachette, 1965), p. 264.
[18] Introduction to *Scènes de la vie privée* (Béchet, 1835) and to the *Études philosophiques* (Werdet, 1835).
[19] *Journal des Femmes*, 1 July 1835.
[20] *Bulletin littéraire et scientifique* (Genève-Paris), III. 80.

were levelled at *Le Contrat de mariage*:[21] 'Rien n'arrive à sa conclusion; l'intrigue et les personnages sont maladroitement abandonnés, moitié à Paris, moitié en pleine mer; tout est laissé incomplet dans cette œuvre où aucune précaution ne vient déguiser un subit avortement.'[22] Emmanuel Gonzalès summed up this general line of criticism when he wrote that Balzac's greatest failing 'est de toujours faillir au dénouement, après avoir été trop pompeux à l'exorde'.[23]

In his article of 1834, Sainte-Beuve had made two points which came to be repeated again and again by hostile critics in the later 1830s. Balzac's popularity, according to the critic, rested on the flattery of women implied by the plots of his stories. Chaudes-Aigues, for example, was merely repeating Sainte-Beuve when he ascribed Balzac's popularity to 'son attention assidue à flatter les femmes. Ce sont les femmes seulement qui ont établi et proclamé son succès.'[24] The link between popularity and feminine interest in fiction of this period is a theme that goes well beyond Balzac criticism. Stendhal had much to say on the subject in his letter to Salvagnoli on *Le Rouge et le noir*.[25] Balzac's exploitation of this link was brought up by Sainte-Beuve, but presented as ignoble only by subsequent critics like Chaudes-Aigues.

The second of the points made by Sainte-Beuve was that the distortion and exaggeration of reality in Balzac's novels was unacceptable. This argument was reoffered as a conclusion to a review of *Le Père Goriot* in a major daily newspaper. Balzac's main fault, the reviewer claimed, was exaggeration: 'Le premier trait de l'auteur est vrai, il est pur; mais il le charge ensuite tellement, que la figure grimace ... [Balzac] ne se règle pas quand il écrit, il s'abandonne, il s'emporte. S'il a de l'élan, il manque de mesure et de méthode.'[26]

Coexisting with these criticisms of exaggeration in the 1830s was a general willingness to grant Balzac a profound 'perception des choses extérieures',[27] a 'grande finesse d'observation',[28] and it is in Sainte-Beuve's article, once again, that the first major statement of this theme

[21] Called at this time *La Fleur-des-Pois*.
[22] E. Guinot, in *Le Charivari*, 12 Dec. 1835.
[23] *La Revue du théâtre*, Feb. 1836, p. 244.
[24] *La Revue du XIXe siècle*, 29 Oct. 1836, p. 412.
[25] See the Garnier edition of the novel (ed. Martineau, 1960), pp. 509–14.
[26] *Le Constitutionnel*, 23 Mar. 1835.
[27] Ibid.
[28] T. Muret, *Le Voleur*, 15 Jan. 1835.

is to be found. The novelist's talent was often likened to that of Teniers and Gérard Dow, the painters of sober and minutely detailed interior scenes.[29] Correspondingly, it was *Eugénie Grandet* that critics of the 1830s considered to be Balzac's masterpiece (to the author's reputed annoyance). This too was an evaluation first made by Sainte-Beuve, though there is a characteristic note of deprecation and irony in his claim that it was *almost* a masterpiece: 'oui, un chef-d'œuvre qui se classerait à côté de tout ce qu'il y a de mieux et de plus délicat *parmi les romans en un volume*'.[30]

Sainte-Beuve's article was reprinted in 1836 in the third volume of his *Critiques et Portraits littéraires* in more or less its original form, with one additional footnote comparing Balzac to 'un Pigault-Lebrun de salon, le Pigault-Lebrun d'un très beau monde'.[31] It was in 1836, too, that arguments of a socio-political nature arose in reaction to Balzac's growing opus. Writing for the royalist *Gazette de France*, Alfred Nettement attacked the subject-matter of the novels. Balzac, he claimed, simply wrote from his memory of ten years spent on the shady fringes of business and journalism. (This vague knowledge of Balzac's career before 1830 is yet another debt owed to Sainte-Beuve's 1834 article.) Some of the subjects were, in Nettement's view, intrinsically immoral; and it was not impartiality that guided Balzac's choice of 'reminiscences', but indifference to art and morality. He described for the sake of describing, 'et l'on pourrait dire qui'l ne marche pas dans le royaume de l'intelligence, mais qu'il s'y promène'.[32] Balzac's espousal of both straightforward materialism and Swedenborgian mysticism proved, for Nettement, that the novelist had no firm philosophy of his own. Ignoring such well-established works as *Le Médecin de campagne* (1832), the critic concludes, with a distinctly political implication, that Balzac had abandoned 'la plus belle mission du talent, qui est d'agir sur ses semblables par les royales influences de la pensée'.[33] The general view expressed here that Balzac's ideas have no intrinsic worth remained a major theme of Balzac criticism and was repeated by such keen campaigners as Taine and Émile Zola. It is worth noting, however, that the rejection of Balzac as

---

[29] Cherbuliez, *Bulletin littéraire et scientifique* (Genève-Paris), III. 80.

[30] Sainte-Beuve, art. cit.

[31] *Critiques et Portraits littéraires* (Renduel, 1836), III. 56–89 Changed to 'Le Pigault-Lebrun des duchesses' in 1846.

[32] *La Gazette de France*, 16 Feb. 1836.

[33] Ibid.

a thinker, and by strong implication as a political ally, originates in a right-wing, royalist view, and not with the political left.

Balzac's preface to *La Maison Nucingen* (1838) brought upon him sharp criticism for flaunting personal and financial grievances in public.[34] The following year, the second part of *Illusions perdues* appeared: and the press reacted precisely as the reader of this bitter indictment of journalistic life would expect—venomously and without any regard for literary merit. A particularly nasty review came from the young Albéric Second, who was not averse, in later years, to publishing fabricated souvenirs of 'Balzac à Angoulême'.[35] There are a number of similarities between Second and the handsome young hero of Balzac's novel, and the critic may have felt he was being got at personally;[36] an alternative explanation is suggested by Asseline, who recounts how young journalists, if they wished to get a toe-hold on either of the two major reviews controlled by François Buloz—the *Revue de Paris* and the *Revue des deux mondes*—were required to begin with a piece 'on', meaning against, Balzac.[37]

According to Second, the description of the world of journalism in *Illusions perdues* was a cheap revenge for the just and fair treatment Balzac's other novels had received from the critics. He had been a novelist, but was now a mere 'machine à romans'. 'Qu'est devenue son imagination si fertile et sa manière si pleine de vie? Sa puissance d'études morales et sa richesse d'observation, que sont-elles devenues? Rien, plus rien ne subsiste.'[38] This sort of outraged condemnation became quite common in the years following the publication of *Illusion perdues*. For example, in a review of *Une Fille d'Ève* which Zola later exhumed,[39] Chaudes-Aigues limited himself to those points which he could deride: the reappearing characters (which show Balzac's inability even to imagine proper endings), the structure of the *Comédie humaine* (intended to force the reluctant reader to buy copies of earlier novels), and so on. All Balzac's heroes are mad; all his heroines wicked; and all his plots plagiats. (The critic had claimed in 1836 that *Eugénie Grandet* was taken from 'un ouvrage allemand dont le nom m'échappe', but in 1839 states its sources to be Molière's *L'Avare*, and *Melmoth*

---

[34] e.g. Sainte-Beuve, *RDM*, 1 Nov. 1838, and A. Pichot, *RDP* 21 Oct. 1838.

[35] See Appendix III, pp. 229, 243.

[36] Like Lucien, Second was fair, young, born in Angoulême, and a novelist as well as a journalist.

[37] *L'Artiste*, 29 Sept. 1844.   [38] *Le Figaro*, 28 July 1839.

[39] See below, p. 125

the Wanderer by Maturin.) French society was far less evil in reality than it appears to be in Balzac's works, and the critic concludes that the novelist, combining 'l'indécision et . . . la maladresse', was a nullity. His rank in the history of literature lay somewhere between Mademoiselle de Scudéry and the infamous Marquis de Sade.[40] Balzac's first play, *Vautrin*, was performed in 1840, and banned after its first night for allegedly taking political satire too far. Critics were baffled by its mixture of farce and intrigue, and could make no sense of it.[41] Jules Janin, for example, considered it 'un lamentable chapître à ajouter aux égarements de l'esprit humain'.[42] A few favourable reviews appeared, mostly in theatrical journals keen to attack the arbitrariness of the censorship and 'moral' judgements on literature.[43] The argument over the morality of the play led Alfred Nettement, who had, by his own admission, neither seen nor read it, to denounce it none the less as an example of the 'dégénération du goût' into which France had fallen.[44] Balzac became associated with 'immorality' and anti-social literature very largely as a result of the performance, suspension, and critical reception of *Vautrin*.

Around 1840, moreover, many critics, once again led by Sainte-Beuve, expressed a growing dislike for the direction in which the French novel had been moving for the past decade. In 1839, Sainte-Beuve had put Balzac among the producers of 'littérature industrielle', or pulp fiction.[45] In 1840, he suggested that the novelist had outstayed his welcome: he had burst on to the scene at a chaotic time, in the wake of the July Revolution in 1830, but 'si de pareils hasards sont précieux, il ne faut pas en abuser, on le sent, ni les prolonger outre mesure, sous peine de faire céder le charme au dégoût'.[46] Sainte-Beuve's disgust was mounting: by 1843 he too associated Balzac with de Sade.[47]

After *Vautrin*, Balzac's alleged materialism and cynicism became a major theme of criticism. Even a favourable assessment such as Girault's ('par la science, par la pensée et par le style . . . Balzac est le premier de nos romanciers') takes as its main argument that '*L'école des faits*, créée par Balzac dans le roman, conclut au matérialisme.'[48]

[40] *RDP* Nov. 1839.
[41] See René Guise, 'Un Grand Homme du roman à la scène', *AB* (1966), 171–216.
[42] *Le Journal des débats*, 16 Mar. 1840.
[43] e.g. in *La Caricature*, 22 Mar. 1840.
[44] *La Gazette de France*, 18 Mar. 1840.
[45] *RDM* 1 Sept. 1839.   [46] Ibid. 1 Mar. 1840.
[47] *La Revue suisse*, June 1843. See below, pp. 68–79, for a more detailed analysis of Sainte-Beuve's views.
[48] *Le Bibliographe*, 25 Apr. 1841.

Girault's analysis is unusual, however, in its favourable attitude to the reappearing characters and to Balzac's style—compared here to Victor Hugo's. Criticism of the 1840s was in general of an extremely low quality—not only hostile, but personal, vindictive, and cheap. A young provincial writer attempted, in these conditions, to re-habilitate Balzac and to present a sober, reasoned account of his literary merits. It is interesting to note just how modest Samuel-Henry Berthoud's assessment was, remembering that the critic was an old friend and faithful admirer.[49] Balzac's literary talent, he considers, belongs to the Flemish school: 'Il se complaît aux tableaux de chevalet, reproduit les figures dans leurs moindres détails . . .'[50] Berthoud disliked the novelist's depiction of 'la boue sociale', and his 'manque d'unité dans la phrase'. None of these points was new, but they had not been combined in a non-hostile assessment since Sainte-Beuve's article in 1834. Indeed, Berthoud's points were laudatory by comparison to Chaudes-Aigues's review of *Le Curé de village* (1841). The catholic message of this rural utopian novel is completely misunderstood; political views and literary style alike are mercilessly derided, and the conclusion is that Balzac's sole motive in writing the book 'a été de correspondre aux goûts du public'.[51]

Accusations of immorality formed the main point of three articles written for Buloz's *Revue des deux mondes* by the soldier–poet Paul Gaschon de Molènes. Balzac was referred to not as 'le plus fécond de nos romanciers' (common in the 1830s), but as 'l'auteur de la *Physiologie du mariage*', and in his novels Molènes found 'une immoralité pédante, érudite, presque inconnue aux gens du monde, celle que les goûts malsains des écoliers leur font déterrer au fond des traités de médecine'.[52] Not only was the style of *Mémoires de deux jeunes mariées* 'diffus, violent et désordonné', full of neologisms and incoherent images, but the story itself 'corrompt et dégrade tous les sentiments auxquelles cette œuvre s'attaque'.[53] Elsewhere, Molènes expressed a general reaction to the contemporary novel that other critics, notably Sainte-Beuve, appear to have felt:

Je hais, et je hais profondément, tous ces poèmes de l'existence parisienne, que les romanciers de ce temps-ci ont maintes fois tenté d'écrire, le tableau

---

[49] See Madeleine Fargeaud, 'Dans le sillage des grands Romantiques: S.-H. Berthoud', *AB* (1962), 213–47.

[50] *Le Musée des familles*, Oct. 1841.

[51] *RDP* May 1841. [52] *RDM* 15 Mar. 1842. [53] Ibid.

des luttes de la vie, l'intervention de l'usurier, l'irruption des affreux spectres de la réalité parmi les doux fantômes de l'imagination.[54]

Molènes admitted, as did nearly all critics from Sainte-Beuve to Berthoud, that Balzac had talent as a 'peintre d'intérieurs et de portraits'; and perhaps because he remembered the generally favourable views expressed by Sainte-Beuve at the end of 1834, he dated the decline in Balzac's qualities from the beginning of 1835.[55] Vanity had brought the novelist down to such abominations as *Les Ressources de Quinola*, so much shallower than Vigny's *Chatterton*: 'Ce que M. de Balzac semble demander, je laisse deviner au nom de qui, c'est de la célébrité et de l'argent.'[56] Vanity likewise and a 'soif insatiable du lucre' had produced the pretentious title and 'bizarre' *Avant-propos* of the *Comédie humaine*, the final term of the novelist's decline.[57] Throughout the 1840s the *Revue des deux mondes* and the *Revue de Paris* continued to attack Balzac's new publications systematically in this vein. In 1842, *Albert Savarus* was suspected of being a rehashed early work ('un secret plagiat de Balzac sur Lord R'Hoone'),[58] and *La Rabouilleuse* was described as 'ridicule à force d'immoralité';[59] in 1843, *David Séchard* (the third part of *Illusions perdues*) was 'conçu sans proportion, composé sans methode'[60] and similar comments were made on *Une Ténébreuse Affaire* (1842),[61] *La Muse du Département* (1843),[62] *Honorine* (1843),[63] *Modeste Mignon* (1844),[64] and *Les Paysans* (1844).[65]

It was not only in these reviews that the theme of Balzac's immorality was propagated. Louise-Laure Ozenne, for example, declared that 'un apprêt musqué, sous lequel circule une chaude dépravation . . . est la réalité la plus palpable dans le talent de M. de Balzac'.[66] This reputation of being both a ladies' novelist and an immoral one (itself an interesting reflection of attitudes to women in the nineteenth century) was widely, but not universally, accepted. It was deplored by a religious critic, who found in *Le Curé de village* 'un résumé touchant des triomphes du catholicisme'.[67] It was not until the 1890s that this opinion gained any wide acceptance, but the theme is present even in the overwhelmingly hostile 1840s.

[54] *RDM* 1 Apr. 1842.   [55] Ibid. 1 Nov. 1842.
[56] Ibid. 1 Apr. 1842.   [57] Ibid. 1 Nov. 1842.   [58] Ibid.
[59] *RDP* 13 Jan. 1843 (the novel was then called *Un Ménage de garçon en province*).
[60] *RDM* 1 Dec. 1843.   [61] Ibid. 15 June 1843.
[62] Ibid.   [63] Ibid.   [64] *RDP* 4 May 1844.
[65] Ibid. 28 Dec. 1844.
[66] *Mélanges critiques et littéraires* (Didot, 1843), p. 160.
[67] A. de Barthélémy Lanta (?), *Écho de la littérature et des beaux-arts*, 25 Nov. 1841.

Not all the Paris press was controlled by François Buloz, and not all French critics followed Sainte-Beuve's tastes and distastes. There were exceptions to the general hostility towards Balzac in the early 1840s, as the last-mentioned article shows. Alfred Asseline, a member of the Hugo clan (he was Adèle's cousin) and therefore disinclined to take Sainte-Beuve on trust,[68] denounced the campaign against Balzac as vindictive. The antagonism had originated, he thought, in the 'procès du *Lys*' in 1836, which set Buloz against Balzac in the law courts.[69] Louis de Cormenin, who later played Sancho Panza to Gautier's bawdy Quixote on the tour of Italy immortalized in the *Lettres à la Présidente*,[70] tried to show that Balzac could not be criticized for the 'missing conclusions' in his novels: 'Si les caractères ont eu leur entier développement, M. de Balzac trouve superflu de dénouer l'intrigue et de compléter la fable, et la dernière ligne lui semble une explication suffisante.'[71] Cormenin argues that the two contradictory aspects of Balzac's descriptions—his attention to detail and his 'exaggerations' of reality—are integral and compatible parts of his technique. In direct contradiction of Nettement, Cormenin states that Balzac expressed his own quite definite social and political ideas through the novels. Furthermore, Cormenin dismisses the fiascos of *Vautrin* and *Les Ressources de Quinola* as irrelevant. He was sure that one day Balzac would succeed in the theatre, and in this he turned out to be right.

Cormenin's article was in many senses exceptional and prophetic, for it adumbrates the combinations found in the attitudes of writers, rather than critics, in the 1850s, and in particular the attitudes of Gautier and Baudelaire towards Balzac's use of detail and exaggeration and towards his dramatic gifts. The connections of friendship may not be irrelevant to this similarity.

Cormenin maintained that the real subject of the *Comédie humaine* was the contemporary bourgeoisie. Philarète Chasles made the same point in an article published the following year.[72] For the rest, however, Chasles is in fundamental disagreement with Cormenin. No

---

[68] See A. Billy, *Sainte-Beuve, Sa vie et son temps* (Flammarion, 1952), I. 76–175, for an account of the friendship and final enmity between Hugo and Sainte-Beuve.

[69] *L'Artiste*, 29 Sept. 1844. Note that Muret's attack in 1835 precedes the 'Procès du *Lys*' by several months, and that Asseline was himself the author of hostile reviews of Balzac's novels.

[70] Quintal associés, Montréal, 1970.   [71] *L'Unité*, 6 May 1843.

[72] *Dictionnaire de la Conversation* (Garnier, 1844), supplément, II. 413–15 (article signed V. Caralp).

longer a close friend and literary comrade-in-arms of Balzac's, as he
had been in 1831, Chasles had become harshly critical of the *Comédie
humaine* by 1844.[73] The common themes of vanity leading to care-
lessness, of financial ambition leading to overproduction, and of
comparisons with 'infamous' writers like Restif de la Bretonne (though
not de Sade) are baldly repeated by this lapsed Romantic.

A shift occurs in Balzac criticism after 1845 or thereabouts. Weinberg sees a new 'period' of high critical esteem beginning in this year,[74]
but that is something of an overstatement. The novelist, certainly,
was no longer the subject of quite such hostile articles as before: but
one must add that he was no longer the subject of very many articles
at all. Balzac remained a notorious, rather than a famous writer, but
his notoriety paled beside that of Eugène Sue and his immensely
popular *romans-feuilletons*, and his many imitators.

A certain consensus of opinion can be seen to exist in the later
1840s. Balzac had a 'rare faculté d'observation'[75] which prompted
comparisons with painters of the Flemish school.[76] He had a slow
and painstaking method, and found it difficult to produce his novels.[77]
The novelist's view of mankind was held to be pessimistic, and his
systematization of life in the *Avant-propos* was disliked. Above all
there was agreement that Balzac was a materialist: but more and more
this was presented as an *unconscious* feature of his works. According
to J. L. E. Lerminier, 'M. de Balzac ne s'est pas aperçu que tout en
ayant l'intention de rendre un éclatant hommage au catholicisme, il
en niait la nécessité.'[78] The 'real sense' of the *Comédie humaine* began
to appear as a contradiction of the novelist's professed allegiance to
Church and Throne. This conflict on the level of the meaning of the
works formed a parallel to the aesthetic contradiction, first pointed
out by Sainte-Beuve, between the 'conscious' techniques of detailed,
realistic description and the 'unconscious' or involuntary romantic
exuberance of Balzac's imagination. Only Louis de Cormenin, between 1834 and 1846, had argued that these opposites were complementary rather than contradictory.

---

[73] See C. Pichois, *Philarète Chasles et la vie littéraire au temps du romantisme* (Corti,
1965), p. 2 and *passim*.
[74] 'There was a sharp, almost spectacular swing of opinion in Balzac's favour' in 1846
(Weinberg, op. cit., p. 67).
[75] E. Pelletan, *La Presse*, 30 Nov. 1846.
[76] e.g. by J. L. E. Lerminier, in *RDM* 15 Apr. 1847.
[77] Pelletan, art. cit.   [78] Lerminier, art cit.

These two sets of opposing features form a structure of thought which underlies, in one way or another, nearly every interpretation of Balzac in the nineteenth century. Significant changes in Balzac criticism result from different resolutions of the four conflicting themes. Favourable evaluations often depended on a simple denial of the existence of one of these poles—for example, Taine cut Balzac off from his political views; unfavourable evaluations usually argued that the conflicts were not soluble. In other words, the fundamental criterion applied was that of unity—unity of meaning and unity of style or register. Despite very great changes in what critics thought they were doing, from Sainte-Beuve to Brunetière evaluations of Balzac continued to be based on the classical criterion of unity.

I   Morality and politics in Balzac criticism from *Les Parents pauvres* to *Madame Bovary*

DISCUSSIONS of Balzac in the early 1850s were dominated by arguments about contradictions in the meaning of his work; whereas arguments about the novels' aesthetic aspects come to the fore in the later 1850s. One of the reasons for this order of progression can be found in the sequence of events in the last years of Balzac's life.

The original publication of Sainte-Beuve's review of *La Recherche de l'absolu* in 1834 marked Balzac's arrival as a writer of note: but its second re-publication in 1846 can be seen to mark the end of the novelist's public career. In 1840, the critic had predicted (hopefully) that Balzac would end very soon in the obscurity from which he had sprung, 'par cent romans que personne ne lira'.[1] By introducing in 1846 additional remarks and footnotes, all of them snide if not positively hostile, to the text of his article, Sainte-Beuve was helping to fulfil his own prophecy.[2] It had in any case been partly realized already, for the enormous success of the *roman-feuilleton* had drawn attention away from the *Comédie humaine*, which grew more slowly in the 1840s than it had in the previous decade. With the completion of the seventeen volumes of the *Comédie humaine* in 1846, Balzac found himself no nearer the rank of *maréchal littéraire* than he had been previously. As André Lorant has shown, Balzac tried to exploit the form of the *roman-feuilleton* in his last two great novels in order to regain his lost celebrity.[3] Thus when *La Cousine Bette* and *Le Cousin Pons* appeared at the end of 1846 and early in 1847, they were immediately seen in the context of a new literary genre firmly associated with Eugène Sue—the most successful practitioner of serial fiction—and with his well-known 'socialist' ideology. Yet the last two novels (collectively known as *Les Parents pauvres*) are more strikingly pessimistic, and more powerfully religious, than any of Balzac's previous

---

[1] 'Dix Ans après en littérature', *RDM* 1 Mar. 1840; *Portraits contemporains* (1870), II. 482–3.
[2] See Chapter 3, pp. 72–3, below.
[3] *Les Parents pauvres. Étude historique et critique* (Droz, 1967), I. 320–3.

works, with the possible exception of *Le Curé de village*. Not surprisingly, therefore, the critical reaction to *Les Parents pauvres* centred on arguments about Balzac's political and religious significance. Such arguments usually claimed to be concerned with 'morality', but their political basis is none the less clear.

The attack on Balzac's morality by Hippolyte Castille has become quite well known. Castille, who later became a serious historian, was in 1846 a young man imbued with early socialist ideas about the moral influence of literature on society. On the one hand he is full of enthusiasm for Balzac's novels, but on the other hand he sees 'vice' as the predominant feature of the *Comédie humaine*. Not only are there more vicious characters than virtuous ones in the novels, but, Castille claims, they are portrayed with greater vividness and colour.[4] Balzac wrote a somewhat ironical reply to this article in *La Semaine*, in which he drew up lists of 'good' and 'evil' characters in his novels to show that the former, not the latter, are more numerous.[5] Baudelaire took the novelist's reply to Castille in all seriousness, and wrote glowingly in his gossip column for the semi-humorous *Tintamarre* that Balzac,

qui, pour être génie, ne manque pas d'esprit, vit dans cette affaire une nouvelle occasion de donner au public des explications sur la *Comédie humaine*, et il l'a fait avec un esprit superbe, une dialectique souveraine, et cependant à la portée des simples de *La Semaine*.[6]

Other critics, however, remained unconvinced by Balzac's arguments. Hippolyte Babou, for example, levelled very similar criticisms at Balzac a few months later. Although a friend of Baudelaire and antagonistic to Sainte-Beuve, Babou agreed with Castille that Balzac succeeded in his portrayal of evil characters, but failed when dealing with the virtuous ones. Therefore, the young critic argued (he was barely a major in 1846), the novels of the *Comédie humaine* are in effect immoral and unchristian—or 'pagan', as Babou puts it:

. . . et s'il en fallait une preuve tirée des *Parents pauvres*, je montrerais comment il vous a été impossible de fixer autour du front de Madame Hulot le nimbe mystique des saintes femmes . . . au contraire, vous réussissez à merveille lorsque vous découvrez l'épaule de Valérie [Marneffe] pour qu'elle pose en Dalila . . .[7]

It is in the reviews that Alexandre Weill wrote of these novels that the theme of 'immorality' acquires an unambiguously political sense.

---

[4] *La Semaine*, 4 Oct. 1846.   [5] *Éd. déf.* XXII. 361.
[6] *Le Tintamarre*, 24 Oct. 1846.   [7] *La Revue nouvelle*, 1 Feb. 1847.

Weill had rejected his strict Jewish upbringing to espouse the utopian political philosophy of Fourier, and had become editor of the movement's newspaper, *La Démocratie pacifique*.[8] Balzac's works, he said, were immoral because they lacked progressive ideological content; the views that they put forward were outdated and degenerate. However, the actual picture of society drawn in the *Comédie humaine* was in conflict with the author's professed religious and political opinions. The novels themselves showed the decay of traditional values and revealed the need for change: 'ce qui prouve que votre génie est plus progressif que votre science et votre volonté.'[9] Castille, Babou, and Weill all see a failing in the *Comédie humaine*, and for all three that failing is a lack of unity between the conscious intention of the novelist and the deeper meaning of what he created. Castille expresses the conflict in terms of moral vice and virtue; Babou in terms of Christian and pagan values; Weill in terms of outdated opinions and progressive 'genius'.

Alexandre Weill grew ever more hostile to Balzac, despite the fact that he moved politically towards the right and was by 1850 editor of the royalist *Gazette de France* and author of a work on *Le Génie de la Monarchie*. It was above all the political and religious incoherence he perceived in Balzac's works that made him rank the novelist lower than Eugène Sue;[10] and Balzac's most Sue-like work, *La Dernière Incarnation de Vautrin*, provoked a veritable onslaught from *La Démocratie pacifique*.[11]

Critics of right-wing persuasion did not need, at this stage, to find contradictions in the meaning of *Les Parents pauvres* in order to attack it. The corrupt nature of the major protagonists of *La Cousine Bette* was taken unquestioningly as an indication of the author's immoral intention in writing the book. The almost unrelieved pessimism of the two novels produced reactions of shock and disgust: 'Est-ce que votre odorat blasé a besoin des senteurs putrides de la corruption, et les parfums empestés qui sortent de ces sépulcres blanchis dont parle L'Écriture, sont-ils maintenant les seuls qui puissent produire quelque impression sur votre sensibilité émoussée?' asked Alfred Nettement in the *Gazette de France*.[12] Eugène Marron declared that an 'excès de vérité' was dangerous in literature: 'Certes, nous ne nions pas la vérité des mœurs que M. de Balzac a décrites dans les *Parents*

[8] See A. Weill, *Ma Jeunesse* (1870) and *Introduction à mes mémoires* (1890).
[9] *La Démocratie pacifique*, 12 Dec. 1846.
[10] Ibid. 5 Jan. 1847.   [11] Ibid. 9 Jan. 1847.   [12] 11 Dec. 1846.

pauvres, pas plus que l'exactitude de ses observations; mais était-il nécessaire de peindre de pareilles mœurs?'[13] Nettement and Marron appear simply not to notice the references to catholicism in *Les Parents pauvres*, and not to have read the *Avant-propos* to the *Comédie humaine*, where Balzac stated that he was writing 'à la lueur de deux vérités éternelles: la Religion, la Monarchie . . .'[14] Ten years earlier Nettement had claimed that Balzac had no philosophy or 'message' (see p. 10, above), and he developed this view in 1845–6 in an attempt to explain the degeneracy of contemporary fiction.[15] There were, he wrote, three distinct stages in this process of decay: the first was an upsurge of woolly utopian dreams, represented in politics by the July Revolution of 1830 and in fiction by George Sand; the third was the cynical attack on all the values of established society by hack-writers like Eugène Sue; and Balzac was a man of the second, intermediate stage, disillusioned by the early ideals yet not explicitly anti-social. The second stage, in Nettement's neat analysis, was typified by the money-grubbing, philistine bourgeois in society, and in literature by the materialistic, morally indifferent, intellectually neutral novels of Balzac.[16] He is a product of a society 'vouée au culte matérialiste du veau d'or'; he treats vice and virtue alike, 'comme un anatomiste sans pitié'. What Nettement is here holding up to criticism is curiously almost identical—even in the image used—to what Taine and Zola would claim to admire twenty and thirty years later. The theme remained constant, but its valency changed. Marron, too, used this theme in his unfavourable review of *Les Parents pauvres*—'c'est . . . toujours la même constatation de faits se servant à elle-même de moralité'[17]—despite his condemnation of the novels' 'immorality'.

Balzac's literary production declined sharply after *Les Parents pauvres*, and his life ended with two years almost complete silence. (For much of the time he was abroad, on Mme Hanska's estate in the Ukraine.) The reactions to *Les Parents pauvres* form the last significant group of articles published whilst Balzac was still alive and in good health, and the arguments they contain on the meaning and intention of the *Comédie humaine* as a whole constitute the starting-point of Balzac criticism for the following ten years.

There were four events during the life of the Second Republic (1848–52) which prompted articles about Balzac, though none of them was to

[13] *La Revue indépendante*, 25 Jan. 1847.   [14] *Pl.* I. 9.
[15] *Études critiques sur le feuilleton-roman* (Perrodil, 1845–6), 2 vols.
[16] Ibid. I. 36 ff.   [17] *La Revue indépendante*, 25 Jan. 1847.

do with prose fiction as such. In 1848, Balzac's fourth play, *La Marâtre*, was performed; in 1850, his first play, *Vautrin*, was revived; in August 1850, Balzac died; and in August 1851, his last play, *Le Faiseur*, was performed under the title *Mercadet*. The first of these events caused little stir. *La Marâtre* is a highly moral piece in the style of the *drame bourgeois*, and despite very favourable reviews by Théophile Gautier[18] and even Jules Janin,[19] the play failed to provoke much comment. It was irrelevant to the dominant themes of Balzac criticism; and it was performed in May 1848, in the middle of great social and political upheavals.

Paris was in the middle of a political conflict, though not an upheaval, when *Vautrin* was staged in April 1850, but the character of Vautrin was at the very centre of the arguments about Balzac's depiction of vice and his political meaning. The play's revival thus provoked a great deal of critical comment, most of it devoted to Balzac in general rather than to the play in particular.

The first performance of *Vautrin* in 1840 had created a furore, and the play was banned after its first night. The wig of the actor Frédérick-Lemaître, it was said, too closely resembled the pear shape used to caricature the monarch.[20] The play itself was therefore associated with political opposition, and the character of Vautrin, in the novels, had been used many times as evidence of Balzac's predilection for 'evil' characters, of his indifference to morality, and of his materialism. Hippolyte Castille had mentioned Vautrin in this way, but it was above all in Nettement's *Études critiques sur le feuilleton-roman* that Balzac's 'grand forçat' had supported attacks on his creator. The main aim of the *Études critiques* was to discredit Eugène Sue and the ideas he was held to represent. The argument against Balzac, outlined above, had a supporting role in Nettement's book: the novelist is even referred to as 'cet esprit remarquable, malgré ses défauts'. None the less, the long passage on the immorality of Vautrin in volume II tars Balzac with the same brush as Sue.[21]

In April 1850 Sue was standing as the radical-socialist candidate for the parliamentary by-election in Paris. The right-wing press attacked with an extraordinary campaign of denigration[22]—and Nettement's *Études critiques* reappeared in the bookshops. They were serialized

[18] *La Presse*, 29 May 1848.
[19] *Le Journal des débats*, 29 May 1848.
[20] See R. Guise, 'Un Grand Homme . . .', *AB* (1966), 171–216, for further details.
[21] *Études critiques*, II. 26–33.
[22] See J. L. Bory, *Eugène Sue* (Hachette, 1962), pp. 338–46.

in Nettement's newspaper, *L'Opinion politique*, and promoted by huge, half-page advertisements.[23] This coincidence of literary and political events had an obvious and direct effect on the critical response to the new production of *Vautrin*, and in the longer term a considerable influence on the whole course of Balzac criticism.

The basic plot of *Vautrin* is similar to that of *Splendeurs et misères des courtisanes*. The arch-criminal attempts to mastermind the marriage of his protégé, here called Raoul de Frescas, into the noble Montsorel family; but Raoul is eventually recognized as Madame Montsorel's long-lost son, and all ends happily. This absurd plot was seen by many critics to imply the possibility of rehabilitation for an 'evil' criminal character like Vautrin, and this notion was stated by Charles Matharel, for example, to be an immoral one.[24] One may note that it was also a predominantly socialist notion.[25] Jules Janin thought that in this play Balzac had been trying to exploit the popularity of *Robert-Macaire* (a boulevard melodrama about a witty and lovable villain, written and performed by the famous actor Frédérick-Lemaître).[26] However, literature which mocks at the law, at moral standards, at the monarchy itself, was not without danger. Balzac might well not have realized this in the untroubled atmosphere of 1840, but in 1850, Janin considers, the dangers have become obvious. Therefore the revival of this 'drame mort-né' was an even greater evil than its original composition.[27] Some of the critics who subscribed to Janin's general view of *Vautrin* as an anti-social play threatening the stability of society and prophesying its collapse none the less thought it had become relatively harmless with the passing of time. Édouard Thierry, for example, declared that everything had collapsed already, and the satirical *Charivari*, in a similar vein, found that 'ce fameux *Vautrin* n'émeut absolument personne'.[28] Only two critics thought that the play's inoffensiveness derived from its lack of literary or dramatic qualities;[29] but there were many who thought that despite these failings the work remained 'dangerous' and 'immoral'.

The former Saint-Simonian, Hippolyte Lucas, described the whole

[23] Extracts published on 28, 29 April, 1 May 1850. Advertisements on 1, 13, 17, 18 May. The publisher advertising this book in 1850 was Lagny, rue Bourbon-le-château; but the edition carries the name Perrodil.

[24] *Le Siècle*, 29 Apr. 1850.

[25] See H. J. Hunt, *Le Socialisme et le Romantisme en France* (Oxford, 1935), pp. 10–11.

[26] See R. Baldick, *The Life and Times of Frédérick-Lemaître* (London, 1956).

[27] *Le Journal des débats*, 29 Apr. 1850.

[28] *L'Assemblée nationale*, 29 Apr. 1850; and *Le Charivari*, same date.

[29] *L'Union* and *La Gazette de France*, 29 Apr. 1850.

intrigue of *Vautrin* as criminal. To put a noble thought in the mind of a criminal, as Balzac had done, and to claim that this absolves the man of all his crimes (as Lucas thought Balzac had claimed) 'est un jeu plus dangereux qu'on ne croit pour le repos public'.[30] Lucas condemns all those writers—Dumas and above all Sue are meant, as well as Balzac—who indulge in overt social criticism. These authors, he argues, 'n'ont pas compris la portée de leurs œuvres', and their characters of crime and revolt, such as Vautrin, 'ont produit leurs imitateurs . . . La société est devenue à son tour le miroir d'une littérature privée un moment du sens moral par la folie de ses auteurs.' French literature of the July Monarchy had failed in its task of purifying and ennobling man's baser nature; and thus the catastrophe of 1848. Lucas concludes pessimistically that 'la dépravation intellectuelle a entraîné la dépravation physique; la société a été doublement dégradée . . . Nous sommes sur une pente funeste.'[31] This morbid over-reaction to the 1850 production of *Vautrin* shows the extent to which Balzac criticism had already become independent of the actual content of the novelist's works. The attacks on Sue and all that was associated with him explain more adequately than the lines of Balzac's play *Nérée Desarbres's* claim that *Vautrin* was an outright threat to 'la paix civile'.[32] The connection of Balzac to some sort of destructive and revolutionary tendency was fostered, as these examples show, by opponents, not partisans, of revolutionary and radical change: the Fourierists had rejected Balzac's thought in their reviews of *Les Parents pauvres*. However, *La Démocratie pacifique* responded to the politically motivated attacks on *Vautrin* in a belated review that picks up the main thread of Weill's earlier arguments, but with an entirely new conclusion. The author of this important piece, Antony Méray, agreed with Nettement's view that the *Comédie humaine* lacked a 'message' or a philosophy. Like Nettement, too, Méray puts Balzac in a transitional phase of the modern novel—between the 'positive affirmations' of Sand and the 'conclusions' of Sue. Yet Méray is not unaware of Balzac's religious and political intentions. Though he considers that the novelist mocks at and destroys all the aspects of society which he portrays, 'il conclut presque toujours au respect des idoles qu'il abat'.[33] 'Not to have a message' in Méray's language clearly means in ours 'to have the wrong message'. Méray is none the less convinced that Balzac was at some deep

---

[30] *Le Moniteur du soir*, 28 Apr. 1850.
[31] Ibid.   [32] *L'Ami du peuple*, 29 Apr. 1850.
[33] *La Démocratie pacifique*, 7 May 1850.

or unconscious level at least a socialist, if not a phalansterian: and he cites the way in which Balzac sets up psychological and social conflicts on the basis of economic conflicts (e.g. David Séchard's quarrel with his father, Goriot's relationship with his daughters) as evidence of this. 'Et partout, et toujours il manque une conclusion.' Méray hazards the guess that Balzac only realized his true opinions late in life, when he was too old to change course; but the lack of an 'explicit moral' is unimportant, he thinks, for after a reading of *La Comédie humaine*, 'bien aveugles ceux qui chercheraient à restaurer les anciennes croyances!'[34] Similar thoughts were expressed in a then unpublished essay by a provincial journalist, Émile Chevalet.

Royauté constitutionnelle, fonctions du représentatif, libéralisme mesquin, religiosité égoiste, tribunaux de commerce, concurrence anarchique de l'industrie et du commerce, le célèbre romancier a critiqué tout cela avec une puissance de raison qui l'élève presque à la hauteur du socialiste éminent Proudhon.

For Chevalet, the epigraph of *Les Paysans*—'Qui terre a, guerre a'— was equivalent in meaning to Proudhon's dictum, 'La propriété, c'est le vol.' But Balzac was surely wrong, he continues, to think that the remedies of the past were apposite to the present situation: 'Quelle grande composition il pourrait faire avec l'idée socialiste!'[35] Méray's comments on *Vautrin* itself form only a small part of his article, but like his general remarks they are a mixture of insight and intentional distortion. The play's plot, he says, is impossible and Vautrin's plans absurd: no noble family would be deceived by such a patent villain for a moment. The recognition of Raoul as the countess's son is ridiculous, but even so, 'il y a dans ce drame une pensée perdue au milieu des richesses du dialogue'. The 'lost thought' is that criminals are such by force of circumstance alone, and *by nature* as honest as the next man. Rehabilitation of the criminal is thus always possible; and this (romantic and socialist) notion 'eût dû faire la pensée principale de la pièce'. The play would have been improved, in Méray's argument, had it in fact conformed to the mythical *Vautrin* that Janin, Lucas, and the right-wing press were attacking. It thus appears reasonable to describe Méray's long article as an attempt at the political recupera-

---

[34] *La Démocratie pacifique*, 7 May 1850.
[35] Émile Chevalet, 'De Balzac à Proudhon', MS. copy, Lovenjoul Library, Chantilly, A.361, fol. 8–17. Dated 1848–9 by Lovenjoul. Published in *L'Avenir républicain* (Issoudun), 21 June 1894.

tion of Balzac, despite the unfavourable remarks in it on the novelist's political views. What is more, Méray's article is not the only review of *Vautrin* to take this line of argument. A few days previously, Paul Meurice, co-editor (with Auguste Vacquerie) of *L'Évènement*, had put forward a similar view of the 'true sense' of Balzac's play. *L'Évènement* belonged to Victor Hugo, and it is Victor Hugo who is credited with inventing the idea of 'Balzac révolutionnaire', in the funeral oration he delivered at the novelist's graveside on 21 August 1850. In April 1850, however, his disciple Meurice was moving towards the same idea, expressed in extravagant rhetoric reminiscent of his master's prose style:

Vautrin, pour être vrai, n'en est pas moins poétique, et pour être moderne, n'en est pas moins éternel. Quand une vaste intelligence, quand une puissante énergie, se tourne contre l'ordre social, qui a tort? Évidemment, l'ordre social qui n'a pas su comprendre ou qui n'a pas su pardonner. Devant Dieu, sans doute, l'homme est toujours coupable du crime; mais la société, dans ce cas, est coupable du criminel.[36]

This is in effect the same argument as Méray's, with the difference that Meurice does not make it clear whether these ideas are present in the play or not. Meurice is even vaguer when he associates Balzac with the democratic left. Vautrin, he says, is the first literary hero to be concerned not with making things but with the creation of a man—and will not the art of Democracy be precisely that, 'de produire des libertés, de créer des âmes, de faire des hommes?' Méray at least had a real point to make about the economic infrastructure of Balzac's fictional world in his argument that the novelist was 'unconsciously' left-wing; Meurice's insubstantial rhetoric is almost meaningless—but not insignificant. It constitutes the first clear attempt to make Balzac an ally of the political left; in all probability, it prompted the Fourierists of *La Démocratie pacifique* to revise their earlier rejection of Balzac; and it may quite possibly be the expression of the views of Victor Hugo—or if it was not, then it must surely have been the source from which the poet drew them.

The coincidence of a political struggle with the revival of *Vautrin* in April 1850 had a notable effect on Balzac criticism as a whole. Unlike the production of the dramatically superior *Marâtre* in 1848, Hostein's venture at the Gaîté brought the novelist out of the obscurity into which he had fallen; and unlike the publication of *Les Parents*

[36] *L'Évènement*, 29 Apr. 1850; 6 May 1850 in some copies.

pauvres in 1846 it set the left against the right in their interpretations of Balzac's 'real meaning'.

News of Balzac's death first appeared in the Paris papers dated 20 August 1850. The only newspaper to carry more than a bare announcement of the facts and the details of the funeral arrangements for the following day was Hugo's *L'Évènement*. Its leading article was devoted to a high-flown lament on the loss of a great author; all other news was relegated to the lower columns. Meurice, who as editor in August 1850 probably wrote the piece on Balzac, declared that details of the journey of the President (Louis-Napoléon was touring the provinces at the time) and news of political manœuvres were trivial besides the death of a great writer. Hugo made much the same point in the funeral oration he delivered the following day at the Père Lachaise cemetery: 'Nous sommes bien fâchés si, devant une telle perte et le regret d'un tel génie, tous vos évènements et tous vos hommes paraissent si petits!'[37] It is in this speech, too, that the idea of Balzac as an unconscious revolutionary received its first well-known rendering: 'A son insu, qu'il le veuille ou non, qu'il y consente ou non, l'auteur de cette œuvre étrange et immense est de la forte race des écrivains révolutionnaires.' This vague but forceful argument had been foreshadowed not only by the articles already mentioned in *L'Évènement* and *La Démocratie pacifique*, but also by the postscript to a long disquisition on the movement of modern literature that appeared in an obscure left-wing paper, *Le Peuple de 1850*. The author of this piece was Taxile Delord, former editor of the satirical *Charivari* who moved on to the respectable opposition newspaper *Le Siècle* under the Second Empire.[38] In this article Delord brands the romantic movement as royalist and reactionary, and he considers critics like Janin and Cuvillier-Fleury to be part of the movement. The 1848 Revolution had ended the sway of these backward-looking writers and critics, he argues, and new literature would be 'revolutionary'. In the postscript, he makes it clear that Balzac was part of the new, revolutionary wave:

> La mort de Balzac est une perte pour les lettres, et, disons-le, pour la Révolution, à laquelle M. de Balzac a été utile, en peignant avec la verve, l'instinct et l'indépendance involontaire du génie l'époque actuelle. M. de Balzac ne partageait aucune de nos opinions politiques ou philosophiques, et pourtant il a contribué s'en [sic] s'en douter, à ébranler la vieille société.

37 Victor Hugo, *Actes et Paroles.—Avant l'Exil* (Imprimerie nationale, 1937), p. 296.
38 See R. Bellet *Presse et journalisme sous le Second Empire* (Kiosque, 1967), p. 308.

C'est là, du reste, l'histoire de tous les esprits vigoureux de ces temps-ci. Qu'ils en aient conscience ou non, ils travaillent pour la Révolution.[39] This article came out in the issue dated 21 August, which presumably appeared before Hugo gave his speech at 3 p.m. that day.[40] This does not permit the conclusion that Hugo took his ideas on Balzac's revolutionary meaning from this article or indeed from *L'Évènement*: it is quite as likely that Hugo's views had been expressed in conversation and had influenced the journalists on papers close to the poet's political position, and in the case of *L'Évènement*, owned by him. What is clear, however, is that the celebrated lines of Hugo's funeral oration do not constitute a unique, isolated illumination twenty years before Zola's invention of a socialist Balzac. They represent the view of a whole section of the left in response to Balzac's death.

The Fourierists were rather slow to express their reaction, but the obituary that eventually appeared in *La Démocratie pacifique* attempts to establish an orthodox line on Balzac, just as their article on *Vautrin* earlier that year had seemed to be a definite conclusion to the reviews of the play. Indeed, Méray's *Vautrin* article was reprinted at the foot of the obituary notice as if it were the definitive expression of the Fourierist line. In the obituary, Méray pursued the main points of his earlier article: Balzac had attacked all sides of contemporary society, described its corruption more accurately than any other writer, and was thus 'le chef de cette glorieuse phalange de littérateurs modernes dévorés sciemment ou instinctivement d'un esprit de critique sociale que rien n'arrête'.[41] Of course, the *Comédie humaine* lacked a 'conclusion'—but since Balzac had been patently unable to produce one, his death was no great loss to literature. Méray then launches into an exaggeration of his earlier speculations on Balzac's 'real' political beliefs. He states that the novelist had in fact become a socialist and had attended a 'fête phalanstérienne': 'Là il avoua qu'il avait trop vécu déjà et trop écrit dans les idées du vieux monde pour oser jamais changer officiellement de croyances.' Some modern scholars believe that Méray is here telling the strict truth.[42] It must be pointed out, however, that no other nineteenth-century critic or biographer took up Méray's point; that no evidence has been found to support the

[39] *Le Peuple de 1850*, 21 Aug. 1850.
[40] *L'Évènement*, 24 Aug. 1850, gives the times of ceremonies.
[41] *La Démocratie pacifique*, 25 Aug. 1850.
[42] e.g. J.-H. Donnard, *Les Réalités économiques et sociales dans la Comédie humaine* (Colin, 1961), pp. 447–9.

claim; and that Méray's words are embroidery on the speculation he put forward in April 1850, and which is discussed above. Furthermore, the editor of *La Démocratie pacifique*, Alexandre Weill, wrote memoirs in which he describes a dinner he gave for Heine, Sue, and Balzac, but no mention is made of any 'fête phalanstérienne' at which the novelist was present. Méray may in fact be referring to this dinner, at which the conversation turned to politics: but according to Weill, Balzac defended Church and Throne with his usual ardour.[43] All the available evidence therefore points to Méray's story of a conversion to socialism being a complete fabrication.

At the opposite extreme of the political spectrum in August 1850, Barbey d'Aurevilly took it for granted that Balzac was a catholic and royalist: 'Il était catholique, apostolique et romain, et c'était un royaliste. Les idées politiques et religieuses d'un homme sont les meilleurs moules de la force de son cerveau.'[44] Others attempted to resist the left-wing appropriation of Balzac's name less by categorical affirmations *à la Barbey* than by reasoned argument. Amédée Achard, for example, conceded that much of Balzac's work was vitiated by the romantic conventions he followed—but it was romanticism, and not Balzac's 'real nature', that had produced the emphasis on vice and evil in the *Comédie humaine*. Had he lived, the novelist would no doubt have overcome this inheritance. Balzac was no flatterer of 'popular instincts' like Sue, Achard continues, but was as critical of the peasantry as he was of the middle and upper ranks of society. Unlike Sand, he had painted the lower classes in their true colours in *Les Paysans*, and from this depiction 'un vif sentiment de la règle, du devoir, de l'autorité, de la hiérarchie s'exhale . . . comme une bonne odeur, et c'est par là qu'il appartient à l'école des écrivains royalistes'.[45] Speculation as to what Balzac would have become 'had he lived longer' also form the basis of the argument put forward by the moderate royalist *Gazette de France*, which at that time enjoyed the apparently impossible collaboration of Alexandre Weill as general editor and Alfred Nettement as literary editor. On Balzac, however, the two critics had never been very far apart, and either could have subscribed to the obituary notice which stated that there was no 'message' or moral to the 'tohu-bohu original' of the *Comédie humaine*—but had Balzac lived longer, he would have given his work a conclusion, 'et nous aimons à croire

[43] A. Weill, *Souvenirs intimes de Henri Heine* (Dentu, 1883), p. 119.
[44] *La Mode*, 24 Aug. 1850.
[45] *L'Assemblée nationale*, 25 Aug. 1850.

qu'elle eût été conforme aux principes que nous défendons'.[46] This argument was refined two days later in an attack on Hugo's funeral oration: the poet had been wrong to claim Balzac as a revolutionary, the *Gazette* states, since the ultimate form and meaning of the *Comédie humaine* must remain a mystery. Since Balzac's work is incomplete, it must be judged by its 'best' parts alone—*Eugénie Grandet, La Recherche de l'absolu* and *César Birotteau*.[47] This kind of 'reductive' argument—reducing Balzac to the author of a small set of his complete works—came to be the common feature of most favourable critical writing on the novelist over the next fifty years. Taine and Zola cut out the metaphysical novels, Faguet and Brunetière cut out *Le Lys dans la vallée* and the *Physiologie du mariage*. Yet Hugo had produced no argument at all for regarding Balzac as an unconscious revolutionary.

Hugo's speech was given wide publicity, with many papers reproducing it in full, and all the others having some sort of résumé.[48] It provoked a good deal of controversy, mostly concerned of course with the claim that Balzac was 'de la forte race des écrivains révolutionnaires'. Charles de Mazade, for example, objected to the bombast, and aptly commented that 'M. Hugo a des façons de s'exprimer qui font toujours croire qu'il parle de lui-même'.[49] Other newspapers, as has been seen, tried to argue the point; and some simply made contrary affirmations: 'Monarchiste, l'auteur du *Lys dans la vallée* n'a pas cessé de l'être; catholique, il l'a été jusque dans ses dernières heures; . . . homme d'ordre . . . etc.'[50] Critics and journalists of the right were in the ridiculous position of having to argue that a famous novelist who had never made a secret of his catholicism and monarchism was not a revolutionary. They had largely created the situation themselves, by refusing to take Balzac seriously, by accusing him of 'immorality' and by associating him with the opinions, not just the literary techniques, of Eugène Sue, thereby giving the left-wing journalists of *L'Évènement*, *La Démocratie pacifique*, and *Le Peuple de 1850* all the arguments they needed to show that Balzac had really been a revolutionary. Hugo had expressed this view to a wider audience and had made it essential to recuperate Balzac as a supporter of the old order. In three years, the situation had been turned upside down: for in 1847 the Fourierists had

---

[46] *La Gazette de France*, 23 Aug. 1850.   [47] Ibid. 24 Aug. 1850.
[48] Full text in *L'Évènement, La Gazette de France, La Patrie, La Presse, Le Siècle, La Silhouette.*
[49] 'Chronique', *RDM* 1 Sept. 1850.   [50] *Le Corsaire*, 24 Aug. 1850.

dismissed Balzac as much as the political right dismissed him; yet in 1850, every faction was eager to appropriate the novelist's name. This development cannot be accounted for in terms of a general change in 'taste' or of trends in criticism. It was created by a precise sequence of events against a particular political background.

The view that Balzac was morally dangerous and politically undesirable was quick to return after the controversy over Hugo's funeral oration had died down. In August and September 1850, not one newspaper of moderate or right-wing persuasion[51] either agreed with Hugo that Balzac was 'revolutionary' or rejected the novelist's political position: yet after 1850 many critics and journalists of professed anti-Republican, royalist, or Bonapartist views criticized Balzac harshly on religious, moral, and political grounds.

In 1851, the Académie de Châlons-sur-Marne awarded 'prix de critique' to two essays on the influence of the literature of the July Monarchy on 'l'esprit public et les mœurs'. Both essays were published and reviewed in the Paris press—and both of course argue that the literature of the preceding twenty years had had a far-reaching and pernicious effect on public morals and political events. The two authors, Charles Menche de Loisne (secretary-general of the Lyons police) and Jules Jolly, do not really produce any arguments, but point to supposedly parallel features in literary and social history and conclude that the one, therefore, influenced the other.

Sand, Hugo, Dumas, and Sue provide these two critics with the bulk of their material, but Balzac is included in the general condemnation of the romantic movement. Menche de Loisne regards the Church as the mainstay of society, and is more concerned with finding evidence of disbelief, scepticism, and rationalism; whilst Jolly concentrates on the issues of crime and family. Both essayists accept that the role of the novelists and playwrights of the July Monarchy was similar to that of the *philosophes* under the Ancien Régime: they had prepared its downfall by undermining its values. In Balzac's works, Menche de Loisne sees the results of irreligion, for they contain no 'enseignement' or 'moralité'; nor is there any mention of an afterlife. Vautrin is taken as Balzac's spokesman, so that the *Comedié humaine* appears to preach

---

[51] Right-wing papers 'reconnus par la police' were as follows: *L'Assemblée nationale*, *Le Corsaire* (legitimist); *Le Moniteur du soir*, *La Gazette de France*, *Le Journal des débats*, *L'Ordre*, *La Liberté* ('parti de l'ordre', moderate right); *L'Union* (catholic); *Le Pays*, *L'Ami du peuple* (Bonapartist). Not recognized were the monarchist *La Mode* and the Bonapartist *Le Pouvoir*.

that wealth is the criterion of virtue; and Rastignac is treated as if he were a disciple of Voltaire. Moreover, some of Balzac's novels are actually anti-religious, in Loisne's opinion: is not *Les Célibataires* an attack on the celibacy of priests, and thus on the whole edifice of the Church? When Granville declares, in *Une Double Famille*[52] (one of the shorter *Scènes de la vie privée*), that he cannot love both his wife and Christ, is this not a further attack on the Church? *La Peau de chagrin* provides Loisne with more examples of irreligious statements, and he concludes that the novelist was an unbeliever: 'Incrédulité! C'est là la conclusion de toutes les œuvres de M. de Balzac.'[53]

Jules Jolly is perhaps a little less obtuse than his competitor. The France of the *Comédie humaine* appears to him 'un abîme sans issue' in which crime pays and virtue does not. The criminal society depicted in the play *Vautrin* is like a 'réunion d'honnêtes gens' besides the morally despicable characters of Balzac's 'respectable' society. This inversion of moral values could not but contribute to the decay of French society, in Jolly's view. Similarly, in *La Femme de trente ans*, that pillar of family life, the husband, is left out of account, thus turning moral values upside down. In *La Physiologie du mariage* Balzac seems to ignore 'tout ce qu'il y a de pureté, de sainteté, de joies ineffables dans cette vie intérieure de famille'—which joys Jolly proceeds to describe at length. The one-sidedness of Balzac's portrayal of family life, and the inversion of values in his treatment of crime and honesty, contributed to the disarray that made the 1848 Revolution possible.[54]

There were other essays in this vein in the early 1850s which attempted to show how literature had fashioned the disasters of society. No doubt the political activities of the great romantic poets, Lamartine and Hugo, and the career of the novelist Eugène Sue, gave a surface plausibility to such arguments. Balzac was less clearly associated with the disaster of 1848 than Sand, Sue, or Hugo, whom Edouard L'Hôte, for example, considered mere propagandists and 'démolisseurs de parti'; and thus his role in shaping events was variously described as indirect or shallow. None the less, the original arguments of Hippolyte Castille were repeated: the preponderance and attractiveness of evil

---

[52] Loisne actually uses the early title, *La Femme vertueuse*, which suggests he had not read it in the Furne edition.

[53] C. Menche de Loisne, *Influence de la littérature française sur l'esprit public et les mœurs* (Garnier, 1852), p. 350.

[54] Jules Jolly, *De l'Influence de la littérature et du théâtre sur l'esprit public et les mœurs pendant les vingt dernières années* (Amyot, 1851), pp. 36-9.

characters in the *Comédie humaine* 'semble donner raison au vice contre la vertu, à la dépravation contre la moralité'.[55] L'Hôte goes further, however, and renders his argument absurd by claiming that 'l'école des *Vautrin* . . . a formé bon nombre d'élèves pour la *tire* et les barricades'. In fact few if any of the young men on the barricades in 1848 could have seen the single performance of *Vautrin* in 1840, and the allegedly subversive lines of the play had been added by the actors and were not in the printed text which the censor passed. Yet *Vautrin* conjured up images of barricades and revolution in the minds of rightwing critics like L'Hôte—and in young poets like Baudelaire. In May 1848, together with Champfleury and Toubin, he had brought out a news-sheet which demanded 'que le théâtre de la Porte Saint-Martin reprenne au plus vite et *L'Auberge des Adrêts* et *Robert-Macaire* et surtout cette belle pièce de *Vautrin* de notre grand romancier, le citoyen Balzac'.[56] For Baudelaire, as for Menche de Loisne, Jolly, and Edouard L'Hôte, Balzac was an 'opposition' writer—in some way connected with revolutionary tendencies. The strongest and most frequently mentioned point of connection was the character of Vautrin in the play and the novels.

The essays of Menche de Loisne and Jolly were reviewed in 1851 by J. L. E. Lerminier, a critic whose views on Balzac's meaning typify the ambiguity of the right at this time. On the one hand he contradicted Hugo in August 1850: 'Sans aucun doute, Balzac n'est pas révolutionnaire', and repeated the argument of Amédée Achard, discussed above, that the novelist had been even-handed in his gloomy description of the different classes, unlike Sand and Eugène Sue.[57] Moreover, Lerminier felt Balzac was a victim, not an instigator of political turmoil, and that his premature death at the age of fifty-one was 'encore une perte à mettre au compte et à la charge de la Révolution'.[58] The novelist had tried to turn his back on the events of February 1848 'qui l'ont surpris dans ses travaux et troublé dans sa vie', but he had none the less been 'presque démoralisé' by the ensuing chaos.[59] It is perhaps not irrelevant to mention Lerminier's own troubles under the Second Republic. As Professor of 'Histoire générale et philosophique des

[55] Édouard L'Hôte, 'De l'Influence de la littérature et du théâtre sur l'esprit public et les mœurs depuis vingt ans', *L'Artiste*, 15 Feb. 1853.

[56] *Le Salut public*, Nᵒ. 2.

[57] *L'Assemblée nationale*, 2 Sept. 1850.

[58] Letter to Cᵗˢˢᵉ Merlin (?). Damescéno Morgand catalogue, May 1956, item 146. Copy kindly shown to me by M. Roger Pierrot.

[59] *L'Assemblée nationale*, 25 Aug. 1850.

législations comparées' at the Collège de France, he had been shouted
down when he tried to lecture on 23 January 1849, and was only able
to give his course on the twenty-seventh with the protection of 1,000
foot-soldiers (commanded by no less than a general), a large cavalry
detachment, a commissioner of police, and eighty policemen. On the
thirty-first he resigned his chair—and in his remarks on Balzac, he may
simply be imputing his own feelings to the novelist, whom he had
met socially.[60] In his review of Menche de Loisne and Jolly, Lerminier
castigates these provincial authors for their ignorance of Balzac's views
on religion and science, and quotes passages from the *Avant-propos*
to the *Comédie humaine* for their benefit. Yet on the other hand
Lerminier agrees that Balzac's religious feelings did not go very deep,
and he repeats an earlier judgement on the disunity between the intention of the novelist and the effect of the novels: 'Il ne s'est pas aperçu
que tout en ayant l'intention de rendre un éclatant hommage au
catholicisme, il en niait la nécessité divine.'[61] From this lack of deep
religion springs Balzac's 'universal pessimism', his view of life as 'ruse,
fiction, sordide intérêt'. Moreover, Lerminier shared the general right-
wing view that this bleak portrait of a society bent on evil and ir-
remediably corrupt had exercised 'sur tous ses contemporains, écrivains
et lecteurs, une maligne influence'. So although he criticized the shal-
lowness of the essays by Loisne and Jolly, Lerminier himself considered
Balzac's works to be not only evidence, but also a cause, of the decay
and corruption into which French literature, like French society, had
fallen.

The question of Balzac's influence on the imaginations and lives
of real people became a central theme of criticism under the Second
Empire (1852-70). This theme represents a development of the
questions on the 'real meaning' of the *Comédie humaine* which we have
discussed; it is of course also part of the reaction to romanticism that
we have seen informing much of the Second Republic criticism, and
of which *Madame Bovary* is on one level a striking example (for
Emma's tragedy arises from the influence of romantic novels on her
imagination); and it is closely associated with the belief, held by an

[60] See J. Pommier, 'Balzac, écrivain révolutionnaire', *AB* (1967) for sources of these
details on Lerminier. In this article, Professor Pommier gives an account of the genesis of
the left-wing view of Balzac without taking the reception of *Vautrin* into account. My
reply, 'Du nouveau sur Balzac, écrivain révolutionnaire', *AB* (1969), deals with some of the
material of this chapter.

[61] 'Chronique', *L'Assemblée nationale*, 29 Oct. 1852; see also *RDM* 15 Apr. 1847,
quoted on p. 16, above.

extremely wide range of critics and writers in that age of technological and material progress, that France was set on a course of decadence and spiritual destruction. Whatever the wider causes for this almost universal gloom and pessimisn, there are certain detailed factors affecting the literary life of the 1850s that confirmed and promoted this view among journalists and critics.

The press laws of the Second Empire created a gulf between 'political' and 'literary' journalism. Political papers were subject to stringent financial controls, but those that were sufficiently cautious to escape the censors' wrath (or which had protection in the entourage of the Emperor, like the liberal *Siècle*) became increasingly profitable. It became virtually impossible to found new political papers, and some actually disappeared—the royalist *La Mode*, for example, and the legitimist *Assemblée nationale*.[62] Literary journals suffered less severe financial restrictions, but they did not have the right to mention even obliquely any matters deemed to be political. Only the first offence against this law was punishable by a fine: the second brought suspension. Moreover, any new paper had to establish itself by subscription sales alone before it was allowed to be sold 'sur la voie publique'—but literary papers, containing no topical comment or reference, could hardly hope for large subscriptions. The result was not a limited number of literary newspapers, as one might have expected in the face of all these impediments to free expression: on the contrary, the only means by which a new writer could hope to break the monopoly on literary fame held by the decreasing number of established journals was to found his own literary sheet. There was in fact an enormous output of ephemeral 'journaux littéraires' in Paris in the 1850s, and no less than 159 different titles are listed by Firmin Maillard for the year 1856 alone.[63] The majority of these lasted for no more than a few issues.

The laws of the Second Empire divorced 'literature' from 'politics', and they favoured the fragmentation of literary ideas into a large number of minor 'schools' and factions, each represented by its own literary newspaper. Cut off from political comment, the journalistic 'bohème' tended understandably to reject notions of the social responsibility of the artist. This tendency, represented in creative writing by Gautier, for example, and in serious literary journalism by the

---

[62] See R. Bellet, *Presse et journalisme*, pp. 13 ff. on the press laws and their effects.

[63] *Histoire anecdotique et critique des 159 journaux parus en l'an de grâce 1856* (chez l'auteur, 1857).

Revue fantaisiste and the new *Revue de Paris*, coupled with the flood of newspapers each one representing some different 'school' or even a single individual, like the *Gazette de Champfleury*, Dumas's *Mousquetaire*, or Alphonse Karr's *Les Guêpes*, created an impression of total disarray. 'Entre la littérature et la société il y a en ce moment un singulier désaccord', wrote one critic for the *Revue des deux mondes* in 1851.[64] The older critics of the established journals could no longer see where French literature was going, and assumed that it was going to the dogs; so they offered prizes for essays on how best to restore French letters to their former glory.[65]

Critics also looked to the past to find the causes of the decadence they perceived in contemporary literature. Just as Menche de Loisne and Jolly had argued that Balzac contributed to the political catastrophe of 1848, so others, in the 1850s, presented the novelist as the source of later decadence. The most virulent exponent of this development of Balzac criticism was Armand de Pontmartin, an aristocrat proud of his descent, a society novelist and prolific critic who saw himself as the defender of the old order and a natural enemy of anything new. In Balzac he found 'un aliment, et pour ainsi dire une note correspondante à tous les vices, à toutes les erreurs particulières à notre époque'.[66] These particular errors and vices were three in number: the 'cult of success', the confusion of moral good and evil, and (worst of all) an amateur approach to politics.

Pontmartin's major article on Balzac was a long and systematic denigration of the novelist's alleged 'apotheosis', and was written in response to the publication of the first chapters of *Madame Bovary* in the *Revue de Paris* in October 1856. Flaubert's novel, rightly or wrongly, was seen as the most scandalous product yet of the '*réaliste*' movement; and Pontmartin's hatred of the new fed his hatred of Balzac, whom he saw was the ancestor of 'ces petits bohêmes, ces réalistes avortés'.[67] Without the example of the *Comédie humaine*, the literary riff-raff would not have realized that 'on peut se jouer de tout sentiment moral' and none the less remain 'un puissant inventeur et un conteur éminent'. Pontmartin believed that scribblers like Flaubert were admirers of Balzac, and that this was an evil fetish. It was thus his duty to expose 'l'immoralité et le genre d'immoralité de l'œuvre

[64] P. Rollet, 31 Jan. 1851.

[65] Laurent-Pichat, 'Un Prix de 2500 francs', *RDP* 1 Jan. 1855.

[66] *L'Assemblée nationale*, 29 Oct. 1853.

[67] 'Les Fétiches littéraires. I.—M. de Balzac', *Le Correspondant*, Nov.–Dec. 1856; *Causeries du Samedi* (Michel Lévy, 1857), p. 33.

de Balzac' and so discredit his imitators. (Precisely why Pontmartin sincerely believed that Flaubert and the realist school were conscious imitators and admirers of Balzac, which they did not claim to be, will be discussed in the next chapter.)

To show Balzac's immorality, Pontmartin takes up Sainte-Beuve's argument that the novelist exaggerated his material and thus falsified and invalidated his work. 'Ideal' in the *Comédie humaine* turns into mysticism, alchemy, Swedenborgian heresy; the 'côté réel et bas' of life becomes glorified ugliness, a 'débauche de réalisme'. The only characters held up for the reader's admiration are 'ces bizarres héros, galériens ou dandys, artistes ou hommes d'état, qui marchent à leur but *per fas et nefas*, traitant le monde en pays conquis'. The immorality of these bizarre heroes—Vautrin, Henry de Marsay, Rastignac—is proved, for Pontmartin, by their real-life imitators. Sainte-Beuve had first given actual examples of the real world copying the *Comédie humaine*, though in a fairly light-hearted vein, when he mentioned that Venetian and Russian aristocrats had dressed up as characters from the novels.[68] (Sainte-Beuve appears to have been duped into believing this by Jules Lecomte, who was attempting to discredit the critic.)[69] There is some corroboration for Pontmartin's claim that Balzac's heroes were taken as models to be emulated in real life, as in this letter from Flaubert to Louise Colet:

Les héros pervers de Balzac ont, je crois, tourné la tête à bien des gens. La grêle géneration qui s'agite maintenant autour du pouvoir et de la renommée a puisé, dans ces lectures, l'admiration bête d'une certaine immoralité bourgeoise à quoi elle s'efforce d'atteindre. J'ai eu des confidences à ce sujet. Ce n'est plus Werther ou Saint-Preux que l'on veut être, mais Rastignac ou Lucien de Rubempré.[70]

Perhaps the source of these 'confidences' was Flaubert's companion, Maxime du Camp, who made a similar comment: 'Être Rastignac ou Marsay, Vautrin ou Lucien de Rubempré, ce fut le rêve de plus d'un'.[71] Du Camp in fact provides an example of this dream in his account of Collet-Meygret, the man who as director of the *sûreté générale* from 1854 was in charge of enforcing the press laws of the Second Empire. Collet-Meygret had read Balzac, had studied him, 's'en était impregné comme bien des hommes de son époque', and above all believed in these fictions. According to Du Camp, Collet-Meygret was brought

[68] *Le Constitutionnel*, Sept. 1850.   [69] See below, p. 73.
[70] Dated 26 Sept. 1853. Flaubert, *Correspondance* (Conard, 1927), III. 353–4.
[71] *Souvenirs littéraires* (Hachette, 1883), II. 52.

to Paris in 1852 as a reward for having founded a Bonapartist news-paper in Lyons (*Le Président*), and then as police chief built up a file of information with which he tried to blackmail the Emperor himself—who retired him to the provinces in 1858. Having failed as a compound of Rastignac and Vautrin, Collet-Meygret rose again after 1870 to emulate Mercadet on the stock exchange, but went bankrupt and was convicted of fraud. He ended his days in 1876 shortly after being re-leased from the Sainte-Pélagie prison.[72] What influence the *Comédie humaine* actually had over Collet-Meygret cannot be known, but it was that kind of career under the Second Empire which lent material to critics like Pontmartin who were convinced of the direct influence of literature on the way men lived.

Balzac's novels had this sort of real-life effect, in Pontmartin's view, because they contained no gradation of moral right and wrong: the hero is simply the one who 'succeeds', by whatever means, and the novels produce no sense of remorse. Balzac's descriptions of married life went beyond the bounds of decency, and were far more corrupting than the open satires of his *Physiologie du mariage* or the *Petites misères de la vie conjugale*; and the advocacy of catholicism in the novels was 'cent fois pire que des insultes'. Pontmartin does not point to a contradiction between the stated intentions of Balzac and the 'real meaning' of the novels to make this point, as previous right-wing critics had done; instead he perceives a contradiction in the *Avant-propos* itself. Balzac's claim that Catholicism was 'un système complet de répression des tendances dépravées de l'homme' and thus 'le plus grand élément d'Ordre Social'[73] reduces the Church to a temporal power, according to Pontmartin, and thus reveals that the novelist was fundamentally an atheist and materialist.[74]

Another, rather more subtle, right-wing critic also attacked Balzac at this time for his materialism and implicit atheism. Eugène Poitou cannot accept the argument of *Louis Lambert* on the unity of the spiritual and material worlds—indeed, he finds the whole book ridiculous. Yet underneath the philosophical ramblings of *Séraphita* and of Louis Lambert himself there is 'un fond d'idées très-sérieuses, c'est le matérialisme même'.[75] Balzac's intellectual forebears are not the mystical Saint-Martin and Swedenborg, but the atheist *philosophes*, Helvetius and Diderot. Poitou, like Lerminier, sees this lack of

---

[72] Most of these details are confirmed by the *Dictionnaire de biographie française*.
[73] *Pl.* I. 8.   [74] Pontmartin, op. cit., p. 44.
[75] E. Poitou, 'M. de Balzac, étude morale et littéraire', *RDM* 15 Dec. 1856.

religious faith as the source of Balzac's pessimism and immorality. By describing a familiar, bourgeois setting in his novels, Balzac rendered them dangerous, for he thereby lent a 'cachet de réalisme' to his imaginary, corrupt universe 'où devoir . . . semble un mot, le dévouement une folie'. In common with most right-wing critics of the period, Poitou takes particular exception to Balzac's treatment of the family. All its values are degraded by the novelist: paternal love in *Le Père Goriot*, maternal love in *La Rabouilleuse* by Madame Bridau's 'inexplicable' preference for her worthless son Philippe. The discussion of the problems of marriage in the *Mémoires de deux jeunes mariées* is abhorrent, and *Le Lys dans la vallée* is described as 'du libertinage au musc'.

Poitou devoted a book to the popular subject of the influence of romantic literature on society, and in it he repeated—though with a much greater degree of polemical skill and intelligence—the arguments of Menche de Loisne and Jolly. That is to say, he sees Balzac as an indirect or involuntary propagator of harmful socialist doctrines, and in particular of the idea of 'le droit au bonheur'. Poitou is not unaware of Balzac's professed legitimism, as Loisne appeared to be, but he considers it so exaggerated as to be insincere.[76] Pontmartin did not suggest that Balzac was insincere in his political views, but that he was deluding himself. The novelist's admiration for the aristocracy, like his allegiance to the Church, was based on the wrong reasons and had to be rejected by the catholic and aristocratic Pontmartin. In *La Duchesse de Langeais*, Balzac had attempted to give 'la peinture exacte de la grande dame du faubourg Saint-Germain pendant la Restauration', and he had failed utterly. The novelist was a mere *goujat*, according to the critic, and had never met any real 'grandes dames'; his only contact was with 'patriciennes déchues', and he had mistakenly assumed that these exceptions were the rule. Thus in his portrayal of the Duchesse, Balzac had calumnied the aristocracy by exaggerating the evil in his model and by producing an inversion of the 'noble courtisane'.[77] In one sense, Pontmartin is right, for *La Duchesse de Langeais* was written partly as revenge for the shabby treatment Balzac had received from the Duchesse de Castries; it was not intended to flatter the aristocracy.[78] Pontmartin's defence of the aristocracy

[76] E. Poitou, *Du Roman et du théâtre contemporains et de leur influence sur les mœurs* (Durand, 1857).

[77] Pontmartin, op. cit., pp. 55–8.

[78] See A. Maurois, *Prométhée ou la vie de Balzac* (Hachette, 1965), p. 230.

verges on the absurd, however, when he attacks the forthright statements of the Abbé Gondrand on the temporal role of the Church (in *La Duchesse*) as a calumny of the noble classes: no aristocrat, he claims, could ever subscribe to such materialistic opinions.

The question arises as to the justification of the attacks on Balzac's morality which are made in the articles discussed above. The author's intention is not relevant to the question, for the 'morality' of a work lies in the effect of its finished form on its readers. Of course, cranks and imbeciles might be inspired to 'immoral' acts by any fiction; but it does appear to be the case that novels like *Le Père Goriot*, with its blurred authorial viewpoint and open conclusion, gave rise to 'immoral' readings on the part of otherwise sane and reasonably intelligent men. Evidence of a sort has been presented to show that the successful, unscrupulous young heroes of the Parisian novels were taken as models to be emulated, with often disastrous consequences. Indeed, it may not be misreading *Le Père Goriot* to draw from it a powerful admiration for unscrupulous fortune-hunters and ladykillers. In a general discussion of morality in fiction, C. Wayne Booth is adamant that an author has an obligation to be as clear about his moral position as he can be.[79] Balzac's professions of faith and intention, in the *Avant-propos*, in the reply to Castille, in the many asides in the *Comédie humaine* itself, were obviously of insufficient clarity, and failed to overrule the implications drawn from the plots and structure of his novels. The critics who attacked the *Comédie humaine* for its immorality were of course politically motivated for the most part, but their motivations are not relevant to the truth or value of what they said. Their conclusions can only be tested against historical reality, but this reality—lives poisoned or perverted from their natural course by the effect of Balzac's fictions—is not verifiable because it mostly went unrecorded. The problem remains intractable, and has no solution; but as a problem in criticism it slowly evaporated as a more Flaubertian attitude to fiction spread to critics and theorists of literature. (Though Flaubert himself, as has been seen, tells us that 'les héros pervers de Balzac ont tourné la tête à bien des gens'.) The critics who attacked the morality of the *Comédie humaine* cannot be dismissed as simply wrong. Independently of each other, a great number of them 'misread' the novels in the same way; so that one is indeed entitled to speculate

[79] C. Wayne Booth, *The Rhetoric of Fiction* (Chicago, 1961).

on whether Balzac, whatever his intentions, had not in fact created an immoral work by mistake.

Barbey d'Aurevilly's views on Balzac's political and religious meaning were exceptional, indeed unique, in the early 1850s—as were so many aspects of this bizarre and flamboyant writer. Barbey, like Pontmartin and Poitou, was a catholic and a royalist; but unlike all other critics of the 1850s he acclaimed Balzac as a great catholic and royalist writer. For Barbey, Balzac was 'le romancier même du XIXe siecle',[80] 'une majesté intellectuelle',[81] 'le premier homme littéraire du XIXe siecle',[82] superior in the unity of his conceptions even to Shakespeare.[83] Moreover, Barbey saw Balzac's religious and political opinions as an integral part of his work and as the source of its quality:

Religieux, catholique, absolu d'idées comme tout penseur, Balzac est de cette grande école d'autorité qu'on rencontre à une certaine hauteur dans toutes les sciences et dans les œuvres humaines. Le Catholicisme n'a besoin de personne, mais le catholicisme, nous osons le prévoir, réclamera un jour Balzac comme un de ses écrivains les plus dévoués car, en toute thèse, il conclut comme le Catholicisme conclurait.[84]

This view of Balzac did not become generally acceptable until the end of the century, when France was a secular state and ardent catholics could recognize that a pessimistic description of an evil society was not necessarily anti-religious. In the 1850s, however, the right wing could not countenance the allegiance of Barbey's almost feudal image of Balzac. He was recruited by the novelist's executor, Armand Dutacq, to compile a selection of *Maximes et pensées tirées de la Comédie humaine*, and he did so with great thoroughness. Dutacq read the manuscript and reported to Madame Ève de Balzac:

C'est un livre nouveau et d'une très grande importance.

Par exemple pour la *Religion* M. de Balzac pense mieux qu'un père de l'Église. Et cependant les catholiques de *l'Univers*, de la *Gazette de France*, de *l'Union*, et de l'*Ami de la Religion* ne l'ont jamais accueilli et encore aujourd'hui ils lui sont contraires. Ils devront désormais se rendre à l'évidence.[85]

The serial rights of the *Maximes et Pensées* had already been sold to *Le Pays*, 'journal de l'Empire', but Dutacq was afraid that they would

[80] *Le Pays*, 25 May 1854.   [81] Ibid. 13 July 1853.
[82] Ibid.   [83] Ibid. 11 May 1864.   [84] Ibid. 25 May 1854.
[85] Unpublished letter dated 7 Apr. 1854. MS. autograph, Lovenjoul Library, Chantilly, A.273, fo. 122–3.

go back on their contract once they saw the political and religious tenor of the selection Barbey had made. 'Je crains des difficultés. Nos amis les écrivains du *Pays* sont des endormeurs, ils s'attachent à ne froisser aucune opinion, aucun système . . .'[86] The editor of *Le Pays* was the same Vicomte de la Guéronnière who had refused to accept *Les Paysans* in 1845. He did in the end publish some of the *Maximes*, but inserted the following note with the second instalment:

la direction est loin de partager toutes les opinions émises par l'éminent écrivain . . . et croit même devoir protester contre certaines particulièrement hasardées, paradoxales ou fausses, que nos lecteurs, qui connaissent bien nos principes politiques, distingueront facilement . . .[87]

Barbey had nothing but scorn for those who refused to accept his picture of a catholic, absolutist Balzac, and he maintained that his selection was not '*du Balzac arrangé par d'Aurevilly*'.[88] None the less, Dutacq's guess that there would be difficulties was correct. *Le Pays* published only a few, sporadic sections of Barbey's manuscript and eventually ceased the series altogether. Barbey's *Maximes et Pensées* never appeared in book form in France, and the (probably abbreviated) version that came out anonymously in Brussels in 1856 was never acknowledged by the author.[89] Balzac's views as presented by Barbey were too far to the right for 'le journal de l'Empire'. It was Hippolyte Taine who captured in a nice formula the view that underlay the rejection of the *Comédie humaine* by *Le Pays*, Pontmartin, Poitou, and the others, when he said that 'Balzac, en politique comme ailleurs, a fait un roman.'[90]

In the decade following the publication of Balzac's last important novels, critics of his works struggled to resolve the conflict that they nearly all perceived between the intentions, as stated in the *Avant-propos*, and the meaning of the novels themselves. 'Right' and 'left' agreed that the picture of modern society drawn in *La Comédie humaine* was not a favourable one—and under the influence of *Les Parents pauvres* tended to exaggerate the gloom and harshness of Balzac's world. Except for a brief period in August–September 1850,

[86] Ibid., fo. 123.   [87] *Le Pays*, 19 May 1854.

[88] Letter dated 25 Aug. 1854, in *Lettres à Trébutien* (Bernouard, 1927), III. 103.

[89] For further details of this 'lost' work, see G. Courville's article in *Études balzaciennes*, 1959, and my forthcoming article, 'Barbey d'Aurevilly et les *Pensées* de Balzac', in the *Cahiers Barbey d'Aurevilly*.   [90] *Journal des débats*, 3 Mar. 1858.

all right-wing critics considered Balzac undesirable on political, religious, and moral grounds (apart from Barbey d'Aurevilly, of course).
Except for a brief period between April and August 1850, left-wing
criticism of Balzac was infrequent, and invariably dismissed the novelist
as politically hostile to the cause. Apparently neutral criticism from
moderates like Nettement and Lerminier simply argued that the lack
of clear political or religious commitment in the *Comédie humaine*
rendered it somehow faulty and immoral. In this general context the
favourable arguments of 1850 appear no more than a squabble for the
propaganda value of Balzac's name at the time when all great men have
their sins forgiven—when they die.

2 Truth and vision in the *Comédie humaine* in the 1850s

BALZAC'S novels contain a great deal of detailed description; yet they are also the product of an exuberant imagination. Few critics before Taine could accept or condone the presence of these two opposing poles, or could find a way of resolving what was seen as an aesthetic paradox. In the 1850s, many followed Sainte-Beuve in believing that the artistic value of the *Comédie humaine* lay in its qualities of observation, and thus felt the imaginative aspects of the works to be aesthetic faults. Others, such as Cormenin and Baudelaire, came to see Balzac's imagination as the source of truth and beauty, and thus felt that the detailed observation of real life was irrelevant to the novels' artistic quality. Only Hippolyte Taine went beyond the paradox to argue that observation and imagination were complementary, mutually enhancing features of the *Comédie humaine*.

Most critics of the early 1850s regarded Balzac as a phenomenon that required explanation, but not as a writer of great literary importance. The idea that Balzac's works were above all a store-house of information about French society was common long before Taine, to whom the notion is now often (and falsely) attributed.[1] This view of Balzac as a 'realist' (in the weakest sense of the word) carried a variety of evaluations in this period. Hippolyte Castille, for example, thought that mere truthfulness did not constitute literary merit. Even if Balzac had written works 'où nos petits-fils iront chercher la reproduction fidèle et détaillée . . . des mœurs', he was not a 'génie dans un sens complexe'. Praise of that sort is reserved for Stendhal alone among the novelists of the July Monarchy.[2] Stendhal's complete works were being published in 1853, when these remarks were written, and his reputation was for a while much higher than Balzac's. In the first book-length critical study of Balzac to be published, the young Armand Baschet wrote that the novelist's principal merit was to have

[1] By R. Sealy, for example. See 'Montégut, Brunetière—and George Eliot', *MLR* Jan. 1971.
[2] *Les Hommes et les mœurs en France sous le règne de Louis-Philippe* (Henneton, 1853), pp. 313–14.

given documents that would be indispensable for all future historians of 'la très-étrange et très-originale époque qui est la nôtre'.[3] Paul de Musset, the poet's elder brother, had stated with the intention to praise that 'M. de Balzac restera comme un document à consulter sur les mœurs du XIXe siècle';[4] whilst the venomous Gustave Planche intended a restrictive and not particularly laudatory sense when he described Balzac as 'ce conteur ingénieux, cet observateur pénétrant, qui a laissé sur notre temps des études pleines de vérité'.[5] In an unpublished essay once again condemning the *Comédie humaine* for its immorality, Hippolyte Lucas concedes that Balzac was a great writer in virtue of his ability to describe external, material reality in precise detail.[6] Alfred Nettement also spoke of Balzac's 'don de l'analyse infinitésimale' as his distinctive literary merit, and likened his descriptions of interior scenes to genre paintings of the Flemish school.[7] Although the theme of 'Balzac observateur' in criticism of the early 1850s was widespread, as these examples show, it did not carry any particular evaluative association, nor a necessary association with the *réaliste* movement in literature. Castille, Lucas, and Planche do not use this term in the passages quoted from above; Baschet refers vaguely to Balzac as 'ce merveilleux réaliste'; Nettement considers the novelist to be the 'chef de l'école réaliste', but for reasons of a different order. Balzac's language, he writes, is sometimes stilted and artificial, and he lacks a concept of 'l'idéal': in this sense, and not because he was a careful and accurate observer, Balzac can be seen as the leader of the realists.

The publication of *Madame Bovary* in October 1856 gave rise to prolonged polemics on *le réalisme* as well as on immorality in the novel, and Balzac was mentioned frequently in both connections. The term *réalisme* had first been used in an artistic context by the painter Courbet, but it rapidly acquired a derogatory meaning and was applied liberally to anything vaguely connected with the artistic and literary *bohème* that met at the Brasserie Andler. Baudelaire, Champfleury, Buchon, Duranty, Courbet were all *réalistes* in this sense. Since it was 'immoral', *Madame Bovary* was 'realist' from the point of view of its attackers, but not according to the *réalistes* themselves. The

---

[3] *Variétés littéraires: H. de Balzac.—Étude variée. Généralités de La Comédie humaine* (Blosse, 1851), p. 14.

[4] *Le National*, 29 Apr. 1850.   [5] *RDM* 1 May 1855.

[6] First published in *Annales romantiques* X (1913), 228; dated 1854 by Weinberg, op. cit., p. 225.

[7] *Histoire de la littérature française sous le gouvernement de juillet* (J. Lecoffre, 1854), II. 242-4.

literary ideas of Duranty, the most extreme of the *réalistes*, editor of a newspaper entitled *Le Réalisme*, were of a Calvinistic strictness. The novelist should invent nothing, copy life as he found it, arrange his material as little as possible, avoid all effects of style and rhetoric. He should not preach or even interpret the meaning of his work, but present the bare truth, sober and unadorned.[8] The ideas of Champfleury[9] and Buchon were not enormously different, but Flaubert and Balzac are, obviously, far removed from this sort of literary programme. None the less, Pontmartin attacked Flaubert as a realist, and considered Balzac to be the realists' 'fétiche littéraire', the model they tried, but failed, to imitate. Duranty's reply to this rabid onslaught is one of the most interesting pieces in the 'querelle du réalisme' sparked off by *Madame Bovary*.

The political and class criteria used by Pontmartin are of course pointed out by Duranty, but he agrees with the catholic critic that the *réalistes* failed to imitate Balzac. The author of the *Comédie humaine*, he says, 'n'est pas un réaliste, quoiqu'il soit souvent réaliste'. By this distinction Duranty means, I think, that when Balzac meets the *réaliste* criteria of literary excellence it is by chance and not design. The novels, he continues, are not objective portrayals of reality but compulsive outpourings dictated by personal manias: 'Balzac est tourmenté par une foule de rêves qu'il est obligé d'écrire pour se soulager.' Duranty also agreed with Pontmartin that Balzac misunderstood most of the philosophical ideas that he tried to deal with in his novels—mysticism in particular. The novelist will be used as a source of historical documents, Duranty thinks, but will not be remembered as a literary figure: 'On puisera dans ses œuvres de nombreux détails sur la société de ce temps, mais on ne croira à aucune de ses inventions, à cause du manque d'équilibre de son esprit.' Balzac's desire 'de tout savoir, de pouvoir dire, j'ai touché à tout' is his most obvious sign of madness. His descriptions were careless and inaccurate, and though he contributed indirectly to *le réalisme* by broadening the range of subject-matter in the novel, his *Comédie humaine* is dismissed as a heap of scrap-iron, 'où l'on voit deux ou trois belles choses'.[10]

Duranty was not very lucky with his literary predictions, for he was sure both Balzac and Flaubert would sink into obscurity within a few years. None the less, one must admire the consistency of his argument.

[8] See M. Crouzet, *Un Méconnu du réalisme. Duranty* (Nizet, 1964), p. 441.
[9] See Champfleury, *Le Réalisme* (Michel Lévy, 1857).
[10] 'Le Remarquable Article de M. de Pontmartin', *Le Réalisme*, Nº 2 (15 Dec. 1856).

If the only legitimate way of writing was to present the literal truth in a calm descriptive manner, then the *Comédie humaine* had to be rejected. Other articles in the newspaper *Le Réalisme* reinforce this attitude to Balzac: Henri Thulié, for example, argued that the writer should study and assess his environment and give the result to the public 'sans parti-pris, sans torture d'esprit, sans café, sans excitant, mais naïvement, sincèrement, comme il a vu et jugé'.[11] The coffee is a reference to Balzac's well-known manner of fuelling his imagination; and the 'parti-pris' and 'torture d'esprit' probably refer to him as well. In another article, Thulié describes Balzac as an enthusiast and an exaggerator:

le moindre détail, le moindre bonhomme lui fait entrevoir des évènements formidables, un homme plus grand que nature . . . il aime les gens extravagants, il a donne dans beaucoup d'utopies, beaucoup de superstitions, il a peint plutôt un monde qu'il a dans la tête que le monde réel.[12]

The rigorous ideology of realism produces, in the end, an assessment of Balzac that critics as apparently diverse as Sainte-Beuve, Baudelaire, and Maurice Bardèche would have signed: 'il a peint plutôt un monde qu'il a dans la tête que le monde réel'. The ascetic school of Duranty rejected Balzac in general—yet Balzac continued to be attacked by others as the 'father of realism'. There is some small evidence that the association of Balzac was partly accepted by the young extremists of *Le Réalisme*, for Jules Assézat, the future editor of Diderot, wrote in a review that with Rabelais, Montaigne, Molière, and Voltaire, Balzac was a moulder of modern scepticism, 'et nous ne renions pas nos aïeux'.[13] Baudelaire was connected with the group on the level of friendship at least (he too was termed a *réaliste* by hostile critics), and his admiration for Balzac was very great indeed. However, the most obvious reason for the assumption that Balzac was the model of the *réalistes* can be found in the person of Champfleury.

François-Jules Husson, alias Champfleury, was the oldest and most creative of the *réaliste* group of writers. He certainly regarded Balzac as a great novelist and treated him, in the dedication of *Feu Miette* (1847), as a kind of hero-figure. Balzac recognized that he was being imitated by the younger writer, and praised him for it. When Paul Meurice retailed this news to Champfleury, it sent him into transports

---

[11] 'Du Roman', *Le Réalisme*, N⁰ 1 (15 Nov. 1856).

[12] 'M. Champfleury', *Le Réalisme*, N⁰ 4 (15 Feb. 1857).

[13] *Le Réalisme*, N⁰ 4. Thulié also praises the 'reality' of Balzac's Grandet and Birotteau in issue N⁰ 2.

of delight.[14] Whether it was the same admiration for Balzac's taste that made Champfleury become the lover of the novelist's widow is not known, but the *liaison*, which lasted from 1850 to 1852, was hardly a secret. Madame Ève de Balzac employed Champfleury as a secretary, and he was entrusted with sorting out the novelist's posthumous papers. It was probably he who gave Baudelaire the Balzac manuscript referred to in one of the poet's letters.[15] It was Champfleury who was commissioned to write the preface to an edition of Balzac's *Pensées et Maximes*,[16] who wrote the prospectus for the Houssiaux edition of the *Comédie humaine*,[17] who published fragments of unknown plays and poems by the novelist—who was, in a word, the first 'Balzacien'. Champfleury alone suffices to explain the way in which Balzac and *le réalisme* were constantly linked in the 1850s; yet the author of *Les Bourgeois de Molinchart* was ambiguous and sketchy in what he actually said about the *Comédie humaine*. Most of his articles on Balzac's early works and ephemera consist almost entirely of quotations,[18] as does his *Journal intime*, or what remains of it. His 'notes historiques' appended to Armand Baschet's book on Balzac in 1851 are but anecdotal reminiscences. In fact, only two of Champfleury's articles are of any relevance to Balzac criticism. In 1840, Balzac had written a long and favourable review of *La Chartreuse de Parme*,[19] and this was reprinted in the 1851 edition of Stendhal's novel.[20] The vogue for Stendhal in the early 1850s thus created a minor vogue for Balzac as a literary critic, and Champfleury participated in this chorus of praise.[21] What was

---

[14] J. Troubat, *Sainte-Beuve et Champfleury* (Mercure de France, 1908), p. 114.

[15] *Correspondance générale* (Conard, 1947), I. 141.

[16] By Mme Ève de Balzac. See J. Troubat, op. cit., p. 124. This preface was probably never written, however, for in the copious lists of his own work and of payment received that Champfleury drew up in his *Journal intime* (now in Columbia University Library, N.Y.) no mention is made of such a preface.

The collection of maxims from the *Comédie humaine* referred to here is not the same as the one made a few years later by Barbey d'Aurevilly. Balzac signed a contract with Plon for such a publication in 1845, which was fulfilled posthumously in 1852. However, the compilation was serialized in *L'Illustration* from 6 Dec. 1851, and the first instalment was preceded by an unsigned (and uninteresting) introductory note.

This collection of maxims may have been made by Balzac himself, by one of his assistants, or by Mme Ève de Balzac—or by all three.

[17] Listed as one of Champfleury's works in the *Journal intime* (no pagination visible on microfilm).

[18] Particularly the articles in *La Gazette de Champfleury* (1856) and *Le Réalisme* (1857).

[19] In *La Revue parisienne*, reprinted in *Éd. déf.* XXIII. 567–776.

[20] Reprint of the 1846 Hetzel edition, with a preface by Romain Colomb.

[21] See Charles de Matharel in *Le Siècle*, 2 Sept. 1850; Amédée Rolland in *Le Nouveau Journal*, 13 Feb. 1852; and Louis Ulbach's preface to *Suzanne Duchemin* (Didier, 1855).

needed, he said, was a complete edition of Balzac's *Œuvres diverses* 'qui formeraient le code littéraire du XIXe siecle'.[22] Champfleury only once came near to saying anything about Balzac as a writer, when he replied to provincial criticism of his own depiction of the clergy. The novels of the *Comédie humaine*, he says, had also been criticized for their lack of a moral conclusion. Prejudice had simply blinded Balzac's critics, he continues, for the attentive reader can easily learn 'les secrets du Tourangeau sceptique et rieur que l'hypocrisie de son temps a obligé de prendre plusieurs masques, mais dont la figure réelle est dessinée à chaque ligne des *Contes drolatiques*'.[23] This is rather odd as an argument, since Champfleury seems to be saying that 'prejudiced' critics were right, not wrong, in denouncing Balzac as a sceptic and materialist. Champfleury has been described as 'aussi laid au moral qu'au physique';[24] from the point of view of Balzac criticism, he was simply insignificant, whatever his role in unearthing a number of the novelist's early works. It seems a pity that so much argument at cross purposes over Balzac's relation to the realist movement should have centred on the ambiguities of such a weak writer and critic, 'qui procède de Balzac comme l'apprenti laborieux et intelligent procède du maître' (Cuvillier-Fleury).[25]

The debate in the 1850s over 'observation' and 'imagination' in the *Comédie humaine* involved not only the criterion of unity, but also the criterion of truth. Pontmartin and Duranty, whose attitudes to realism were diametrically opposed, both found the novels of Balzac untruthful. For Louis Ulbach, however, who saw himself as a new romantic, truth lay simply in the description and analysis of the conflict between the real and the ideal world. The idea that art should show a conflict, not a resolution (and in terms which strangely prefigure Northrop Frye)[26] allows Ulbach to view Balzac in a very favourable light. He is the precursor of 'cette voie d'analyse dans laquelle nous entrons', and in ten years will be 'l'écrivain le plus admiré, le plus imité mais non peut-être le plus adoré: car on lui en veut des vérités qu'il jette à pleines mains à travers les déchirures du cœur'.[27] Balzac, the critic says, is neither 'left' nor 'right', but '*humain* par la nature de son talent'. One element of the novelist's truthfulness was of course his detailed de-

[22] *Le Messager de L'Assemblée*, 14 June 1851.
[23] *Le Figaro*, 10 July 1856.   [24] Jules Troubat, op. cit., p. 82.
[25] *Le Journal des débats*, 2 July 1854.
[26] *Anatomy of Criticism* (Princeton, 1957).   [27] *RDP* Mar. 1853.

scription of everyday objects and manners: *La Comédie humaine*, says
Ulbach, is 'l'empreinte la plus exacte de notre société'. None the less,
the copying of reality does not of itself produce art, and the *réalistes*
who practise it have little artistic merit. Like Pontmartin, Ulbach was
under the misapprehension that Duranty and his school were attempting to imitate the Balzacian novel, and he thus makes a contrast between the two. Balzac, he writes, made a religion of 'l'imagination . . .
l'idéal . . . cet héroisme . . . ce je ne sais quoi de surhumain et d'inconnu
qui nous ravit loin de ce monde', whereas all that the *réalistes* either
want or achieve is a 'calque servile de la réalité', devoid of ideas and
emotions. 'Cette école se croit fille de Balzac; elle n'est que la filleule
de Paul de Kock.'[28] After this polemic, Ulbach comes to his main
point about Balzac. What the novelist had done was to introduce not
historical truth, but *psychological* truth into the novel. By this Ulbach
means that the novels of the *Comédie humaine* present new insights into
the actual workings of the human mind and emotions through the
problems of their characters. Ulbach believed in progress and was
searching for ways in which literature could contribute to solving the
problem of 'le bonheur de tous', which he saw as the only possible
aim for 'cette seconde révélation du romantisme' which Balzac had
initiated. Thus he is dogmatic that all new literature must follow 'la
route psychologique tracée par Balzac' if it is not to go up a blind alley.
Thirty years later, Paul Bourget made the idea of fiction as psychology
the basis of his criticism and practice; and for Paul Bourget too Balzac
was the initiator of the modern novel. The notion that Balzac was a
master of the analysis of the minds and emotions of his characters
was usually restricted, in the 1850s, to his treatment of the novels'
heroines, and often had an unfavourable weighting. Ulbach's argument was then an unusual one for the period in which it was written,
but it does not for all that step outside the terms of the debate on
whether Balzac was truthful or not.

Like so many topics and themes of Balzac criticism, the debate on
truthfulness in the *Comédie humaine* goes back to Sainte-Beuve. The
conclusion of his review of *La Recherche de l'absolu* in 1834 had been
negative, and this remained his opinion in the obituary he composed on
Balzac in 1850. As the occasion demanded, however, Sainte-Beuve
masked his criticisms with a layer of judicious praise. He willingly
granted Balzac a mastery of detail and extraordinary perceptiveness,

<hr />

[28] L. Ulbach, *Suzanne Duchemin* (Didier, 1855), Préface.

and to stress the uncanny scope and power of the novelist's observation Sainte-Beuve adopted a phrase that Philarète Chasles had used a few days previously,[29] to the effect that Balzac 'n'était pas un analyste, c'était un voyant'. Saint-Beuve also talked of a 'gift of second sight' to express his appreciation of the accuracy and range of normally hidden detail that the 'seer' Balzac brought into his portraits and descriptions. Far from praising Balzac as an imaginative or visionary writer, Sainte-Beuve is using the term 'voyant' as a hyperbolic rendering of the theme of 'Balzac observateur'. Philarète Chasles, who appears to be the inventor of the phrase, had meant something rather different. The novelist, he wrote, had been entirely wrapped up in his own fictional universe; he was an artist intoxicated by his own thoughts. 'Les hommes vivants ne vivent plus; ce sont les Nucingen, les Marneffe et les Vautrin qui existent seuls.' The basic material for the novels of the *Comédie humaine* may well be the result of observation, Chasles admits, but Balzac did not simply transcribe observed reality: 'Il se plongeait et s'absorbait dans les faits observés. Ce n'était pas un analyste, c'était un voyant.'[30] Both Chasles and Sainte-Beuve mix praise and criticism in their obituaries; and neither of them liked the imaginative side of Balzac's works. Sainte-Beuve thought that the less grandiose, more 'realistic' novels of Charles de Bernard were superior; and when he mentioned that 'Balzac inventait et rêvait bien souvent' he was chiding the author for departing from mimetic sobriety. Chasles, likewise, considered the high colour and grandiose dreams of the *Comédie humaine* as features to be criticized and deplored; his assessment of the novelist's rank in French literature was a modest one: 'Ne comparons ni à Molière ni à Shakespeare le vigoureux et subtil écrivain que nous venons de perdre.'

Chasles's phrase that Balzac was a 'voyant' achieved a certain currency in the 1850s, but was mostly used without its original sense. Gustave Desnoiresterres, author of a monumental biography of Voltaire and of the first life of Balzac to be published, used the phrase more or less as Sainte-Beuve had done: 'Ce qu'on a écrit de plus juste sur M. de Balzac, c'est que c'était un *voyant*. Rien ne peint mieux en effet cette faculté d'observation organique . . .'[31] Armand Baschet referred to Balzac as a 'voyant' and a 'remarquable peintre' in the same sen-

---

[29] *Le Journal des débats*, 24 Aug. 1850.

[30] Ibid. For confirmation of this interpretation, see Chasles's *Mémoires* (Charpentier, 1876), I. 303–8.

[31] G. Desnoiresterres, *Honoré de Balzac* (Paul Permaint, 1851).

tence,[32] presumably meaning, like Louis Lurine in 1856,[33] that Balzac was exceedingly perceptive of detail. Sainte-Beuve was obviously the source of this transformation of the meaning of 'voyant', but ironical justice was done when Armand de Pontmartin reused Sainte-Beuve's remark on Balzac's 'don de seconde vue' in the wrong sense. Pontmartin considered this 'second sight' as unbalanced mental ramblings, deriving from 'un défaut complet d'équilibre dans les facultés de son cerveau';[34] whereas Sainte-Beuve had simply meant by 'second sight' Balzac's great power of accurate observation. Like Sainte-Beuve and Chasles, however, Pontmartin thought that the only merit of Balzac's techniques and range of subjects would have been to portray accurately and soberly 'le côté de la vérité accessible par en bas'. The hostility to all that smacked of romanticism was shared almost equally by the traditional critics and the *réalistes* themselves. The bitter polemics between the factions over realism seem to owe as much if not more to the situation of the parties than to any fundamental difference in aesthetic presuppositions: for the criteria of unity and truth, and the rejection of imagination as a source of truth, were common to nearly all critics of the early 1850s.

Louis de Cormenin, like those other exceptional figures, Ulbach and Barbey d'Aurevilly, seemed to be expressing a much more personal opinion in his writings on Balzac than the general run of critics in daily and weekly newspapers. In the 1850s, he wrote for the new *Revue de Paris,* with which Gautier was closely involved, and which published Flaubert's *Madame Bovary.* For Cormenin, Balzac was

non le pharmacien vulgaire, mais l'alchimiste de génie de la civilisation actuelle. Il l'a regardée d'un œil monstrueux, plein d'éclairs et de ténèbres, et sa *Comédie humaine,* si une et si complexe, si hybride et si simple, si fantasque et si réelle, à la fois, est le procès-verbal apocalyptique de la société . . . La réalité exagère ses proportions, déplace ses lignes, transpose ses contours sous le champ de sa loupe. Il fait bien plus qu'observer, il communique à ses personnages une vie étrange, diabolique. Il est vrai d'une vérité qui sans cesser de demeurer criante est imaginaire.[35]

This 'strange, diabolical life' of Balzac's characters had been noted the previous year by the theatre critic Auguste Lireux, who thought the atmosphere of *Le Lys dans la vallée* was nightmarish, 'd'une intuition

[32] Baschet, op. cit., p. 92.   [33] *La Semaine,* 4 May 1856.
[34] *Causeries du samedi* (Michel Lévy, 1857), p. 63.
[35] *RDP* 1 Mar. 1854.

presque satanique'.[36] Cormenin's final point, however, that the truth of the *Comédie humaine* was the product of imagination, was to receive a systematic (though often misinterpreted) exposition in 1858, in Hippolyte Taine's celebrated *Étude sur Balzac*.

Hippolyte Taine is often credited with the invention of a 'scientific' theory of literature and criticism. He expounded his general views most clearly in the Introduction to his *Histoire de la littérature anglaise* which appeared in 1863. In its crudest form the theory states that works of art are products, like vice and virtue, like sugar and vitriol; and the principal determinants of artworks are 'la race, le milieu et le moment'. This idea was in fact fairly common before even the *Étude sur Balzac* of 1858: Philarète Chasles's obituary uses precisely the same schema in 1850. The *Comédie humaine*, Chasles wrote, owed its particular nature to Balzac's links of blood and upbringing with Touraine (the southern origins of Balzac's ancestry were not yet known), to his environment at the Collège des Oratoriens at Vendôme and in his early poverty-stricken years in his Parisian garret, and to the whole atmosphere of modern life. This last factor, Taine's 'moment', was given particular emphasis by Chasles: 'Bonne ou mauvaise, cette œuvre est du XIXe siècle.'[37] Of course, it was Balzac himself who most noticeably presented character (thought not art) in terms of environment and, to a lesser extent, heredity. Zola later remarked that Taine's so-called method was no more than an application of Balzac's presuppositions to the study, rather than the creation of literature.[38] In its strong form, Taine's theory is untenable, since it fails to distinguish what is literary from what is not; and it is also circular, since literature provides the evidence from which to deduce the nature of the 'factors' that 'produced' it. In its weak form—that works of art and socio-historical factors are related to each other through the artist—it is good common sense, and only a formalization of the approach used by Sainte-Beuve in his literary-biographical sketches.[39] The declaration which opens Taine's study of Balzac—'les œuvres d'esprit n'ont pas l'esprit seul pour père; l'homme entier contribue à les produire'[40]—could be taken as a manifesto of Sainte-Beuve's critical

[36] *Le Constitutionnel*, 20 June 1853.

[37] *Le Journal des débats*, 24 Aug. 1850.

[38] *Le Roman expérimental* (Charpentier, 1880), p. 222.

[39] See P. Moreau, *La Critique selon Sainte-Beuve* (S.E.D.E.S., 1964).

[40] *Nouveaux Essais de critique et d'histoire* (Hachette, 1864, dated 1865), p. 62. Originally published in *Le Journal des débats*, 3 Mar. 1858.

method as well as of Taine's. Crucial to such a method is actual knowledge of 'l'homme entier'—of his character, career, contacts, background, and so forth. Several volumes appeared in the early 1850s purporting to provide such information about Balzac, but none of these early biographies could command very much respect. The details repeated by Mirecourt[41] were too obviously sifted out of the novels themselves (*Louis Lambert* and *La Peau de chagrin* in particular were assumed—not only by Mirecourt—to be virtually autobiographical); Gustave Desnoiresterres's volume was a rush job brought out only weeks after Balzac's death;[42] and the brochure by Cayla was no more respectable than the other works in his series of short, scandalous, and pot-boiling biographies of popular figures.[43] Balzac's eccentricities, which had provided *Charivari* with so much material in the 1830s, continued to be written about in the press, most notably by Léon Gozlan, who collected his anecdotes on 'le propriétaire des Jardies' in two volumes, *Balzac chez lui* and *Balzac en pantoufles*.[44] For all the light they throw on the novelist's more amusing quirks, these books provided no greater base of real information than the other works mentioned above.

In 1856, however, Balzac's sister, Laure Surville, published the first part of a work of considerable importance: *Honoré de Balzac, Sa Vie et ses œuvres d'après sa correspondance*. The apparent documentary evidence of the letters and the fact that the work was written by a person who had known the novelist longer than anyone else gave Laure's volume an authoritative status. None of the many errors and inaccuracies in it were discovered until the end of the century, and it provided the basic facts which Taine and Gautier, in his life of Balzac, quoted extensively.

The portrait that Laure gives of her brother shows him as a dreamer and visionary. Balzac's introverted childhood, and his secret, voracious reading at the Collège de Vendôme are shown to lie behind the fiction of *Louis Lambert*; the novelist's fantasy and good humour in the rue Lesdiguières garret are made memorable by the letter concerning the servant 'moi-même', which Laure reproduces; and above all she emphasizes and brings out in a dozen details Balzac's total belief in the

---

[41] *Les Contemporains: H. de Balzac* (Rivoyre, 1854). For a scathing criticism of this work, see Altève Morand, *Eugène de Mirecourt et 'les Contemporains'* (C. Nolet, 1855).

[42] Serialized in *L'Ordre* on 11, 12, and 13 Sept. 1850.

[43] *Célébrités européennes*, pt. IV (1854).

[44] Lévy, 1862, and Collection Hetzel (Brussels), 1856.

reality of his fictional characters. In an article on Dickens that appeared before the first instalments of Laure's biography, Taine had already suggested that the French novelist lived in 'le pays de la pure logique et de la pure imagination'.[45] The biography could only confirm this view: and the central point of the *Étude sur Balzac* is not that Balzac was a realist (precisely how this myth developed in twentieth-century scholarship would be worth a study in itself), but that he drew his literary greatness from the power of his imagination.

Taine's *Étude* is a major event in Balzac criticism; conversely, it marks also an important development in Taine's own critical methods. His first important work, written originally as a thesis, was the celebrated *La Fontaine et ses fables* of 1853. The choice of subject and the manner of argument owe a lot to Geoffroy Saint-Hilaire's idea of the 'unity of the species', which Balzac had also proclaimed as true in the *Avant-propos*. The zoological terminology of the *La Fontaine* came to be replaced, in the 1860s, by a more chemical and medical jargon, but the real development lay in a movement from what I have called the 'strong' form of Taine's theory to its 'weak' form. That is to say, the critic progressively abandoned the attempt to account for works of literature as the product of identifiable determinants. More and more, the character of the writer himself, or his particular ability—which Taine called his 'faculté maîtresse'—is invoked as the key to the unity of the work of art with its social and historical background. The *Étude sur Balzac*, written in 1858, shows the scientific determination and the romantic, Hegelian idea of the unity of artistic and social phenomena in more or less equal balance.

Taine's first premise is that Balzac was 'un homme d'affaires endetté'. Thus the novelist understood that 'l'argent est le grand ressort de la vie moderne', and this 'effect' was one of the causes of his popularity:

Les lecteurs se sentaient glisser sur une nappe d'or. De là une partie de sa gloire. Il nous représente la vie que nous menons, il nous parle des intérêts qui nous agitent, il assouvit les convoitises dont nous souffrons.[46]

Secondly, Balzac was a Parisian. Taine expands this point with an evocation of the city as the feverish centre of intellectual and financial activity that is strongly reminiscent in style and content of the bravura passage on 'l'or et le plaisir' in Balzac's *Histoire des Treize*.[47] It would seem that an 'effect' is being presented here as a 'cause' of itself.

45 *RDM* 1 Feb. 1856, p. 636.
46 Taine, *Nouveaux Essais*, p. 67.   47 *Pl.* V. 255–69.

Further effects of the influence of Paris include the complicated in-
trigues of the *Comédie humaine*, its 'paradoxes de style', 'expressions
dévergondées', 'anecdotes crues', and its monstrous, nightmarish
characters, 'plus vivants que les physionomies réelles'.[48]

Although Taine explains Balzac in terms of 'causes' and 'effects',
he is not entirely uncritical of the novelist's own use of descriptive
teleology. Art is not science, he states, yet 'Balzac commençait à la
façon non des artistes mais des savants. Au lieu de peindre, il dis-
séquait.[49] Thus the long portraits and descriptions become catalogues,
and 'l'artiste se fait trop attendre.' The accumulation of material detail does not of itself render the *essence* of a subject. Of course, Taine
believes that Balzac is objectively correct in his conception of character
revealed through external detail: 'l'homme intérieur laisse son empreinte dans la vie extérieure, dans sa maison, dans ses meubles, dans
ses gestes, dans son langage; il faut expliquer cette multitude d'effets
pour l'exprimer tout entier'.[50] None the less, the aim of such an explanation of external effects must be, in art, to *express* the unique and
individual essence of a character. The acuity of Balzac's observation,
the accuracy of his details are not in Taine's view the key to his
greatness. It is in the manner in which he organizes his detail around
a strong, central theme that Balzac rises to the level of a Shakespeare:
'S'il est si fort, c'est qu'il est systématique . . . Il voit, avec les détails,
les lois qui les enchaînent.'[51] In his better novels, then, Balzac gives the
essential nature of a character—his *faculté maîtresse*, in fact—made
credible by the systematic build-up of realistic detail.

Imagination thus plays a very different role in Taine's analysis of
Balzac's achievement from that which previous critics had given it.
For Sainte-Beuve and Chasles, imagination was at the root of the
novelist's faults. For Taine, however, it gives a dominant centre to the
disparate external details that Balzac observed, it constitutes his 'génie
visionnaire', 'source unique de la vérité'.[52] Laure Surville had shown
how Balzac believed in the reality of his fictions, and Taine takes up
this point to argue that the concentration of Balzac's 'ideas' in his
characters produced a powerful 'effect' of truth; the novelist's hallu-
cinations make these fictional heroes develop with the consequence
and logical necessity of living people.[53]

The pseudo-scientific jargon of Taine's *Étude*, with its constant

[48] Taine, op. cit., p. 73.   [49] Ibid., p. 80.
[50] Ibid., p. 85.   [51] Ibid., p. 86.
[52] Ibid., p. 95.   [53] Ibid., p. 94.

abuse of terms like 'cause', 'effect', 'logic', 'necessity', and so on, has obscured the real significance of his interpretation of the *Comédie humaine*. Taine's praise of Balzac is not uncritical, nor does it embrace all that the novelist wrote; but the critic argues at length and systematically that the supreme quality of Balzac, his unique source of truth, was his powerful imagination. Baudelaire is often credited with the invention of this theme of Balzac criticism, but by the time the poet expressed this view it was hardly original.

Laure Surville's *Balzac d'après sa correspondance* is dated 1858, but the book actually appeared in November 1857;[54] and much of it had already appeared in the *Revue de Paris* in May–June 1856. Taine's *Étude* appeared in the *Journal des débats* in February and March 1858; and Théophile Gautier's *Honoré de Balzac* was serialized in *L'Artiste* and *Le Moniteur universel* in March, April, and May.[55] In September, Hippolyte Babou published a 'Lettre à Mme Surville' in which he attacked the notion of Balzac as an 'observateur, copiste, photographe . . .' and claimed that the author of the *Comédie humaine* was 'un homme d'imagination. . . . N'est-ce pas à l'imagination que ses écrits empruntent toute leur puissance?' Like Taine, Babou also dismisses the question of morality and influence. Certainly he sees that the Second Empire was a Balzacian age, full of characters inspired by the *Comédie humaine*—

La fièvre les tient, ils calculent; l'Imagination les enlève, ils combinent; le Diable les emporte, ils vendent et achètent, ils marchandent! Ils sont inévitablement et absolument fantastiques dans un milieu tout saturé de réalité.

But if one reproaches Balzac for having influenced society as well as for prophesying its development, 'Il faudrait lui reprocher son génie de visionnaire, tout son génie!'[56] By the end of 1858, then, praise of Balzac's 'génie visionnaire' was an established, if recent, theme of criticism that had originated in Laure Surville's portrait of her brother, had been propagated by Gautier as well as Babou, and had been most fully argued in Taine's *Étude*.

In 1859, Baudelaire contributed to the series of studies on contemporary writers that *L'Artiste* was publishing under the heading *Galerie du XIXe Siècle*, with a long article on Théophile Gautier, to

[54] Registered in the *Bibliographie de la France* on 14 Nov. 1857.
[55] See Appendix III for the exact dates.
[56] *La Revue française*, 1 Sept. 1858.

whom he had dedicated *Les Fleurs du Mal*. Gautier's *Honoré de Balzac*, which Baudelaire mentions, is a sympathetic and stylish rendering of the material Surville and Gozlan had already published, with a number of personal reminiscences added. It accepts as a matter of course that Balzac was a writer of the imagination; and it was published in book form in Brussels in 1858 in a volume that included Taine's *Étude*.[57] Unless he had kept back numbers of *L'Artiste*, Baudelaire could only have consulted Gautier's biography in this edition when he was preparing his own article on the poet; and it seems reasonable to suppose that he also read Taine's *Étude* following it.

Baudelaire's celebrated passage in the Gautier article on 'Balzac visionnaire' requires some explanation not only because of the importance other historians of literature have given it but because it marks a very sudden break with all that Baudelaire had previously written on the novelist. It is not in order to accuse the author of *Les Fleurs du mal* of plagiarism that I have suggested how he might in fact have taken his ideas from Taine, but rather to show that all successful critics are 'plagiarists', working within traditions and themes that go beyond individual expression. Like Hugo's claim in 1850 that Balzac was 'à son insu . . . de la forte race des écrivains révolutionnaires', Baudelaire's conclusion in 1859 that the novelist was 'visionnaire, et visionnaire passionné' was not an isolated case of miraculous illumination.

Where Baudelaire was ahead of his time was in his admiration of Balzac as a man, rather than as a writer. He saw the novelist's life as a poignant example of 'le guignon'; Balzac was 'un héros de la volonté', 'aux prises avec l'adversité'.[58] He had put his theory of will-power into practice in his own life, and Baudelaire wished he could imitate his habit of always working: '[mais] jusqu'ici je n'ai de commun avec lui que les dettes et les projets.'[59] One of those projects was in fact to write a full-length study of Balzac, but it never came to anything.[60] The few fragments on the novelist that were written before 1859 are fairly conventional: Baudelaire sympathetically ridicules Balzac's obsession with money,[61] and his habit of rewriting;[62] like Sainte-Beuve, he compares the caricatures of Gavarni and Daumier to the

[57] *Balzac, sa vie, son œuvre*. Biographie par Théophile Gautier. Analyse critique par Hippolyte Taine (Bruxelles, Dumont, 1858).
[58] C. Baudelaire, *L'Art romantique* (Conard, 1925), p. 347.
[59] *Correspondance générale* (Conard, 1947), I. 141.
[60] See *L'Art romantique*, p. 279.   [61] *L'Écho des théâtres*, 23 Aug. 1846.
[62] *L'Esprit public*, 15 Apr. 1846.

Comédie humaine;[63] he describes the novelist as 'un savant, un inventeur et un observateur'.[64] Not one reference in all that Baudelaire wrote before 1859 prefigures the justly celebrated passage in the article on Gautier. Here he considers that Balzac had ennobled the lowly genre of the novel by the sheer force of the personality he threw into his works. He was not a mere observer, but a 'visionnaire, et visionnaire passionné'. Though the characters he created were composed of realistic elements, they were exaggerated in their traits, larger than life: 'Bref, chacun, chez Balzac, même les portières, a du génie.' The central principle informing the novelist's own life and that of all his characters was will-power: 'Ce sont des âmes chargées de volonté jusqu'à la gueule.' To express his heightened vision of people and things, Balzac 'a noirci leurs ombres et illuminé leurs lumières'. His prodigious taste for detail required him to emphasize 'les lignes principales, pour sauver la perspective de l'ensemble'.[65] This heightened rendering of reality—which Sainte-Beuve so disliked—constitutes, for Baudelaire, Balzac's greatest quality.

Aesthetically, Balzac's novels were as ambiguous to critics of the 1850s as they were politically. For Duranty and Baudelaire, the *Comédie humaine* was the fruit of imagination only; for Castille, it was solely a work of observation. Other critics, as we have seen, tried to assess which of the two poles was dominant, without denying the presence of both. For Cormenin and for Taine, imagination was the prime source of truth in Balzac; for Sainte-Beuve, who will be more fully discussed in the next chapter, the only truth in the *Comédie humaine* was the observation of detail. The resolutions given to this perceived conflict of 'inner' and 'outer' truth were not unrelated to the answers given by critics to the question of Balzac's meaning. B. Jouvin pointed this out as early as 1851. Critics, he wrote, contradict themselves by hailing Balzac as 'l'observateur le plus vrai, le plus exact', and at the same time accusing him of 'exaggeration' and 'paradox'. This reproach, Jouvin declares, 'est étayé sur la passion politique'.[66] Balzac was never attacked for *being* a *réaliste*, but he was attacked as the misunderstood source of realism: thus right-wing criticism

[63] *L'Art romantique*, p. 64.   [64] *Œuvres posthumes* (Conard, 1939), I. 246.
[65] *L'Artiste*, 13 Mar. 1859. On the question of Baudelaire's attitude to Balzac, see P.-G. Castex, in *RSH* (1958), pp. 139 *passim*; and on Baudelaire and Taine, see J. Cabanis in *Le Figaro littéraire*, 7 Oct. 1965.
[66] *La Chronique de Paris*, 4 Sept. 1851.

(Pontmartin, Poitou) both rejected Balzac's politics as the result of his unreliable and untruthful imagination, and claimed that the *avant-garde* had misunderstood the novelist. The literary and political left, from Weill to Duranty, with the exception of Hugo, were as adamant as their detractors that Balzac's imagination and politics were faulty. Approval of Balzac's 'inner' meaning of social criticism accompanied praise of his 'outer' truth in observed detail (Méray, Delord). Disapproval of Balzac's observation of detail (only Pontmartin and Duranty really belong here) accompanied attacks on both his politics and his imagination; but by far the commonest combination, between 1846 and 1858, was praise of Balzac's handling of 'outer' truth, criticism of his imagination, and (except for a brief period after August 1850) rejection of his political meaning, both 'inner' and 'outer'. Hippolyte Taine did not shatter the established themes, but altered the possible combinations by praising Balzac's imagination as the prime source of truth in his novels, whilst still emphasizing the importance of his observation of detail and simply dismissing his philosophy and politics as fictions. The combination was an implicit possibility in Balzac criticism from 1846 on, and was actually realized in part by Cormenin, Lireux, Ulbach, and even Hugo had hinted at it. Yet it came to the fore in 1858 not because of Taine's 'method' but because Taine was no longer shackled with objections to romanticism, like Weill and Duranty, or with objections to realism, like Pontmartin, Poitou, and Nettement; nor was he grinding a 'party' axe like Ulbach. Taine was a critic of a new generation, and his essay gives a powerful impression of freshness, vigour, and youth, delighting in the discovery of new facts and ideas. The new facts, and even some of the ideas, had been provided by Laure Surville's biography, the importance of which cannot be overstated in any history of Balzac's reputation.

3 Popularity and criticism

So far we have looked at Balzac criticism of the late 1840s and 50s mainly in terms of two controversies, over the novels' political meaning in Chapter 1, and over the source of their truth, in Chapter 2. The texts referred to show a growing acceptance of Balzac as a great writer through the decade: but criticism does not progress in a smooth and united flow, nor does it jump from one set of themes and evaluations to another at specific dates. One can certainly characterize the 1890s, for example, as a period far more favourable to Balzac in general than the 1850s; or the 1870s as a decade more interested in the novelist than the 1860s. But if one tries to define periods in Balzac criticism in terms any less vague than these, one falls into sterile arguments about an imaginary consensus opinion and circular propositions about changes in taste. If one tries to establish dates for changes between two periods, one falls into an even greater trap. Weinberg, for example, in his pioneering study of critical reaction to French realism, sets October 1856 as the divide between two periods, the earlier characterized by muted hostility to Balzac, the later by a general acceptance of the novelist as a writer of the first rank.[1] Straightaway he has to juggle his evidence and put Eugène Poitou's hostile diatribe of December 1856 into the earlier period, despite its date.[2] The choice of October 1856 is not hard to explain, for it was then that *Madame Bovary* began to appear. How comforting it would be for the literary historian if that epitome of realism in the novel had indeed changed opinion in favour of its forebear, the *Comédie humaine*! The truth is not necessarily complicated, but chronology is not its only dimension. To represent criticism as a string of separate reactions set on the thread of time alone is to flatten and distort the picture, and later in this chapter I shall discuss two rather large distortions made by the imposition of 'period-divisions' on Balzac criticism of the Second Empire. Firstly, however, the question of alternatives to purely chronological periodization must be considered.

An author as prolific and diverse as Balzac might be expected to give rise to an enormous diversity of opinions and critical arguments. What is surprising, in the eighty pieces by fifty different authors so far

---

[1] Weinberg, *French Realism*, pp. 74, 81.   [2] Ibid., p. 242.

considered, is not their diversity but the similarity both of the questions they seek to answer about the *Comédie humaine* and of the structure of their arguments. It is as if they were, with rare exceptions, working like scientists in a given field on a set of common hypotheses; and as if their subject was not Balzac but the themes of Balzac criticism. Thus new criticism of the novelist is related not only to a reading of the works, nor just to the most recent expressions of critical opinion, but in the first place and above all to the structure of thought underlying all actual examples of Balzac criticism. In the introduction I suggested that this underlying system consisted of a set of propositions about the novelist which I have called 'themes' and a set of rules governing the ways in which themes could be combined. Criticism changes when new themes are added, but above all when the rules are altered. Thus Taine, who showed that approval of Balzac's imagination could be combined with approval of his observation of detail, operated a greater change in criticism than the *querelle du réalisme*, which added new themes of comparison and contrast between the *Comédie humaine* and the theories and works of Duranty, Champfleury, and Flaubert.

The structural dimension of a system of thought such as Balzac criticism exists within chronology, of course, but the sequence of time does not have to dominate the way in which that system is described any more than it need dominate the writing of social and political history.[3] The objection can be raised that to distill 'themes' from a wide variety of different critical appreciations distorts the true picture as much as the imposition of a rigid chronological progression. It is indeed true that in the preceding chapters I have necessarily left out much of what the critics in question actually wrote in order to concentrate on what seem to be the central topics, not of their articles, but of Balzac criticism. However, the aim of this book is to make sense of the development of Balzac's reputation, not to make nonsense of perfectly intelligent critics who happened to write in an earlier age. The conception of critical thought as a system or structure makes better sense of their work than the idea of a progression through chronological periods towards a 'better understanding' of Balzac's novels.

THE FATE OF 'MERCADET'

A purely chronological description of Balzac criticism would be obliged to dismiss a number of switchback situations as 'exceptions'

[3] See, for example, Theodore Zeldin's *France, 1848–1945* (Oxford, 1973).

to the general trend. The reception of *Mercadet* in August 1851 provides an example of almost rapturous approval in a period characterized by Weinberg as one of muted hostility; yet in 1868, in a period supposedly highly favourable to Balzac, the play was not well received and the production closed after a short run.[4] In 1888, when some critics were already proclaiming Balzac a classic, *Mercadet* was a total flop and closed after its first night.[5] The success of *Mercadet* in 1851 cannot therefore be accounted for by general trends, but it can be explained as the result of an interaction between themes of Balzac criticism and specific events related to the play's performance.

The play performed in 1851 and throughout the nineteenth century was not all Balzac's work. The original five-act text of *Le Faiseur* had been adapted into a three-act comedy by Adolphe d'Ennery, whose untiring pen and accurate judgement of public taste earned him a fortune of twelve million francs by the end of his long career as a theatrical 'arranger'.[6] Théophile Gautier, whose judgement can be respected in this matter since he was not only a professional theatre critic but also one of Balzac's few really loyal and sympathetic friends, thought d'Ennery had done a very skilful job in adapting the play.[7] The public that flocked to nearly 100 performances of *Mercadet* may have been appreciative as much of d'Ennery's stagecraft as of Balzac's dramatic genius. The last line of the play, where the hero exclaims 'Enfin, je suis créancier!' was held to be the wittiest—and it was of course d'Ennery's line, not Balzac's. In the original play, the situation is as uncertain at the end as it is at the beginning, and Mercadet is still waiting for his associate Godeau to return from the Indies; but in the version that was performed Godeau does return with vast sums of money that allow the intrigue to be untied, and cascades of banknotes were showered on to the stage for the celebration of such a happy ending.

In the second place, the production of *Mercadet* and the critical acclaim it received can be seen, with historical hindsight, as an atonement for Balzac's drab and unsuccessful funeral. The first night of the play took place a few days after the first anniversary of the novelist's death on 18 August 1850. A picture of what had happened on 21 August 1850 can be pieced together from diverse contemporary

[4] See F. Béchard, '*Mercadet*', *La Gazette de France*, 16 Nov. 1868.

[5] See R. Dorsel, 'Le *Mercadet* de Balzac', *Le Moniteur universel*, 16 Apr. 1888.

[6] See D'Ennery's obituary in *La Gazette de France*, 22 Jan. 1899.

[7] *La Presse*, 1 Sept. 1851

sources. There had been a sparse attendance as the procession passed from the church of St. Philippe-du-Roule, where the service was held, to the Père Lachaise cemetery.[8] It was a grey and drizzly afternoon, despite the season, and the Minister of the Interior, Baroche, represented the President who was touring the provinces.[9] Victor Hugo was suffering from a throat infection, and his oration which reads so grandiloquently in print was delivered in a barely audible whisper.[10] The vice-president of the Société des Gens de Lettres spoke after Hugo, but was actually booed for using the occasion to call on the government for legislation to protect 'la propriété littéraire'.[11] Though great men were present—Hugo, Sainte-Beuve, Baroche—the funeral procession and burial ceremony were far from magnificent and ended in a thoroughly undignified manner.

The press treated the event as an occasion for polemics over Balzac's 'morality' and political meaning, and though all were eager to appropriate the novelist's name to whichever faction their paper represented, only Hugo and Barbey d'Aurevilly wrote with unreserved admiration for the *Comédie humaine*. Most critics were grudging in their praise. Chasles, for example, was settling old scores in the obituary he wrote; and Sainte-Beuve's hostility was only thinly veiled. The general impression made by this collection of articles on the novelist is a drab and unflattering one.

Many of the reviews of *Mercadet* in August 1851 pointed out the anniversary, and treated the opening night at the Gaîté theatre as a Paris society 'event'. It had had a lot of advance publicity in the press, and there is some evidence of official encouragement from high authority to regard the production favourably.[12] It was as if Paris were preparing to atone for its past injustices to Balzac in a characteristically Parisian manner. There were of course some unfavourable criticisms of the play, but no outright attacks of the sort which had been customary. Jules Janin, for example, was notorious for his hostility to the novelist in earlier years, and wrote a sharp criticism of the morality of *Mercadet*. (According to Julien Lemer, Janin had suffered 'un accès de conscience' in August 1850, had spoken warmly

---

[8] See *Le National*, 27 Aug. 1850, where other papers are criticized for exaggerating the size of the crowds at the funeral.

[9] See *L'Indépendance belge*, 1 Sept. 1850, for a description of the weather.

[10] See *L'Évènement*, 20 Aug. 1850; and V. Hugo, *Correspondance*, II. 16.

[11] *Le Corsaire*, 24 Aug. 1850. Desnoyer's speech reprinted in *L'Évènement*, 23 Aug. 1850.

[12] See Ange Galdémar, 'La Malechance de Balzac', *Le Gaulois*, 5 Dec. 1894.

of Balzac at a dinner party and vowed to bury the hatchet for evermore. This review of *Mercadet* suggests either that Janin's opinions were volatile, or that Lemer invented the story—the latter being marginally more likely than the former).[13] All of Balzac's heroes, Janin said, were crooks and 'faiseurs' like Mercadet, and he gave the following explanation: 'Balzac aime le *faiseur* parce qu'il aime l'argent!'—and so on for several column inches.[14] Apart from the intention to insult, Janin's piece on money in Balzac's life and works is altogether like Taine's chapter on the subject. Even Janin had to conclude, none the less, that *Mercadet* was an extremely amusing comedy and a great success with the public. According to one trade journal, *La Revue et Gazette des Théâtres*, Balzac's play was 'le plus grand succès du moment', with full houses every night.[15] The President himself finally came to see it,[16] despite the fact that his Minister of the Interior had temporarily suspended the production after the first night. However, once he had read the manuscript the Minister allowed the play to reopen almost immediately.[17] The whole story is reminiscent of the *Vautrin* scandal, for once again it was, allegedly, additions made by the actors that had caused the fuss.[18] The left-wing journalist Taxile Delord, whose opinions remained as trenchantly revolutionary as in August 1850, thought that the Minister should have confirmed the suspension. Balzac's comedy, he wrote, was a cruel but accurate satire of the men who then held power in France—the criminal speculators. Thus the authorities, were they to be logical in their censorship policies, should ban a play which ridicules the very source of their power and wealth.[19] Obviously, Delord's remarks are quite unrelated to Balzac's intentions in the play which was written before the Bonapartists rose to power; but they are clearly related to the themes of criticism which had come to the fore in left-wing writing on the *Comédie humaine* a year previously. My personal guess is that the suspension of the play was a *coup monté*, suggested by the *Vautrin* scandal of 1840, and intended to increase the publicity surrounding the play, which was in any case enormous.

Janin was not the only critic to consider that *Mercadet*'s happy ending made it an immoral play, given the criminal characters involved.

[13] J. Lemer, *Balzac, sa vie, son œuvre* (Sauvaître, 1892).
[14] *Le Journal des débats*, 25 Aug. 1851.
[15] See issues of 4 and 7 Sept. 1851.
[16] Reported in the *Revue et Gazette des Théâtres* on 21 Sept. 1851.
[17] Ibid. 28 Aug. 1851.
[18] Ibid.   [19] *Le Charivari*, 27 Aug. 1851.

Auguste Lireux thought it gave encouragement to the pernicious doctrines of realism and art for art's sake (the two concepts were more or less interchangeable in 'moral' criticism of the 1850s)[20] but that it was none the less a good play. He concluded therefore 'qu'il faut admirer M. de Balzac et ne le point imiter'.[21] According to Théodore Muret, 'Cette œuvre, il est aisé de le voir, fut conçue sous le dernier régime', which explains its immorality.[22] For Paul de Musset, *Mercadet* was 'une hideuse création', yet extremely well written and a dramatic success.[23] B. Jouvin thought that Balzac had something of Molière in him: 'Balzac est pessimiste et triste au plus fort de sa gaîté, rien n'est plus vrai!'[24] Wholeheartedly enthusiastic reviews were written by Eugène Cellié,[25] Edouard Thierry,[26] Louis Lurine,[27] Théophile Gautier,[28] and Philippe Busoni.[29] It must have been on a very partial reading of the press that Baudelaire lamented to his mother: 'Les hommes qui ont tant tourmenté Balzac l'insultent après sa mort. Si tu lis les journaux français, tu auras cru que *Mercadet* était une chose abominable. C'est simplement admirable.'[30] The 1851 production of Balzac's fifth play was so successful with the public that it became something of a legend.[31] After that, it more or less disappeared for fifty years, until in 1899 it was added to the repertoire of the Comédie française as part of the celebration of the centenary of the novelist's birth. This switchback effect would be difficult to account for in any simple chronological description of Balzac criticism. Yet the production of *Mercadet* was not without influence on the subsequent nature of the themes of criticism, even if it had no general or lasting effect on the novelist's reputation. It provided another double-sided proposition about Balzac's dramatic genius: for *Mercadet*'s popular success showed that he was a capable dramatist, yet the fact that his text had had to be adapted showed to others that he was not a competent playwright.

---

20 '*Gautiérisme*' was used as a synonym for '*réalisme*' by Levallois as late as 1877. See below, p. 137.

21 *Le Constitutionnel*, 25 Aug. 1851.

22 *L'Union*, 25 Aug. and 1 Sept. 1851.   23 *Le National*, 25 Aug. 1851.

24 *La Chronique de Paris* (mensuel), 4 Sept. 1851.

25 *Revue et Gazette des Théâtres*, 24 Aug. 1851.

26 *L'Assemblée nationale*, 25 Aug. 1851.

27 *Le Messager de l'Assemblée*, 25 Aug. 1851.

28 *La Presse*, 1 Sept. 1851.   29 *L'Ordre*, 25 Aug. 1851.

30 *Correspondance générale*, I. 141.

31 See Albéric Second, 'La 100ᵉ représentation de *Mercadet*', *Le Constitutionnel*, 18 June 1852.

THE CASE OF SAINTE-BEUVE

Another feature of criticism which militates against rigid or even meaningful periodization is the survival of early arguments and conclusions into later decades. Of course, in some cases this feature can be explained away as the fossilization of attitudes in ageing but long-lived critics. Armand de Pontmartin, however, only started writing criticism in the late 1840s, and his first articles on Balzac date from the mid-1850s. His opposition to Balzac crystallized as a reaction to the publication of *Madame Bovary*, and though the religious, political, and 'moral' considerations he deals with are not dissimilar to themes of earlier Balzac criticism, Pontmartin is not as a man or as a writer a survival from an earlier age. Though Taine's *Étude* was influential over some critics, it made no impact whatever on the author of *Les Samedis*. The Franco-Prussian War, in 1870, and the Paris Commune of 1871 provided Pontmartin with yet more 'reasons' for deploring Balzac—'un homme aussi extraordinaire dans son influence posthume que dans l'ensemble de sa vie et de ses œuvres'.[32] The continued decadence of both public morality and literature (for which the events of 1870–1 were both evidence and retribution) proved to Pontmartin that he had been correct in his attacks on Balzac and realism in 1856. His only regret was that he had not succeeded in stopping the rot; but since he had failed, the increasing popularity of the novelist was for Pontmartin direct proof of his evil influence. Lovenjoul's scholarly *Histoire des Œuvres de Balzac* appeared in a second edition in 1886 and might be taken as an indication that the novelist had risen to the status of a classic, but to Pontmartin the book showed precisely how confused, disorganized and unhealthy the novelist's mind had been—for Lovenjoul catalogues with minute care all the changes of title and all the different versions of Balzac's stories. 'Je me fais du génie une idée plus simple . . .'[33] Pontmartin's views were unusual in the 1880s and few other critics agreed with him at that time. None the less, he was not merely repeating old arguments, since the material provided by Lovenjoul was largely new. What made him 'exceptional' was that he had not adopted the new rules that his contemporaries obeyed for their combinations of the themes and evaluations of Balzac criticism.

Whether a forgotten literary jouster like Pontmartin should be

---

[32] *Le Correspondant*, XLVIII (1871), 22.
[33] *Souvenirs d'un vieux critique* (Calmann-Lévy, 1887), VII. 216.

considered an exception or not might be thought a trivial matter. Of much greater importance to Balzac criticism and to literary history in general is the case of Charles-Augustin Sainte-Beuve, whose influence on critical attitudes from the 1830s on was without equal in France. The evolution of his view of Balzac goes against what might be thought the general trend, for his opinion of the novelist grew steadily worse. Any periodization of Balzac criticism on the basis of the balance of opinion would make Sainte-Beuve as much of an exception in the 1830s as he was in the 1860s. It can hardly be wise to reduce the greatest critic of the nineteenth century to a figure on the sidelines of the history of taste; nor would it be easy to square up this 'exceptional' development with the fact that the origin of many of the controversies of Balzac criticism can be found in Sainte-Beuve's writings.

The review article on *La Recherche de l'absolu* that the critic published in 1834 has been referred to many times. In it, Sainte-Beuve gives a survey of the achievement so far of 'le romancier du moment par excellence'. It was only since *La Peau de chagrin* (1831), he says, that Balzac had come to the public's notice, since when 'il l'a remué, sillonné en tous sens, étonné, émerveillé, choqué ou chatouillé en mille manières'. Apart from the 'coups de trompette' for *La Peau*, he had not been helped very much by press publicity but had created a vogue for his novels by his own efforts, with each new work 'servant, pour ainsi dire, d'annonce et de renfort au précédent'. Balzac had women behind him: and on this Sainte-Beuve quotes an earlier review by Jules Janin which suggests that the novelist's special gift was for analysing the feelings of the fair sex. Sainte-Beuve suggests that Balzac was read and admired by provincial women in particular for this reason. He was also read in the provinces, the critic continues, because of the provincial settings of many of his novels. Thus his fame was greater in all corners of France than it was in Paris, where doubts had been expressed over his qualities as a 'poète . . . artiste . . . écrivain'. Yet Balzac had worked hard to achieve higher standards, Sainte-Beuve claims, and he gives some details of the early works to show how much the novelist had improved. The critic obviously disagrees with those who take the mere existence of the uncreditable novels of the 1820s as 'une objection péremptoire à la réalité de ses perfectionnements récents'. An author capable of works of the quality of *Louis Lambert* and *Eugénie Grandet* cannot be ignored, whatever else he has written.

Sainte-Beuve then tries to sketch the evolution of Balzac from a hack-writer to a major novelist, relying heavily on *Louis Lambert* as a source of information on Balzac's own life. With uncanny perception he suggests that the novelist was really from the south of France, not from Tours (though Sainte-Beuve could not have known about Balzac's ancestry at this time) and considers that just as Louis Lambert wanted to be 'un alchimiste de la pensée', Balzac was the alchemist of fiction, painfully producing gold from the baser metals of his early works. The novelist's most original feature, he continues, is to always have thirty novels in his head when he was writing one. (Note that the 'reappearing characters' and the plan and title of the *Comédie humaine* had not yet been invented, let alone announced, when Sainte-Beuve wrote this.) Balzac also had the ability to bring provincial scenes to life, and to animate material and detailed descriptions. Some of his works are 'presque admirables', with a fine comic touch; but others are a 'pêle-mêle effrayant'. Mostly, the stories begin well, but do not always keep a high level to the end. Balzac, Sainte-Beuve argues, is not yet sure of his manner. It is *Eugénie Grandet* which contains all of his qualities and the fewest faults: this is the manner he should keep to.

Sainte-Beuve is less favourable to Balzac's style than to his qualities of observation. Balzac has no purity of line; he uses metaphors and images that are 'unclean'; the very details he describes are often repugnant. Yet he took a great deal of trouble over his language, according to Sainte-Beuve. Sometimes he improves on his first version, but at other times he actually spoils 'une première rédaction plus franche et plus simple'. The novelist should avoid neologisms, keep clear of long, breathless, syntactically muddled sentences (of which examples are given), and stop his misuse of the partitive pronoun 'en'.

La Recherche de l'absolu was not one of Balzac's best works to date, in Saint-Beuve's judgement. It contains fine examples of observation and characterization, but also a cruel and stupid idea—Claës's desire for 'genius or nothing'. The excess of wealth and bric-à-brac in the Claës household is typical, the critic suggests, of Balzac both as a writer and as a man. Sainte-Beuve disapproves of the apparent praise in the novel of the hero's monomania, and he quotes a recent autobiographical brochure on the same subject (alchemy) to show that the picture Balzac gives is inaccurate and exaggerated.

Now this long and considered article can hardly be described as an unfair assessment of Balzac's achievement in 1834. The remarks on *La Recherche* itself may represent a misreading of the novel, certainly, but most of the article is favourable, sympathetic, and relatively well informed. In 1836, it was reprinted, but with an additional footnote in which 'un homme d'esprit' is quoted as suggesting that Balzac was in many ways similar to Pigault-Lebrun (1753–1835), a prolific author of *romans gais* under the First Empire and Restoration, whose biography had just appeared.[34] This was meant as a derogatory comparison. In 1838, Sainte-Beuve began to think that Charles de Bernard was much better at writing Balzacian novels than Balzac himself: for though he had found 'un filon heureux', his almost magical power of observation 's'obscurcit tout d'un coup, et se perd, en croyant se continuer, dans toutes les aberrations de l'invraisemblable'.[35] Balzac's career may end the way it began, the critic speculates, and Bernard could take over as the reigning novelist. A month later, a scathing review of *La Torpille* appeared (though it may not be by Sainte-Beuve, it is usually attributed to him[36]), attacking its style and unreal storyline. The following year, 1839, Balzac appears as a producer of 'littérature industrielle'; and in 1840, Sainte-Beuve's increasing distaste for the *Comédie humaine* becomes very apparent. He was now sure that the novelist 'allait finir come il a commencé, par cent volumes que personne ne lira'.[37] His transitory fame had been due to a particular moment in French social history, just after the July Revolution, when it had become possible to write about personal and private matters. 'Mais si de pareils hasards sont précieux, il ne faut pas en abuser . . . sous peine de faire céder le charme au dégout.' Balzac was incapable of stopping the excesses which he had developed: 'ce n'est plus le poète dérobant les fins mystères, c'est le docteur indiscret des secrètes maladies'. It was this indelicate treatment of personal relationships, and in particular of women's emotions, that Sainte-Beuve was to refer to more and more as Balzac's major fault. In 1843, the critic saw 'un fond de De Sade masqué mais non point méconnaissable' in the inspiration of 'deux ou trois de nos romanciers',[38] and he confirmed in a letter to Juste Olivier that he meant above all Balzac.[39] The following year, he complained of the impact of money on contemporary writing: Balzac was a representative of the age, for he had 'le véritable

---

[34] Jean-Nicolas Barba, *Vie et aventures de Pigault-Lebrun* (Barba, 1836).

[35] '*Gerfaut* et *Le Nœud Gordien* de M. Charles de Bernard', *RDM* 15 Oct. 1838.

[36] The cumulative index of the *RDM* brought out in 1857 gives Charles Labitte as the author, but in a footnote says that Labitte collaborated with Sainte-Beuve. The article was included in the 1875 edition of Sainte-Beuve's *Premiers Lundis*, II. 360–7.

[37] 'Dix Ans après en littérature', *RDM* 1 Mar. 1840.

[38] 'Quelques Vérités sur la situation en littérature', *RDM* 1 July 1843.

[39] *La Revue suisse*, June 1843.

alliage' of 'un grand amour de l'argent et une excessive vanité littéraire'.[40]

The re-publication of the review of *La Recherche de l'absolu* in 1846
has already been mentioned as a significant event. One footnote was
added comparing the novelist to a seller of fine clothes—but grease-
stained, second-hand clothes.[41] Another note was added to expand a
remark on Balzac's revelations of the 'mystérieux détails privés'. 'Un
ami plus sévère que moi' is quoted as saying that the novelist was like
an impertinent doctor. 'Il a des arts secrets, de certains tours de main,
comme en a l'accoucheur, le magnétiseur. Bien des femmes, même
honnêtes, s'y sont prises. On l'eût traduit en jugement autrefois pour
maléfice.'[42] (It is as if the physically impotent critic were transferring
the responsibility for his past fiasco with Adèle Hugo to a novelist
who had more than one affinity with the hated husband and poet.)
Sainte-Beuve also altered his view of Balzac's constant invention of
new plots and of links between his novels. The idea of the reappearing
characters, he says, is quite wrong: 'rien ne nuit plus à la curiosité qui
naît du nouveau et à ce charme de l'imprévu qui fait l'attrait du roman.'[43]
He also alters his praise for Balzac's treatment of provincial life by
adding that 'il méconnaît le plus souvent et viole ce que ce genre de
vie, avec la poésie qu'elle recèle, a de discret avant tout, de pudique
et de voilé'.[44] Finally, he emphasizes the disappointing nature of the
novel's endings and the 'dirtiness' of their descriptive passages.[45]

Sainte-Beuve's dislike of Balzac may originate, as J. F. Jackson
suggests,[46] in the fact that he did not figure on the list of twelve 'literary marshals of France' invented by the novelist in 1840. It was also
in that year that Balzac made his harsh and unjustified attack on Sainte-
Beuve's *Port-Royal*.[47] The examination of the changes made between
1834 and 1846 in the critic's expressed views, however, suggest that
Sainte-Beuve was growing more and more sensitive to explicit mentions of female sexuality in the novel. Over the ensuing twenty-five
years a different basis can be shown to underly the critic's worsening
opinion—that of moral and political bias.

In a postscript to the 1869 version of the review of *La Recherche de
l'absolu*, Sainte-Beuve claimed that the piece seemed to him a fair and

[40] *La Revue suisse*, 2 Nov. 1844.
[41] *Portraits contemporains* (Didier, 1846), I. 444.   [42] Ibid.
[43] Ibid., 451.   [44] Ibid., p. 453.   [45] Ibid. 454–5 and 457–8.
[46] 'Balzac and Sainte-Beuve', *PMLA* XLV (1930), 918–38. See also J. Hytier, 'Balzac
et Sainte-Beuve', in *Questions de littérature* (Geneva, 1968).
[47] In the *Revue Parisienne*. Reprinted in *Éd. déf.* XXIII. 634–59.

objective judgement of the novelist. However, he had just made further changes and additions to this article, which inreased its hostility beyond even that of the 1846 version discussed above. He also recommended, in this postscript, his own obituary of Balzac as a more general and rounded survey of the writer. Sainte-Beuve is trying to portray the evolution of his attitude as the reverse of what it was. The 1850 obituary was at the time of its appearance the most hostile piece he had written on Balzac. It is 'fairer' than the 1869 version of the earlier review, but no more generous than the 1846 version of the same piece. Balzac's sister Laure evidently feared that the critic would take a harsh line in his obituary, and wrote a letter begging Sainte-Beuve to consult her before he put pen to paper.[48] Another critic seems to have been more successful in influencing him—or at least, in feeding him information. Jules Lecomte recounted in the Brussels newspaper, *L'Indépendance belge*, how he had been standing behind the great critic at the funeral service for Balzac at the church of St. Philippe-du-Roule. Referring to himself in the third person, Lecomte continued: 'Cet écrivain raconta donc sur M. de Balzac diverses choses peu connues, porta quelques jugements et, il faut le dire, s'exprima très intentionellement de façon à influer sur les dispositions du critique …'[49] Lecomte repeated details of 'les mœurs et les goûts russes *à la Balzac*, l'anecdote sur une société vénitienne inspirée de lui' which he wrote about in another article for *L'Indépendance belge*.[50] And true enough, Sainte-Beuve inserted these anecdotes in his obituary. These two stories had a long and varied career. Apart from inspiring one of the silliest remarks ever made that Balzac was 'le régénerateur de Saint Pétersbourg',[51] they provided first Sainte-Beuve, and then Pontmartin and others, with specious evidence of the influence of literature on real life: 'C'est ainsi que ce qui avait pu paraître d'abord exagéré finit par n'être plus que vraisemblable.'[52] Not only because he believed in this influence, but also because like so many men who had lived through 1848, he feared it, Sainte-Beuve concluded his obituary of Balzac with a sigh of relief. The age of the exuberant novel, he thought, was now over; 'remettons-nous un peu' by having novels no less magnificent but 'plus apaisés, plus consolants'.

[48] See A. Billy, 'Balzac, sa sœur et Sainte-Beuve', *Le Figaro littéraire*, 29 June 1950.
[49] *L'Indépendance belge*, 8 Sept. 1850.
[50] See issue of 23 Aug. 1850.
[51] G. Richard, in *Le Courrier de la Gironde*, 18 Dec. 1850.
[52] Sainte-Beuve, 'M. de Balzac', *Le Constitutionnel*, 2 Sept. 1850.

Such undisguised relief at the death of a man is unusual in obituaries, and it can be taken that Sainte-Beuve intended here to be read seriously. The obituary is a genre where praise is *de rigueur*, so that reservations and criticism carry more than their usual weight. A bad example of the genre is provided by Philarète Chasles, who tacked two paragraphs of manifestly insincere laudatory prose to the end of a fairly stiff criticism of all that Balzac achieved.[53] Sainte-Beuve was more subtle, and skilfully mixed apparent praise with implicit criticism. The import of these criticisms, if read properly, goes very far. Balzac, he says, was very popular: he flattered a large class of novel-readers by inventing the 'woman in her prime'. At the same time, *La Femme de trente ans* relies on a popular theme of eighteenth-century pulp literature. The meaning of these remarks is that literary merit had nothing to do with Balzac's success: it was the result of a market-oriented and borrowed 'invention'. Secondly, Sainte-Beuve pours veiled scorn on three of the novelist's principal aims: to portray society faithfully, to link his novels through the reappearing characters, and to be a thinker as well as a story-teller.

The sharpest point of sarcasm is reserved for the way in which Balzac mixes fiction and reality. There is a moment, Sainte-Beuve writes, 'où, dans son analyse, le pléxus véritable et réel finit, et où le pléxus illusoire commence, et il ne les distingue pas . . .' This he surmises is no doubt the result of his mystical leanings: 'c'est dire qu'il est sujet à illusion'. Balzac was an inventive, restless, energetic creator, but he lacked completely the ability to dominate and order his own creation—that is to say, he lacked true genius. Sainte-Beuve takes Steinbock, the artist of *La Cousine Bette*, as Balzac's spokesman, and quotes him as saying in defence of constant work that all artists have lived 'en concubinage avec La Muse'. Sainte-Beuve's rebuke is characteristically prudish: 'Non, Phidéas et Homère n'ont pas vécu *ainsi en concubinage* avec la Muse; ils l'ont toujours accueillie et comme chaste et sévère.'

In this obituary notice, Sainte-Beuve pounced with savagery on what he called his 'gibier favori',[54] and attacked with sarcasm many of the features which distinguish the *Comédie humaine* from, for example, the works of George Sand—whom the critic considered a finer writer.[55] The moderation of language is a result of the constraints of

[53] *Le Journal des débats*, 24 Aug. 1850.   [54] *Mes Poisons* (Plon, 1911), p. 111.
[55] 'un plus grand, plus sûr et plus ferme écrivain que M. de Balzac'; Sainte-Beuve, *Le Constitutionnel*, 2 Sept. 1850.

the obituary genre; and Sainte-Beuve's reference to this article as a fair and general portrait of Balzac is only justifiable in the context of later, not earlier, attitudes expressed by the critic.

After this article, moreover, the critic's hostility to Balzac became almost legendary. In *Le Feuilleton d'Aristophane*,[56] a satire by Banville and Boyer that was staged in 1852, Sainte-Beuve (in the thin disguise of Aristophanes) is treated to a long lecture on the virtues of Balzac and the *Comédie humaine*. (Courbet appears in this play as Réalista, and enters the stage with the line: 'L'Art, c'est moi.')

There are no later articles from Sainte-Beuve's pen devoted solely or mainly to Balzac, but the development of his attitude can be studied in references made to the novelist in articles on other subjects, from changes made to the three main pieces of 1834, 1838, and 1850 in their various re-editions, and finally from other more indirect sources.

In 1855, the philanthropic millionaire Dr. Véron donated ten thousand francs to the Société des gens de lettres to be distributed as prize money for four essay competitions, one of which was to be on the subject: *Étude sur Honoré de Balzac*. Sainte-Beuve was chairman of the panel of judges for this particular competition. However, only six scripts were presented, and none was deemed worthy of the prize. Unfortunately, the Société say they have no records of this contest in their archives: unfortunately, since one of the six entrants may well have been Barbey d'Aurevilly. Barbey was under no illusion about the outcome. He wrote to Dutacq that the judges 'sont les ennemis de Balzac. Il a transpiré des noms d'une hostilité connue.'[57] He must presumably have meant Sainte-Beuve, since he continued that the only approach likely to be favoured was 'le poison sucré de l'article de Sainte-Beuve du *Constitutionnel*' (i.e. the obituary). Despite all this, Barbey declared he was not averse to entering the contest, and may well have done so. Not even Barbey, however, foresaw quite how farcical the Concours Véron would be. At its *séance solennelle* on 16 April 1856, the Society's President, Louis Lurine, read out a report on the competition—but this 'report' was in fact Lurine's own essay on Balzac, and the panel of judges, who were present, immediately declared he had won and awarded him the not inconsiderable prize of 2,500 francs.[58] The proceedings were irregular—and the content of the

---

[56] Published by Michel Lévy, 1853.

[57] *Lettres intimes* (Bernouard, 1929), p. 101.

[58] See ' Échos parisiens' in *L'Abeille impériale*, 1 May 1856, for an account of the proceedings.

essay itself reveals extraordinary bias. Through a fog of circumlocution, Lurine's essay apes the more elegant *double-entendres* of Sainte-Beuve's 1850 article on Balzac. Lurine points out the importance of description in the novel, but promptly criticizes its 'excesses'; he exercises heavy sarcasm at the expense of Balzac's 'exaggerations of reality'; and, like Sainte-Beuve, Lurine mentions the novelist's 'don de seconde vue'—giving the theme a sarcastic twist: 'Lorsque Balzac ne trouve pas, il devine; il voit les yeux fermés et l'on a eu raison de l'appeler un voyant.'[59] Lurine's derogatory remarks on Balzac's interest in science, his paragraphs on style, on proper names in the *Comédie humaine,* and on the life with which inanimate objects are endowed are all imitations of passages on the same topics in Sainte-Beuve's writings.

This 'report' thus contains very large borrowings from the work of the man who then awarded it a prize: so one may reasonably assume that the additional material in Lurine's report met with Sainte-Beuve's approval. It always was the critic's habit to attribute his harshest thoughts to someone else—in the Balzac articles, he had used Janin, Chasles, Jean-Jacques Ampère, and 'un sévère ami—j'ai toujours cet ami-là à mes côtés'. Thus it can be argued that Sainte-Beuve was almost speaking by proxy at the Concours Véron.

What Lurine added—and all that he added—to the material drawn from Sainte-Beuve's obituary was a comparison between Balzac and Rousseau. Both, he said, had had a considerable influence on society, for they had flattered men's vices, made forms of evil socially acceptable, and perverted the minds and manners of their readers. The same comparisons were made by Menche de Loisne and Poitou[60]—critics whose political and religious criteria of judgement were quite clear. Sainte-Beuve had spoken with praise of Rousseau in 1850, but only as a stylist. As Roger Fayolle shows, 'l'admiration professée par le lundiste est ambigüe et lourde d'arrière-pensées politiques'.[61] That Sainte-Beuve's critical judgements derived from political and 'moral' criteria can be shown also by the conclusion to the appendix he wrote for the second edition of *Port-Royal* in 1860. The critic does not refute the ill-informed attack that Balzac had made on the book twenty years before, but launches instead into a diatribe against the morality and

---

[59] L. Lurine, 'Discours', *La Semaine,* 4 May 1856.

[60] 'Rousseau est le vrai père de tous nos déclamateurs modernes', E. Poitou, op. cit., Introduction.

[61] R. Fayolle, *Sainte-Beuve et le XVIIIᵉ siècle, ou Comment les Révolutions arrivent* (Armand Colin, 1972), p. 233.

influence of the *Comédie humaine*. The novelist's popularity with the public in no way acquits him from the charge of immorality:

Car la société actuelle, ne l'oubliez pas, les générations présentes aiment et préconisent dans Balzac l'homme non seulement qui leur a peint leur vice, mais qui le leur a chatouillé, c'est pourquoi je les récuse comme juges en dernier ressort: ce sont des complices.[62]

Sainte-Beuve used a very similar kind of argument in one of the additions he made in 1869 to his review of *La Recherche de l'absolu*. Balzac should not have used the 'particle of nobility' (his real name was Honoré Balzac, not *de* Balzac), the critic says, but by doing so 'il a mis à la mode cette manie de tant d'hommes de notre génération et que depuis n'a fait que de croître et d'embellir—de se donner pour ce qu'on n'est pas'.[63] This is moralizing and personal criticism that does not fit the image that Sainte-Beuve liked to project of himself— of a literary 'naturalist', objectively classifying works and authors into 'les grandes familles naturelles de l'esprit'. The critic's references to Balzac sound increasingly inspired by Armand de Pontmartin: he notes that the surgeon Ricord will soon be needed to cut away the cancerous growth of the novelist's reputation;[64] and the literary movements of the Second Empire, he wrote, damn themselves by their 'admiration enthousiaste et comme frénétique . . . les gloutons pour Balzac, les délicats pour Musset'.[65]

A prudish distaste for the treatment of women's lives and emotions in the *Comédie humaine* continued to inform Sainte-Beuve's remarks on the novelist. In an article on the caricaturist Gavarni, the critic mentions Balzac's descriptive manner as a literary counterpart to the artist's sketches of contemporary life. But though he was an expert on 'les mœurs du jour, et certaines mœurs en particulier, où il est expert et passé maître', the novelist allowed his material to get out of control. 'Il s'enivre du vin qu'il verse et ne se possède plus . . .'[66] Sober accuracy was what Sainte-Beuve required from contemporary fiction—thus his praise of Charles de Bernard and, later, of Flaubert. The Goncourt

---

[62] C. A. Sainte-Beuve, *Port-Royal* (Michel Lévy, 1860), I. 559.

[63] *Portraits contemporains* (Michel Lévy, 1869), II. 332.

[64] *Mes Poisons* (Plon, 1911), p. 111.

[65] *Mes Cahiers* (Lemerre, 1876), p. 134.

[66] *Le Constitutionnel,* 12 Oct. 1863. A few days earlier Henri Delaborde had made the same comparison in the *RDM* (1 Oct. 1863, p. 589). Note also that Faguet misquoted this article in his *Balzac* (Hachette, 1913), writing 's'emporte et manque de goût à tout moment' where Sainte-Beuve had put 's'emporte et manque à tout moment'.

brothers reported the following conversation in their diary entry for
11 May 1863:

La causerie touche à Balzac et s'y arrête. Sainte-Beuve attaque le grand
romancier:
— Balzac n'est pas vrai . . . C'est un homme de génie, si vous voulez,
mais c'est un monstre!
— Mais nous sommes tous des monstres, riposte Gautier. Alors, qui a peint
ce temps-ci? où se retrouve notre société? dans quel livre? si Balzac ne l'a
pas représentée?
— C'est de l'imagination, de l'invention, crie aigrement Sainte-Beuve, j'ai
connu cette rue de Langlade, ce n'était pas du tout comme ça.
— Mais dans quels romans trouvez-vous la vérité? Est-ce dans les romans de
Madame Sand?
— Mon Dieu, fait Renan, qui est à côté de moi, je trouve beaucoup plus
vraie Madame Sand que Balzac.
— Pas possible, vraiment!
— Oui, oui, chez elle les passions sont générales . . .
— Et puis Balzac a un style! jette Sainte-Beuve, ça a l'air tordu, c'est un
style *cordé* . . .[67]

The argument of this long examination of Sainte-Beuve's attitude
to Balzac is that the critic's views did not stagnate. Some scholars
have been deluded into thinking that they did by their failure to examine the changes that Sainte-Beuve made to his earlier articles. The
movement in the views of the author of *Volupté* was not based on a
dislike of all new literature. He did not participate in the hounding of
Flaubert, and was sympathetic to Baudelaire. The change was partly
related to a growing prudishness in Sainte-Beuve in the 1840s, but
much more firmly related to a change in political outlook after 1848.
After Balzac's death Sainte-Beuve became a venomous, moralizing,
and increasingly militant critic of the man whose reputation he had
helped more than anyone to establish. Roger Fayolle has demonstrated how Sainte-Beuve's concern, between 1848 and 1852, was not
to give an objective picture of French literature, but to separate the
right from the wrong.[68] His criteria of judgement were hidden, but
none the less firmly political. Although he never actually said so, and
would probably have denied it if asked, Sainte-Beuve shared the general view of right-wing 'moral' critics that Balzac was not without
influence on the events of 1848; and like Pontmartin, he believed that
by denouncing Balzac he was denouncing the evil that was rooted in

[67] Edmond et Jules de Goncourt, *Journal*, II. 89–90.
[68] Op. cit. and also 'Défense de la socio-critique', *Le Monde*, 18 Sept. 1970.

the writings of Rousseau and which was responsible for the decadence of French society.

The examples of Sainte-Beuve and Pontmartin show just how unreal it is to make any period-divisions in the history of Balzac's reputation. To treat these two critics as exceptions would introduce an unacceptably arbitrary element into the periodization itself. None the less, it is true that more and more critics came to regard Balzac as a major writer and to approve of him in the course of the Second Empire, and that the 1860s in that sense seem to be a different 'period' from the early 1850s. Weinberg's division of Balzac criticism into periods may be open to many objections, but it does for all that describe one aspect of a change that really took place. What requires clarification, then, is not only the process of periodization but the things or aspects that are being periodized.

The term *criticism* refers to a wide variety of different kinds of writing, ranging from short reviews in the daily press to scholarly books resulting from years of study and reflection. Both these extremes, and all intermediate forms of criticism, have in common the status of mediators between the producers and consumers of literary texts. Some critics claimed to be neutral mediators: Sainte-Beuve and Lanson, for example, based their authority on objective detachment. It was more frequent in the nineteenth century, however, for critics to be explicitly biased. Pontmartin, Scherer, Biré, Faguet, and Brunetière stated that their function was to direct consciences, and the direction they sought to impose derived from political and broadly ideological considerations. Whether explicit or not, all criticism is ideologically motivated—Sainte-Beuve's as much as Pontmartin's, as the preceding analysis has demonstrated. The simple fact that a critic has to select what he writes about means that he imposes a particular direction on his own public. The selection of books by a critic may be made on the basis of loyalties towards an individual publisher or writer; it may be an inherited selection from previous critical traditions; but it is always fundamentally a function of the critic's ideology, be it formulated or unconscious. Actual criticism of the *Comédie humaine* represents a relationship between the underlying ideology of the critic and the underlying themes of Balzac criticism. Both poles of the relationship are subject to change, both are 'variables'. The relationship itself can thus be seen as a complex variable, the evolution of which can only be described as the conjoint result of the double evolution of the bases of critical thought and of the content of critical themes.

Another way of showing how an author's reputation is a highly complex variable is to consider the ways in which critics rank him in the literary system. A comparison of Balzac and De Sade only has an evaluative meaning if we know what system the comparison derives from—in Sainte-Beuve's image of French literature De Sade has a negative rank, but not in the minds of, let us say, Mario Praz or Georges Bataille. In 1836, Saint-Marc Girardin compared *Le Père Goriot* to *King Lear*, and found the latter a better treatment of the problems of paternity,[69] as might any present-day critic. However, the place occupied by Shakespeare in the image of world literature held by a French academic of the July Monarchy is quite different from his position today, so that the evaluative content of Saint-Marc Girardin's comparison is also quite different. In 1850, Philarète Chasles denied that Balzac could be compared to Shakespeare; in 1858, Taine wrote that 'Avec Shakespeare et Saint-Simon, Balzac est le plus grand magasin de documents que nous ayons sur la nature humaine.' Both Chasles and Taine were well versed in English literature, but their disagreement on the evaluative relationship between Balzac and Shakespeare is a function of differences over two separate ideas—the status of Balzac and the nature of Shakespeare.

The term 'reputation' thus covers an extremely complex set of relationships. Furthermore, it must be distinguished from what is usually called 'popularity'—the degree to which the book-reading public, as opposed to the critics, approve or disapprove of an author's works. It is well known that what the public actually reads bears little relationship to what the critics write about. And so it would be quite wrong to try to fit changes in critical evaluations and changes in popularity into the same periods.

Weinberg's periodization of Balzac criticism relies on the term 'reputation' being understood as a conflation of popularity, rank, and evaluation. A more interesting, though more complicated description of the novelist's 'vie posthume', as Pommier called the subject,[70] can be gained if the highly abstract idea of a 'reputation' is exploded into a number of separate relationships. One of the relationships referred to above is that which obtains between the themes of criticism and the ideology of the critic. The themes of Balzac criticism in the 1850s can

[69] His lecture was reprinted in the *Cours de littérature dramatique*, I. 241–5, in 1843.
[70] *AB* (1967), p. 258.

be analysed in greater or lesser detail. A crude set of four propositions was suggested in the first two chapters, namely: (1) Balzac was a revolutionary; (2) Balzac was not a revolutionary; (3) Balzac was an observer of reality; (4) Balzac was a writer of the imagination. As has been shown, these themes are in themselves evaluatively neutral. A closer analysis would describe more concrete statements as themes, for example: (5) *Eugénie Grandet* is Balzac's best novel; (6) *Les Parents pauvres* is Balzac's best novel; (7) *Vautrin* is a bad play; (8) *Mercadet* is a dramatic success. This second set of themes consists of comparative value-judgements, which none the less remain evaluatively neutral in the sense that (5), first proposed by Sainte-Beuve, is frequently used by critics hostile to the *Comédie humaine*; (6) was used in conjunction with (1) by the left with a positive general judgement of the novelist, but in conjunction with (2) by writers like Lerminier who saw the novelist as a pessimist and atheist; (7)—the truest of these statements— was both an accusation and an excuse; and (8) could be adduced as proof of Balzac's inability to write plays since *Mercadet* had been adapted for the stage by someone else. It has been suggested that the evaluations implied by actual uses of these themes derive ultimately from the ideology of the critic using them—ideology being understood in the widest sense. There is something more concrete than ideology, however, which actually prompts a critic to write about a particular author on a particular day and to use particular themes in doing so. Obviously the most frequent stimulus to critical activity in daily and weekly papers is the publication of a new book by the author in question, but in the case of Balzac criticism after 1850, of course, this reason only applied in a small number of instances (about 12 of the 1,000 items in Appendix III are reviews of previously unknown Balzac texts). There was in fact a wide range of different events which provoked critical activity on the *Comédie humaine*: performances of Balzac's plays, of dramatizations of his novels; publications of new books by other writers (e.g. Flaubert, Zola); political events, such as the various peripeteia of the Dreyfus affair; and so on. Critics replied to other critics, and the whole activity sometimes acquired its own dynamic for a while. Now it seems pertinent to ask whether there are any reasons for certain events to provoke critical writing on Balzac, and for others not to; and also to inquire whether there is any relationship between the provoking event and the themes of the criticism thus provoked. *Madame Bovary* once again provides a clear answer: because one of the major themes of criticism up to 1856 was the im-

morality of the *Comédie humaine* and because Flaubert's novel was
sufficiently immoral to be tried in a court of law for 'outrage à la
pudeur', therefore the publication of *Madame Bovary* provoked
articles on Balzac. The link is one of theme and event, not of literary
comparison. The appearance of *L'Éducation sentimentale* was not
accompanied by any critical articles on the *Comédie humaine*.

The relationship between the themes of criticism and the events
that provoke actualizations of the themes in critical writing is an in-
teractive one—that is to say, it works in both directions. It is of course
not only the event itself—such as the production of *Vautrin* in 1850—
but the whole political and social situation in which that event takes
place that has a determining effect on the kind of criticism that results.
Nor is it just the themes themselves, but their links with other ideas
that play a determining role in making some events the source of
criticism and others not.

Change in Balzac criticism can, then, be shown by the changing
nature of the events which stimulated it, much more easily than by the
development of its themes, which remained remarkably constant
throughout the century. To describe the change of the novelist's
rank within the literary system requires a major study of the system
itself, which would be outside the scope of this book. On the other
hand, it is possible to describe change in Balzac's popularity in the
second half of the nineteenth century without going too far afield.

An author's popularity with the public is, at least in theory, the one
dimension of the literary system that can be quantified without begging too many questions. Even here, however, it is not immediately
clear that we know which set of numbers most truly represents popularity; and not all the figures are easy to unearth.

For example, present-day publishers assess the popularity of their
books by conducting surveys into how many people read each copy
bought. This is taken to indicate the potential market and thus the
'true' popularity of the work. Another simpler measure is provided
by the number of copies actually sold, and it is on a sample of such
figures that best-seller lists are compiled at the present time. The results of this method are not always identical to the results of the survey of each copy's readership. An even cruder index of popularity is
the print-order of a book: this tells us what the publisher estimated
the *profitable* market size to be, but cannot inform us whether he was
right or not. The simplest but most widespread way of guessing at the
popularity of a book is to count up the number of times it was reprinted

over the years. Of these four measures of popularity, the last is without doubt the least significant, for it does not distinguish between large and small editions. It is also the only measure which has been available for historical periods, and the only check ever used against the not always reliable claims of critics and historians about writers' popularities. However, the third measure—that of the number of copies printed at each reissue—is available for books produced in France in the years between 1817 and 1881. The Napoleonic legislation which put the burden of censorship and control on printers, rather than publishers, was maintained throughout this period in one respect: namely, that printers were obliged to make a declaration of each printing job they did and to include on their declaration the print-order of the work.[71] These declarations were made to the Ministry of the Interior (in the provinces, via the *préfet*) and are now to be found with that Ministry's papers at the Archives nationales. There are thus well over half a million slips of paper at the French national archives which, one hopes, will one day be sorted out and analysed properly to provide a more complete picture of the tastes of the reading public in the nineteenth century—or rather, of the publishers' expectations of these tastes.[72] Publishers may have made mistakes, but in general one can assume that a second edition of a work means that the first has been sold out. Thus the print-order figures for all but the *last* issue (in 90 per cent of cases, this is also the first) can be taken as either the true or less than the true level of the book's popularity.

A number of factors complicate the interpretation of the figures for Balzac's works (and no doubt for other writers too). Houssiaux, who re-published the entire *Comédie humaine* in the 1850s, was not allowed by Mme Ève de Balzac, who had inherited her husband's literary estate, to print as many copies as he wanted to. He wanted in fact to double the printing of all twenty volumes from one to two thousand: but as Mme Ève explained to her business manager Dutacq, 'ces vingt mille volumes tiendront une place dans le commerce de la librairie et feront obstacle à toute nouvelle édition . . .',[73] and thus she refused her permission.

Printers are not likely to have lied on their declarations—one can

---

[71] See D. M. Bellos, 'The *Bibliographie de la France* and its sources', *The Library*, Mar. 1973.

[72] See my paper on 'French printing statistics' in *Proceedings of the VII*th *Congress of the International Comparative Literature Association* (forthcoming).

[73] *Petit Cahier d'Ève de Balzac*, Lovenjoul Library, Chantilly, A.275, fo. 6.

TABLE I

Ledger	Reg. no.	Date	Author	Title	Printer	Print-order
39	7262	30. 8.50	Balzac	*Histoire des Treize*	Lange-Lévy	1 000
39	7263	30. 8.50	Balzac	*César Birotteau*	Lange-Lévy	1 000
39	7272	30. 8.50	Balzac	*Les Parents pauvres*	Lange-Lévy	1 000
39	7652	14. 9.50	Balzac	*Pensées et maximes*	Plon	2 000
37	2183	14. 3.50	Dumas	*La Régence*	Bureau	4 000
38	3677	30. 4.50	Dumas	*Joseph Balsamo*	Lange-Lévy	6 000
38	4098	14. 5.50	Dumas	*Joseph Balsamo*	Lange-Lévy	6 000
39	7011	23. 8.50	Sue	*Les Mystères du peuple*	Dondey-Dupré	6 600
60	1105	2. 2.55	Balzac	*Mémoires de deux jeunes mariées*	Voisvenel	500
60	1103	2. 2.55	Balzac	*Maison du chat-qui-pelote*	Voisvenel	500
60	1162	5. 2.55	Balzac	*Les Contes drolatiques*	Bernard	10 000
60	1977	28. 2.55	Balzac	*Eugénie Grandet*	Voisvenel	500
60	2358	10. 3.55	Balzac	*Les Employés*	Voisvenel	500
60	508	16. 1.55	Stendhal	*Le Rouge et le noir*	Dondey-Dupré	6 600
60	710	22. 1.55	Dumas	*La Reine Margot*	Voisvenel	6 000
60	2047	1. 3.55	Soulié	*Les Mémoires du diable*	Morvis	10 000
60	2840	24. 3.55	Stendhal	*Mina de Wangel*	Blondeau	2 500
60	2979	16. 3.55	Dumas	*Vingt Ans après*	Dondey-Dupré	6 600

Note

Compiled from the ledgers of the *Surveillance de l'imprimerie et de la librairie*, Archives nationales F18*II, 37–177. Fourteen of these 140 ledgers were examined: nos. 37, 38, 39, 40 (for the year 1850); 60 (for 1855); 84 (for 1860); 108, 109, 110 (for 1865); 129, 130 (for 1869); 131, 132 (for 1870); 177 (for 1881). Every Balzac printing mentioned has been included in Table 1, as well as a selection of other printings for comparison.

84	3133	28. 3.60	Balzac	La Recherche de l'absolu	Voisvenel	500
84	3134	28. 3.60	Balzac	La Peau de chagrin	Voisvenel	500
84	3644	13. 4.60	Balzac	Maison du chat-qui-pelote	Voisvenel	1 000
84	3646	13. 4.60	Balzac	Mémoires de deux jeunes mariées	Voisvenel	1 000
84	2961	23. 3.60	Féval	Les Enfants de la nuit	Blot	100 000
108	1042	7. 2.65	Balzac	Eugénie Grandet	Voisvenel	500
108	1043	7. 2.65	Balzac	Le Lys dans la vallée	Voisvenel	500
108	1465	17. 2.65	Balzac	Scènes de la vie parisienne	Voisvenel	500
108	2153	9. 3.65	Balzac	Scènes de la vie privée	Voisvenel	500
108	4000	5. 4.65	Balzac	Mémoires de deux jeunes mariées	Voisvenel	500
108	858	3. 2.65	Z. Carraud	La Petite Jeanne		15 000
108	1705	25. 2.65	Sue	Les Mystères de Paris		2 200
109	5195	18. 5.65	Balzac	Les Contes drolatiques	Pillet	1 500
109	5196	18. 5.65	Balzac	Scènes de la vie privée	Pillet	1 500
109	5467	27. 5.65	Balzac	Une Fille d' Ève	Voisvenel	500
109	5468	27. 5.65	Balzac	La Paix du ménage	Voisvenel	500
109	5469	27. 5.65	Balzac	Scènes de la vie privée	Voisvenel	500
109	5669	6. 6.65	Balzac	Béatrix	Voisvenel	500
109	5980	17. 6.65	Balzac	Honorine	Voisvenel	500
109	5982	17. 6.65	Balzac	Le Père Goriot	Voisvenel	500
109	5983	17. 6.65	Balzac	Scènes de la vie parisienne	Voisvenel	500
109	5984	17. 6.65	Balzac	Le Curé de village	Voisvenel	500
109	6032	19. 6.65	Balzac	La Femme de trente ans	Pillet	1 400
109	6533	4. 7.65	Balzac	La Femme de trente ans	Voisvenel	500
109	4579	29. 4.65	Féval	Les Drames de la mort	Poupart-Davyl	20 000
109	4621	1. 5.65	Goncourt	Germinie Lacerteux	Claye	1 500
109	5029	12. 5.65	Diderot	Le Neveu de Rameau	Dubuisson	6 000
109	5558	31. 5.65	Erckmann-Chatrian	Mademoiselle Thérèse	Voisvenel	26 500

continued overleaf

TABLE I—*contd.*

Ledger	Reg. no.	Date	Author	Title	Printer	Print-order
110	7670	5. 8.65	Balzac	*La Peau de chagrin*	Voisvenel	500
110	8241	29. 8.65	Balzac	*Ursule Mirouet*	Voisvenel	500
110	8282	29. 8.65	Balzac	*Le Lys dans la vallée*	Voisvenel	500
110	8878	18. 9.65	Balzac	*La Recherche de l'absolu*	Voisvenel	500
110	6802	13. 7.65	Z. Carraud	*La Petite Jeanne*	Lahure	11 000
110	8770	13. 9.65	Hugo	*Notre-Dame de Paris*	Bonaventure	15 000
129	9862	24. 8.69	Sue	*Attar-Gull*	Voisvenel	500
129	10908	28. 9.69	G. Sand	*Indiana*	Dupont	11 000
129	10909	28. 9.69	G. Sand	*François le champi*	Dupont	16 500
129	10910	28. 9.69	G. Sand	*La Marquise de Villemer*	Dupont	16 500
129	11389	16.10.69	Flaubert	*L'Éducation sentimentale*	Claye	2 000
130	12392	10.12.69	Sue	*Les Légendes du peuple*	Lahure	10 000
132	4460	3. 6.70	Balzac	*Scènes de la vie parisienne*	Voisvenel	300
132	4466	3. 6.70	Balzac	*Scènes de la vie privée*	Voisvenel	300

see no reason why they should—but some sets of figures in the archives are so surprising as to cause suspicion. Voisvenel, for example, printed many of the cheaper editions of Balzac's novels published in the 1850s and 1860s by Michel Lévy's *Librairie nouvelle* and by the newspaper *Le Siècle*. In the majority of cases he declared a very low print-run of only 500 copies, and in two instances of only 300. New novels by unknown authors were commonly brought out in runs of 1,000 copies; and Voisvenel declared much higher figures for printings of novels by Balzac's contemporaries—Dumas, Sue, Sand, and so forth. Other printers of Balzac also declared rather higher and much more variable figures than Voisvenel. There is no other source of information that might give direct corroboration of these figures, and they must therefore be accepted as the only evidence we have of public demand for the novels of the *Comédie humaine*. None the less, it is possible that Mme Ève de Balzac limited these cheap editions as she did the complete works; or that for some reason unknown to us Voisvenel was under-declaring. Finally, it may be that Michel Lévy found it more convenient, given the very frequent reprintings of many of the novels, to keep the printer's 'beds' and to run off a few hundred copies each time the stocks ran low, instead of printing a big edition and then having to recompose the text at a later date.

In Table 1 on pages 84-6 I have set out all the declarations of Balzac titles found in a selection of registers in the archives (a note on p. 84 explains exactly how the material was selected), together with a few declarations for books by other authors for comparison. The largest printing discovered of a Balzac text was for the *Contes drolatiques* in 1855, where the figure is 10,000. This was the edition illustrated by Gustave Doré: an unillustrated edition was printed in a run of 1,500 ten years later. The difference is not a measure of a decline in the work's popularity, but an indication of the saleability of any book illustrated by Doré.

No other work by Balzac in these registers was printed in a run of over 2,000. Yet moderately successful works by other authors were printed in quantities higher even than that of the illustrated *Contes drolatiques*. Dumas's *Joseph Balsamo* totalled 12,500 copies in 1850; Hugo's *Notre-Dame de Paris* had a single printing of 15,000 in 1865. Really best-selling novels reached considerably higher figures: 19,500 for *François le Champi* in 1869; *Mademoiselle Thérèse*, by the regional novelists Erckmann-Chatrian, had a printing of 26,500 in 1865; and Paul Féval reached 'le mur des cent mille' in 1860 with *Les Enfants de la nuit.* Even the 'happy few' were in the opinion of Stendhal's publisher as numerous as 6,600 in 1855.

The material from which these figures are drawn represents a 10 per cent sample of all books printed between 1850 and 1881 (14 out of 140 registers were examined exhaustively). It would be a strange statistical quirk indeed if they were all exceptional. The discrepancy between printings of Balzac and printings of other novelists is too large and too constant to be a distortion introduced by a rough and ready sampling method. The conclusion is inevitably that Balzac was at no point between 1850 and 1881 a best-selling author. His popularity, measured in this way, was far lower than that of Sand, Sue, or Dumas.

None the less, Balzac's novels were very frequently reprinted, at least until the late 1860s. In the block-graph on p. 89 (Figure 1), the number of Balzac volumes announced in the official *Bibliographie de la France* has been shown in vertical columns for each year from 1850 to 1910. Figures for the works of Dumas and Sand are represented as lines. As can be seen, the heyday of all three writers lies between 1855 and 1870. All three fell from favour at the end of the Second Empire, and between 1875 and 1890 re-publications were at a very low ebb. Eugène Sue, whose 'popularity curve' has been left out of the graph, disappeared completely after 1880. In the 1890s, however, a substantial revival occurs in the number of Balzac titles re-published. (Unfortunately print-order figures are not available for this period.) George Sand and Alexandre Dumas do not enjoy a similar revival.

Balzac's popularity, then, was different from that of his closest contemporary rivals in the novel. The market for his works was smaller at the time they were all in demand, but unlike his rivals, Balzac survived the trough of the 1880s to emerge as a classic. This feature would appear to be common to all authors who 'survive': as Robert Escarpit has shown, on the basis of much wider evidence than ours, every writer 'has a rendez-vous with oblivion in the ten, twenty or thirty years after his death'.[74] What is of interest to Balzac criticism is to see how this picture of one part of the novelist's reputation can be related to others.

The combination in the 1850s and 1860s of a high number of re-publications with low printing figures is not paradoxical, for it corresponds to the picture created by other more traditional sources of information on his popularity. Towards the end of the 1840s, Balzac and Stendhal were the favourite authors of the pupils at the École

[74] *The Sociology of Literature*, translated by E. Pick, 2nd edition (1971), p. 22.

Normale Supérieure—that is to say, of the élite of the generation that reached maturity and influence in the period from 1855. Octave Gréard, one-time Minister of Education, recounts in his biography of the political theorist Prévost-Paradol that it was an established custom to

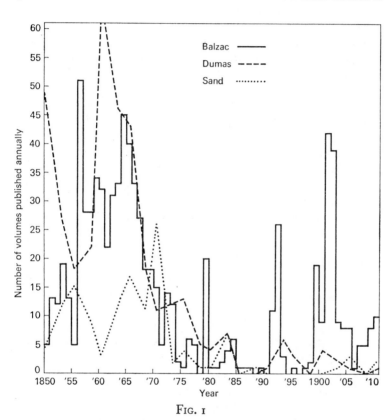

FIG. 1

Note. Compiled from the *Bibliographie de la France*. The figures represented are the number of volumes published, not titles. Balzac's output is entered on a yearly basis, Sand's and Dumas's at alternate two- and three-year intervals. Figures do not include translations, plays, or dramatizations

slip a volume of the *Comédie humaine* to any boys unlucky enough to suffer detention.[75] Of the boys who passed through the rue d'Ulm at this time many made contributions to Balzac criticism: Taine, of course, Edmond About, Jules Vallès, Francisque Sarcey, and Philoxène

[75] O. Gréard, *Prévost-Paradol* (Hachette, 1894), p. 14.

Boyer. According to Jean Mélia, the passion for Stendhal and Balzac among the pupils was due to the influence of a single teacher, Paul Jacquinet.[76] Be that as it may, Philoxène Boyer went on to spend himself and his considerable fortune in a conscious imitation of Balzac's Raphaël de Valentin; he also composed a vertiable panegyric to the novelist in his satire on Sainte-Beuve, *Le Feuilleton d'Aristophane*, and gave a public lecture on Balzac in 1858.[77] (The text of this lecture has not been found.) It was to men of this sort who imitated Balzac's fictions in their own lives, as well as to writers like Champfleury who appeared to imitate him in their novels, that Babou was referring in 1859 when he talked of a school of 'Balzaciens . . . et sous-balzaciens'.[78] Journalists frequently used pseudonyms from the *Comédie humaine*: Louis Lambert, Rastignac, and Raphaël de Valentin, as well as Foedora and Madame de Mortsauf in later years. Two newspapers were founded with the title of *La Comédie humaine*,[79] one with the same title was projected,[80] and one called *Le Balzac* actually appeared.[81] In the literary and journalistic world there does indeed seem to have been a group of men who were, like Guérin of *Gil-Blas*, '[des] Balzaciens qui savaient Balzac par cœur'.[82] The high esteem in which they held the novelist became itself a theme of Balzac criticism. Nearly every event related to Balzac in the fifty years that followed his death was referred to by one critic or another as 'la véritable apothéose du roman-cier'. Like the immorality of *Vautrin*, the popularity of Balzac itself became a myth.

Corroboration can also be found for the low demand from the public for the novels of *La Comédie humaine*. The cheap edition of the works published in the 1850s by Michel Lévy at 1 fr. 25 per volume, and which was printed (as has been shown) in very small runs, did not sell well. One journalist claimed in 1884 that the edition was still not sold out.[83] In 1860, *Le Monde illustré*, which shared offices on the

---

[76] *Stendhal et ses commentateurs* (Mercure de France, 1911), p. 235; and p. 242, where Sarcey is quoted as saying: 'Balzac était notre Dieu . . .'

[77] Reported in the *Gazette d'Augsbourg* and even the London *Times*.

[78] *La Revue française*, July 1859.

[79] *La Comédie humaine*, journal hebdomadaire, 1881–2; and *La Comédie humaine*, journal politique, 1891–2. [80] See Chapter 4, note 1, below.

[81] *Le Balzac*, journal politique, littéraire et artistique, 1884–5. The only complete run is at the Lovenjoul Library, Chantilly, B. 1342. The Arsenal Library, Paris, possesses a single copy of another *Le Balzac*, containing only extracts from the *Comédie humaine*. In 1900, the first *Balzac* was resurrected by G. H. Renault as a right-wing political and literary monthly.

[82] M. Talmeyr, *Souvenirs de la Comédie humaine* (Perrin, 1927), p. 7.

[83] E. Lepelletier, 'Les Balzaciens', *L'Écho de Paris*, 8 Sept. 1884.

Boulevard des Italiens with Lévy's publishing companies, carried the following announcement at regular intervals:

Le Mondé illustré offre . . . aujourd'hui une nouvelle prime à ses abonnés. QUARANTE-CINQ VOLUMES, grand in-18°, éditées par la Librairie Nouvelle, forment la seule édition complète des ŒUVRES DE BALZAC. Cette édition, la seule classée d'après les notes de l'auteur lui-même, et dont le prix est de CINQUANTE-SIX FRANCS, sera envoyée franco moyennant TRENTE-CINQ FRANCS à toute personne qui prendra un abonnement de 21 francs pour un an au *Monde illustré*.

The works could hardly have been selling well in the bookshops if they were used in this way as a cut-price enticement to subscribe to a periodical.

In the 1880s, when public demand for Balzac's works was at a low ebb, Edmond Lepelletier tried to repopularize the novelist by serializing *Ferragus* and *La Fille aux yeux d'or* in his newspaper, *Le Réveil*. Sales dropped sharply both times, and the serials were quickly abandoned.[84] However, he later succeeded in publishing all of *La Femme de trente ans* as a serial in *Le Réveil-Matin*.[85]

Ferragus had seemed the most 'popular' of Balzac's novels to Lepelletier, which was why he chose it in the first place for his *feuilleton*. One dimension of popularity that must be recognized in the case of an author as prolific as Balzac is the differential in demand for his various novels. To see whether Lepelletier's belief, and others like it, have any basis in fact, I have broken down the figures of annual re-publications of Balzac's works into the subtotals for the major novels, grouped into ten-year periods. The results (Table 2) do not tally entirely with the totals in Figure 1, since I have excluded re-publications in genuine complete works series (Houssiaux, Calmann-Lévy) but included the *Librairie nouvelle* editions. Other discrepancies arise over *Les Parents pauvres*, counted as two entries in Table 2 (one for *La Cousine Bette*, one for *Le Cousin Pons*) even when it appeared as a single volume; and over *Splendeurs et misères des courtisanes* which has been counted in Table 2 each time any one of its constituent parts appeared, and which is thus over-represented. Even so, *Splendeurs et misères* only comes out as the most-published novel in the 1850s, and yields first place to *Le Lys dans la vallée* in the 1860s, to *Le Père Goriot* in the 1870s, and to *Histoire des Treize* (of which *Ferragus* is a part) in the 1890s. Over the whole fifty-year period, *Splendeurs et misères* is equal

[84] *L'Écho de Paris*, 12 June 1887.   [85] From 12 June to 31 Aug. 1887.

with *Le Lys dans la vallée* at twenty-two re-publications each, followed by *Eugénie Grandet* with twenty and *La Peau de chagrin* and
La Cousine Bette with nineteen. What is remarkable about these
figures is their even spread: exactly half of the twenty-eight separate
titles listed were re-published between sixteen and twenty-two times—
which is a very narrow band of variation. Just over one third of the
578 publications listed in all is made up of 'other titles'—plays other
than *Mercadet*, early works, *œuvres diverses*, the shorter stories from
the *Études de mœurs*, and some less popular novels like *Séraphita*.

As was to be expected, those works most criticized for their im-

TABLE 2

Title	1850–9	1860–9	1870–9	1880–9	1890–9
1 *Splendeurs et misères des courtisanes*	10	10	2	0	0
2 *Mémoires de deux jeunes mariées*	7	11	0	0	0
3 *La Peau de chagrin*	7	10	2	0	0
4 *La Cousine Bette*	7	9	2	0	1
5 *Le Lys dans la vallée*	6	13	2	0	1
6 *Eugénie Grandet*	6	11	1	1	1
7 *Ursule Mirouet*	6	9	0	1	0
8 *Le Médecin de campagne*	6	9	1	0	1
9 *La Rabouilleuse*	6	8	1	0	1
10 *Le Père Goriot*	6	7	3	1	1
11 *Histoire des Treize*	5	10	1	0	2
12 *Le Curé de village*	5	9	1	0	1
13 *La Recherche de l'absolu*	5	6	0	0	1
14 *Le Cousin Pons*	5	5	2	0	0
15 *Illusions perdues*	4	8	1	1	1
16 *Modeste Mignon*	4	8	0	0	1
17 *César Birotteau*	4	6	2	0	1
18 *La Physiologie du mariage*	4	3	0	0	0
19 *La Femme de trente ans*	3	11	1	0	1
20 *Béatrix*	3	11	1	0	1
21 *Les Employés*	3	2	0	0	1
22 *Les Contes drolatiques*	2	7	2	1	1
23 *Les Paysans*	2	3	0	1	1
24 *Honorine*	2	3	2	0	0
25 *Louis Lambert*	2	2	0	1	1
26 *Albert Savarus*	2	1	0	0	0
27 *Les Chouans*	2	2	0	1	1
28 *Mercadet*	6	3	0	0	0
29 Other Titles	52	88	20	8	27

morality—*Mémoires de deux jeunes mariées, La Peau de chagrin,* and *La Cousine Bette*—rank among the leaders in the 1850s and indeed over the whole half-century. Less expectedly, *Eugénie Grandet* has a high rank in the 1860s and comes third over all, perhaps suggesting that Sainte-Beuve was not entirely out of touch with the novel-reading public. The position of *Illusions perdues* is not very high: and indeed this novel, now seen as perhaps the greatest Balzac wrote, has hardly been mentioned in the critical material dealt with so far.

The figures presented in the three tables show that public demand for Balzac's works up to the 1890s was small, but that it embraced a very wide range of his novels more or less equally. At the same time, there is evidence that Balzac's reputation was 'carried' through the inevitable trough in his popularity by a small band of influential enthusiasts centred on the élite of the generation that passed through the École Normale Supérieure at the end of the novelist's life. This is not to say that all of Balzac's 'vie posthume' can be accounted for by generation change and conspiracy theory, but to add a previously unexplored dimension to the history of his survival. The extent of his re-emergence in the 1890s is best shown in Figure 1, since many of the volumes published in that decade were parts of complete works series and have thus not been counted up in Table 2. The kind of publication in which Balzac's novels appeared at the end of the century was indeed very different from the earlier popular decades. On the one hand, the *Comédie humaine* had acquired snob value: the novels became suitable texts for those luxuriously bound and richly illustrated volumes intended to grace the bourgeois bookcase or coffee-table.[86] On the other hand, Balzac was, by the 1890s, part of the educational publishing world. As will be seen in Chapter 5, Balzac had become a classic; and in 1886 the Académie française set for its *prix d'éloquence* the subject: *L'Œuvre d'Honoré de Balzac*. Three years later, *Eugénie Grandet* was put on the required reading list for the 'agrégation de l'enseignement secondaire spécial'. Thus all high-grade *lycée* teachers trained in the 1890s had an academic knowledge of at least one of Balzac's novels, and they presumably passed some of this knowledge on to their pupils. It became feasible for Lévy to put the first *Pages choisies d'Honoré de Balzac,* with an introduction by Lanson, on to the market in 1895. The revival in Balzac's fortunes measured by the number of re-publications

---

[86] For example, *Les Chouans,* avec eaux-fortes par Julien le Blant, préface par Jules Simon (Testard, 1890); *La Maison du chat-qui-pelote,* préface par Francisque Sarcey (1899).

Popularity and criticism

is thus inseparable from his institutionalization as a classic and 'teach-able' author.

It is not easy to correlate changes in popularity with changes in other dimensions of a writer's reputation. The only aspect of Balzac criticism that can be quantified simply is the number of different articles on the novelist published each year—and this is a very crude and inaccurate way of describing change in his reputation. However, the annual totals based on Appendix III at the end of this book have been set out in Table 3, parallel to the figures for annual re-publica-tions of Balzac's novels that are also represented in Figure 1. The number of articles published in 1863, 1868 and 1869 was very much higher than in the other years of that decade because there were per-formances of *Les Ressources de Quinola*, *Mercadet*, and *Vautrin* re-spectively in those years. Nearly every newspaper reviewed nearly

TABLE 3

Year	Number of re-publica-tions	Number of critical items listed	Year	Number of re-publica-tions	Number of critical items listed
1850	5	70	1875	1	8
1851	13	58	1876	6	30
1852	12	21	1877	5	12
1853	19	43	1878	0	16
1854	13	34	1879	20	22
1855	5	21	1880	1	27
1856	51	39	1881	1	10
1857	28	29	1882	2	29
1858	28	23	1883	4	31
1859	34	41	1884	6	13
1860	32	8	1885	1	14
1861	22	7	1886	1	16
1862	31	14	1887	1	27
1863	33	35	1888	0	28
1864	45	11	1889	1	8
1865	40	14	1890	0	11
1866	33	17	1891	11	10
1867	27	4	1892	26	8
1868	18	29	1893	3	9
1869	18	30	1894	0	22
1870	15	6	1895	1	8
1871	5	6	1896	0	15
1872	14	10	1897	1	12
1873	12	3	1898	2	29
1874	2	3	1899	19	122
			1900	9	38

every Paris theatre's productions, but most were far more selective in the books they chose for criticism: thus the old hierarchy of the genres produces a distortion in the figures, and the entries for 1863, 1868, and 1869 can be disregarded as indices of general critical activity concerning Balzac. (This does not mean that the reviews of the plays are themselves without considerable interest.) Apart from the three rogue years, there was little Balzac criticism written between 1860 and 1875. From 1876 to the end of the century, there was a much steadier stream of articles and books, culminating in the huge number of assessments, anecdotes, and reminiscences in the centenary year, 1899, and for the fiftieth anniversary of Balzac's death in 1900. The reason for the higher figure in 1876 was the appearance of the long-awaited *Correspondance*. Like Laure Surville's biography of 1856, the correspondence had a considerable influence over Balzac criticism, and provided material and impetus for a whole brood of Balzaciens, from Paul Bourget to Spoelberch de Lovenjoul. Between 1879 and 1881, Zola's campaign for naturalism kept Balzac's name in critical polemics, and in 1883 and 1887 proposals for a Balzac monument in Paris gave rise to a large number of newspaper articles on the novelist. Many of the articles between 1898 and 1900 in fact deal with one of the chapters in the story of the Balzac monument, namely the scandalous work submitted by Auguste Rodin.

Making due allowance for the peaks in critical activity created by such events, it is obvious that there is a difference between the evolution of Balzac's popularity with the reading public and of his popularity as a subject of criticism. The level of critical writing falls off well before the decline in the number of re-publications noted towards the end of the 1860s; it rises after 1875 and continues at a fairly high level during the years when almost no novels from the *Comédie humaine* were being reprinted; and it responds to the centenary in a statistically more impressive way than do the re-publication figures. In each up and down, however, the change of the level of critical activity prefigures by about ten years the development of public demand. It seems most unlikely that there was any causal link over such a large time-lag. Indirectly, of course, the establishment of Balzac's classicism in the 1880s contributed to the level of demand for his novels in that it resulted in at least *Eugénie Grandet* becoming a set text. Yet the *myth* of Balzac's popularity which exaggerated the level of public demand for his works, was a potent force in Balzac criticism, and is perhaps the real dynamic link between the different dimensions of his reputation which the tables seek to quantify. There may be a parallel here with Stendhal, who himself created the myth of his own unpopularity, providing his critics not only with a major theme but with two reasons for writing about him—to mark themselves as members of an élite, and to bring his works to a wider public.

The enormity of the popularity myth by the end of the century is easy to demonstrate. Jules Huret, an enterprising and usually reliable journalist, claimed in 1900 that Michel Lévy frères had been regularly paying the sum of 80,000 francs each year to Mme Ève de Balzac, and after her death in 1882 to her heirs, as royalties for Balzac's works.[87] Lévy surely paid nothing of the sort in 1878, 1888, 1890, and 1896, when neither he nor anyone else published anything by Balzac. Even in 1856, when fifty-six volumes appeared, Lévy would have been foolish to pay on average some 1,600 francs per volume when the total *retail* value of many of these, printed in runs of 500 and sold at 1 fr. 25 a copy, was only 625 francs. Huret's figure is then quite ridiculous, and shows how disproportionate was the myth to reality. Armand Dutacq, Balzac's *exécuteur testamentaire* and his widow's business factotum, offered to buy the entire rights to the novelist's literary estate for only 40,000 francs.[88] A five per cent return would probably have been considered adequate on a moderately safe investment of this sort (as Dutacq no doubt believed it to be), so that the figure offered suggests he expected about 2,000 francs a year on average for the royalties over the fifty-year period in which they were payable. This is one-fortieth of the figure Huret put forward.

All the same, Huret was only giving voice to a general belief when he talked of Balzac as a best-seller. Lucien Muhlfeld implied the same thing when he tantalizingly announced that 'on a calculé le chiffre atteint par le tirage des romans de Balzac depuis sa mort . . . C'est un fameux chiffre.'[89] On the basis of the figures in Table 1 and Figure 1, one can guess that Dumas had a score about six times as high. Finally, one further aspect of the *fin de siècle* myth of Balzac's popularity must be considered: that the great revival in publication of his works around 1900 was due to the end of the period in which royalties were payable. Balzac's works entered the *'domaine public'* in August 1900, but the second cycle of popularity had begun some years earlier, in 1891 and 1892. Perhaps publishers were holding back in the years 1894–8, but

[87] 'L'Œuvre de Balzac et le domaine public', *Le Figaro*, 2 Mar. 1900.
[88] *Petit Cahier d'Ève de Balzac*, Lovenjoul Library, Chantilly, A.275, fo. 5–6.
[89] *Le Gaulois*, 18 Aug. 1900.

if so their patience did not last out, for more Balzac volumes appeared in 1899 than in 1900 itself. It is true that the real rise comes in 1901 and 1902 (with 42 and 39 publications respectively), and these figures may include some volumes held over from before 1900 by publishers eager to maximize profits. What the figures show, none the less, is that the new demand for the novels of the *Comédie humaine* was not the result of an incidental and temporary factor but part of a larger cycle. The first cycle of Balzac publishing lasted fifty years—from 1830 to 1880—but the second has yet to end. The following chapters explore the ways in which Balzac's reputation emerged transformed from the trough between these two cycles.

4   The impact of Émile Zola

BALZAC became a classic to save him from being a Naturalist. This is of course a simplification of the tastes and aims of those critics who developed the notion of 'Balzac classique' in the 1880s and who will be studied in detail in the next chapter. It must also be said that Zola and the Naturalists considered Balzac a classic author in the weaker sense of the word; and that, as will be seen from the theatre reviews dealt with in this chapter, this appears to have been a widely accepted attitude even in the 1860s. Despite these substantial reservations, it remains true that the explicit establishment of Balzac's classical traits as an author and his promotion to the rank of an accepted 'classic' can only be fully appreciated in the context of Zola's appropriation of the *Comédie humaine* to the prehistory of Naturalism in the novel. This appropriation was forcefully argued from scores of newspaper articles, and resisted fiercely by opponents of Zola's 'subversive' and 'obscene' literary school. Naturalism in France was, after all, more than just a tendency: it was a group with a particular political colouring, with its own newspaper (*Le Voltaire*)[1] and its meeting place (Zola's country retreat at Médan), and its campaigns were mounted in almost military style. The group was held together by a certain kind of discipline, and there were mutinies and ceremonial drummings-out.[2] It was held together also by a certain view of literary history as much as of literary practice, and in this Naturalist history Balzac occupied a place of central importance. In this chapter, therefore, we shall examine how Zola evolved his very particular view of the *Comédie humaine*, in detail commensurate to the very great influence, both direct and indirect, that his attitudes had.

ZOLA AND BALZAC IN THE 1860S

Zola's view of Balzac was drawn in the first instance from Taine, who was in all things the novelist's *maître à penser* in the middle 1860s.

[1] Until 1880 only. A new naturalist paper was projected at that time, to be called *La Comédie humaine* (H. Céard, letter to É. Zola, MS. aut. Bibliothèque nationale, Paris, N.a.fr. 24516, dated 30 Oct. 1880).

[2] For example, the 'Manifeste des cinq' in 1887. See M. Raimond, *La Crise du roman* (Corti, 1967), p. 25.

According to J. C. Lapp, Taine was personally acquainted with Zola as early as 1864.[3] According to Zola himself, he first read Taine around 1864–5.[4] The first proper French edition of the critic's *Étude sur Balzac* appeared in 1864 in the *Nouveaux Essais de critique et d'histoire* and it was in that year also that Taine brought out the first volume of his *Histoire de la littérature anglaise* with its aggressive and deterministic introduction. Zola wrote a series of letters to his former schoolfriend Antony Valabrègue in the summer of 1864 in which he sketched out a theory of artistic creation that has some important points of contact with Taine's ideas. For Zola, personality and individuality were of paramount importance: 'On ne saurait être trop personnel . . . Un livre, un article, n'est jamais que l'opinion d'un seul . . . Ce que nous cherchons dans une œuvre, c'est un homme.'[5] The artist's personality is, he continues, like a screen or prism through which reality is refracted into art. Thus the quality of the work results from the quality of the screen ('Écran')—that is to say, from the greatness of its creator's personality. Formal perfection is an irrelevant concept for evaluating works of art in this analysis, and doubly so for Zola since the rules of form are, he says, simply extrapolations of the actual practice of great writers. 'Les règles n'ont leur raison d'être que pour le génie, d'après les œuvres duquel on a pu les formuler; seulement, chez ce génie, ce n'étaient pas des règles, mais une manière personnelle de voir, un effet naturel de l'Écran.'[6] Now Taine had begun his study of Balzac by declaring that the man, not just his mind, was the father of the work; and in the third chapter of the *Étude* he had vigorously defended Balzac's use of language and the structure of his novels as the necessary and logical result of his personality and purpose. Zola's idea of the artist as a prism is very close in its function to Taine's notion of the *faculté maîtresse*, and both ideas allow the critics to defend a writer who 'breaks the rules' in the name of genius.

The connection between the early theory of *L'Écran* and Balzac becomes apparent in a review Zola wrote in 1865 of the novels of Erckmann–Chatrian. Here he restates the argument that an artist's vision of reality is created by his particular personality: 'il ne saurait reproduire ce qui est dans sa réalité: il n'a aperçu les objets qu'au travers de son propre tempérament'.[7] 'Pour me mieux faire comprendre,' he

---

[3] J. C. Lapp, 'Taine et Zola', *RSH* (1957), pp. 319–26.

[4] Interview with Louis Trébor in *Le Figaro*, 6 June 1893.

[5] É. Zola, *Correspondance. I. Les Lettres et les Arts* (Charpentier, 1908), pp. 7–8; letter dated 18 Aug. 1864.

[6] Ibid., pp. 16–17.   [7] *Le Salut public* (Lyon), 29 Mar. 1865.

continues, 'je citerai la *Comédie humaine* de Balzac.' What he then quotes is in fact Taine's chapter on 'Le Monde de Balzac', suitably compressed to the dimensions of a newspaper article. The world of the *Comédie humaine*, Zola states, is not a copy of the real world, but a human creation, an invention of Balzac's mind. As well as enthusiasm, Zola expresses reservations for this Balzacian world:

La vie de ce monde, il est vrai, est factice parfois; le soleil ne s'y joue pas librement; on étouffe dans cette foule où l'air manque; mais il s'en échappe des cris de passion, des rires et des sanglots d'une telle vérité humaine que l'on croit avoir devant soi des frères en douleur et que l'on pleure avec eux.[8]

Taine had made much the same reservations about Balzac's fictional world: the accumulation of detail, he objected, often obscured the story-line, 'et on est vite suffoqué par une odeur de greffe, d'amphi-théâtre et d'échoppe'.[9] It is from Taine likewise that Zola's criterion of 'vérité humaine' is derived. Throughout his study of Balzac, Taine had emphasized the human truth of extreme characters such as Hulot, Valérie Marneffe, and Rastignac; and his conclusion was that the *Comédie humaine* was one of the greatest stores of knowledge about human nature. Zola's reference to the 'human truth' of the passions of the characters of Balzac's universe is clearly derivative from Taine. Most striking of all, however, is the resemblance between Zola's emphasis on the role of the personality in shaping a work of art (in the letters to Valabrègue) and Taine's insistence in the Balzac study that the 'source unique de la vérité' of the *Comédie humaine* was the intensity of Balzac's personal 'hallucination', or imaginative obsession with his fictional characters.[10]

Taine had of course also made much of Balzac's descriptive method and of his use of material detail. Among other things, he maintained that the *Comédie humaine* was an invaluable document for social historians, and something in the nature of an inquiry into social organization. Taine had argued vigorously for the novelist's right to portray all sides of life, however nasty, by likening the role of the writer to that of a scientist or naturalist: 'Il dissèque aussi volontiers le poulpe que l'éléphant.'[11] The significance of Taine's defence of Balzac's right to portray the seamier side of life can only be fully appreciated in the context of the attacks on the 'immorality' of his works which had been current in the years immediately preceding the composition

---

[8] *Le Salut public* (Lyon), 29 Mar. 1865.
[9] Taine, *Nouveaux Essais de critique et d'histoire* (Hachette, 1864), p. 82.
[10] Ibid., p. 95.   [11] Ibid., p. 117.

of this study. Taine is not in fact entirely in favour of Balzac's apparent predilection for evil and sordid characters: 'L'idéal manque au naturaliste; il manque encore plus au naturaliste Balzac.'[12] The two themes of Taine's *Étude* that have been isolated—the theme of Balzac as a powerful visionary, and the theme of Balzac as a dispassionate naturalist—are not contradictory themes, but require, and receive in Taine's work, some skilful blending. The surest evidence that Zola had read Taine, but had not read much Balzac, by Spring 1865 is that he separates out the two themes and makes them appear to contradict each other.

In his article on Erckmann–Chatrian, Zola sets up Balzac's fictional world as a criterion by which to judge the value of a novel. After a discussion and rather unfavourable judgement of Erckmann–Chatrian's novels in the light of this criterion, Zola then returns to Balzac—but in a quite different vein of argument:

L'œuvre de Balzac a la sécheresse d'une analyse exacte; elle ne prêche ni n'encourage; elle est uniquement le compte-rendu brutal de ce que l'écrivain a observé. Balzac regarde et raconte; le choix de l'objet sur lequel tombent ses regards lui importe peu, il n'a que le souci de tout regarder et de tout dire.[13]

This contradicts in direct fashion the earlier passage on Balzac's intensely personal vision of the world. It also indicates little familiarity with the novels themselves, for how else could Zola claim that Balzac 'ne prêche ni n'encourage'? In later years, in fact, Zola was to take the greatest exception to Balzac's preaching of a social and religious message in the *Comédie humaine*.

In the mid-1860s, then, it appears to be Taine, and above all Taine's medico-scientific jargon, that captivated Zola's imagination, rather than Balzac's works themselves. The jargon was applied fairly liberally and at the risk of self-contradiction. In one place, it is Balzac who is described as 'un simple anatomiste qui taille en pleine chair',[14] but in another article, it is Flaubert who becomes 'un chimiste poète, un mécanicien peintre, qui s'est contenté d'analyser les faits moraux et physiques, et d'expliquer le jeu des tempéraments et des milieux'.[15] In order to distinguish Flaubert's originality, Zola is forced to present Balzac in different terms, and so switches back to his other Tainian theme of imagination and exaggeration in the *Comédie humaine*.

---

[12] Ibid., p. 118.   [13] Zola, in *Le Salut public* (Lyon), 29 Mar. 1865.
[14] *Le Salut public* (Lyon), Mar. 1866.   [15] *L'Évènement*, 25 Aug. 1866.

The delight that Zola took in imitating Taine's bold, 'naturalist' jargon is quite evident. In 1866, for example, Zola read a paper entitled *Deux Définitions du roman* to the 33rd Congrès Scientifique de la France. Here he opposes the 'classical' novel of abstract types to the 'modern' novel of observation and analysis. Balzac, not Flaubert, is presented as the culmination of the development of the modern novel, which is in itself significant—for Taine had never written about Flaubert. The Balzac of Zola's text, however, is a curiously deformed version of Taine's Balzac:

> Si j'avais demandé à Balzac de me définir le roman, il m'aurait certainement répondu: Le roman est un traité d'anatomie morale, une compilation de faits humains, une philosophie expérimentale des passions. Il a pour but, à l'aide d'une action vraisemblable, de peindre les hommes et la nature dans leur vérité.[16]

Only the last sentence, of course, could conceivably have been uttered by Balzac. Zola is tacking on his own, as yet tentative, approach to the novel when he attributes to Balzac the idea of 'une philosophie *expérimentale* des passions'—which not even Taine had suggested was the aim of Balzac's, or of any other writer's novels. The criterion of 'vérité', with which Zola ended the passage quoted above on the Balzacian novel, does however derive not only from Taine, but through Taine from the preoccupations of novel-criticism of the preceding decade; and the jargon of this text, Zola himself admitted, was inspired directly by the author of the *Histoire de la littérature anglaise*: as he wrote to Valabrègue, 'Je suis content—lisez très content—de ce petit travail où j'ai largement appliqué les méthodes de Taine.—En un mot, des affirmations carrées et audacieuses.'[17] At this time, Taine was an intellectual father-figure for Zola. In 1866, he declared himself Taine's 'humble disciple'.[18] It is obvious, from the material cited above, that Zola knew the *Étude sur Balzac* rather better than he knew the *Comédie humaine*: the inconsistencies in his references to the novelist are therefore explicable and at the same time of little real consequence. What was of considerable consequence, however, was the fact that Zola's first views on Balzac were formed under the powerful influence of Taine's very particular opinions—for the role of Taine's ideas in shaping Zola's developing idea of the novel itself was a very substantial one indeed.

---

[16] Published by G. Robert, 'Trois textes inédits de Zola', *RSH* (1948), pp. 181–207.
[17] Zola, *Correspondance*, I. 37.   [18] *L'Événement*, 25 July 1866.

In 1867, Zola claimed to be rereading Balzac; the obvious strength of his reactions upon reading the novels was such that it is reasonable to consider this his first real initiation into the *Comédie humaine*. His enthusiasm has the authentic ring of a first meeting:

Lisez aussi dans Balzac quelques admirables pages sur la vie de province. —A propos, avez-vous lu tout Balzac? Quel homme! Je le relis en ce moment. Il écrase tout le siècle. Victor Hugo et les autres—pour moi—s'effacent devant lui. Je médite un volume sur Balzac, une sorte de roman réel.[19]

Zola's reactions to this reading of Balzac, are, then, threefold: first, an immense admiration for the personality of the novelist (Quel homme!); secondly, a desire to turn this admiration to a literary end, the creation of a 'sorte de roman réel'; and third, a reordering of his literary hierarchy. The first two reactions are characteristic of the great writers of the nineteenth century: Barbey d'Aurevilly, Baudelaire, Gautier, Taine, Bourget—all were fanatical in their enthusiasm for the personality of Balzac, and all either projected or actually wrote studies of his life or works. It is only to be expected, of course, that a young man as impregnated as Zola was with Taine's article on Balzac should react to the *Comédie humaine* with an immense admiration for its author; and unsurprising that a critic-cum-journalist with literary aspirations, as Zola was in 1867, should want to put this reaction to literary use.

What is particular and characteristic of Zola in this reaction to Balzac, however, is his immediate reordering of literary preferences. It is not just that this is evidence of his movement away from romanticism, 'Victor Hugo et les autres'. At this stage, as throughout his life, Zola evidently felt the need for some sort of literary-historical 'system' which would not only make sense of past developments, but point the way to the future. This need for a system accounts at least in part for the strong hold that Taine exercised over Zola's mind; and the nature of Taine's system itself can also account in part for Zola's need to break away and develop a system of his own.

Taine's critical method was essentially a historical one. His arguments were built up from material that was enclosed in the past; they provided an interpretation of literary works in the context of a closed set of social, political, racial, and environmental factors. This is true of Taine's method whether it is viewed as a deterministic philosophy of creation or, as René Wellek suggests, simply as a romantic and

[19] *Correspondance*, I. 49 (29 May 1867).

Hegelian way of expressing the unity of an age through social and literary phenomena. It is not a method that can be applied intact to contemporary new writing. Zola's main activity was precisely as a reviewer of new books, and though Taine exercised much influence over his way of thinking and, as Martin Kanes has shown,[20] over one aspect of his actual working method, he could not in any proper sense apply Taine's methods in his criticism. The practical similarity between the two critics was in their apparent analytic rigour, for Taine and Zola both began their articles by splitting works into component elements. In Zola's case this was a convenient framework that allowed him to deal with a large number of books in a consistent manner. For Taine, however, the point of such an analysis was to isolate those elements in the work which could be accounted for by extra-literary factors. In an 'open-ended' situation such as the appearance of a book by a new writer, about whom little is known and whose life is in any case unfinished, it is simply not possible to explore the interrelations between his works, contemporary society, and his life.

Taine, consequently, rarely wrote about contemporary writers. What is more, the nature of his critical method limited his notion of literary excellence to the products of past ages: in other words, it was a method that created its own conservatism in matters of taste. Unable to apply his method to novelists of any generation later than Balzac's, roughly speaking, Taine was unconvinced of the merits of departing from Balzac's novelistic techniques. All new departures appeared to Taine to be evidence of literary and social decadence—for they could not (yet) be fitted into any Tainian pattern.[21] It is not surprising, then, that Zola, who had found Taine so stimulating in the early and mid-sixties, began to strain under this intellectual yoke when he embarked upon his own career as a serious novelist.

After the appearance of *Thérèse Raquin*, Taine wrote a long letter to Zola in which he presents Balzac as the paragon of the novel and the model Zola should imitate. *Le Cousin Pons*, Taine affirmed, was a better novel than *Thérèse Raquin* because it was more of a social panorama:

... un livre doit être toujours, plus ou moins, un portrait de l'ensemble, un miroir de la société tout entière; il faut à droite, à gauche, des biographies, des

[20] 'Balzac, Zola et la *Fortune des Rogron*', *French Studies* (1964), p. 303.
[21] See A. E. Carter, *The Idea of Decadence in French Literature, 1830–1900* (Toronto, 1958), pp. 51–5.

personnages, des indices qui montrent le grand complément, les antithèses de toute sorte, les compensations, bref, l'au-delà de votre sujet.[22]

Taine's idea of the Balzacian novel is, evidently, his idea of the novel *tout court*. Obviously, Zola could only accept Taine's views and advice in this case if he was willing either to regard himself as a bad novelist or to simply imitate the *Comédie humaine*. Zola's need to reject Taine, then, is intimately bound up with his attitude to the Balzacian novel.

Zola replied to Taine's advice on *Thérèse Raquin* in the preface he wrote for the second edition of the novel in 1868. Zola here justifies his right to abandon the social panorama of the Balzacian novel by invoking the scientific method and by claiming that his novel was a scientific inquiry into a limited topic. Thus Zola's scientific reading and interests at that time led him away from Taine, and not vice versa.[23] A further point that follows from this is that Zola's attempts, in 1868–9, to formulate a literary 'programme' were made in the context of a conflict between Taine and the idea of the novel as a social panorama on the one hand, and the idea of 'science' on the other. The formulation of this new literary 'programme' was made in sets of notes,[24] where Zola attempted to draw the outline of his future achievements and to reassure himself that he was embarking on a project that was quite distinct from what Balzac had done before him. Through a close examination of the second and third sets of notes, it is possible to date this formulation of aims fairly precisely.

The *terminus a quo* is provided by a text which is known to date from 1869:[25] the *Premier plan remis à l'éditeur Lacroix*. A reference to Balzac in this text reveals an intention little removed from Taine's idea of the novel: 'Je ferai, à un point de vue plus méthodique, ce que Balzac a fait pour le règne de Louis-Philippe.'[26] Of course, in a proposal to a publisher Zola was no doubt eager to present as respectable a literary ancestry as he could, and thus the reference to Balzac may not be entirely sincere. None the less, it does seem that this text precedes the notes entitled *Différences entre Balzac et moi*, where Zola states that his object in writing the as yet unnamed *Rougon-Macquart* is quite different from Balzac's aim in the *Comédie humaine*. Zola's rethinking of his

[22] See J. C. Lapp, art. cit., p. 322.

[23] See M. Raimond, *Balzac vu par les romanciers français de Zola à Proust*, p. 34.

[24] Published with minor omissions in the Bernouard edition of Zola's works (1927), I. 353–7.

[25] See F. W. J. Hemmings, *Émile Zola* (2nd edition, Oxford, 1970), p. 54.

[26] Zola, *Œuvres complètes* (Bernouard, 1927), I. 358.

attitude to Balzac came, then, between the composition of the *Premier plan* at the beginning of 1869 and the composition of *Différences*. An event in January 1869 may have precipitated this change of attitude: namely, the appearance of the first volume of Calmann-Lévy's 'Definitive Edition' of the *Comédie humaine*. Zola's review of this publication is of the greatest interest, for in it he quotes in full Baudelaire's appreciation of Balzac, from the 1859 article on Gautier. Now, it is certainly not admiration for Baudelaire as poet or critic that prompted Zola's tribute, but rather what might be called the 'Tainian content' of the passage on 'Balzac visionnaire': 'Baudelaire avait mis le doigt sur la vérité, ce qui lui arrivait rarement: si l'œuvre de Balzac est grande, c'est que cette puissante personnalité s'y est jetée tout entière.'[27] In other words, this review corroborates the impression given by the *Premier plan*, namely that in January 1869 Zola's view of Balzac was still very much impregnated with the themes of Taine's *Étude*.

The volumes of the Calmann-Lévy edition appeared at monthly intervals in 1869, and Zola reviewed several of them. From these reviews it is evident that he reread much of the *Comédie humaine* with some care. The *Différences entre Balzac et moi* show that he reread the first volume with attention, for the first sheet of this text is a précis of Balzac's *Avant-propos* to the *Comédie humaine*. These notes could not have been made in 1867, when Zola had 'reread' Balzac for the first time; nor could they have been made from memory. This is the third piece of evidence, therefore, that confirms the dating of the *Différences* as after 30 January 1869—the date of the appearance of the first volume of the *Édition définitive*, containing the *Avant-propos*.

The *Différences entre Balzac et moi* constitute the third set of notes bound into a volume of Zola manuscripts kept at the Bibliothèque nationale, Paris. The pages of the first set of notes, entitled *Notes sur la marche générale de l'œuvre*, are numbered 1 to 7 in Zola's hand; the second set, the *Notes générales sur la nature de l'œuvre*, written in a slightly different ink, are paginated 1 to 4 in Zola's hand, the numbers being overwritten 9 to 13; and the *Différences* were also originally numbered independently and subsequently renumbered to fit their place in the bound volume. It is clear, therefore, that these three sets of notes were not originally written as a continuous series, but as separate pieces at separate times. The order in which these notes are placed, on the other hand, is probably the order in which they were composed. There is a clearly perceptible progression from the general-

[27] *Le Gaulois*, 4 Feb. 1869.

ities of the *Notes sur la marche générale* to the crux of the matter in the *Différences*. In the first set of notes, much the untidiest of the three, Zola is putting down attitudes rather than projects. Neither Taine nor Balzac is mentioned; but it is perhaps significant that Zola crossed out the sentence: 'Seulement je suis l'historien des fièvres de l'époque.'[28] Other remarks in this text also suggest that Zola is attempting to reject the idea of the novel as social history, as he had done in reply to Taine's criticism of *Thérèse Raquin*. None the less, it is already clear to Zola that his novels will contain much that is social history, and he justifies this by saying: 'C'est dire que cette famille, née dans un autre temps, dans un autre milieu, ne se serait pas comportée de la même façon.'[29] A depiction of the social and historical background is justified, then, because it constitutes one of the factors acting upon the behaviour of the characters—and not because the novel *is* social history.

The second set of notes, on the *Nature de l'œuvre*, is devoted to more precise topics, and in particular to marking off the project in hand, that was taking shape as *La Fortune des Rougon*, from confusion with Taine and Balzac.[30] 'Taine dit cependant: Faites fort et général. Faire général ne m'est pas permis, par la construction même de mes livres. Mais je puis faire fort le plus possible . . .'[31] Zola declares that he will abandon Balzac's 'analyse courante'—by which he means, perhaps, the discursive element in the omniscient author's descriptions and digressions in the *Comédie humaine*. 'Tout le monde réussit en ce moment l'analyse du détail; il faut réagir par la *construction solide des masses* . . .'[32] On characterization, Zola rejects Taine's advice to portray general types of humanity, and considers exceptional characters as more worthy of an artist's attention: ' . . . en sortant du général, l'œuvre devient supérieure (*Julien Sorel*); il y a création d'homme, effort d'artiste; l'œuvre gagne en intérêt humain ce qu'elle perd en réalité courante'. Taine's admiration for Stendhal, Zola remarks, contradicts his advice to 'faire général', for all of Stendhal's heroes are exceptional creations.

Zola then sets out the reasons for having a philosophical tendency underlying his future novels—'Non pour l'étaler, mais pour donner une unité à mes livres.' Just as Taine had done, Zola ridicules the uses to which Balzac put his philosophy in the *Comédie humaine*: 'On a dit

---

[28] N.a. fr. 10345, fo. 3. [29] Ibid., fo. 4.
[30] Zola concluded the first set of notes by stating that he had found his 'direction': 'La famille ira au contentement de l'appétit *fortune* ou *gloire*.'
[31] N.a.fr. 10345, fo. 10. [32] Ibid., fo. 11.

qu'il n'y avait pas un grand romancier qui ne contînt un philosophe; oui, une philosophie absurde, à la façon de Balzac. Je préfère être seulement romancier.' However, there is no doubt that Zola was concerned lest he be accused of imitating Balzac and the Goncourts. He thus fixed his intention to restrict the scope of his novels to a small number of characters: 'Ainsi j'échapperai à l'imitation de Balzac.' The Goncourts, on the other hand, will be so outmatched by the sheer power and inexorable logic of the novel he has in his head 'qu'on n'osera pas m'accuser de les imiter'.

The next stage in Zola's reassessment of his literary projects is represented by the third set of notes, the *Différences entre Balzac et moi*. Here Zola faces squarely the question of his debt to the *Comédie humaine*, instead of skirting round it as we have seen him do in the preceding notes. The first page of the *Différences*, as has been mentioned, consists of a fairly pedestrian analysis of the *Avant-propos* to the *Comédie humaine*, and dates from 30 January 1869 at the earliest, and not from 1868 as has been claimed.[33] In the following pages, Zola goes on to define the differences between his projects and Balzac's achievements. In a flat rejection of Taine, he declares that

Mon œuvre sera moins sociale que scientifique . . . Le cadre en sera plus restreint que celle de la *Comédie humaine*. Je ne veux pas peindre la société contemporaine, mais une seule famille, en montrant le jeu de la race modifié par les milieux. *Si j'accepte un cadre historique, c'est uniquement pour avoir un milieu qui réagisse.*[34]

The political, moral, and religious 'message' of Balzac's novels will be absent from Zola's projected work: 'Je me contenterai d'être savant, de dire ce qui est en en cherchant les raisons intimes.' There will be no need for reappearing characters; and Balzac's separation of 'les hommes, les femmes et les choses' (in the *Avant-propos*) will be reordered: 'Je soumets les hommes et les femmes aux choses.'

In these notes, then, Zola defines his projects in opposition to Balzac's works, and, in particular, in opposition to Taine's presentation of the Balzacian novel. The young writer is throwing off the shackles that he had willingly endured under the powerful intellectual domination of Taine for the preceding five years. At the same time, Zola was composing *La Fortune des Rougon*, a novel which in its final form bears a remarkable resemblance to Balzac's *Pierrette*—as Martin Kanes has

---

[33] By M. Raimond, for example. Op. cit., Bibliographie.
[34] N.a.fr. 10345, fo. 15.

elegantly and irrefutably demonstrated.[35] The provincial *milieu*, the political situation on the eve of a revolution, the family quarrel over the division of inheritances, the resemblances between Balzac's Jérôme-Denis Rogron and Zola's Pierre Rougon, down to the similarities between the names themselves, all point towards substantial borrowings from Balzac in the first novel of the *Rougon-Macquart*. *Pierrette* appeared in the fourth volume of the *Édition définitive* in May 1869, and it is one of the few volumes of this edition that Zola did not review or even mention in his newspaper columns. This omission may, indeed, be significant. In the light of these substantial borrowings from Balzac in *La Fortune des Rougon*, moreover, Zola's private protestations of *Différences entre Balzac et moi* take on added meaning. It is not that Zola can be accused of lying in these notes: there are immense differences between his treatment of Plassans, in *La Fortune*, and Balzac's portrayal of Provins in *Pierrette*. It is less certain, however, that Zola would have needed to define his own methods and devices in opposition to Balzac's had he not been in the process of making substantial borrowings of situation, character, and name from one of Balzac's novels.

The *Différences* can then be seen as a counterpart to the elaboration of the plot of *La Fortune des Rougon*. For this view to have any validity, it must include the notion that the *Différences* were written after the appearance of *Pierrette* in May 1869. On the other hand, the text must predate the completion of *La Fortune*, as it must predate the article on *Le Cabinet des antiques* that Zola published in October 1869, for reasons that will shortly be explained. This close examination of Zola's view of Balzac in early 1869 allows us on the one hand to give a new and fairly accurate dating to the *Différences*—namely, between May and October 1869, and probably nearer May than October—and on the other hand it provides a very special example of change in critical themes: a change that springs from the creative needs of a major writer. None the less, it is only too evident that this change also was provoked by an extra-critical event, the appearance of the *Édition définitive*, and that the nature of that event profoundly affected the nature of the change in Zola's views. There is no reason to suppose that he would have read the *Avant-propos* in January, or *Pierrette* in May 1869, had the relevant volumes of the *Édition définitive* not appeared then; and there is every reason to suppose that Zola's views

[35] M. Kanes, art. cit.

would not have advanced in the same way if he had not experienced those two texts at that time.

The article that Zola wrote in October 1869 discusses the 'real' political significance of *La Comédie humaine* and presents *Le Cabinet des antiques* as an unconscious depiction of the forces of the proletariat and of the inevitability of a future democratic revolution. These are ideas far removed from the Tainian disdain for Balzac's politics that Zola repeated as late as the *Différences*. This turn around in Zola's views may have been closely bound up with the writing of *La Fortune des Rougon*. In its finished form, this depiction of provincial life is a denunciation of the bases of political power in France and an attack on the 1852 *coup d'état*. If a novel drawn from Balzac's *Pierrette* led to the elaboration of a political message, Zola may have surmised, then perhaps there was a hidden political message in Balzac's works themselves. The change in Zola's attitude between July and October 1869 is complete. His review of *La Rabouilleuse* in July harks back to his early theories and to Taine's admiration for the power of Balzac's 'strong' heroes—Philippe Bridau is described as 'la plus belle brute, le tempérament lâché le plus librement dans la vie, qu'un écrivain ait jamais osé créer'.[36] In October, the politically oriented, 'Naturalist' Balzac makes his first appearance. Though it took Zola ten years to complete his annexation of Balzac to the Naturalist movement, the political interpretation of *Le Cabinet des antiques* in October 1869 is, unmistakably, the first stone in the new edifice.

This second change in Zola's views does not seem to spring, like the first, from the writer's creative needs, but, rather, from his actual creation. Always eager to find a coherent literary system, Zola can be seen altering his literary and critical views to fit his own works.

Taine's *Étude sur Balzac* occupied an important place among the forces that influenced the development of Zola's attitudes towards Balzac, towards the novel, and towards his own projects as a novelist. This influence was at first direct, and subsequently indirect, as Zola reacted against it. Zola, however, was not the only critic to take note of what Taine had said; nor were the themes of the *Étude* the only ones current in Balzac criticism of the 1860s. In order to set the view of Balzac as a Naturalist in its proper perspective, it is necessary first to consider the general course of Balzac criticism between 1858 and the end of the Second Empire.

[36] *Le Gaulois*, 31 July 1869. See ch. v of Taine's *Étude*, where Bridau is described in similar terms.

THEMES OF THE 1860S

Taine's *Étude*, as we have seen, inspired Baudelaire and Babou to see in Balzac a writer of the imagination and a poet of truth. It also put Balzac criticism in general on a more serious and intellectual level. Moral criticism continued to flourish in the 1860s, but it was mostly far more subtle and well informed than the diatribes of 1856 from Poitou and Pontmartin. Of course, the simple passing of time also contributed to this growing seriousness, for as memories faded and as death took its toll Balzac became less of a subject for news and gossip columns. It would be wrong, on the other hand, to think that he was abandoned by daily newspapers. Of the items listed in Appendix III, but excluding reprinted articles, the percentage of Balzac criticism appearing in daily newspapers rose from 43 per cent in the decade 1850-9 to 46 per cent in the decade 1860-9. For the remainder of the century, too, the proportion of new articles appearing in the daily press remained at just under half of the total, the other half being shared more or less equally between books and the non-daily press. The rising seriousness of Balzac criticism through these decades cannot therefore be accounted for by any significant change in the medium of publication of the criticism in question.

The higher level of seriousness in Balzac criticism after Taine is exemplified by the long study of the novelist that Elme-Marie Caro, the spiritualist thinker, published in 1859.[37] The exposition and preliminary arguments of this article are closely modelled on Taine; none the less, Caro makes a number of original and penetrating comments on, among other things, Balzac's philosophy. With more acuity than Taine, he demonstrates the contradictions between the statements about the guiding principles of Church and Throne in the *Avant-propos* and the implications of Balzac's plots in his novels. Caro's aim, however, is quite different from Taine's: he wishes to investigate not only whether Balzac succeeded on his own terms, but whether he succeeded in conforming to 'les conditions éternelles de l'art'. In other words, Caro announces his intention of applying the Sainte-Beuvian and traditional criteria of taste to Balzac, without rejecting out of hand the aspects of Balzac's genius that Taine (whom Caro never mentions by name) had uncovered.

[37] *La Revue européenne*, 1 and 15 Oct. 1859; reprinted in *Poètes et romanciers* (Hachette, 1888). Page references are to the book edition.

Caro lays great emphasis on the power of Balzac's imagination, and on the degree to which his belief in his fictional characters is communicated to the reader. It is in this, Caro thinks, that the reason for Balzac's persuasiveness as a story-teller lie. He does not use the weakness of many of Balzac's virtuous characters as an argument against the morality of the *Comédie humaine*, but reasonably suggests: 'Peut-être pourrait-on dire que le mal prête à l'art des ressources plus variées, et, en ce sens, une plus riche matière que le bien.'[38] He makes an intelligent criticism of what he sees as Balzac's real heroes, Marsay and Vautrin: 'La vraie force se doit à elle-même de ne pas s'étaler, la vraie finesse est celle qui a l'air de s'ignorer . . . Professer sa corruption [as de Marsay and Vautrin do] c'est en perdre tous les bénéfices.'[39] His judgements on Balzac's lack of 'mesure' and balance, however, hark back to Sainte-Beuve. For Caro, only *Eugénie Grandet* and *La Recherche de l'absolu* are 'perfect' works: apart from these novels, 'Je n'aperçois dans son œuvre que des ébauches ou des ruines . . .'[40] In Caro's analysis, what Balzac most lacked was 'le goût'. His style is 'comme son art, plein de brusqueries et de disparates, immodéré, exorbitant'. Its brilliance may be patchy, but its brilliance cannot be denied. It may be an 'art inférieur', but it is 'réel et puissant' just the same. These are reasonable views, which in many ways anticipate the qualified and selective admiration of Faguet and Brunetière towards the end of the century. Where Caro is less reasonable is in his remarks on the mystic novels. The critic allows his own interests in spiritualism to persuade him that Balzac's greatest descriptive 'paysage' is that of Norway, in *Séraphita*—a decidedly idiosyncratic opinion. Caro does not minimize the power of Balzac's language—its 'impérieuse magie', as he calls it—but is forced by his own criteria to conclude rather regretfully that it lacked taste and moderation. The final chapter of Caro's study is devoted to a consideration of Balzac's influence.[41] It is necessary, in his opinion, that a critic should reach a conclusion on the influence of the author he is studying: not to do so (as Taine had failed to do) is easy but 'sans utilité'. In other words, Caro thinks that a critic should be explicit about the direction he is seeking to impose on his public, and he proceeds to sum up Balzac's influence in harsh terms:

[38] *Poètes et romanciers*, p. 325.
[39] Ibid., pp. 331–2.
[40] Ibid., p. 349.
[41] Chapter V, incorrectly marked IV in the Hachette edition.

Dans son ensemble, l'œuvre de Balzac est une œuvre malsaine d'inspiration, malsaine d'influence. Balzac est, à mes yeux, le plus grand corrupteur d'imaginations qu'ait produit le demi-siècle littéraire qui s'achève à sa mort.[42]

That inspiration was, in Balzac's own words in *La Fille aux yeux d'or*, 'l'or et le plaisir'. The meaning of the *Comédie humaine* could be summed up by Hobbes's dictum, *Homo homini lupus*: 'On pourrait l'inscrire en lettres de fer au frontispice de la *Comédie humaine*.'[43] Balzac's treatment of money and of women in his novels are compensation fantasies: 'C'est une orgie qu'il se donne à lui-même'—and in these fantasies good and evil count for naught. Only 'la force, la grandeur' are made admirable in Balzac's novels; and they are associated with evil characters, not with good. Balzac's lack of 'le moral et le goût' deforms his entire fictional universe; his immorality 'n'est pas . . . dans la perversité exagérée des types; elle est tout entière dans la nature des impressions que Balzac impose à l'imagination de ses lecteurs'.[44] Caro's assessment is then quite different from Pontmartin's, for virtually all the features selected by Taine as being qualities rather than faults— such as Balzac's power of imagination and persuasion, his fascination with strength, his brilliant but patchy use of language—are not disputed by Caro. Pontmartin had written a denunciation of Balzac, but Caro, whose moral prejudices were not far removed from Pontmartin's, has to argue for a judgement—for he is writing after Taine.

A considerable number of minor critics in the 1860s followed Caro's general argument and conclusions, without adding any particular refinements to them. An anonymous writer of 1860 found Balzac's 'admiration vicieuse . . . pour l'égoisme triomphant' his greatest fault;[45] in 1864, J.-E. Combes concluded that Balzac 'n'éprouve aucune sympathie personnelle pour le bien, aucune antipathie pour le mal', and that the *Comédie humaine* was nothing more than 'Enfantin qui dogmatise dans le roman'.[46] Louis Combes, in 1865, followed Caro in considering that Balzac's most lasting influence was to have corrupted the imagination of a generation;[47] and Benjamin Gastineau[48], as well as the celebrated feminist Maria Deraimes, wove variations on this apparently inexhaustible theme.[49]

[42] Ibid., p. 359.   [43] Ibid., p. 363.   [44] Ibid., p. 368.
[45] In *Varia* (Michel Levy, 1860), p. 195.
[46] *La Revue contemporaine*, Sept. 1864. In this article, J. E. Combes manages to find traces of Saint-Simon and Enfantin in almost every writer of the July monarchy.
[47] *L'Amateur d'autographes*, 1 July 1865.
[48] *Les Génies de la liberté*, 1865.   [49] *Le Nain jaune*, 24 Mar. 1866.

One important theme of Caro's article on Balzac which has not yet
been mentioned is concerned with the political significance of the
Comédie humaine. After the appropriation of Balzac by the left in 1850
and the weak riposte of the right-wing *Gazette de France*, the political
edge of Balzac criticism had remained fairly blunt throughout the 1850s.
Of course, as has been made clear, political considerations influenced
quite substantially the reactions of various critics, particularly over the
querelle du réalisme in 1856–7; and Barbey d'Aurevilly had not abandoned his view of Balzac as the intellectual leader of the extreme right.
Caro, however, reintroduced the distinction that had been made in
1850 between Balzac's professed political opinions (which for once
are presented reasonably accurately in his article) and the political
implications of the *Comédie humaine*, which are in his view democratic
and revolutionary.[50] Alphonse Pagès assembled another collection of
Pensées extraites de la Comédie humaine a few years later in order to
demonstrate that Balzac was a moralist and a democratic, left-wing
thinker. He explains the contradiction in the following manner:

> . . . je vois en Balzac deux hommes qui se livrent un combat perpétuel,
> l'homme du passé, l'homme de l'avenir. Balzac se disait, non sans une
> certaine ostentation, catholique et légitimiste; Balzac a soulevé les problèmes
> favoris du socialisme et leur a donné souvent les mêmes solutions que nos
> plus hardis novateurs.[51]

It does not strike Pagès that the doctrines of the early socialists were
very similar, in many ways, to the views of right-wing thinkers, and
so he mistakenly presents Balzac's support of free trade, for example,
as a contradiction of his monarchist opinions. Jules Claretie, for one,
was not surprised by the democratic leanings that Pagès extracts from
the *Comédie humaine*: 'Il y a longtemps que j'avais deviné ces dispositions chez l'homme qui a créé le type de Z. Marcas.'[52] Two years later,
Claretie repeated Pagès's distinction between the two Balzacs in an
essay that purports to be a review of the 1868 revival of *Mercadet*:
'Révolutionnaire par son style, par son ironie qui soufflette les hontes
sociales, par ses révoltes contre les fatalités de la misère ou des derniers
servages, Balzac est réactionnaire en toutes choses . . .'[53] In 1864,
Camille Chancel had given a more precise parallel between certain
aspects of Balzac's works and the ideas of the early socialists. Charles
Fourier had studied the vices of individualism 'dans l'ordre économ-

[50] Caro, op. cit., pp. 309–10.   [51] A. Pagès, *Balzac moraliste* (Michel Lévy, 1866).
[52] *Le Figaro*, 12 Mar. 1866.   [53] *L'Opinion nationale*, 15 Aug. 1868.

ique'; Balzac studied the same vices 'dans l'ordre passionnel et moral'. He showed how society had created and excited needs and desires 'sans s'inquiéter de les satisfaire'. In this respect, Balzac's work went beyond liberalism, 'pour tendre la main aux plus avancés':

> Hostilité universelle, déperdition de forces, absence de pensée générale et de protection efficace pour les petits, beaucoup de droits abstraits prodigués à l'individu, très peu de devoirs effectifs imposés à l'État. Ce bilan social, est-ce un phalanstérien qui le dresse? Non, c'est Balzac lui-même, en plusieurs passages de la *Peau de chagrin*, du *Père Goriot* et du *Médecin de campagne*.[54]

Not all the critics of the 1860s were concerned either with Balzac's morality and influence or with the interpretation of his political message. Paul Dollfuss, for example, cast wise doubts on the extent of literature's real influence over society:[55]

> Les écrivains, et surtout les écrivains influents, ne sont pas des hommes à part des autres et vivant à part; bien loin de là, ils n'ont d'influence que par la conformité de leurs opinions avec les opinions du temps. C'est de l'esprit de leur temps qu'ils sont imbus non pas d'infatuations personnelles, ceux qui arrivent à une grande renommée.[56]

It is quite ridiculous, he argues, to consider Balzac immoral and not Sophocles as well. Everything is permitted to writers of antiquity: nothing, it appears, to the writers of the July Monarchy. The reason for this discrimination, Dollfuss suggests, is the 1848 Revolution, which had become a myth distorting critics' views of the period which immediately preceded it. Much of Chapter 1 of this study confirms Dollfuss's perception.

In the 1860s, Balzac's pessimism began to be accepted rather than contested. August Avond, for example, remarked that 'Balzac voit l'humanité à travers un prisme noir qui pourrait bien être, hélas! le prisme de la vérité . . .',[57] which echoes the conclusion to Lamartine's chapters on Balzac: 'Balzac est parfait, mais il est triste. Est-ce que le monde est gai?'[58] Written in 1859, Lamartine's piece on Balzac was published separately in 1866 as *Balzac et ses œuvres*.[59] Despite many factual inaccuracies, Lamartine paints a memorable portrait of Balzac as a man; as for politics, the novelist had had the good sense, Lamartine remarks, to avoid personal involvements. The poet considered the

[54] *La Nouvelle Revue de Paris*, 15 Aug. 1864.
[55] Signed Dollfuss, but the index of *L'Artiste* has *Deltuf*.
[56] *L'Artiste*, 15 Oct. 1864.   [57] *La Critique française*, Nov. 1862.
[58] *Cours familier de littérature* (1859), ch. xviii, pp. 273–527.   [59] Michel Lévy.

three main features of Balzac's talent to be 'la vérité, le pathétique et la
moralité', and demonstrates these qualities in *Eugénie Grandet* and *Le
Père Goriot*. Like Taine, however, Lamartine thinks that *Les Parents
pauvres* was Balzac's greatest work and constitutes 'le chapitre le plus
vaste, le plus divers et le plus véridique de sa *Comédie humaine*'.[60]
Taine, Baudelaire, Gautier, Babou, Lamartine, Dollfuss—the list of
writers who, between 1858 and 1870, appreciated Balzac's works without having recourse to political or overtly moral arguments is not an
unimpressive one. Very few of the reviews of *Paméla Giraud* and *La
Marâtre* in 1859, of *Les Ressources de Quinola* in 1863, of *Mercadet*
in 1868 or of *Vautrin* in 1869 treat the plays as having anything more
than a purely literary interest. Of these revivals, only *La Marâtre*
had any great success with the public: the commonest reactions to
Paméla Giraud and *Les Ressources de Quinola* was one of disappoint-
ment;[61] while *Mercadet* seemed badly acted and badly produced, particularly to those who had seen its first triumphant run in 1851.[62]
La Marâtre, on the other hand, was not just a pious exhumation of a
forgotten play, but a venture that captured the taste of the theatrical
world. It was produced at the Théâtre de Belleville, in the Paris
suburbs, shortly after its run at the Gymnase; then at Bordeaux and at
Nantes. For a short while it was playing to full houses in all four
places at once.[63] One reviewer, it is true, did mention revolution in the
context of *La Marâtre*, but a literary revolution was meant: 'Chapeau
bas, s'il vous plaît: c'est le réalisme qui prend possession du théâtre.'[64]
Quinola, not surprisingly, provoked few remarks about Balzac's realism, but was rather used as evidence of his strangely exaggerating
imagination. This line, of course, enabled reviewers to account for the
unsatisfactory nature of the play without having to abandon the purple
prose of praise that had by then become a more or less obligatory
feature of reviews of Balzac's plays or of adaptations of his novels.

[60] Op. cit., ch. xlix.

[61] Typical of reaction to *Paméla Giraud* was Paul de Saint-Victor's remark (in *La
Presse*, 10 July 1859) that it was a play 'que le maître a signé de son nom, mais non de sa
griffe'; and Philibert Audebrand on *Quinola*: 'Balzac est mort et enterré, ainsi que l'a
prouvé Mlle Essler le soir de la reprise . . . N'en parlons plus . . .' (in *Le Nain jaune*,
14 Nov. 1863).

[62] The actor Geoffroy had brought out Mercadet's *bonhomie* in the 1851 production,
but in 1868, Got played the character as an outright swindler. According to D. Bernard
(*L'Union*, 26 Oct.) and L. de La Combe (*L'Époque*, 24 Oct.) the leading ladies were ugly
and incompetent.

[63] See *La Revue et gazette des théatres* on 4, 8, 9 15, 22, 25, and 28 Sept.; and on 9
and 24 Oct. 1859.

[64] Francisque Sarcey, in *L'Opinion nationale*, 12 Sept. 1859.

The themes of Balzac criticism in the 1860s were far from homogeneous. While Pontmartin's views remained unchanged from 1856, while Sainte-Beuve became ever more hostile, while Taine had introduced a new attitude free of political or moral criteria that was followed by a number of younger critics, there was also a substantial body of opinion which regarded Balzac as a classic, whose qualities could be discussed but not disputed; it is in the theatre reviews that this view is most abundantly expressed. This is perhaps because professional literary critics do not write unless they have either a cause to do so or something new to say; whereas theatre reviewers are not professional critics of novels, and are obliged to write something on every new production. One might tentatively conclude from this that the view of Balzac as a classic was becoming the generally accepted view among the literate public in the mid-1860s.

The theme of Balzac as a revolutionary was not a major one in the 1860s, either numerically or in terms of the influence of the critics who used it, with one notable exception, that of Jules Vallès. Vallès had been a pupil at the École Normale Supérieure at a time when, as Octave Gréard recounted,[65] the *Comédie humaine* was always slipped to anyone unfortunate enough to suffer the 'consigne du jeudi ou du dimanche'. Vallès, one of the most unruly, turbulent, and protesting characters ever to pass through the institution of the rue d'Ulm, must have had ample opportunity to read Balzac's works. Much of what he said later about the influence of Balzac on the minds of imaginative young men refers back to this period and to Vallès's experiences as a hot-headed adolescent in 1848.

Most of Vallès's references to Balzac do in fact deal with the deleterious effect of the novels on talented young men. The *Comédie humaine* constitutes a 'cours d'ambition sceptique', according to Vallès—but the lessons are not always well learnt:

Ah! sous les pas de ce géant, que de consciences écrasées, que de boue, que de sang! Comment il a fait *travailler* les juges et pleurer les mères! Combien se sont perdus, ont *coulé*, qui agitaient au-dessus du bourbier où ils allaient mourir une page arrachée à quelque volume de la *Comédie humaine*![66]

The vehemence of Vallès's denunciation of Balzac's influence in real life is a function not so much of any hatred on Vallès's part as of the

---

[65] Octave Gréard, *Prévost-Paradol* (Hachette, 1894), p. 14.

[66] *Les Réfractaires* (A. Faure, 1866), p. 197. Adapted from 'Les Victimes du livre', *Le Figaro*, 9 Feb. 1862.

immense literary power and genius of Balzac, which he willingly admitted and admired. Balzac, for Vallès, 'résume la grandeur du livre *et ses dangers*'. The danger is in Balzac's glorification of heroes whose activities, if carried out in the real world, are neither noble nor glorious and which lead in all but exceptional cases to sordid ends. Balzac is no realist, but an epic poet 'qui a autant la manie des grandeurs que l'amour de la vérité'.[67] These reactions to Balzac are not in substance original, but unlike Pontmartin, Poitou, or Caro, Vallès puts the unmistakable ring of sincerity and lived experience into his denunciation—for he was himself one of the 'victimes du livre' about whom he writes, a victim of the illusions of grandeur and facile success that the novels of Balzac and George Sand had fostered. In that he awakens desires that cannot be satisfied in society as it stood, Balzac became, for Vallès, a powerful agent in the precipitation of revolutionary desires: and as a writer whose work stimulated revolution, he was—whatever his professed opinions—a revolutionary.[68]

On Sunday 15 January 1865, Vallès gave a lecture on Balzac to the *'société Entretiens et Lectures'*. Under the Second Empire public lectures had become an extremely popular form of education and entertainment. Though they were in theory as strictly controlled as the press, and were restricted to literary and general education subjects, effective control of the spoken word was not easy to enforce, and the very existence of the regulations invited the lecturers to cock a snook at authority. There were three main lecture-societies, the most successful of which took place at the salle du Grand-Orient, rue Cadet, which is where Vallès's 'Cours libre' on Balzac was given.[69] The evening was to have begun by a reading of *Hernani* by the actor Beauvallet. Though hardly political dynamite in itself, *Hernani* was by the author of *Napoléon le petit:* public acclaim for the Emperor's most prestigious enemy was considered 'dangerous' by the authorities, and so Duruy, Minister of Public Instruction, banned the reading. The public, who had flocked to express their opposition to the Empire by applauding Hugo, had to be content with *Cinna*.[70] Vallès's lecture followed this reading, and it caused a stir in the audience (some of whom nearly walked out)[71] and in official circles when word got back. Unfortun-

---

[67] *Le Courrier du dimanche*, 17 Sept. 1865.

[68] See also J. Vallès, 'La Révolution littéraire', *Le Réveil*, 24 July 1882.

[69] See Vallès's description of these 'Cours libres' in *Le Courrier du dimanche*, 12 Feb. 1865.

[70] Gaston Gille, *Jules Vallès, 1832–1885* (Flammarion, 1941), pp. 116, 117.

[71] See Vallès, *L'Insurgé* (Charpentier, 1885). In the 10/18 edition (1962), p. 29.

ately, no text of the actual lecture has been preserved, so that press reports are the only source of information concerning its contents. Gaston Bell's *compte-rendu* hardly reveals that the lecture was about Balzac: most of it is devoted to what must have been Vallès's preamble, on the specific advantages of the novel over other literary genres as an expression of society in an 'époque démocratique comme la nôtre'.[72] Hector Pessard, in *Le Temps*, gave a fuller account of the lecture:

Le roman est la seule forme littéraire dans laquelle un écrivain puisse suivre les développements d'une passion ou d'un sentiment, peindre dans toute sa vérité et sous tous ses aspects l'espèce humaine. Dans cette forme, Balzac est et reste le maître à tous, précisément parce qu'il n'a point hésité à prendre tous ses personnages dans la vie ordinaire, à les présenter avec leurs qualités et leurs défauts, grands et petits, capables de toutes les lâchetés et de tous les courages. À son insu, et malgré sa volonté d'être royaliste, catholique et autoritaire, Balzac, selon M. Jules Vallès, est un grand révolutionnaire . . .[73]

Hommage was paid in the end to Victor Hugo that evening: for Vallès brought back into currency, in almost the same words, the poet's celebrated dictum that Balzac was 'à son insu, qu'il le veuille ou non, qu'il y consente ou non, de la forte race des écrivains révolutionnaires'. The legend grew up that this lecture turned to a shambles and that the police had to be called in to quell the first flicker of a riot. Although this did not in fact happen,[74] the lecture certainly made an impact: Vallès recounts himself how he went on from talking of 'Balzac mort, pour parler des vivants' and waved before the audience 'non point seulement le drapeau rouge, mais aussi le drapeau noir'.[75] The lecture brought Vallès no money, but opened the doors of a number of newspaper offices—as well as losing him his job as a clerical civil servant. Gréard, the Inspecteur de l'Académie, had reported the political tenor of Vallès's speech to higher authority, and Vallès was banned from public speaking; a circular was also issued warning organizers of literary lectures not to allow them to be used for political ends in future.[76]

'BALZAC NATURALISTE'

Zola, involved as he was in the world of journalism and criticism, could not have been ignorant of Vallès's lecture, nor of the legend that grew up about it. Yet there is no evidence to suggest that this political interpretation of *La Comédie humaine* made the slightest

[72] *La Presse*, 18 Jan. 1865.
[74] See G. Gille, op. cit., p. 117.
[76] G. Gille, loc. cit.

[73] *Le Temps*, 18 Jan. 1865.
[75] Vallès, *L'Insurgé*, loc. cit.

impression on him. The following year, he reviewed Pagès's collection of left-wing 'Pensées' taken from the *Comédie humaine,* and exhibited a characteristically Tainian disdain for Balzac's philosophy and politics. Despite their occasional flashes of brilliance, Zola writes: 'Ces *Pensées* n'ont pas été assez travaillées pour être ainsi présentées à part. Je préfère de beaucoup Balzac romancier à Balzac moraliste.'[77] Until October 1869 Zola remained, as it were, insulated both against taking Balzac's politics seriously and against political interpretations of the significance of Balzac's work. By October 1869, however, Zola was on the staff of a left-wing newspaper, *La Tribune,* and author of an as yet unpublished novel attacking the men who founded the Second Empire. A reading of *Le Cabinet des antiques* when it appeared in the *Édition définitive* that autumn sufficed to suggest to him that Balzac's politics might not after all be as inimical to his own position as they had seemed.

Le cas est curieux. Voilà un homme qui, pendant les trente années d'une production littéraire incessante, s'est inclinée chaque jour devant la royauté et le catholicisme. Voilà un homme qui a peut-être cru en mourant qu'il laissait un magnifique plaidoyer en faveur des rois et des prêtres. Et aujourd'hui . . . nous n'y sentons plus souffler qu'un large souffle révolutionnaire.[78]

The *Comédie humaine,* Zola continues, was written by a 'démocrate sans le savoir', and to prove this assertion he analyses *Le Cabinet des antiques,* with its decayed and derelict aristocrats overshadowed by 'ce brave fils du peuple', Chesnel.

Je ne sais quelle a été la vraie intention de Balzac. . . . Mais, malgré lui, c'est le fils de l'ancien valet qui grandit dans son œuvre . . . Chesnel, c'est l'activité, l'intelligence, la vie, c'est le peuple qui est appelé à renouveler la société et à prendre le pas sur ses anciens maîtres . . .

Zola believes that the whole of the *Comédie humaine* is amenable to this sort of analysis: 'Les Rastignac, les de Marsay, les Maxime de Trailles, tous ces débris ironiques et pourris de la noblesse font la plus honteuse mine devant le flot sourd du peuple qu'on entend gronder au fond de la *Comédie humaine.*' This is going much further, obviously, than Vallès, for example, who presented Rastignac and his like as revolutionary forces only in the desires they aroused in the reader. For Zola, it is not that Balzac was unwittingly writing works which turned out to be useful to the left: it was that he would not admit what he knew to be his real political sympathies. 'Balzac aimait trop la vigeur, les énergies herculéennes pour ne pas admirer les forces vives de l'humanité.' Whether Zola had by this time read *Les Paysans*, where the rural proletariat is portrayed more as the deadweight than as the 'force vive' of humanity, is not known. Zola's explanation of Balzac's monarchist pronouncements is interesting in the way it illuminates Zola's idea of the literary mentality: 'Balzac voulait régner, sans conteste, sur les écrivains, et il entendait aussi faire manœuvrer les personnages du monde qu'il avait créé, comme d'humbles sujets, dociles sous sa main.'[79] Thus Balzac's advocacy of a monarch who would control the nation in that way is but a transposition of his literary ambition into the real world. These political opinions go by the board, however, as soon as he actually observed reality: for the reality was, and is for Zola, in the rise of the oppressed classes. Zola ends this article with a battle-cry that was to be repeated *ad infinitum* by the Naturalist writers of the 1870s:

S'il est regrettable qu'un esprit de cette trempe n'ait pas travaillé franchement à la Révolution, il y a une grande consolation à penser qu'il était avec nous quand-même. Sur son drapeau, où il a écrit: Royauté, Catholicisme, nos enfants liront le mot: République. Toute son œuvre est là pour crier: Ne l'écoutez pas, il se ment à lui-même, il a travaillé pour l'avenir, il a raconté les premiers bégayments [sic] de la démocratie universelle.[80]

In more ways than one, this article on Balzac is the first stone in the edifice of Naturalist critical theory that Zola was to construct—and to think of in terms of 'construction' and 'monument'. In this article of October 1869, Zola speaks for the first time in the first person plural ('Balzac . . . est avec nous . . .'), revealing a new awareness of leading and creating a group. For the first time, too, he analyses a book not to judge its qualities but to show the direction to which its author belonged. Of course, the partisan tone of this article may be partly due to the partisan nature of the newspaper for which it was written: but this crusading, aggressive style is none the less an essential and characteristic feature of later Naturalist criticism as a whole.

Throughout the 1870s Zola led a vigorous, extraordinarily active literary campaign to win recognition for the Naturalist novel. What

[79] Cf. Louis Joly's review of Balzac's *Correspondance* in *Le Moniteur universel* (21 Jan. 1877): 'Son respect pour la légitimité, son culte pour l'aristocratie n'était en réalité qu'une attitude, qu'une pose, une affectation *littéraire*.'
[80] Zola, in *La Tribune*, 31 Oct. 1869.

success this campaign had was due to the fact that it was systematic—both in its organization and in the ideas it attempted to propagate. Zola professed to believe that great works of literature were not the products of random individuals, but belonged to an ordered progression which had evolved in a necessary, logical and comprehensible way. One element of this attitude—that literature somehow belonged to a wider pattern of social and historical development—Zola owed to Taine; another element—the idea of literary 'evolution'—became current in the 1870s and after through the writings of Brunetière. For Zola, the function of a critic was not to assess the qualities of literary works according to any criteria of taste or perfection, but to guess and to predict the influence that particular works would have over subsequent developments—in other words, to feel the 'true direction' of new writing. This, of course, was where Sainte-Beuve as well as Taine had failed: they had not perceived 'la véritable puissance des écrivains qui doivent un jour déterminer une évolution dans la littérature nationale'.[81] Zola himself, it might be noted, also failed signally to predict the *future* course of French literature; Naturalism appears in his critical writings as the ultimate stage of the novel's evolution, beyond which only degeneracy is possible. Zola's system, however, was geared to the needs of the moment, which was to refute or otherwise confound his adversaries, and the insistence on Naturalism as an evolutive stage, as a necessary and inevitable literary development, was of the greatest use in this respect. Zola effectively wrote his own fragmentary literary history, which concentrated on the major novelists, in order to show that he was obeying the same irresistible movement towards scientific realism that had dominated and determined the works of novelists of past ages and whose greatness was not seriously disputed. At the same time, he could stigmatize his own critics by pointing out the similarities between what they said of the *Rougon-Macquart* and what earlier critics had said, mistakenly and unfairly, of his predecessors—of Balzac, for example. Zola was of course quite justified in claiming that he owed much to Stendhal and Balzac: but it must be noted that his system, subordinated to the requirements of a campaign fought in a political—indeed, almost military—style, involved not only praise of Balzac, but also substantial criticism.

The important thing about Balzac in orthodox Naturalist doctrine is that he was a precursor of the ultimate in the novel, and not, as Taine had thought, the ultimate itself. The Naturalist tradition ex-

[81] *Le Voltaire*, 13 Mar. 1880.

tended into the past beyond Balzac to Diderot. The Romantics, coming between these two masters, represented a temporary aberration in the evolutive process: '... rêveurs surexcités ... qui ne représentaient rien de net ... Le siècle appartenait aux naturalistes, aux fils directs de Diderot ... La chaîne se renouait, le naturalisme triomphait avec Balzac.'[82] It was, however, only in his better moments that Balzac was a triumphant Naturalist. Zola cannot see how the entirety of his literary production was to last: to begin with, he had written too much, and experience showed that 'les œuvres légués par les siècles sont toutes relativement courtes'.[83] Moreover, *La Comédie humaine* lacked neatness and system: 'L'idée première manque, il ne s'appuie pas sur une vérité scientifique pour en déduire des jugements logiques.'[84] In a splendid example of the pot calling the kettle black, Zola accused Balzac of lacking all 'sens critique'. The earlier novelist had been unaware of his role in literary evolution, and his literary criticism was that of a 'dormeur éveillé'.[85] Particularly heinous as an offence against Naturalist theory was Balzac's attack on Victor Hugo's style: for Hugo, assigned a minor role in literary evolution, was granted the rank of the greatest French lyric poet and stylist of the nineteenth century.[86] The comparison between Balzac and Hugo was a theme Zola returned to time and time again in his critical writings: on the one hand, a poet who achieved immense success in his own time, the acknowledged leader of a literary movement, but whose literary posterity was more or less nil; on the other hand, a novelist, unappreciated in his own lifetime, without a 'school' or even disciples, but whose work had none the less laid the foundations of the modern novel.[87] Zola could not understand why Balzac had not founded a 'school', and thought, in 1872, that the *Correspondance*, when it appeared, would reveal Balzac's secret desire for 'la domination ... de la littérature française'.[88] This theme was not taken up after 1876, when the *Correspondance* appeared, for obvious reasons. It is an example of what has been called 'grafting'—of ideas and in this case desires being attributed to Balzac which properly belong to the critic in question. It is also interesting to see Zola attempting to justify his

---

[82] *Viestnik Evropi* (St. Petersburg), Jan. 1879 (in Russian). See Appendix III for details of re-publications of this and all other Zola articles in French and in book form.
[83] *Viestnik Evropi*, Mar. 1880.
[84] *Le Voltaire*, 27 July 1880.   [85] Ibid., and also 3 Aug. 1880.
[86] *Viestnik Evropi*, May 1879.   [87] *Le Voltaire*, 4 Apr. 1879.
[88] *La Cloche*, 15 June 1872.

own desire for literary domination on the basis of an illustrious precedent.

Naturalist attitudes to Balzac's imagination were somewhat ambiguous. On the one hand, the power of Balzac's novels was admitted to be a consequence of the power of his personality and of his imagination: 'La puissance, la puissance, entendez-vous! cette force créatrice sans laquelle il n'y a pas de génie',[89] but on the other hand, Zola, like Sainte-Beuve, criticized the invented, exaggerated, imaginative features of the *Comédie humaine*:

Il y a en Balzac un dormeur éveillé, qui rêve et crée parfois des figures curieuses, mais qui ne grandit certes pas le romancier. J'avoue ne pas avoir d'admiration pour l'auteur de la *Femme de trente ans*,[90] pour l'inventeur du type de Vautrin dans la 3e partie des *Illusions perdues* et dans *Splendeurs et misères des courtisanes*. C'est là ce que j'appelle la fantasmagorie de Balzac. Je n'aime pas davantage son grand monde qu'il a inventé de toutes pièces et qui fait sourire . . . En un mot, l'imagination de Balzac m'irrite plus qu'elle ne m'attire.[91]

It is in the treatment of these 'romantic' aspects of Balzac's works that the Naturalist movement was most critical. In many references and articles, of course, Balzac's imagination is simply not mentioned; where it is discussed by the Naturalists, imagination is equated with extravagance and *invraisemblance*.[92] It is curious, and perhaps significant to a consideration of Zola's awareness of his own methods as a novelist, that the author of the *Rougon-Macquart* was unable to reconcile, in his critical writings, the real with the imagined. Balzac's role in the evolution of the novel had been to introduce the observation of reality. This was not compatible with his also being a romantic or imaginative writer, and thus the latter aspect of his achievement is simply lopped off in Naturalist theory. Zola was much subtler as a novelist, it will be agreed, than he was as a critic.

Perhaps because of its lack of subtlety, Zola's presentation of Balzac was extremely influential over the subsequent course of Balzac criticism. There were in fact two identifiable levels to the appropriation of the

---

[89] *Le Voltaire*, 13 Mar. 1880.

[90] One of Zola's *bêtes noires*. See also *Le Voltaire*, 25 Mar. 1879.

[91] *Le Voltaire*, 20 Aug. 1878.

[92] Zola's son-in-law, Maurice Le Blond, gave an extreme version of this theme together with some curdling images: 'Balzac a vécu dans le Romantisme et il en a respiré le poison par tous ses pores. Il a fait rutiler devant nous les violents vermillons de faces terribles. Il a su lui aussi incarner le vice en des héros qu'il a sculptés dans de la brique et peints de sang. Mais il a créé des monstres . . .' (*La Plume*, 15 Mar. 1898).

Comédie humaine to the prehistory of the Naturalist movement. On the first and more justifiable level, Balzac and Stendhal were presented as the major precursors of Zola, in that they had turned the novel away from artificiality and convention, towards observation and analysis of reality. In so doing, they had *determined* the subsequent evolution of the novel in the nineteenth century. Even at this level there is an element of circularity, not to say intellectual trickery, in Zola's argument. If Zola and the Naturalists were justified in their 'dissection of reality'—indeed, obliged by the irresistible force of literary evolution to write as they wrote—because Balzac had determined that evolution, then how can Balzac at the same time enjoy a position of greatness solely because he determined what later writers would do? Zola's argument is self-justifying, but lacks any element to justify his claims about Balzac's literary qualities.

The second level in the Naturalist appropriation of Balzac consisted in making him a second image of Émile Zola himself. He was presented as the first martyr of the Naturalist evolution; the cruelty of his contemporaries and their incomprehension of his new kind of fiction were emphasized:

Stendhal et Balzac ne mentaient pas, avaient une saveur amère, désagréable au premier abord. Ils furent peu lus, ils moururent avant d'assister à leur triomphe. Mais ils apportaient la vérité qui triomphe toujours.[93]

With evident glee, Zola exhumed the criticisms of Janin and Chaudes-Aigues, and pointed out the parallels between these biased, hostile pieces on Balzac and the sort of attacks he had himself suffered. Implicit in this is a parallel between Balzac and himself as novelists.[94] It is at this point that Zola's arguments about Balzac became undeniable distortions, at the point, that is, where Zola identifies himself with Balzac and Balzac with the Naturalist novel.

Further along this line of appropriation, Zola presented Balzac as a scientist in literature. It is true that Balzac was interested in the sciences of his day, and intentionally vulgarized what he thought to be the latest advances in knowledge[95]; but it is false—and Zola probably knew it to be false—to make the following claim:

Balzac et Stendhal faisaient par le roman l'enquête que les savants faisaient par la science. Ils n'imaginaient plus, ils ne contaient plus . . . Balzac étudiait

---

[93] *Le Figaro*, supplément littéraire, 22 Dec. 1878. A few months later, Balzac became 'lapidé et crucifié, comme le messie de la grande école du naturalisme' (*Le Voltaire*, 4 Apr. 1879).
[94] *Le Voltaire*, 16 Mar. 1880 and 26 July, 1880.   [95] *Pl.* I. 12.

les tempéraments, reconstituait les milieux, amassait les documents humains, en prenant lui-même le titre de docteur ès sciences sociales.[96]

Zola often repeated this claim that Balzac excluded mere story-telling from his works. The character of old Grandet is, he says, 'une application absolue de la théorie des milieux' and just as scientifically true as Taine's application of the theory to history: 'Le romancier part de la réalité du milieu et de la vérité du document humain; si ensuite il développe dans un certain sens, ce n'est plus de l'imagination à l'exemple des conteurs, c'est de la déduction, comme chez les savants.'[97] The disadvantage of this sort of claim is that it can be contradicted by fact: in this case, for example, by the fact that Saumur was not the 'milieu' in which Balzac studied the 'document humain' of old Grandet.[98]

Not only did Zola claim that Balzac employed methods of documentation and 'scientific' inquiry that were properly his own, he also presented one of Balzac's novels, *La Cousine Bette*, as a 'roman expérimental': 'Dès qu'il a eu choisi son sujet, il est parti des faits observés, puis il a institué son expérience en soumettant Hulot à une série d'épreuves, en le faisant passer par certains milieux, pour montrer le fonctionnement du mécanisme de sa passion.' The scientific jargon in this passage at least can be accepted as figurative language; but not in the following claim:

Il est donc évident qu'il n'y a pas seulement là observation, mais qu'il y a aussi expérimentation, puisque Balzac ne s'en tient pas strictement en photographe aux faits recueillis par lui, puisqu'il intervient d'une façon directe pour placer son personnage dans des conditions dont il reste le maître.[99]

This argument is not compatible with the initial position of Naturalist theory on the role of Balzac in the evolution of the novel, namely, that he abandoned the artificial convention of authorial arrangement and intervention in the plot to introduce observation and 'truth'. Zola goes further than this in contradicting his premises when he allows the parallel of literature with science to carry him into speculations on the social utility of 'experimental' novels such as *La Cousine Bette*. The progression of events in that novel, Zola argues, is determined by Hulot's 'tempérament amoureux', and this single gangrenous member

---

[96] *Viestnik Evropi*, Jan. 1879.   [97] *Le Voltaire*, 27 May 1879.
[98] See P.-G. Castex's introduction to the Garnier edition of *Eugénie Grandet* (1965), p. xxvi.   [99] *Viestnik Evropi*, Sept. 1879.

endangers the entire 'circulus social'. Hulot's temperament is given such close scrutiny by Balzac

parce qu'il s'agissait de se rendre maître du phénomène de cette passion pour la diriger; admettez qu'on puisse guérir Hulot ou du moins le contenir et le rendre inoffensif, tout de suite le drame n'a plus de raison d'être . . . Donc, les romanciers naturalistes sont bien en effet des moralistes expérimentateurs.

In politics, too, Zola grafted ideas of his own on to the author of the *Comédie humaine*. The naturalist movement was unavoidably left-wing:[100] the Empire had made it impossible for any *avant-garde* literary movement to associate itself with anything other than the left wing in politics. Zola's personal opinions on political parties and topics are not what is under consideration here, but the general position of Naturalism as a phenomenon in public life. Since Zola had presented the novel in terms of a necessary and logical evolution, it was essential for him to show how Balzac, one of the originators of Naturalism and precursors of the novels of the Médan group, had been working in the same direction as they. Zola's initial appropriation of Balzac to the left was made as early as 1869, with the article on *Le Cabinet des antiques* that has already been discussed. The same article, with a few modifications, was re-published in 1872,[101] its arguments were included in the long review of Balzac's *Correspondance* originally written in 1877,[102] and which was reprinted in *Les Romanciers naturalistes* in 1881.[103] The material on this subject is not very varied, but it was frequently brought to the public's attention.

Despite the internal contradictions that can be pointed out in it, Zola's interpretation of Balzac had enough external coherence to impose itself on a whole generation of writers and critics. The idea of Balzac as the first novelist to introduce observation, documentation and the 'théorie des milieux' into fiction remained alive, as M. Raimond has remarked,[104] well beyond the disintegration of the Naturalist movement itself; and in its weak form the notion that Balzac was a precursor of Naturalism contains a considerable element of truth. In its strong form, Zola's idea of Balzac as a 'naturaliste sans le savoir', as an experimental novelist, and as a prophet of revolution, is very wide of the mark. Many of the attacks on Zola's literary theory and

---

[100] Cf. Edmond Biré's claim: 'Le Naturalisme est essentiellement *révolutionnaire*', in *L'Univers*, 13 July 1887.

[101] *La Cloche*, 2 Oct. 1872. [102] *Viestnik Evropi*, 1 Jan. 1877.
[103] Charpentier. [104] M. Raimond, op. cit., p. 64.

practice are for good reason particularly harsh on his appropriation of Balzac.

The Naturalist Balzac was built up in the course of the 1870s, and the campaign for Naturalism reached a climax of publicity and polemic in 1879–81. Other writers, such as Huysmans, had already followed Zola's lead on Balzac, claiming in 1876 that 'le chef véritable de notre école, celui devant lequel il faudrait s'agenouiller, c'est l'analyste profond, l'observateur merveilleux, qui, le premier, a créé dans le roman moderne cette qualite maîtresse en art, c'est Balzac'.[105] In Huysmans's tract, the Naturalist novel is above all a rejection of romantic 'fantoches plus beaux que nature', and an attempt to introduce 'real life' into literature. In a spirited defence of Zola's morality, Maurice Guillemot even invented a passage on Balzac which he attributed to Zola: 'Balzac est le vrai . . . Il travaille sur le corps humain sans pitié pour ces chairs pantelantes, ces secousses nerveuses des muscles, ce craquement de toute la machine. Il constate et il expose . . .'[106] Naturalism, Guillemot states, is not 'né d'hier'; it is a term that denotes 'cette littérature exacte, scrutatrice, inventée par Balzac, continuée par les de Goncourt, Flaubert, Champfleury, et enfin aujourd'hui, Zola et son école'.[107] Another Naturalist disciple, Harry Alis, presented Zola's movement as inevitable. The merit of its leader, therefore, was not to have invented Naturalism—for he could not have done otherwise—but to have explained the evolutive process of which he is a part:

Avant M. Émile Zola, d'autres écrivains, notamment Balzac et Champfleury, avaient pressenti cette évolution fatale de la littérature. Sans en poser les principes et sans les discuter, ils les avaient mis à l'exécution. Mais M. Zola, le premier, et ce sera sa gloire, eut l'audace d'établir les règles de cette transformation. Il apprécia Balzac à sa réelle valeur et prédit que l'avenir serait à ceux qui suivraient la même voie . . .[108]

Other journalists writing in defence of Zola frequently drew parallels between the *Rougon-Macquart* and the *Comédie humaine,* as well as between their authors; Zola is constantly praised for having set Balzac in his true perspective.[109] Among the considerable diversity of

---

[105] *L'Actualité* (Brussels), 1876.
[106] *La Revue moderne et naturaliste,* 1 Feb. 1880.
[107] Ibid. 1 May 1880.
[108] Ibid. 1 May 1879.
[109] See for example F. Champsaur, *La Revue moderne et naturaliste,* 1 June 1879.

opinion on Zola's practice in his own novels, one theme binds virtually all Naturalist critics together: that Zola was right about Balzac.

MARGINAL CRITICISM: MAUPASSANT AND FLAUBERT

There were of course exceptions to this in the wider circle of writers associated with Naturalism. Maupassant, for example, expressed views almost totally opposed to those of the author of the *Rougon-Macquart*. However, the Naturalist movement considered as a campaign fought in the press and orchestrated by Zola with the help of several lesser writers and journalists, did present a consistent and systematic view of Balzac's place in the evolution of the novel, and made this a central point in the arguments for the Naturalist novel. Opponents of Naturalism, such as Brunetière and Michiels, regarded this reinterpretation of Balzac as central, also, to their arguments against Émile Zola. In other words, Zola succeeded in determining the framework of arguments for and against Naturalism, and the presence of Balzac at their centre is evidence of the growing prestige of the *Comédie humaine*.

Guy de Maupassant did not take Zola's theoretical pronouncements very seriously. The doctrines of Naturalism, he admitted privately in 1877, were worthless in themselves, and served only to give expansion to Zola's personality, just as 'Romanticism' had only existed in France as an extension of Victor Hugo.[110] None the less, Maupassant did subscribe to the general Naturalist view of Balzac's place in the history of the novel. Balzac and Stendhal, he wrote, are 'les deux romanciers . . . de qui date la réelle évolution de l'aventure imaginée à l'aventure observée, ou mieux, à l'aventure racontée comme si elle appartenait à la vie'.[111] The second point is in fact more subtly accurate than anything Zola ever wrote on the subject; and Maupassant's opinion of Balzac is more sincerely admiring than Zola's. Stendhal, he thought, was only a precursor, a 'romancier de second plan'; whereas Balzac was a writer of truly colossal stature: 'le géant des lettres modernes, aussi énorme que Rabelais, ce père de la littérature française . . .' Balzac is as a god to later writers, and though he had his faults—particularly in his use of language which only reaches perfection in passages written 'avec une furie de cheval emporté' and left uncorrected—it would be almost impious to criticize him: 'Un croyant oserait-il reprocher à son dieu toutes les imperfections de l'univers?'

---

[110] Maupassant, *Chroniques, études, correspondance*, ed. R. Dumesnil (Gründ, 1938), pp. 223–6.
[111] *La Revue de l'Exposition universelle de 1889*, II. 245–8, Sept. 1889.

Balzac, Maupassant continued, had the creative energy of a demiurge, as well as the slips, the hastiness, and lack of proportion of a creator, 'qui n'a pas le temps de s'arrêter pour chercher la perfection'. Balzac's ability to create the illusion of reality in his novels comes not from observation, Maupassant argues, but from his genial intuition. The codification of the literary devices used by Balzac was made after his death, by Champfleury and Duranty 'qui, s'autorisant de ce que Balzac écrivit mal, n'écrivit plus du tout . . .'[112] The arguments of this article of 1889 on the evolution of the novel can be used to illuminate Maupassant's real attitude to Balzac at a much earlier date. In October 1876, an article on Gustave Flaubert appeared over the signature of 'Guy de Valmont' in the *République des lettres*.[113] In it, Balzac is referred to in glowing terms:

. . . un innovateur étrangement puissant et fertile et un des maîtres de l'avenir, écrivain imparfait, sans doute, gêné par la phrase, mais l'inventeur de personnages immortels qu'il faisait mouvoir comme dans un grossissement d'optique, les rendant par cela même plus frappants et en quelque sorte plus vrais que la réalité!—*Madame Bovary* parut, et voilà tout le monde bouleversé.—Pourquoi? Parce que M. Flaubert est un idéaliste mais aussi et surtout un artiste . . .

The remarks on Flaubert seem strangely disconnected from the preceding appreciation of Balzac. The reason is that Henri Roujon, an editor of *La République des lettres*, had changed whatever it was that Maupassant had originally written. Maupassant wrote to Roujon saying that he was sending a copy of his article to Flaubert himself:

mais comme je ne veux pas recevoir la mercuriale qu'il m'adresserait infailliblement, j'ai soin de lui dire que vous avez fait à la dernière heure quelques changements qui modifient un peu ma pensée sur Balzac; car je sais qu'il le juge absolument comme moi, et que, tout en admirant son incontestable génie, il le considère non point comme un écrivain imparfait, mais comme pas écrivain du tout. En outre, ce que je dis ensuite de Flaubert ne répond plus parfaitement à ce qui précède.[114]

If what Maupassant had written about Flaubert in the original text had corresponded perfectly to what preceded on Balzac, then it seems reasonable to suppose that the main and final argument about Balzac had been that he was not an artist. Maupassant's remarks in the letter to Roujon—that he shared Flaubert's view that Balzac was not just

---

[112] *La Revue de l'Exposition universelle de 1889*, II. 245–8, Sept. 1889.
[113] Maupassant, *Chroniques* . . ., p. 3.   [114] Ibid., p. 216.

'un écrivain imparfait, mais pas écrivain du tout'—confirm this sup-
position, as does the text of the 1889 article on the evolution of the
novel. There, Balzac's style is condemned briefly, but broadly: for
those passages which Balzac wrote 'avec une furie de cheval emporté'
and did not subsequently correct are few and far between. In another
study of Flaubert, written as a preface to the 1884 edition of Flaubert's
letters to George Sand,[115] Maupassant presents the appearance of
Madame Bovary in 1856–7 as having constituted 'une révolution dans
les lettres'; for although Balzac had previously created powerful novels
overflowing with life, he had been hardly a true artist.

. . . il écrivait une langue forte, imagée, un peu confuse et pénible. Emporté
par son inspiration, il semble avoir ignoré l'art si difficile de donner aux
idées de la valeur par les mots, par la sonorité et la contexture de la phrase. Il
a dans son œuvre des lourdeurs de colosse; et il est peu de pages de ce très
grand homme qui puissent être citées comme des chefs-d'œuvre de la langue,
ainsi qu'on cite du Rabelais, de la Bruyère, du Bossuet, du Montesquieu, du
Michelet, du Gautier, etc. Gustave Flaubert, au contraire . . .[116]

Whatever his 'lourdeurs', none the less, Balzac remained for Maupassant a 'colosse', a 'très grand homme'. In his review of Balzac's
Correspondance for *La Nation*, Maupassant writes of Balzac's immense
'bonté' and naïve, generous good nature in a way quite reminiscent of
George Sand's preface to the first issues of the Houssiaux *Œuvres
complètes illustrées*.[117] In this text more than in any other, Maupassant
separates himself from the view of Balzac as a Naturalist: the author of
the *Comédie humaine*, he says, is 'avant tout un remueur d'idées, un
spritualiste; il le dit, l'affirme et le répète. C'est un inventeur prodigieux
bien plus qu'un observateur; seulement il devinait toujours juste.
. . . Il ne visait qu'à l'âme. L'objet et le fait n'étaient pour lui que des
accessoires.'[118] Maupassant was, of course, involved in the Naturalist
battle in some of its fiercest moments; in 1882, he was among Zola's
most vigorous defenders in the affair over the appearance of *Pot-
Bouille*.[119] He knew what Zola was doing with his literary polemics,

---

[115] Charpentier, 1885.　　　　　　[116] See Maupassant, *Chroniques* . . ., p. 139.
[117] This is a rare bibliographic item, and the only copy known to me is in the Lovenjoul library. Mme Ève de Balzac objected to George Sand's tone and had the preface
removed from all the copies she could lay her hands on. The text is, however, reproduced
in Sand's *Autour de la Table* (Lévy, 1876), pp. 197–213.
[118] *La Nation*, 22 Nov. 1876.
[119] Maupassant signed about four articles a month in *Le Gaulois* between January and
June 1882. Some have been collected. Of these that have not, see articles on 14 Jan. and
18 Mar. for partisan defences of Zola and *Pot-Bouille*.

namely making publicity and venting his need to dominate and lead; he thus regarded the actual content of the polemics on literary and critical topics as intrinsically worthless. At the same time involved and yet detached, Maupassant was the only writer to be on Zola's side, as it were, and to hold independent views on the place of Balzac in French literature in the late 1870s and 1880s. It is not well established, however, whether Maupassant went so far as to regard Balzac as 'le génie du vague', as 'Mme X' recounted in 1912. The remarks this former ladyfriend claimed Maupassant made about Balzac towards the end of November 1884 have little in common with what Maupassant said either before or after that date.[120] It is of course possible that Maupassant's visits to the mental hospital of La Salpetrière, which began towards the end of 1884, did persuade him to see in Balzac a 'scientific visionary' as 'Mme X' claimed. It is also possible that these opinions, which became very current by the end of the century, were 'Mme X's' own. It is therefore rather rash to assume as M. Raimond does[121] that Maupassant prefigured the themes of the spiritual and occult that enter Balzac criticism in the later 1890s.

Maupassant's view of Balzac, then, owes little to Zola; on the other hand, it is very evidently derivative from the opinion of Gustave Flaubert. The only direct evidence that we have of Flaubert's opinion, however, are the few remarks he made on this subject in his correspondence. Maupassant was right in saying to Roujon that Flaubert regarded Balzac as 'pas écrivain du tout' if 'écrivain' means, as it did for Flaubert, artist and stylist. One of his fears when composing *Madame Bovary* was of letting his style fall into 'le Paul de Kock ou de faire du Balzac chateaubrianisé'[122] In 1850, Flaubert had been much saddened by the news of Balzac's death: 'Quand meurt un homme que l'on admire on est toujours triste. On espérait le connaître plus tard et s'en faire aimer. Oui, c'était un homme fort et qui avait crânement compris son temps!'[123] Flaubert regarded observation and accuracy as secondary qualities in the novel, but Balzac had set new standards in this field which had to be kept to;[124] and Flaubert was much tickled by the resemblance that Gautier had perceived between him and Balzac: 'Théo prétendait souvent qu'à m'entendre parler, c'était tout comme, et que nous nous serions chéris.'[125] Flaubert had also been disturbed by strange resemblances he had found between sentences in

---

[120] See *La Grande Revue*, 25 Oct. 1912, pp. 1678, 1685.
[121] M. Raimond, op. cit., p. 55.   [122] Flaubert, *Correspondance* (Conard, 1926), II. 316.
[123] Ibid. II. 256.   [124] Ibid. V. 36.   [125] Ibid. VII. 366.

Madame Bovary and sentences in *Le Médecin de campagne*; as by the similarity in plot of *La Spirale* and *Louis Lambert*.[126] The first set of resemblances is not in fact very substantial, as André Vial has shown,[127] but the second remains a striking coincidence. Flaubert's own reaction upon discovering these similarities[128] indicate that he had feelings as of pupil to master for Balzac: but on the other hand, most of Flaubert's references to the author of the *Comédie humaine* are critical in a fairly fundamental way. Balzac, Flaubert once grumbled, was just as bad as the author of *Uncle Tom's Cabin* in letting political attitudes interfere with his novels;[129] and Balzac was not the Homer the novel-form was waiting for. 'Quel homme eût été Balzac s'il eût su écrire!' After reading Balzac's *Correspondance* in 1876, Flaubert wrote virtually the same letter to three different correspondents, so it can be assumed that he meant what he said. Immensely moved by Balzac's tortured life, Flaubert was none the less shocked by Balzac's preoccupations with material life:

. . . comme il s'inquiète peu de l'Art! *Pas une fois* il n'en parle! Il ambitionnait la Gloire, mais non le Beau. D'ailleurs, que d'étroitesses! légitimiste, catholique, collectivement rêvant à la députation et à l'Académie française! Avec tout cela, ignorant comme un pot et *provincial* jusque dans les moelles: le luxe l'épate. Sa plus grande admiration littéraire est pour Walter Scott.[130]

Flaubert's attachment to Balzac was not, then, a literary admiration, but of an anecdotal, personal variety. He was pleased when he found in either Balzac's life or works details which accorded with his own ideas—such as his misogyny and hatred of marriage. Flaubert repeated the story that Mme Cornu had told him, that Balzac's last words to his sister were ' "Je meurs de chagrin"—du chagrin que lui causait son épouse!'[131] He felt sympathy for Balzac in his sufferings at the hands of the critics[132] and was ready to defend him: 'Je me suis, une fois, emporté, devant témoins, contre Sainte-Beuve, en le priant d'avoir autant d'indulgence pour Balzac qu'il en avait pour Jules Lecomte. Il m'a répondu en me traîtant de ganache! Voilà où mène la largeur!'[133] Despite this, and despite the obvious and substantial influence of Balzac on Flaubert's practice as a novelist, it is not really possible to

---

[126] See E. W. Fischer, *Œuvres inédites de Flaubert* (Leipzig, 1908).
[127] *RHLF* July–Sept. 1948.
[128] Flaubert, *Correspondance*, I. 495 and III. 76–9.
[129] Ibid. III. 61.   [130] Ibid. VII. 384.
[131] Ibid. VIII. 58.   [132] Ibid. VIII. 58.   [133] Ibid. VI. 296.

consider Flaubert as a conscious 'émule' or 'disciple' of the author of the *Comédie humaine*. His view, which changed little throughout his life, was put in a nutshell in a letter to Edmond de Goncourt: 'Au résumé, c'est pour moi un immense bonhomme, mais de second ordre.'[134] Maupassant's view was very similar to that of 'le maître de Croisset'; if he is more generous with his praise for Balzac as a man, it is because he had more occasion than Flaubert to write criticism in the press.

Flaubert and Maupassant held views that reflect their own pre-occupations with style and technique, and which are quite outside the themes of Balzac criticism as a whole. Their views are not, for all that, more balanced or more profound: considering the immense debt Flaubert, in particular, owed to the author of the *Comédie humaine*, what he said about Balzac strikes one as fragmentary and grudging.[135]

With Barbey d'Aurevilly and Flaubert, Maupassant was perhaps the only writer who retained a personal, independent view of Balzac through the 1870s and 1880s. Zola's appropriation of Balzac to the Naturalist school affected virtually all other writing on Balzac in those two decades. The Naturalist faction, as has been shown, held a schematic, apparently coherent view of Balzac, and argued its points in an aggressive, dogmatic manner. The opponents of Naturalism had the advantage of greater knowledge of the history of literature, and, in some cases, greater gifts as writers of literary criticism.

ZOLA'S FIRST OPPONENTS

Zola's success as a novelist in the 1870s not only created controversy, but was to a certain extent itself created by controversy. As a literary leader, Zola revelled in polemic and public dispute. However, the way in which he was attacked played some role in shaping the way he formulated his own literary theories.

Darwin's notion of the evolution of species was applied to the literary context by various critics, whose knowledge of Darwinism remains doubtful, from 1870 on. The idea of history being an evolutionary process rather than a set of discrete, chronologically juxtaposed events was, one might say, in the air of the 1870s, rather than being a definite notion adopted from a specific source. In the literary context,

---

[134] Flaubert, *Correspondance*, VII. 386. See very similar views expressed by . . . Bouvard and Pécuchet (Livre de poche edition, p. 175).

[135] Flaubert was just as harsh on Stendhal: *La Chartreuse de Parme* he considered 'mal écrit et incompréhensible comme caractères et intentions', and he could not understand 'l'enthousiasme de Balzac pour un semblable écrivan'.

it seems obvious that Zola's systematization of the history of the novel as a 'Naturalist evolution' was quite independent of Darwinism, since the roots of the system can be seen in the *Notes sur la marche générale de l'œuvre*, written before Darwin became at all known in France. An article by Scherer on Balzac, written in 1870, is further evidence of the existence of the idea of the 'evolution of the genres' independently of Darwinist influence.

Scherer had been among the first to point out the inconsistencies in Taine's critical method,[136] and his arguments bear a striking resemblance to those of Wellek nearly a century later. In his article on Balzac, Scherer repeated his point that the 'théorie des milieux' had failed to account for what was specifically literary in a work of literature. On the other hand, biographical criticism seemed more relevant to a study of literature, except in so far as it destroyed any real literary history: 'Il n'y manque qu'une chose, l'enchaînement des faits littéraires.'[137] Scherer believed that there was a literary history worthy of the name, and that it consisted of a history of the genres. To evaluate Balzac's place in French literature, Scherer examined what changes he had made in the genere of the novel. This approach to literature has had a long and successful career, and still informs much academic writing. Scherer was one of the first critics to formulate explicitly the criterion of originality within a genre as a measure of literary achievement, and deserves a much higher regard than is usually accorded him in the history of criticism.

For Scherer, the novel-genre was 'avant tout un récit'.[138] In this fundamental respect, Balzac changed nothing; but

Il y a ajouté quelque chose, je veux dire la description. . . . L'accessoire est ici devenu le principal. Ces descriptions, presque toujours trop longues, presque toujours déplacées, n'en forment pas moins l'un des caractères du talent de Balzac. Il y a déployé une incontestable virtuosité. Et il a fait école dans ce genre. Il n'y a plus de romancier aujourd'hui qui ne se regarde comme obligé de décrire tout ce qu'il nomme. Première trace laissée par Balzac dans le roman contemporain.[139]

In the sub-genre of the 'roman sentimental', Balzac added nothing at all: his talent was too heavy and clumsy. It is above all as the renovator

---

[136] 'La Méthode de M. Taine', 1866. Reprinted in *Études sur la littérature contemporaine* (Lévy, 1873), IV.

[137] E. Scherer, 'Balzac', *Le Temps*, 1 Mar. 1870; reprinted in the *Études*. Page references are to the book edition.

[138] Ibid., p. 68.　　　　　　　　[139] Ibid., p. 69.

of the 'roman de mœurs' that Balzac made his contribution to the evolution of the genre. The introduction of 'real life', of observation and accurate depiction of men and manners were his original features: and he showed great virtuosity in creating characters 'qui restent dans le souvenir comme s'ils avaient vécu'.[140] Scherer's notion of the genres is not a sterile critical tool that does not allow value-judgements: on the contrary, it provides a criterion of perfection, or at least of literary quality, in that Scherer extracts from previous practice what the true 'essence' of a genre is. Balzac's contributions to the development of the novel cannot overrule the fact that for Scherer none of his works are perfect as examples of the novel genre. This is left as an unresolved paradox: 'Chose étrange! Balzac n'est pas un artiste, et il est créateur! il n'est pas écrivain, et il a fondé un genre; il n'a pas fait un ouvrage achevé, et toute une littérature procède de lui'. Scherer's article predates Zola's campaign for Naturalism, and his appropriation of Balzac to the Naturalist movement. None the less, it contains the elements that Brunetière and others were to use from 1875 on to attack the Naturalists and Zola in particular: namely, the idea that what Zola had taken from Balzac was his worst features.

Even the well-disposed critic of the *avant-garde* journal, *La Renaissance littéraire*, found that Zola had exaggerated 'le procédé de Balzac et de Flaubert' in his early novels.[141] Description and background should be accessory to the main interest of the novel, and not at its centre. Balzac's pessimism, the critic continues, is fundamentally different from Zola's: the former is infused with sympathy and humanity, and, like Hugo, Balzac 'ne désespère de personne, ne désespère de rien'. Zola, on the other hand, is inexorable in his treatment of vices, and in the name of science becomes fatalistic and irrational. Behind Zola, the *Renaissance littéraire* is attacking Taine and his method, 'inventé par les Allemands, ces fatalistes sans autre idéal que le règne de la force brutale'.

Ferdinand Brunetière, too, laid most of the blame for the defects of the modern novel on Taine, and on his interpretation of Balzac in particular:

Est-il bien étonnant que les romanciers du jour nous fatiguent de leurs descriptions techniques et de leurs détails spécieux quand ils entendent louer Balzac d'avoir si bien embrouillé telle intrigue dans *Une Ténébreuse Affaire* ou dans *César Birotteau* par example, qu'il faille être pour la suivre magistrat ou juge de commerce? On peut croire que ni M. Zola ni M. Malo[t] n'affec-

---

[140] Ibid., p. 64.   [141] Issue of 10 May 1873.

teraient de relier leurs romans les uns aux autres ni d'écrire leur *Comédie humaine* s'ils n'avaient lu quelque part 'que le drame ou le roman isolé, ne comprenant qu'une histoire isolée, exprime mal la nature et qu'en choisissant on mutile' (Taine, *Étude sur Balzac*).[142]

Yet, Brunetière argued, Balzac was not a true realist at all: his object was to transform reality into art, not to copy it; and he organized and arranged his characters and plots with 'une suite que ni les caractères ni les passions ne sauraient avoir dans la vie réelle'. Balzac's alleged imitators changed that aspect, thinking, under the influence of Taine's article, that they were perfecting the Balzacian novel when they were in fact perverting it.

Brunetière's argument rests at this stage on a reinterpretation of Balzac as a romantic and idealist, as he then understood the terms. Taine and the Naturalists, he claims, had failed to appreciate the *Comédie humaine* correctly and had adopted from it all that was inessential and in a literary sense bad. This does not affect Balzac's real place in the evolution of the novel, but merely presents his literary posterity as misguided. Brunetière's arguments are on the same level as Zola's, and differ not in substance but in value-judgement.

Jules Levallois took a line analogous to Brunetière's in an article published in 1877. The Naturalists, he says, 'ne se rattachent à Balzac ni par le procédé, dans ce qu'il a d'essentiel, ni par la direction morale, ni par les origines'.[143] Balzac's 'procédé', Levallois explains, was to use description to back up and reinforce the plot. The Naturalists, who should be called 'néo-romantiques échoués dans le réalisme', describe for the sake of describing, excessively and gratuitously. Théophile Gautier, in Levallois's view, was the source of this quite unBalzacian tradition of writing 'pour ne rien dire'; and *Madame Bovary* was the first major irruption of 'Gautiérisme' in the novel.

Levallois is to a certain extent justified in thinking that there was a fundamental difference between the role of free will and *volonté* in the *Comédie humaine* and the relative passivity of the heroes of Flaubert, the Goncourts, and Zola. Had the latter written *César Birotteau*, the critic speculates, the hero would have finished up drinking himself to death instead of pulling himself out of disaster by his own bootstraps. On the other hand, there are less justifiable but clearly perceptible political undertones to the criticism that both Levallois and Brunetière level at Zola and his interpretation of Balzac. Both critics were of

[142] *RDM* 1 Apr. 1875.   [143] *Le Correspondant*, 10 Apr. 1877.

course writing for right-wing periodicals whose support for the new Republic was far from solid. Levallois cannot avoid criticizing the attacks on the Second Empire in Zola's novels, and he lets his partisan feelings distort his appreciation of Balzac. The latter, he declares, would never have introduced politics into his novels as Zola had done. This is a curious lapse, since there were plenty of arguments available for proving that Balzac, at least, was not a left-wing writer like Zola, without going so far as to state an untruth: for Balzac, of course, introduces a great deal more political *discussion* in the *Comédie humaine* than Zola does in the *Rougon-Macquart*.

Levallois went on to attempt an explanation of how Balzac, whose idea of art, of morality, and of literary techniques he had just shown to be so different from Naturalist conceptions, had come to be as it were the patron saint of the contemporary novel. The root of this posthumous inversion of values, Levallois considers, can be found in Baudelaire's *Salon de 1846*, which marks the first attempt to appropriate Balzac to the 'école Gautier':

Le mal fit des progrès rapides et il atteignit à son apogée lorsque, peu d'années après, on vit la réalité se modeler sur le roman, Rastignac et de Marsay devenir des ministres *pour tout de bon*. Alors, dans les bas-fonds sociaux parmi les désœuvres et les déclassés, commença de grouiller une tourbe pour laquelle Vautrin était un grand homme. Le cri sauvage de cette tourbe a retenti dans un pamphlet . . . *Les Réfractaires*.[144]

The novelists of the day—Flaubert, the Goncourts, and later Zola— could not resist the pressure of public admiration for the politically revolutionary aspect of Balzac's works; so that, despite the fact that their point of departure was quite unBalzacian, they were forced to become 'la queue de Balzac'. It has already been shown in this chapter that Vallès's interpretation of Balzac was of no importance at all as an influence on Zola's theories—and that there is no evidence that the *Comédie humaine* was read widely enough to reach the 'bas-fonds sociaux'. Levallois is quite right to place the peak of Balzac's popularity with the public in the middle Second Empire,[145] and there may be an element of truth in his claim that Zola, at least, was responding to a certain kind of public pressure in writing novels that reveal the evil bases of political power in France, in the same way that Balzac's novels were seen to do.

[144] *Le Correspondant.* On Vallès and *Les Réfractaires*, see above, pp. 117–19.
[145] See Figure 1, above, p. 89.

The brunt of Levallois's attack on Zola, however, is that he misunderstood Balzac; that the *Comédie humaine* was not an immoral work, but that the *Rougon-Macquart* was; that the 'désordres de ces vingt dernières années eussent existé sans Balzac', but that Vallès and Zola were writing insurrectionary literature in the mistaken belief that they were continuing the Balzacian tradition. Despite some rather extraordinary statements on the role of Gautier (who was, as has been seen, one of the few critics to defend Balzac as a moral writer in the 1850s) this article by Levallois does complement the arguments of Brunetière against the Naturalist appropriation of Balzac. Brunetière made Balzac a romantic and an idealist in 1875; in 1877, Levallois adds that he was a moral writer and that his literary devices were essentially adjuncts to story-telling and not exercises in corruption.

Brunetière returned to the attack in 1880, in an article on Flaubert. Here he attempts to pour scorn on those who claim to imitate Balzac by the elegant argument that Balzac is, in his good parts, inimitable; and where he is imitable, 'Il est franchement détestable. . . . Avec cela, l'un des pires écrivains qui jamais aient tourmenté la pauvre langue française. On prétendit, quand parut *Madame Bovary*, qu'il y avait là des pages que Balzac eût signées. Certes! S'il avait pu les écrire!'[146] Champfleury had faithfully imitated Balzac's manner in his descriptions of provincial life, and had produced *Les Bourgeois de Molinchart*, which Brunetière thinks an abysmal novel; and *La Dernière Incarnation de Vautrin* had served as a model for the lamentable *Dernier Mot de Rocambole*. Brunetière's desire to deny literary respectability to writers he considered immoral and misguided, such as Zola, leads him to denigrate precisely that writer he is attempting to wrest from Zola's appropriation. This ambiguity in Brunetière's attitude to Balzac was to remain with him throughout his life: even in his last book on Balzac in 1906, there were two edges to everything Brunetière said about the *Comédie humaine*. In the early years, this curious mixture of admiration and deprecation is partly a result of Brunetière's attitude towards the function of literary criticism in general. He always used it for some purpose that went beyond literature proper, and, as John Clark wrote, 'la critique littéraire a été pour Brunetière un moyen de préciser sa pensée sur d'autres questions qu'il estimait plus graves et plus importantes'.[147] His opposition to Naturalism was religious, moral, and political, more than literary; and his attitude to Balzac, in the 1870s and

[146] *RDM* 15 June 1880.
[147] J. Clark, *La Pensée de Ferdinand Brunetière* (Nizet, 1954), p. 37.

1880s, depended largely on whichever aspect of Naturalism he happened to be attacking.

In 1881, Brunetière reviewed Zola's collection of articles entitled
Les Romanciers naturalistes, and which begins with the long review
of Balzac's *Correspondance* with other articles on Balzac appended to it.
Brunetière's object, here, was to prove that Zola was ignorant of
literary history and inept as a critic. He picks on Zola's expression
of surprise at discovering that Balzac admired Walter Scott, and shows
how little Zola appreciated the importance of 'milieu' in the historical
novel. Balzac, he admits, introduced 'les préoccupations de la vie
matérielle' into the novel, but, Brunetière argues, this was not as
original as Taine had made out in his *Étude*, 'qui pourrait bien avoir
éveillé la vocation de M. Zola'.[148] An assessment more measured than
Taine's must be arrived at, for, far from founding 'notre roman actuel',
Balzac had simply written 'le roman de Balzac. N'est-ce pas assez?' In
order to deny Zola any credit, Brunetière is evidently prepared to
contradict his own nascent ideas on the evolution of the genres. Zola's
systematization of literary history is rejected not only in details such
as the role of Walter Scott in introducing 'milieu' into the novel, but
also in its entire conception: for if all that can be said about Balzac
is that he wrote the 'roman de Balzac', then he has no place in the
history or evolution of the novel. It is doubtful, I think, whether
Brunetière actually believed this in 1881. He was attacking Zola, and
with Zola materialism—and success in that attack took priority over
the expression of Brunetière's own ideas if, as they might have done in
this case, they weakened his arguments by appearing to agree with
Zola's.

Moral outrage and indignation at the 'excesses of Naturalism',
coupled with Zola's appropriation of Balzac to the Naturalist movement, led to two distinct and contradictory themes in Balzac criticism.
The first, most powerfully expressed by Brunetière and Levallois, was,
as we have seen, to emphasize the substantial differences between
Balzac's novelistic practice and Naturalist theory. The second was to
condemn Balzac together with Naturalism. The second, in truth, required very little original thought, as the older arguments of Pontmartin and Sainte-Beuve became once again applicable in this new
context. Marius Topin, for example, did little more than rewrite
Sainte-Beuve's obituary of Balzac,[149] and the Belgian poet Charles

---

[148] *RDM* 15 Sept. 1881.
[149] *Les Romanciers contemporains* (Charpentier, 1876), pp. 37-49.

Potvin repeated the criticisms that Saint-Marc Girardin had made of
Le Père Goriot in his attack on literary 'corruption'.[150] Daniel Bernard
talked of Balzac as a 'puissant et dangereux romancier'.[151] The sense
that should be attributed to 'dangereux' is perhaps explained by
Gaston Feugère: Balzac, he wrote, was a *poseur* whose greatest fault lay
in his 'mélange du réalisme et du raffiné'. Updating Sainte-Beuve's
attitude to Balzac, Feugère made the *Comédie humaine* the source of all
that he saw as evil in modern literature: 'Avec Balzac le roman est
entré dans ces voies du réalisme brutal qui de chute en chute l'ont
conduit à M. Flaubert, et de M. Flaubert à M. Zola—du trottoir au
ruisseau, du ruisseau à l'égout. Peut-il descendre plus bas?'[152]

Thus the impact of Zola and Naturalism on Balzac criticism can be
summarized in the following way. Zola's attitude to the *Comédie
humaine* grew out of a reading of Taine's *Étude* in the first instance.
The pseudo-scientific jargon of Taine remained with Zola as a critic
even when his criticism developed into a reaction against, and in some
respects a rejection of Taine. This reaction was part and parcel of
Zola's growing awareness of himself as a novelist in the years 1869–70,
and his reassessment of Balzac's political meaning in 1869 grew out of
the creation of the first novel of the *Rougon-Macquart* series. Thence-
forth Zola systematized his idea of literary history in such a way as to
make Balzac the focal point of polemics both for and against the theory
and practice of the Naturalist movement. Expressed opinion of Balzac
in the years of the 'Naturalist battle' (1878–81) was more dependent
than ever before on political and ideological criteria, since Zola had
succeeded in making the *Comédie humaine* a justification for what others
saw as alternatively obscene and subversive literature. Thus the themes
of criticism, their combinations and valencies froze, became for a
while perceptibly fixed.

The stagnation underlying this apparent vitality in Balzac criticism
was contemporary with the lowest point of the trough in public demand for the novels of the *Comédie humaine*. It was also the decade in
which the first serious work of scholarship on Balzac was completed—
Spoelberch de Lovenjoul's *Histoire des Œuvres de Balzac*—and the
decade in which the long-awaited *Correspondance* appeared. The latter
publication in particular had an enormous impact on attitudes towards
the novelist, and tended to distinguish Balzac's image very sharply
from that of Zola and his disciples. The opponents of Naturalism dis-

150 *De La Corruption littéraire en France* (Brussels, 1872), p. 233.
151 *L'Union*, 28 Nov. 1876.   152 *Le Français*, 19 Nov. 1876.

cussed in this chapter—Brunetière, Levallois, Feugère—tried to destroy Zola's claim that Balzac was a Naturalist, but did so largely within the framework of arguments set up by Zola himself. That is to say, they either denied any role at all to Balzac in the prehistory of Naturalism; or they condemned the *Comédie humaine* as the source and origin of the abominations of the *Rougon-Macquart*. Other more subtle arguments were to appear which took the debate over Balzac's qualities a step further, or rather backwards to the notion of classicism.

The contribution of Naturalism to Balzac criticism can thus be seen in two ways. On the one hand, the assertion of a historic role for the *Comédie humaine* in determining not only the subsequent course of the novel in France but in moulding social attitudes and awareness became tightly linked with the theme of 'Balzac révolutionnaire'. This combination remains fundamentally the same today in the scholarly works of Bernard Guyon, Jean-Hervé Donnard, and (above all) Pierre Barbéris. On the other hand, the opponents of Naturalism—as will be seen in the next chapter—eventually produced those arguments which guaranteed Balzac's survival and institutionalization, that is to say the argument that Balzac was a *classic*. Whether one sees Zola's major achievement in this field as the direct establishment of Balzac's political and literary relevance or as the indirect provocation of his classicism is very much a matter of taste.

5   'Balzac classique'

THE term *classic* has been used in this book several times, and it requires some definition. The writers of classical antiquity and of the classical seventeenth century in France were seen, throughout the nineteenth century, as having analysed those aspects of human life which were not subject to change—the eternal truths of passion and love in Racine, the eternal types of humanity in Molière. The unchanging nature of their material was seen as the reason for the unchanging and eternal value of their works, and thus there was little need to distinguish what are now two quite different meanings to the word *classic*. Therefore, to point out a feature of Balzac's work as similar or parallel to the practice of one of the great dramatists of the *grand siècle* bore a very strong meaning for all of the nineteenth-century critics discussed in this book. It meant that Balzac was an author worthy of respect and study, and above all it meant that he would survive fluctuations in literary fashions. Now respect was something that was conspicuously missing from nearly all critical writing on Balzac between 1830 and 1875. There are passages even in Taine's *Étude* which are not only lacking in respect but positively sarcastic, and Zola continued to imitate his *maître à penser* in this respect even after he had moved away from his actual opinions. The establishment of Balzac's respectability, though it did not cause the notion of classicism to arise, predated its appearance in criticism by over ten years. It was without doubt a necessary preliminary to the institutionalization of the *Comédie humaine* as part of the classical literary tradition of France.

When Balzac's respectability had been at its lowest ebb in the years 1835–45, the novelist's personality was as much under attack as his works. The assumption of a close and necessary relation between the man and his work was common to all the major critics so far considered, from Sainte-Beuve to Zola, and for all of them (with the exceptions of Gautier, Baudelaire, and Barbey d'Aurevilly) Balzac was to a greater or lesser degree *taré* as a man and as a writer. The appearance of the novelist's correspondence in 1876 had a notable effect on the general image of Balzac as a man, and consequently on the view of his works. Scrutiny of letters never intended for publication is a very searching test of character: but Balzac passed this test, in the opinion of most reviewers, with flying colours. Critics were impressed by the sheer energy of the man, by his constant effort and devotion to his art, by the strange twists and tragic ending of his life; but most of all they were impressed by the warmth, sincerity and simple goodness of his heart:

Ce qui apparait d'abord, c'est une bonté immense, un cœur grand, loyal, sans détour et tendre comme une âme de jeune fille; un esprit naïf et simple.[1]

Enfant il était toujours resté par le cœur, par l'illusion, par la tendresse; aimant à la façon des enfants qui savent aimer et ne savent pas haïr.[2]

L'implacable justicier, le profond docteur que fut le Dante de la comédie humaine, était, de son vivant, *un brave homme*![3]

Sa vie fut héroïque . . .[4]

These quotations indicate the range of reaction to the *Correspondance*: from reverent admiration to pleasurable surprise. These reactions may seem a little exaggerated nowadays, but it must be remembered, first, that many letters that might have produced a different impression had been suppressed by Mme Ève de Balzac and Michel Lévy, and others had been emended with a similar intention;[5] and secondly, that the reviewers of 1876 were reacting in the context of a set of ideas about Balzac that were for the most part fundamentally incompatible with the good sides of the novelist's character that transpire from the letters. The revelation of Balzac's magnanimous character, of his 'heart of gold', could not but affect the themes of Balzac criticism and their distribution in a substantial way. It could not make the objections to the *Comédie humaine* simply evaporate: but it put the objectors in what was then the conceptually difficult necessity of separating the respective values of the man and his works.

The review written by Gaston Feugère exemplifies the awkwardness of many traditional right-wing attitudes to the *Comédie humaine* when confronted with its author's correspondence. He tries to put the least favourable interpretation possible on Balzac's letters: for example, he points out how they show the speed and volume of the novelist's production of literature, which, he says, do not match his notion of the

---

[1] Guy de Maupassant, *La Nation*, 22 Nov. 1876.
[2] Charles Bigot, *Le Journal Officiel*, 18 Nov. 1876.
[3] Henry Laujol, *La République des lettres*, 5 Nov. 1876.
[4] Barbey d'Aurevilly, *Le Constitutionnel*, 27 Nov. 1876.
[5] See R. Pierrot's introduction to vol. 1 of Balzac's *Correspondance* (Garnier, 1960), p. vii.

true artist. Balzac's personality was a shifting one; he adopted 'poses', or artificial tragi-comic roles which he played for his own amusement and conceit. He indulged in all the vices of vanity, self-glorification, self-deprecation, exaggeration, and fantasy. The letters also show how he had no stable qualities of character or intellect, but adopted new poses under the influence of the latest fashionable idea.[6] Yet despite this very unfavourable reading of most of the *Correspondance*, Feugère also praises the letters to Laure Surville and to Mme Hanska for their moving sincerity. He does not try to reconcile the emotional honesty that he praises here with what he saw as the charlatanry of the rest of the *Correspondance*. What he does state as his conclusion is that the favourable impression created by some of the letters 'ne modifierait en rien notre opinion sur la *Comédie humaine* et n'adoucirait pas la sévérité de nos conclusions, s'il fallait les formuler.'[7] These 'severe conclusions', presumably, are the reason for the critic's harsh reading of the letters in general, and so Feugère appears to be doing the opposite of what he announced at the outset of his review, that he would separate Balzac as a man from the nature of his work. Indeed, the objections that he makes to Balzac's personality are but variants of well-established themes in criticism of the novels. The reproach of vanity goes back to Théodore Muret's article of 1835; the argument that Balzac lacked a stable set of ideas and merely followed fashions or personal manias was a theme of Nettement's earlier pieces as well as of Duranty's article in *Le Réalisme*. Feugère was in fact writing for *Le Français*, a small-circulation paper of the extreme right, and thus it is likely that he adopted these themes from Pontmartin rather than from any of the other critics mentioned. They become very awkward to argue when combined with the revelation that in certain respects at least Balzac was a good and loving brother, a solicitous, passionate and patient suitor, and a 'brave homme'.

The review published by the staid but very influential *Journal officiel* was written by its regular literary editor, Charles Bigot. Théophile Gautier, who died four years before the *Correspondance* appeared, had been for many years the *Journal*'s theatre critic, and this may not be irrelevant to the new line on Balzac taken in 1876. Very simply, Bigot states that the letters show Balzac to have been a man of great moral stature, and *therefore* the novels he wrote could not have been immoral.[8] This argument is the inverse of the underlying idea of

6 *Le Français*, 12 Nov. 1876.   7 Ibid. 19 Nov. 1876.
8 Bigot, art. cit., 18 Nov. 1876.

Feugère's article, that since the novels were immoral Balzac must have had a defective personality. Bigot tries to defuse the whole issue of the morality of the Comédie humaine, first by suggesting that it had been exhaustively argued out already, and secondly by restricting the meaning of morality in works of literature to the direct effect they have on people's lives. Balzac only appeared to influence Frenchmen of the 1850s and 1860s, he says, for the July Monarchy itself had been 'gros du Second Empire'. The genius of Balzac had been to perceive the hidden forces in society that came out into the open ten and twenty years later. He had arrived at this perception not through careful observation of detail nor through painstaking documentation—the Correspondance shows that he had been far too busy to have had time for that! The novelist had reached his prophetic truths through imagination and intuition, through a truly artistic creative process, and it is for that reason that 'les peintures de Balzac se sont trouvées plus vraies après vingt années, que le jour où il les faisait'. Bigot thus makes out a case for regarding Balzac as a passive participant rather than an active force in the development of French society. He had exercised little or no direct influence over the changes in public and private morality that took place in later years, but, like all true artists, he had given society an insight into its own evolution. His only crime, if crime it was, was to help the Second Empire 'à prendre la nette conscience d'elle-même'. It would be wrong to attribute this new and favourable official view of Balzac entirely to the publication of the Correspondance, but the impression made by the letters of an honest, loving man certainly made it much easier for the Journal officiel to argue convincingly for a reassessment of the novelist's moral position. Underlying this reassessment is not only the connection with Théophile Gautier, who had for twenty years argued along those lines, but of course the change of political regime. Since the Empire was defeated it was no longer necessary to blame or attack representatives of the regime that preceded it; and there were obvious reasons for reassessing authors who had been attacked or accused under the Empire, such as Hugo and Balzac.

Before the Correspondance was published two posthumous works by Philarète Chasles appeared, and they both contained references to Balzac which are more reminiscent of the tone of 1840s criticism than of the Second Empire. According to Chasles, the novelist lacked 'la charité, la bonté, l'amour de la société où il a vécu'.[9] The theme of the

[9] La Psychologie sociale des nouveaux peuples (Charpentier, 1875) p. 139.

Comédie humaine was not the distinction of good from evil, as in Dante's *Divina Commedia*, but 'la confusion du bien et du mal'. Since literary works survive only by their recognition of moral goodness, Chasles concludes, Balzac's works were doomed to perish.[10] Barbey d'Aurevilly wrote a review of these *Mémoires* before he had read Balzac's correspondence, and though he could hardly have agreed with Chasles he was careful not to oppose too openly a man who had known Balzac intimately.[11] But in his review of the *Correspondance* itself, Barbey welcomes it as 'une immense réplique à Philarète Chasles et à tous ceux qui se sont permis de parler avec plus ou moins de renseignements et de fatuité étourdie, de l'auteur de la *Comédie humaine*'.[12] Barbey does not hide his glee at finding in the letters corroboration for his own long-standing view of Balzac as a man of great moral stature. The novelist had not been a monster, as some of his acquaintances had made out in their anecdotes; he had been a normal human being, exceptional only in the size of his intellect, creativity and character. Of all his heroes, the correspondence shows, it was Balzac himself who had been the largest, the most outstanding and the most 'romanesque'. This final point in Barbey's joyful reassertion of his views was not dissimilar to the reaction of Paul Bourget to the *Correspondance*. Like Barbey, Bourget was devoted to Balzac throughout his life. At the age of fifteen, he had been bowled over by *Le Père Goriot*, and he proceeded to model his life on what he knew of Balzac's. Thus he took to working at night, drank strong black coffee to keep himself awake as he gazed at the two busts on his desk: one of Napoléon and one of Balzac.[13] In 1876, he reviewed the *Correspondance* for the *République des lettres* (edited by Catulle Mendès), and entitled his article *Le Roman de la vie de Balzac*. The novelist, he wrote, had lived in a grandiose, epic dream, full of bizarre characters and outsize emotions.[14] The grandeur of his works was the result of the grandeur of his character and life, and in particular Balzac's energy, rapacity, and thirst for life, which he had passed on to all his fictional heroes, allowed him to create the illusion of life in art. 'Tous les hommes de Balzac sont des gloutons et de faméliques gloutons',[15] he says, echoing

---

[10] *Mémoires* (Charpentier, 1876) I. 303–8.

[11] *Le Constitutionnel*, 31 Oct. 1876.

[12] Ibid. 27 Nov. 1876.

[13] See Bourget's *Nouvelles Pages de critique et de doctrine* (Plon-Nourrit, 1922), pp. 40–2 for autobiographical detail; further information in L. J. Austin, *Paul Bourget* (Droz, 1940), pp. 81–85.

[14] *La République des lettres*, 24 Dec. 1876, p. 2.   [15] Ibid., p. 5.

Baudelaire's thought ('chargés de volonté jusqu'à la gueule') and syntax ('visionnaire, et visionnaire passionné'). Bourget proceeds in this review article to give a biography of Balzac, which is sketchy, careless, and slipshod, even allowing for the deficiencies in his sources. None the less he succeeds, like René Benjamin fifty years later,[16] in communicating an immense admiration for the novelist and in writing an exuberantly romantic tale of a great man battling with the cruelty and incomprehension of ordinary life. For Bourget as for Baudelaire the author of the *Comédie humaine* was 'un héros de la volonté, aux prises avec l'adversité'.

Bourget's principal contribution to the remarkable change in attitudes that came to the fore in reviews of the *Correspondance* was to introduce sympathy for Balzac as a man; whilst the *Journal officiel* had removed the still-present suspicion of immorality. Léopold Derôme, a journalist with a bent for the literary archaeology of the romantic period, used the *Correspondance* to compose a sober and more respectable account of Balzac's life. He too lays emphasis on the novelist's energy, on the incredible volume of his literary production, and on his devotion to his work. Though peppered with jibes at some of Balzac's more outlandish pretentions, Derôme's biography was a serious and respectable piece of work, and made a large contribution to establishing the new official myth of 'Balzac, brave homme'.[17]

The Naturalists did not make much noise about the *Correspondance* when it appeared, for the impression Balzac gave in his letters hardly fitted Zola's nascent literary system. Zola did actually review the publication for the St. Petersburg *Viestnik Evropi* (European Messenger)[18] and fragments of this article appeared in French in 1877.[19] Like Bourget's article, Zola's piece does not bear comparison with Derôme's; and he later admitted that it was entirely unworthy of its subject.[20] What he emphasized in this article was the goodness of Balzac's soul—like nearly all other reviewers of the *Correspondance*; and he criticized the lack of clarity in Balzac's mind, as he was to do more and more in his literary campaign of 1878–81. The only other

---

[16] *La Prodigieuse Vie d'Honoré de Balzac* (Plon, 1925) which inspired the most erudite and thorough of Balzac's modern publishers with his first passion for the *Comédie humaine*.

[17] Published in *Le Soleil*, 11, 16, and 28 Jan. 15 Feb., and 2 Mar. 1877.

[18] Issue of January 1877.

[19] In *Le Bien Public*, 16, 23, and 30 July 1877; in *Le Figaro*, 11 Mar. 1880; in *Le Voltaire*, 27 July and 3 Aug. 1880.

[20] *Les Romanciers naturalistes* (Charpentier, 1881), p. 2.

Naturalist article on the correspondence was a compilation of quotations by the obscure Philippe Gille.[21] The usual team of active polemicists—Céard, Alexis, Huysmans, Guillemot—do not appear to have made any attempt to bring Balzac's *Correspondance* into the Naturalist scheme of things. There is little in these letters to uphold Zola's line on the *Comédie humaine*: little evidence of the patient accumulation of detail, no evidence of left-wing politics or of the desire to found a literary school; and a lot of sentimental effusion. When Zola's *L'Assommoir* appeared in 1877, creating an uproar and scandal as great as that which had greeted the publication of *Madame Bovary* twenty years before, no mention was made of Balzac. The absence of comment and comparison shows how far the *Journal officiel* had succeeded in defusing the question of morality in the *Comédie humaine*. Thanks to the impression created by his letters, Balzac was no longer associated automatically with any literary development that tended towards the scandalous. He had become, in a word, respectable.

Balzac's respectability was not only negative in the 1870s, in the sense that he was not naturally brought to mind by 'immoral', 'obscene' or otherwise unrespectable publications, but also positive, in that he was increasingly considered a subject worthy of study and scholarship. The wealthy Belgian Vicomte Spoelberch de Lovenjoul had already begun his task of collecting and cataloguing Balzac's publications and manuscripts, and of course Champfleury had been publishing fragments of unknown early works since the 1850s. These early Balzacians were joined in the 1870s by several other writers: Léopold Derôme, Descauriet, A.-J. Pons. In 1879, Calmann-Lévy published Lovenjoul's *Histoire des œuvres de Balzac* as a supplement to the definitive edition of the *Comédie humaine*, and a second, much enlarged edition came out in 1886. In that year also Cerfberr and Christophe published their idiosyncratic but painstakingly compiled biographical dictionary of the characters of Balzac's novels.[22] This too went into a second edition, with a preface by Paul Bourget.[23] By 1886–7, nothing could have seemed more remote from the continuing polemics over the Naturalist novel than the *Comédie humaine*.

As early as 1880 Zola seems to have realized that Balzac was somehow escaping his attempts to appropriate him. His proposal that a

[21] Source unknown; reprinted in *La Bataille littéraire* (Havard, 1889), pp. 271–80.

[22] *Répertoire des personnages de la 'Comédie humaine'* (Calmann-Lévy, 1886).

[23] Bourget's preface first published separately in the *Journal des débats*, 2 Feb. 1886.

monument to the author of *Le Père Goriot* should be erected[24] appears to derive from a desire to espouse the changing nature of Balzac's reputation and to present himself as the grateful inheritor of the Balzacian tradition. Nothing came of this particular proposal, just as nothing had come of Alexandre Dumas's attempt to launch a subscription for a Balzac monument in 1854.[25] It was the novelist's widow, Ève de Balzac, who had been directly responsible for quashing Dumas's efforts: she had sued the author of *Monte-Cristo* on the grounds that Balzac's name was her legal property, and had won the nominal damages of one franc.[26] She had also been responsible for quashing Armand Baschet's efforts in 1853 to gather and publish Balzac's correspondence,[27] and for the many delays in the eventual publication of the letters by Calmann-Lévy. In 1882, however, after a long illness, the old lady died, leaving huge debts (mostly due to the profligacy of her daughter, Anna Mniszech). Her creditors pillaged the Hôtel Beaujon, with its treasure of manuscripts, proofs, letters, and *inédits*, before the bailiffs could put legal seals on the property, and thus only part of Balzac's papers were publicly auctioned at the Hôtel Drouot. Lovenjoul rushed to Paris from Brussels, and found that some of the manuscripts had been bought by their weight and pulped down; others were rescued from butchers' shops and even from hotel toilets.[28] There was a good deal of journalistic comment on the fate of Balzac's papers, and though many of the stories told may well have been invented they are symptomatic of the rank then accorded to the novelist —that of one of France's national glories.

Since the articles on the sacking of the Hôtel Beaujon and the sale at the Hôtel Drouot were published in the news columns, they were mostly written by reporters and political journalists rather than by the newspapers' literary columnists. Thus the collection of articles appearing in 1882 are interesting as evidence of a general, non-specialist attitude to the *Comédie humaine*, in the same way that the theatre

[24] *Le Figaro*, 6 Dec. 1880.

[25] See *Le Mousquetaire*, 15 Mar. 1854, and subsequent issues.

[26] *Le Mousquetaire*, 5 May 1854.

[27] Barbey d'Aurevilly was in fact the author of the letter signed by Ève's business factotum, Dutacq, which threatened legal proceedings against Baschet. Published in *Le Siècle*, 8 Dec. 1853; original (delightfully vitriolic) draft in Barbey's hand in the Lovenjoul Library, Chantilly, A. 274, fo. 17. Baschet's request for the novelist's letters made in *Paris*, 23 Nov. 1853; see *Le Mousquetaire*, 8 Dec. 1853. See also my article on 'Barbey et les *Pensées* de Balzac' in the *Cahiers Barbey D'Aurevilly* (forthcoming).

[28] These details given by R. de Bonnières in *Le Figaro*, 3 July 1882 and Henry Céard in *L'Express*, 22 June 1882.

reviews of the 1860s were seen to express the conventional or standard themes of that period. Secondly, of course, the authorship of these news items accounts for the reintroduction of political polemic into Balzac criticism. Most journalists wrote long laments on the loss of Balzac's papers; Jules Vallès alone thought that they were unimportant, saying that 'ses livres suffisent pour qu'on le connaisse'.[29] For the novelist Robert Caze, however, Balzac was 'une école pour nous'[30]; for Robert de Bonnières, his reputation 'ne pouvait guère s'augmenter davantage' even by the publication of his *inédits*. Bonnières refers to Balzac as a 'rude réactionnaire'; this is the first example of right-wing acceptance of the novelist's monarchism and catholicism since 1850, with the exception of Barbey d'Aurevilly's many articles. Another journalist had already argued that Balzac was neither reactionary nor revolutionary, but a moderate political theorist. This was an entirely new theme of criticism. Balzac's absolutism, it is argued, was a mere mask, 'et il n'était au fond qu'un partisan très sensé et très-réfléchi du gouvernement des classes moyennes, un homme convaincu qu'il fallait tenir compte des changements accomplis dans la société moderne, et ne pas songer à restaurer le passé ... Son respect pour la légitimité, son culte pour l'aristocratie n'était qu'une attitude, qu'une pose, une affectation littéraire.'[31] Many critics had argued that Balzac's absolutism was more part of literature than of politics (Taine and Zola, for example) but none had argued before that the novelist was 'really' a safe and moderate writer. Even allowing for the fact that the journalist in question was attempting an appropriation of the *Comédie humaine* to his newspaper's faction, this new theme of criticism was highly significant. The mere possibility of making such a claim before the publication of the *Correspondance* in 1876 did not exist.

Balzac's image with critics and journalists between 1876 and 1882 was undergoing a process of sterilization—no longer immoral, no longer politically dangerous—and this process was taking place during Zola's campaign for the naturalist novel, which came to an end in 1881, since, as he said, 'j'ai senti que je m'encanaillais'.[32] This campaign had been far from neutral in morality and politics and it involved Balzac to a great extent. However, it was not until 1883 that these implicitly anti-naturalist evaluations of Balzac as a safe and moderate writer produced themes of criticism concerned with the actual

---

[29] *Le Réveil*, 26 June 1882.   [30] Ibid. 23 June 1882.

[31] L. Joly, *Le Moniteur universel*, 21 Jan. 1877.

[32] Letter to Jules Troubat, 5 Nov. 1881; *Correspondance* (Charpentier, 1908), II. 192.

nature of his novels, and they arose out of the need to distinguish the *Comédie humaine* not from the *Rougon-Macquart* but from the novels of Alexandre Dumas père. The creator of the *Three Musketeers* was about to be honoured by a statue in the Place Malesherbes, but many journalists, commenting on this forthcoming event, thought it wrong to honour Dumas without first honouring Balzac. However, Dumas fils was able to organize a powerful lobby in his father's favour and the Société des gens de lettres agreed to raise the funds for the Dumas monument. By the end of 1883, however, the Société launched an appeal to commission a Balzac monument as well.[33] The arguments in the press for and against Balzac and Dumas had nothing to do with Naturalism, but produced an argument of supreme utility to the anti-Naturalists.

Albert Delpit, a close friend of Dumas père in earlier years, claimed that Balzac had sunk into obscurity whilst the fame of the author of *Monte-Cristo* had grown constantly since his death in 1870. The reason was that the *Comédie humaine* was restricted to a single moment in French history, and its descriptions of clothes, furnishings, and so on had become obscure with the changing of fashions. Dumas, on the other hand, 'a lâché la bride à son imagination féconde. Il a raconté, non pas une époque spéciale, mais des drames de tous les temps . . .'[34] The claim is made, here, that Dumas is classical in that his subjects are eternally interesting ('des drames de tous les temps') even if the phrase might be more accurate if it were read as meaning 'dramas from all periods of French history'. Delpit goes on to praise Sainte-Beuve's 'finesse pénétrante' in predicting Balzac's obscurity. Among younger writers, he says, there are many who have scarcely any knowledge of the *Comédie humaine*. 'Excepté *Les Parents pauvres* et *Eugénie Grandet*, ils n'ont rien lu du grand romancier . . . mais ils connaissent Dumas par cœur!' By 'la jeune génération littéraire' Delpit does not mean the younger Naturalist writers, presumably, nor Paul Bourget; but Joris-Karl Huysmans, who broke away from the Médan group in 1884 with *À Rebours*, gives a degree of corroboration to Delpit's claim. Des Esseintes, the hero of *À Rebours*

avait naguère adoré le grand Balzac, mais en même temps que son organisme s'était déséquilibré . . . ses inclinations s'étaient modifiées. . . . Bientôt même,

---

[33] The president of the society, Emmanuel Gonzalès, had been one of Balzac's detractors in the 1830s (see p. 9) and he delivered a very ambiguous appeal for funds (see *L'Évènement*, 22 Nov. 1883). Gonzalès died the following year, and this, the third project for a Balzac monument, also lapsed. [34] *Le Figaro*, 21 June 1883.

et quoiqu'il se rendît compte de son injustice envers le prodigieux auteur de la *Comédie humaine*, il était venu à ne plus ouvrir ses livres dont l'art valide le froissait.[35]

Delpit's argument that Balzac was dated and unreadable was repeated by many of the journalists in the Dumas lobby, such as Jules Poignand.[36] The counter-argument, that Balzac's achievement was not subject to changing fashions, was put by Gustave Geffroy, a journalist close to Zola but somewhat more independent than most of the younger Naturalists. Geffroy worked on George Clemenceau's newspaper, *La Justice*, and though he thus met the politically sympathetic Médan group a great deal, 'il s'en fit peu à peu le critique, tel un nouveau Sainte-Beuve'.[37] The value of the *Comédie humaine*, he wrote, did not lie in its historical and documentary veracity, but in its creation of universal types and its treatment of general passions. The historical accuracy of its descriptions, in Geffroy's view, did not date the work but acted as an adjunct to its general truth 'qui est la vérité humaine'.[38] Geffroy was not the first critic to mention 'universal types' in the context of Balzac criticism—Louis Lurine had compared the character of Mercadet to Molière's Harpagon in 1851[39]—but from Geffroy's reply to Delpit until the end of the century the nature of Balzac's characterization was presented as the link between the *Comédie humaine* and the classical tradition of French literature. Twenty years later, Geffroy repeated his point in English for the New York *International Quarterly*:

It cannot be denied, it seems to me, that there is a tie which unites the author of the *Comédie humaine* to the French classics of the XVIIth century. He has their precision, their philosophy, their conclusions. Like them, he defines characters in the struggle with life, like them he analyzes emotions. He differs from them in this way, in that he fills in by his definiteness and his amplitude the role of historian . . .[40]

A few weeks after Geffroy's original statement of this theme, another journalist seized upon it to attack the Naturalist novels of Alphonse Daudet. Daudet's characters were slavishly copied from real-life models, it was claimed, whereas Balzac had created *types*. The younger

---

[35] *À Rebours* (Crès, 1922), p. 233.
[36] In *Le Gaulois*, 23 Nov. 1883 (over the signature Montjoyeux).
[37] Charles Beuchat, *Histoire du Naturalisme français* (Corrêa, 1949), II. 335.
[38] *La Justice*, 25 June 1883.
[39] *Le Messager de l'Assemblée*, 2 Sept. 1851.
[40] 'Émile Zola', *International Quarterly* (New York), VI. 370–1 (Dec. 1902).

Thiers had been a springboard for the creation of Rastignac, but Rastignac was much more than Thiers. Had Daudet written *Le Père Goriot*, 'il nous aurait donné un Thiers aussi exact qu'il nous a donné un duc de Morny irréfutable'. Balzac's characters are immortal, the critic argues, because they are types made up of details from diverse individual sources.[41]

The theme of Balzac's classicism was then present in criticism of the early 1880s, and its two first realizations in this period are in articles that attempt to separate Balzac from a representative of Romanticism (Dumas) and a representative of Naturalism (Daudet). In 1887, Émile Faguet published a study of the novelist which argued from beginning to end that Balzac's qualities lay in his 'réalisme classique'. This witty and clever article had as much importance for Balzac criticism as did Taine's *Étude* of 1858, and it merits a detailed analysis.

Balzac was not a writer without faults, in Faguet's assessment. He had a double character, half artistic, half vulgar, but it is in the artist that the critic is principally interested. None the less, he does deal in a fairly sweeping way with what he calls the 'romanesque' side of Balzac's work—all those features of novel-structure, story, characterization, and description which he considers inherently *invraisemblable*. The plots of *Splendeurs et misères* and of *Histoire des Treize* fall into this category of 'romanesque', as does the characterization of Madame de Mortsauf in *Le Lys dans la vallée* and the nature-worship of that novel. These features can be excused as the result of romantic influence on Balzac. The countryside descriptions of *Le Lys*, Faguet suggests, 'sont bien dans le tour d'esprit des paysagistes de 1830 et nous les verrons plus tard s'épanouir, se gonfler, s'étendre et devenir, chez un "romantique" sans le vouloir, l'énorme et fantastique *Paradou* de *La Faute de l'Abbé Mouret*'.[42] Faguet is here striking at the heart of Zola's public image, and of his self-image too in all probability. Romanticism was what Zola rejected in favour of a development of Balzac's realism; and thus to show (or to claim) that the real link between the two novelists was in their exaggeratedly romantic attitude to nature was to remove all credibility from Zola's version of literary history, and by implication to destroy his arguments for naturalism in the novel. Other critics had tried to score this sort of point, but with much less success than Faguet. Brunetière, for example, had seized on Zola's failure to understand Balzac's admiration for the historical and romantic novels

---

[41] A. Racot, *La Revue générale* (Brussels), Aug. 1883.
[42] Émile Faguet, *Études littéraires sur le XIXe siècle* (Lecène et Oudin, 1887), 424.

of Walter Scott. Local colour, detail, *milieu* entered the novel through Scott's historical fictions, Brunetière states, and Balzac had done for France what Scott had done for English literature: thus his admiration for the author of the Waverley novels.[43] This argument does not turn the tables on Zola as Faguet's did, even if it does show up his ignorance. The strong romantic element in Zola's early novels (before the *Rougon-Macquart*) had been commented on by another critic, who suggested 'period' subtitles for these works—'*Thérèse Raquin, ou la friture criminelle; Madeleine Férat, ou le noyé inopportun* . . . qui feraient la fortune d'un faiseur de l'ancien Ambigu.'[44] Faguet was, however, the first to point out that the streak of romantic exaggeration, of melodrama, of artifice, was common to Zola and Balzac, and that this, as much as the alleged continuity of method in observation of reality and materialistic determinism, could be seen to constitute the real tradition of the nineteenth-century novel in France. This streak was, Faguet states clearly, one of Balzac's faults, but which could be accounted for and excused by the literary atmosphere of the period in which he lived. The reader can infer that Zola's indulgence in romantic fantasies cannot be explained in this way, since he lived in a different era, and that it constitutes a deliberate pandering to the lower tastes of the reading public. This is a much more persuasive denunciation of Zola as an artist than the well-worn theme of Zola's immorality and his debasement of Balzac's techniques of realism.

This argument against Zola is, however, only incidental to Faguet's main case in favour of Balzac. Balzac, he maintains, was a realist in the classical sense. He did not invent literary realism—for it constitutes the great tradition of French literature from Racine and Molière on. Brunetière, in his Sorbonne lecture of 1882,[45] had already spoken of 'Le Naturalisme au XVIIe siècle'. True Naturalism, he considered, was the treatment of universal human types and passions. The object of Brunetière's argument was, of course, to deny Zola the use even of the term *Naturalism*, and not to reinterpret seventeenth-century literature in any particular way. Faguet's notion of classical realism is, in essence, similar to Brunetière's definition of seventeenth-century naturalism, but the use to which he put it rose above mere polemic.

'Le Réalisme', for Faguet, meant presenting the fundamental issues

---

[43] 'Les Origines du roman naturaliste', *RDM* 15 Sept. 1881.
[44] J. Levallois, in *L'Opinion nationale*, 9 Feb. 1869.
[45] Reprinted in *Études critiques* (2nd edition, Hachette, 1888), vol. 1.

of human life in a manner as impersonal as possible. Flaubert had failed to reach the standard of Molière's realism, for the novelist had tinged all his works with his own personal, supercilious irony, thus robbing them of any universal value. Not all of Balzac's works have this universality, and where they fail to meet the standards of classical realism they must be discarded. Only a small part of the *Comédie humaine* can, in Faguet's view, be considered great literature, but this small part is well worth examining. It is not impossible to reconcile this viewpoint with an acceptance of the unitary framework of the *Comédie humaine*, or with the realization that it is more than a series of disparate novels, but it would have been impossible for Faguet to argue that the entire Balzacian opus was of a classical realism—there was too much evidence to the contrary. The notion of classical realism did, on the other hand, permit Faguet to perceive the inequalities in Balzac's works that have often escaped more recent critics. The concept of 'classical realism' is then both an historical abstraction of the qualities that are common to writers admitted to be great; an evaluative tool that allows the chaff to be sorted from the wheat; and a normative rule that Faguet prescribes for the guidance of young writers: '... le réalisme bien entendu est le soutien solide et ferme où l'imagination doit s'appuyer avant de partir, et pour mieux partir'.[46] Classical realism is, in Faguet's view, much more of a general orientation than a set of rules, devices or specific features: 'L'art réaliste consiste à voir exactement, et sans passion, les choses et les hommes, et à les peindre de même.'[47] It might be objected that such a definition is so general as to be useless as a critical tool. It is a definition, also, which leaves immense scope for subjective variations: no two men will necessarily agree whether Balzac, for example, depicted French society 'exactly' and without passion, and political prejudices remain as likely as any to sway the final judgement. None the less, it does represent a considerable step forward in the context of critical method. It escapes the ambiguities and historical strait-jacket of Taine; it is not overtly political, like Brunetière's *ad hoc* methods of literary jousting; and it provides a general framework into which diverse themes can be fitted without systematic distortion.

What Balzac saw exactly and without passion, Faguet thinks, was human society, not as a collection of individuals, but as a body. He portrayed men in groups, obeying group influences. Men considered in groups often follow baser instincts than they would appear to do as

[46] Faguet, op. cit., p. 453.   [47] Ibid., p. 434.

individuals, and thus, Faguet argues, Balzac's apparent concentration on the evil sides of human nature is justifiable, accurate, and necessary. The apparent weakness of his virtuous heroines and good characters generally is likewise not a fault but the result of his exact perception of society: good men and women always do appear a little *niais* in real life.[48]

Realism does not have anything to do with the faithful listing of the external minutiae of objects and appearances, in Faguet's analysis. True, Balzac did believe that the external features of men and objects constituted invaluable indications of their inner souls and essences: but this does not justify or explain the mass of detail that Balzac put into his descriptions, nor does it entitle the detail to be considered an integral part of realism. 'La vérité est qu'il aime les choses, dans tout le détail de leur physionomie, et s'attarde à les decrire parce qu'il s'y amuse infiniment.'[49]

It is in the characterization of his major personages that Balzac appears to Faguet to approach most nearly the ideal of classical realism. Old Grandet, Old Goriot, Balthazar Claës, Baron Hulot, and so on, are powerful and memorable because of their simple contours. More than mere monomaniacs, they are pure, classical types—purer even than Molière's Harpagon, who possessed the complicating factor of being in love as well as being a miser. Balzac's characterization, then, had nothing to do with nineteenth-century '*réalisme*' *à la Duranty*, but was a pure expression of the French classical tradition.[50] Faguet does not suggest that Balzac was able to use this kind of simple characterization only because he provided richness and diversity in other ways—in descriptions, namely, of an eminently nineteenth-century *réaliste* brand.

Where Balzac departs from the canon of classical realism, Faguet considers him worthless—in his liking for exaggeratedly brutal characters, such as Vautrin and Valérie Marneffe,[51] in his atrociously badly carpentered novel-structures,[52] in his over-lengthy expositions which are not 'du réalisme' but merely 'du bavardage',[53] and in his frequent lapses of taste, of language, and of style. All of this must be cast aside, and only novels such as *Eugénie Grandet* and *Le Cousin Pons* can be considered true examples of Balzac's genius.

Faguet's article, though much shorter, can be compared in quality and importance to Taine's 1858 *Étude sur Balzac*. The passage of thirty

48 Ibid., pp. 427–31.   49 Ibid., p. 425.   50 Ibid., p. 440.
51 Ibid., p. 437.   52 Ibid., p. 446.   53 Ibid., p. 447.

years' time between them is sharply evident, for whereas Taine fought with crusading fervour in favour of a much-maligned novelist, Faguet is attempting, with a great deal more calm and reasoned argument, to assess the real value of a much-praised but little-appreciated figure in the history of the French novel. Faguet's literary judgement rests, in the last analysis, on a much firmer sense of taste and tradition than does Taine's, it seems to me. Where Balzac can be argued into the comforting, seemingly immutable framework of classical literature, Faguet is prepared to accept him; where he cannot, Faguet is equally ready to discount him. The fact that so much of Balzac's work could be considered 'classical', even in the broad sense that Faguet used the term, would not have occurred to Taine—and would indeed have seemed incompatible with his theory of literary creation.

One of the themes of criticism which Faguet attempted to neutralize was the proposition that Balzac wrote badly. Sainte-Beuve, Flaubert, Maupassant, and above all Faguet's rival and colleague Ferdinand Brunetière had at different times used this argument to deny value to the *Comédie humaine*. There was a considerable change in the way this theme was used in 1880s. Faguet's comments on it resolve nothing, of course, but tend to defuse the issue, just as Bigot's remarks on Balzac's morality, in the *Journal officiel* of 1876, simply dismissed the question as no longer relevant. Of course the novelist wrote badly, Faguet admits, but it hardly matters. His style has to be discarded together with much of what he wrote; but the *Comédie humaine* still contains enough material of the first order for it to survive as a classical monument of French fiction.

Defenders of Balzac's use of language had been few before the 1880s: only Francis Girault, Louis de Cormenin, Hippolyte Taine and Théophile Gautier, had written favourably on the subject. The latter had also defended the novelist's right to invent the language he required to express his material and thought: 'Il avait, bien qu'il ne le crût pas, un style et un très-beau style,—le style nécéssaire, fatal et mathématique de son idée.'[54] Paul Bourget later took up this argument and attempted to show that the novelist 'avait un style de premier ordre'. Balzac cannot be blamed for not having 'la phrase sobre et simple d'un La Bruyère et d'un Pascal'; in order to express his complex, modern world he needed a language that was 'opulente et complexe, qui ne redoutât ni les termes techniques, ni les formules d'argot—une

---

[54] Théophile Gautier, 'Préface', in the later issue of the 1855 Houssiaux edition of Balzac's *Œuvres complètes*.

langue à longues et larges périodes . . .'[55] It is thus the harmony between the 'fond' of Balzac's novels and the 'forme' of his language that Bourget, like Gautier, sees as giving quality to his style. Correspondingly, the wide range of subject and mood in the *Comédie humaine* created a wide range of different styles, and this diversity was what disconcerted earlier critics: 'Le seul malheur de Balzac, c'est qu'il est trop touffu et trop riche, et que tous les tons se rencontrent sous sa plume, sa rhétorique déconcerte nos jugements traditionnels.'[56]

The rejection of the idea of 'style' as a particular kind of literary language goes back to the romantics, and was not unfamiliar to Sainte-Beuve; but it took a long time to percolate down to the general run of journalists and critics who contributed to Balzac criticism. After Bourget's article, the diversity of Balzac's stylistic registers and the harmony between his style and his subjects become frequent, indeed regular features of journalistic comment. In the news items on the saga of Balzac's statue in 1883, one writer exclaims '. . . de quelle souplesse [la langue de Balzac] est douée, et quels effets étonnants elle arrive à produire'.[57] In a later chapter of the same saga, in 1887, Maurice Talmeyr proposed a distinction between 'le style' et 'la correction'. Style consists of expressive and picturesque natural language, he argues, and in that sense Balzac has style.[58] Talmeyr was a cultural nationalist, and he introduces an element of eccentric patriotism into his notion of style by the examples he gives: characters such as Corentin, Peyrade, and Marche-à-terre (all from *Les Chouans*) 'have style', in that they too are picturesque and expressive of the French soul. It is at this point that Balzac criticism departs into the realm of mild lunacy, which the anti-Dreyfusards rendered acute in later years. The novelist became the incarnation of Frenchness, and *Les Chouans* was reinterpreted as an anti-republican tract: thus a certain Dr. Henri Favre declared that Balzac was 'celui des nôtres qui se dresse le plus droitement en face de la Germanie au nom de la race, par la valeur du génie, par la portée l'œuvre. . . . C'est à titre de Celte que j'ai à propos de rappeler l'œuvre de Balzac, . . . (etc.).'[59]

A more serious, if less picturesque, attempt to account for the nature of Balzac's style was made by Maurice Souriau, a critic who,

---

[55] P. Bourget, *Le Parlement*, 29 Nov. 1883. [56] Ibid.

[57] André Theuriet, *Le Parlement*, 10 Dec. 1883.

[58] *Le National*, 4 May 1887. Cf. Alexandre Weill, *Introduction à mes mémoires* (Dentu, 1890), p. 141: 'Le style n'est pas dans la langue mais dans le caractère de l'homme'.

[59] *La France en éveil* (Marpon et Flammarion, 1888), pp. 4–5.

like Faguet, was also an academic. He sees two main reasons for the
faults in the language of the *Comédie humaine*: the speed with which the
novels were written, and the epoch in which Balzac learnt to write.
The novelist's neologisms and pseudo-scientific terms were typical of
the fashionable language of the First Empire, and he can hardly be
blamed for adopting the fashions of his (very early) youth.[60] Souriau
and Faguet do not go as far as Bourget in re-evaluating Balzac's language, but the way in which they deal with the problem is significant.
Faguet simply sweeps the question aside; Souriau takes the sting out of
the view that Balzac wrote badly by explaining why he wrote the
French he did.

One aspect of the *Comédie humaine* that Faguet hardly mentions in
his 1887 article is that the novels are linked together by the reappearing
characters. Maurice Souriau's long-winded and ponderous study,
which came out the following year, can be seen as an extension and
correction of Faguet, in this and other respects. Balzac's dénouements
are classed by the critic as one of the 'durable beauties' of his work, for
they are supremely living. Death is the only end to a story from life,
so a novel drawn from life must either leave the reader's curiosity un-
satisfied or end in a hecatomb which strains the reader's belief. Balzac,
he says, solved this problem by the grandiose plan of his *Comédie
humaine*. Each novel leads into another, and they do not need therefore the artificial endings of other romantic fictions; and the reader's
curiosity can be satisfied by reading the next novel. This is just like
life, Souriau argues, and constitutes one of the greatest advances ever
made in novelistic technique.

Another of the 'durable beauties' which Souriau pedantically lists
(after a long section on the 'défaillances de l'œuvre') is Balzac's depiction of 'strong' or forceful characters, in particular Vautrin.
Faguet had continued to pour scorn on this aspect of the novels, as so
many critics had done before him, and Souriau here seems to be aiming
his reassessment directly against Faguet. For it is in the paragraphs on
Vautrin that he rejects specifically the idea that Balzac had created
'types' in a classical mould: the arch-criminal was admirable, according
to Souriau, not for his eternal characteristics, but for the concrete detail
and reality of his description. The two poles of humanity in the universe
of the *Comédie humaine* were the 'hommes forts' and the 'femmes de
trente ans', and it is Vautrin who is the real hero of the entire work.

[60] *La Revue de l'enseignement secondaire et de l'enseignement supérieur*, X. 100–7; 1
Sept. 1888.

The third of the 'durable beauties' that Souriau gives also represents an inversion of a traditional theme of criticism. Balzac's descriptions are not mere *hors d'œuvre*, but essential elements in the novelist's analysis of the human mind; they thus constitute a large part of his novels' qualities. Balzac, he says, was in all things a spiritualist: 'il cherche partout la trace de l'âme dans les choses, et dans l'âme la trace des choses'.[61] Now the use of the label *spiritualist* in literary polemic in 1888 was loaded with political associations, and it reveals the fundamental anti-Naturalist orientation of Souriau. Taine had made the same point as Souriau, of course; but the way in which Balzac linked the outer appearance and inner nature of men and things in his descriptions had been thought of as materialism and determinism in the 1840s and 1850s. Souriau terms it spiritualism in order to associate Balzac with fashions acceptable to the right and above all totally un-acceptable to Zola. A similar example of 'loaded labelling' was provided a few years earlier by Melchior de Vogüé, the first translator of Tolstoy and Dostoievsky into French. In his general book on the Russian novel, Vogüé relates his material to the history of French literature. Realism, he writes, originated with Flaubert and reached its nadir in Zola (he does not use the term 'naturalism' in this context at all). The great Russian novelists had taken nothing from French realism, but were the true inheritors of the classical, idealist novel of Balzac. The *Comédie humaine*, he continues, had no historical or documentary in-terest at all; its value lay in its general truth. '*Suivant les préceptes de l'art classique*, ses personnages de premier plan sont poussés tout entiers vers une seule passion; voyez Nucingen, Balthazar Claës, etc.'[62] Thus Balzac comes to be not a naturalist, realist ('synonyme courant de lit-térature infâme', according to Faguet), or even romantic writer, but 'le plus fougueux de nos idéalistes'.[63] The reaction against Zola's novels and against his view of Balzac underlies all these examples of misleading labelling, and there is no doubt that this reaction would have been less strong had the author of the *Rougon-Macquart* been less clearly associated with republican politics. For all its crudeness and all its faults, Zola's 'Naturalist Balzac' did not produce anything quite as lunatic as the following piece, which sums up the underlying motivation of many of the anti-Naturalist critics of the 1880s and 1890s:

Tout ce que depuis trente ans, nous lisons de sain, d'honnête et de beau, est inspiré par Balzac. Tout de qu'il y a de bas, d'impur, d'abject dans notre

---

[61] *La Revue de l'enseignement secondaire et de l'enseignement supérieur*, X. 139.
[62] *Le Roman russe* (Plon, 1886), pp. xxix–xxx. [63] Ibid., p. xxix.

littérature courante provient de ses *prétendus* disciples: faux-Goncourts, faux-Flauberts, faux-Zolas qui—grâce à la complicité d'un certain public— battent monnaie sous le couvert de son nom et de son immortalité.[64]

The themes of criticism that come to the fore in the years 1875–90 in writing not directly or openly concerned with Naturalism are, then, three in number. First, in response to the publication of the novelist's letters, the theme of 'Balzac, brave homme' was widely propagated. This corresponded of course to the views of Gautier, Baudelaire, and Barbey d'Aurevilly in earlier years, but in the later 1870s it made acceptable the view that his works were not immoral. Secondly, the theme of Balzac as a romantic, 'romanesque' hero, also becomes noticeable after the appearance of the *Correspondance*, and the most notable proponent of this cult of Balzac was the fashionable novelist Paul Bourget. The third theme, by far the most important, was that Balzac was not the initiator of the Naturalist novel. To state this as a positive rather than as a negative proposition, Vogüé called him an idealist, Souriau used the term spiritualist, and Faguet invented the all-important notion of classical realism. Faguet's idea was not completely original, as we have seen: very few influential expressions of ideas ever are entirely new. Nor can it be claimed that attaching the label *classic* to the *Comédie humaine* was solely or uniquely responsible for the official acceptance and institutionalization of Balzac that occurred in the following years. None the less, it seems obvious that the idea that he was a classic was a more powerful contribution to Balzac's inclusion among the great and 'teachable' authors of *la critique universitaire* than the topical, fashionable labels put forward by Vogüé, Souriau, and others. The underlying motivation of Faguet in his study of Balzac was to discredit Zola, and this motivation was only in part of a literary nature.

At the beginning of the previous chapter it was claimed that Balzac became a classic to save him from being a Naturalist. This bald statement can now be refined a little. By the mid-1880's, Naturalism was associated on the one hand with 'littérature infâme' and on the other with republicanism and socialism; at the same time the history of literature was becoming a subject taught far more widely and at different levels, under the impact of the educational reforms of Jules Ferry.

---

[64] J.-Nicolas Brusse, in *L'Indépendent littéraire*, 15 July 1888. Naturalist lunacy was of a milder kind: see Jules Christophe, in *La Revue indépendante*, Sept. 1884, and Maurice Guillemot, in *La Revue moderne et naturaliste*, 1 Feb. 1880.

Moral criticism of contemporary fiction was still very much the order of the day, and school and university textbooks of the period present *moral truth* as the factor common to all great literary works of the past.[65] In such conditions Balzac could have sunk into the sort of obscurity enjoyed at that time by Sand, Dumas, and Stendhal; or he could have been presented in a footnote simply as what Zola said he was, one of the precursors of Naturalism. However, this would have meant the absence of all post-revolutionary fiction from the canon of modern classics; and it would not have made any easier the task of demonstrating the decadence of the contemporary novel. Stendhal took rather longer to rehabilitate (though he did have a university thesis devoted to him before Balzac[66]) and it is no doubt because the Naturalists had written so much more about the *Comédie humaine* than about *La Chartreuse de Parme* that Balzac was the first to be institutionalized. In 1886, before Faguet's study appeared, the Académie Française accepted Balzac at last, and set for its *prix d'éloquence* the subject: *L'Œuvre d'Honoré de Balzac*. The winning entry, by a young lawyer called Augustin Cabat, was published in 1888 and entirely deserved this comment from one reviewer: 'Si Cabat voulait s'habituer à penser un peu par lui-même, il irait loin, car ce qu'il pense, il l'exprime souvent très-bien.'[67] In 1889 *Eugénie Grandet* was added to the list of works 'which must be known by all candidates for the *agrégation de l'enseignement secondaire spécial.*'[68] Thus all specialist *lycée* teachers graduating in the 1890s had a knowledge of at least one Balzac novel— and indeed the one that had not only enjoyed a high reputation from Sainte-Beuve's article of 1834, but which even the most venomous of critics, Chaudes-Aigues, had likened to Moliere's *L'Avare*.[69] The link between Faguet's establishment of the classical nature of Balzac's genius and his institutionalization as a 'classic' in the school text sense cannot be illustrated more clearly than by the choice of *Eugénie Grandet* for the *agrégation* reading list.

[65] Before Faguet, Sainte-Beuve's view of Balzac, not Taine's, was the basis for comments in encyclopedias, textbooks, etc. See Pierre Conil's *Encyclopédie populaire* (Poussièlgue, 1880), p. 208; Marius Topin, *Les Romanciers contemporains* (2nd edition, Hachette, 1881), pp. 39–43; Paul Albert, *La Littérature française au XIXe siècle* (Hachette, 1882), II. 245–73.

[66] *De Henrico Beyle sive Stendhal Litterarum Germanicarum judice*, by A. Kontz, 1899. (Quoted by J. Mélia, *Stendhal et ses commentateurs* (Mercure de France, 1911), p. 309.)

[67] S. Boubée, *La Gazette de France*, 17 Nov. 1888.

[68] Raoul Frary, *Essais de critique* (Colin, 1891), p. 277. Souriau's article was presumably a preparation for this change in the syllabus.   [69] See above, p. 11.

6   *Fin de Siècle* criticism

In 1887, Faguet formulated a number of reasons for considering Balzac as a writer of the classical tradition, and very shortly after this, the novels of the *Comédie humaine* came to be institutionalized as 'classics'. The critical theme of 'Balzac classique' turned out to be a potent fertilizer of writing on Balzac from every source and from critics who accepted only the weaker but evaluatively loaded sense of 'classique'. The novelist became a desirable property to acquire and to defend for a wide diversity of political, literary, and philosophical schools in the last years of the nineteenth century. Jean Mélia, the first historian of Stendhal's reputation, claimed in 1900 that 'seuls les socialistes sont, à l'heure actuelle, en droit de réclamer Balzac comme un des leurs'[1]—to which Charles Maurras, the future leader and theoretician of *Action française*, replied: 'Dans ce vol, c'est nous qu'on vole . . . Défendons un bien royaliste.'[2] Balzac criticism did not escape the increasing politicization of intellectual life that the Dreyfus case engendered in *fin de siècle* France: indeed, the perceived and publicized relationship between Zola's *Rougon-Macquart* and the *Comédie humaine* put Balzac once again in the centre of contemporary polemics. The old theme of 'Balzac révolutionnaire' was split into a number of factional appropriations—claims were made that Balzac was a Marxist, a democrat, a republican, a socialist, and a supporter of Le Querdec's movement for social catholicism. The opposing notion, that Balzac was a supporter of the 'old order', was diversified into arguments that he was a Boulangist, an anti-Dreyfusard, an anti-Semite, a royalist, an anti-republican, and a clerical. The reaction of the 1890s was also expressed by renewed interest in the minor attachments of the romantic movement, and thus there were articles on Balzac as a romantic, mystical, spiritualist writer, on his knowledge of the occult and of animal magnetism. The *Comédie humaine* was analysed from many non-literary and slightly lunatic points of view: as a Celtic work, as an anti-German work, as a support for various medical, physiological, and psychological theories. Balzac acquired a 'feminine soul' as well as a reputation of total sexual abstinence. More importantly, however, and underlying all these different appropriations of his name, Balzac's

---

[1] J. Mélia, 'Balzac révolutionnaire', *La Petite République*, 15 Aug. 1900.
[2] C. Maurras, 'Balzac royaliste', *La Gazette de France*, 19 Aug. 1900.

novels became accepted not only as modern classics, but as the classical examples of the novel as a literary genre. His relationship to other fiction writers was seen as analogous to Shakespeare's position in English drama or Molière's in French comedy. Balzac became the touchstone by which the qualities and defects of other novelists were judged, the paragon and model for all fiction.

The underlying view that unites nearly all Balzac criticism of the 1890s must be differentiated from the claim made by Taine, and repeated by Zola in the 1860s, that the novelist was the most perfect exponent of a literary system. Certainly Taine regarded Balzac as a novelist whose work could not be improved upon, as his letter to Zola on *Thérèse Raquin* shows;[3] but for Taine the *Comédie humaine* was an extreme, it represented the ultimate limit of a method. In the 1890s, Balzac was a paragon because he was *not* extreme in terms of the literary movements of the period. He had steered a course between the Scylla of Naturalist 'excess' and the Charybdis of symbolist decadence: he was a classic because he was the golden mean. Zola's own 'Naturalist Balzac' differed from Taine's by being not an extreme but a precursor and pathfinder. Although Zola himself and his faithful disciples continued to propagate this view it becomes less and less prominent even in left-wing approaches to Balzac in the 1890s. Critics of other persuasions tended to lump Zola and Taine together. Taine's association with the German philosophers, particularly Hegel, and Zola's republican politics and pro-Dreyfus stand, meant that the view of Balzac 'as a realist', which they were both assumed to have held, became a theme of ridicule and attack from the right. A striking example of this complicated development was provided by the reception of Rodin's sculpture of Balzac, commissioned by the Société des gens de lettres in 1893 for the long-awaited monument. In long, flowing robes, with a broad and vulgar grin and thick limbs on a stocky frame, Rodin's vision of the author of the *Comédie humaine* was an image of sublime force, of herculean vulgarity, of a Tainian Balzac. The novelist Jules Case wrote about the statue when it was unveiled in 1898, and gave his interpretation of the *Comédie humaine*: 'Une idée générale s'en dégage . . . mais elle est intraduisible parce qu' elle est une abstraction: La Force—la force moderne, sans apparat ni décor.' Genius does not need the appearance of technical perfection, he continues. Balzac was neither a politician nor a moralist: 'Ce qui l'impressionna et le fascina, ce fut la force; son œuvre, colossale encyclopédie . . . est un

[3] See Chapter 4, pp. 104-5, above.

autel dressé à cette divinité.'[4] These remarks defend Rodin's image of Balzac as much as they describe the *Comédie humaine* and they are quite recognizably the themes of Taine's *Étude*. So the Société des gens de lettres, when they refused to 'recognize' the sculpture,[5] were not just exhibiting a philistine preference for a purely representational statue, but expressing their rejection of a Tainian view of Balzac's creation. Falguière's sober monument, eventually inaugurated in 1902, was much nearer the sterilized, moderate, classical figure that was wanted.

Balzac's new situation in the literary system as the creator of the 'standard' form of the novel was expressed in diverse ways. Marcel Barrière, for example, contrasted his 'idealism' to the materialism 'qui pourrit les sociétés modernes';[6] whilst the hero of *Le Termite*, a novel of literary life by J.-H. Rosny, contrasted Balzac's 'realism' to the ramblings of the symbolists: 'Il nous faut le réalisme de Balzac . . . C'est net, ça, ça va au but, comme le boulet, . . . Mon vieux, en guerre, Napoléon; en littérature, Stendhal et Balzac; mais tes Chinois brumeux, qu'ils restent en Normandie ou Lorraine, . . . c'est pas des Latins, c'est des Allemands! Et d'eux descendent les menteurs du rambuteau symboli-décadent.'[7] For Huysmans, who broke away from the Naturalist movement in 1884, Balzac was a colossus who blocked the horizon for later novelists.[8] Thus his hero, Des Esseintes, abandons Balzac in his search for new forms of art and experience: 'quoiqu'il se rendît compte de son injustice envers le prodigieux auteur de la *Comédie humaine*, il en était venu à ne plus ouvrir ses livres dont l'art valide le froissait'.[9] Brunetière expressed the view of Balzac as the very incarnation of the novel in a more direct and pedagogic fashion. The essence of the novel genre, he said, was a blending of material description and psychological truth: 'Point de roman, sans une valeur historique ou "documentaire" précise et déterminée, particulière et locale, d'une part, mais d'autre part, point de roman non plus, sans une valeur et une signification psychologique générale et durable.'[10] It was precisely a 'lasting and general psychological meaning' that

[4] J. Case, 'Devant Balzac', *Le Gaulois*, 13 May 1898.

[5] See M. Demaison, 'La Statue de Balzac', *Le Journal des débats*, 20 Mar. 1898, for an account of these events.

[6] *L'Œuvre de H. de Balzac* (Calmann-Lévy, 1890), p. ii.

[7] J.-H. Rosny, *Le Termite* (Savine, 1890), p. 25.

[8] See M. Raimond, *Balzac vu par les romanciers français de Zola à Proust*, p. 57.

[9] *À Rebours* (Crès, 1922), p. 233.

[10] *Manuel d'histoire de la littérature française* (Delagrave, 1898), p. 443.

Brunetière and the right in general denied the Naturalist novel, and which they increasingly credited to the *Comédie humaine*. Brunetière's description of the novel as a genre is more or less identical to his description of the Balzacian novel.

A peculiarly powerful contribution to the emergence of Balzac as the classical novelist of France was made by Paul Bourget. Bourget was seen by his followers in the same light that Zola's disciples considered their master—as the true inheritor of the *Comédie humaine*; but Bourget had fewer reservations about the novelist's talents than Zola, and fostered more directly the association of his name with that of Balzac. A kind of osmosis occurred, whereby in right-wing circles it was impossible to praise Bourget without praising Balzac, and vice-versa. This literary association had considerable political implications and a great effect on the themes used in right-wing writing concerned with the actual nature of the novels.

Bourget's attitude to the Republic in the 1890s was as scornful as Balzac's attitude to democracy in the 1840s. Bourget, moreover, was a supporter of the Church in its conflict with the state over education, and argued that religion should have a social role similar to that proposed by Balzac in the *Avant-Propos* of 1842.[11] He wrote novels that presented human life in terms of a mysterious and idealistic psychology, as well as a great deal of criticism which set up 'psychological truth' as a criterion of quality. As has been seen, Bourget also indulged in a kind of Balzac cult, offering *ex-votos* of muddled respect and biography to the deity of the novel.[12] Thus themes of criticism concerned with the treatment of minds and emotions in the *Comédie humaine* became the exclusive preserve of the political right, and were frequently associated with the spiritual, mystical, and occult ideologies that were fashionable at the end of the century.

Bourget's own writing on Balzac tended to be a defence of the novelist against specific criticisms, rather than an interpretation. He refuted Brunetière's accusation that Balzac did not know how to write;[13] and he argued that the number of 'impossible', romanesque characters, dismissed by Faguet, did not represent a larger proportion of the population of the *Comédie humaine* than such characters do in real life.[14] Significantly, this argument takes 'real life' as a criterion of literary quality, and on a fairly superficial level. Other right-wing critics of the

[11] 'Notes sur Balzac', *Minerva*, 15 Nov. 1902.   [12] See above, pp. 147–8.
[13] 'La Genèse du roman contemporain', *La Vie littéraire*, 15 Aug. 1878.
[14] 'Notes sur Balzac', *Le Parlement*, 29 Nov. 1883.

psychological school extended this approach to interpretations of the entire *Comédie humaine*.

The first and least interesting of these psychological studies on Balzac's novels was Marcel Barrière's long book, dedicated to Paul Bourget as 'le plus délicat et le plus subtil de nos analystes, continuant dignement après Stendhal, après Balzac . . . l'éternelle histoire du cœur humain'.[15] The analyses of the human heart that Barrière finds in the *Comédie humaine* are mostly of women. To defend the moral utility of characters such as Henriette de Mortsauf in *Le Lys dans la vallée*, Barrière claims that they might have existed.[16] Had they been 'impossible' in real life, he implies, an analysis of their emotions would have been without value. This long book constantly reveals in its comments on each novel (taken in the order of the definitive edition) confusions between universals in literature and typicalness in real life, and between psychology and morality. It is a ham-fisted attempt to apply what was not a very profound critical method, that of Paul Bourget. A much more subtle variant of the same set of attitudes was provided by Paul Flat's two books of *Essais sur Balzac*. The actual stuff of the *Comédie humaine* is here treated as material for the psychological investigation of womanhood. Flat states at the outset that he is not assessing Balzac or writing about the form of his work: but since the novelist had described most aspects of 'la sensibilité féminine', 'une étude des principaux types de femme de la *Comédie humaine* se trouvera être en même temps une étude de la sensibilité féminine'.[17] This programme assumes that the characters are 'universal' in real life; and the way in which Flat justifies his method assumes an anti-naturalist viewpoint. The aim of the critic, he says, should be to sympathize with the heroes of fiction and to share this sympathy with the reader. One of the major themes of criticism of Zola had been precisely that the subjects of his novels precluded any sympathy between reader and hero.[18] The English and Russian novelists were consequently held up as examples of realist writers who succeeded, unlike their French counterparts, in creating that sympathy which gave art a moral utility[19] and, for Brunetière, its aesthetic quality.[20] Thus Flat's

[15] *L'Œuvre de H. de Balzac* (Calmann-Lévy, 1890), p. i.   [16] Ibid., pp. 141–6.

[17] P. Flat, *Essais sur Balzac* (Plon, 1893), p. v.

[18] This had of course been a theme of Balzac criticism in earlier years. See E. Pelletan, in *La Presse*, 30 Nov. 1846.

[19] See P. Chasles, *La Psychologie sociale des nouveaux peuples* (Charpentier, 1875), p. 150, for this argument applied to Dickens.

[20] See R. J. Sealy, 'Montégut, Brunetière—and George Eliot', *MLR* Jan. 1971.

invocation of 'sympathy' situates his ideological position firmly on the right, with Bourget and Brunetière.

Flat's concentration on Balzac's treatment of women is also typical of right-wing literary criticism and of the 1890s in general. Far from being the robust and vulgar Parisian businessman that Taine and Rodin admired, that Faguet considered inadmissible but none the less acknowledged, the *fin de siècle* Balzac is a deodorized sentimental hero, entirely safe and entirely moral. His heroism in laying bare the most intricate workings of the mysterious female psyche was made to seem all the greater by the myth of his chastity, which Flat subscribed to and propagated. Balzac himself was partly to blame for the existence of this myth, having been discreet to the point of secrecy about his physical involvements with women. Neither his sister nor his widow had allowed the slightest mention of mistresses to mar the correspondence they published, and Gavarni's anecdotes on Balzac's unwillingness to waste his 'vital fluid' reached a wider audience when the Goncourts' *Journal* was published in 1877.[21] Gautier, Sand, and Lamartine had confirmed the novelist's apparent mistrust of physical pleasures, and Gabriel Ferry had turned the story of Balzac's affairs of the heart into a veritable myth of superhuman purity.[22] The importance of this belief in the novelist's chastity is that it was yet another way of separating Balzac from the crudities of Naturalism, and of associating him with the idealist and moral tendencies of *fin de siècle* criticism. 'Ceux qui connaissent le mieux l'amour sont ceux qui en ont le moins abusé', declares Flat,[23] as if to contradict all experimentalism and scientific knowledge when it comes to the human 'heart'. For Flat, in fact, Balzac was almost a bisexual. If the reader must sympathize with fictional characters in order to understand them, then the writer must do even more than sympathize with his real-life models in order to recreate them. Balzac possessed an ability to feel as a woman, Flat writes, and his soul was endowed with a unique degree of *féminéité*.[24] Thus young male heroes such as Lucien de Rubempré and Calyste du Guénic, in *Béatrix*, lack their creator's will-power, for they are distant from him,[25] whilst Anaïs de Bargeton and Béatrix herself are full-blooded Balzacian characters.[26] Unfortunately for Flat, the *Lettres à l'Étrangère* were published the following year, and he had to

---

[21] e.g. in vol. V, p. 152.
[22] *Balzac et ses amies* (Calmann-Lévy, 1888).
[23] *Seconds Essais sur Balzac* (Plon, 1894), p. 3.
[24] Ibid., p. viii.
[25] *Essais sur Balzac*, pp. 36–7.
[26] Ibid.

do some intricate back-tracking to defend his arguments on the novelist's chastity and feminine soul.[27]

Other critics were inspired by Flat to examine the role of women in the *Comédie humaine*. Paul Souday, for example, took Émile Faguet to task for failing to appreciate the 'relief étonnant' of Eugénie Grandet, or the strength and beauty of Marguerite Claës, in *La Recherche de l'absolu*.[28] Another critic, apparently a woman, sought to refute Flat's notion of the *féminéité* of Balzac's soul. The novelist had always been afraid of not understanding women: '. . . et il les a faites comme il les souhaitait et les craignait: de suprêmes dominatrices'.[29] Madame de Beauséant, for example, is superior to both her lovers, Ajuda-Pinto and Gaston de Nerval; the Duchesse de Langeais leaves Montriveau as the true loser; and Dinah de la Baudraye, in *La Muse du département*, is morally, intellectually, and emotionally superior to the journalist Lousteau. These heroines all have a spark of masculine determination 'qui s'est nommé Napoléon'. Balzac may well be close to them, as Flat believed, but it was not because he was 'feminine' but because Balzac's heroines were in fact men in disguise.[30] There was a reply to this article, also apparently by a woman, which took up the cudgels on behalf of Paul Flat. What had been for Sainte-Beuve a chapter of criticism and for Chaudes-Aigues a lamentable aberration becomes by 1900 a subject of exegesis and praise: 'Si aujourd'hui l'on apothéose l'immortel génie de Balzac, c'est qu'il sut cueillir les plus jolies fleurs du cœur féminin.'[32] And so the banquet to celebrate the centenary of Balzac's birth was entertained by 'les mélodies d'un orchestre de femmes vêtues de rose'.[33]

Approval of Balzac's treatment of women in his novels was often combined in the 1890s with an interest in the mystical novels—just as disapproval of the feminine emotions described in the *Comédie humaine* was often combined in earlier decades with sarcastic remarks on the novelist's 'illusions'. This too was a topical way of separating Balzac from Zola, whose scepticism at the much-reported 'miracles' of spiritualism, second sight, and so on was well known. Max Nordau made this clear in the bilingual *Revue Franco-allemande*:

Ich sehe in Balzac einen monumentalen Beweis, dass die äusserliche Beobach-

[27] See the *Avant-propos* to the *Seconds Essais*.
[28] *La Revue pour les jeunes filles*, 5 May 1899.
[29] 'Les Femmes de Balzac', *Le Gaulois*, 11 May 1899.   [30] Ibid.
[32] 'Les Héroines de Balzac', *La Gazette de France*, 22 Nov. 1902.
[33] 'Les Fêtes de Balzac à Tours', *Le Gaulois*, 8 May 1899.

tung für die Dichtung vollkommen unerheblich ist . . . Man hänge Balzacs Bild an die Pforten der *Kathedrale* des Herrn Huysmans und des *Chat-Noir*, der Rose † Croix Ausstellung und des Théâtre-Antoine, des Wohnhauses von Frln Couesdon und der Bodinière. Alle diese Anstalten hat er ein wenig kommanditiert, in allen ist er ein wenig Hausherr . . . Die einzigen Stellen, wo sein Porträt unberechtigt wäre, sind die Titelblatter von Thureau-Dangins *Geschichte der Julimonarchie* und von Zolas Romanen.[34]

Balzac's interest in the supernatural was the subject of articles in specialist and right-wing newspapers,[35] and a whole book was devoted to those instances in the *Comédie humaine* where 'mind' controls 'matter'.[36] The symbolist poet Charles Morice had mentioned *Séraphita* as Balzac's nearest approach to Art,[37] and the occult masters Papus and Jules Bois considered Balzac an 'initié', capable of 'une beauté ésoterique . . . dans certains fragments'.[38] The most valuable result of this fashionable resurgence of interest in *Séraphita* and *Louis Lambert*, however, was Paul Flat's second volume of essays. Here he sets out to show that Balzac's mysticism was really a metaphysical system that made will the key to the human universe. The theory of the will, as outlined in *Louis Lambert*, is, he says, 'l'essence même de son génie', because it explains the behaviour of all of Balzac's heroes and heroines. The whole *Comédie humaine* can be analysed in terms of conflicts of will-power—*Le Père Goriot*, for example, as a drama created by the difference between the 'facultés volontaires' of Rastignac and Vautrin. Flat's essay is full of dated and complicated arguments about love, concentration, and animal magnetism, but the main drift of it anticipates the argument of Ernst-Robert Curtius and which few present-day critics would wish to refute: that the theory of the will is 'le système nerveux de l'art de Balzac'.[39] It remains to this day, however, a politically loaded aspect of Balzac criticism, as can be seen when the Marxist Pierre Barbéris reproves Maurice Bardèche for being 'idéaliste'.[40]

One final argument from Flat's essays must be discussed, and that is his assertion that Balzac was a poet. Defence of Balzac's style had of

---

[34] *Revue Franco-allemande*, May 1899.

[35] e.g. Gaston Malet, 'Le Merveilleux dans Balzac' published in both *L'Écho du merveilleux* and *La Gazette de France* on 1 June 1898.

[36] E. Baumann, *Le Symbolisme de la vie dans Balzac* (Verne, 1896).

[37] *La Littérature de tout-à-l'heure* (Perrin, 1889), p. 167.

[38] In Jules Huret's *Enquête sur l'évolution littéraire* (Charpentier, 1890), pp. 50, 52.

[39] E.-R. Curtius, *Balzac* (Grasset, 1933), p. 70.

[40] P. Barbéris, *Balzac. Une Mythologie réaliste* (Larousse, 1971), p. 13.

course become a theme of criticism before Flat published his work, and indeed it was Paul Bourget who defended it with the greatest vigour. In the *Contes drolatiques* (left out of account by most nineteenth-century critics) Flat finds that Balzac's style rises to the level of poetry. In the novels generally he sees the quality of the language as its connotative wealth. The associations of Balzac's vocabulary are peculiarly apt, Flat considers, for the evocation of 'états d'âme' and the description of 'le sentiment envisagé dans son essence'. These arguments are once again buried in a mass of fashionable pseudo-science, in what hostile critics (had they existed) would have considered a truly Balzacian manner, but they represent none the less the logical end of the acceptance of the *Comédie humaine* into the canon of respectable literature. The feminine sensitivity, philosophical consistency, and stylistic quality of Balzac are not only reversals of the principal criticisms made of the novelist in earlier years: they are virtual sterilizations of the debatable aspects of his achievement.

Karl Marx's *Das Kapital* was translated into French in 1872, and it contains a number of references to Balzac. The most important is a passage on Balzac's accurate analysis, in *Les Paysans*, of the relationship between peasants and their creditors.[41] Curiously enough, not one of the socialist articles on Balzac that appeared in the 1890s quotes or mentions Marx's comments, but nearly all acknowledge a book published by the left-wing journalist Julien Lemer in 1892. This work consists of a biographical and anecdotal introduction followed, as in Barrière's book, by analyses of the stories of each of the novels of the *Comédie humaine*. It was originally composed to help Zola's campaign for a Balzac monument in 1880, then submitted for the Académie's competition in 1886. Although it could not be given a prize since it did not conform to the required *dissertation* pattern, one of the judges, Ernest Renan, thought it worth publishing.[42] The aim of Lemer's book is quite simple: to show that Balzac was basically an anti-clerical republican. Thus Lemer dedicates his work to Hugo and Zola for reasons similar to those that prompted Barrière to dedicate his work to Paul Bourget; and, like Barrière's, his work is of a mediocre quality. The versions of the stories that he gives are badly distorted, and long passages are quoted in misleading contexts to show the left-wing trend of Balzac's mind. For Lemer, however, Balzac was not an important

---

41 K. Marx, *Le Capital*, traduction de M. J. Roy (Lachâtre, 1872).
42 J. Lemer, *Balzac, sa vie, son œuvre* (Sauvaître, 1892), 'Avant-propos'.

artist, and the value and interest of his novels lay not in their form but in 'le travail du philosophe, du penseur, je dirais volontiers du réformateur'. The literary aspects of the *Comédie humaine* were, he claimed, merely a way of adapting philosophical thought and moral observation 'aux goûts, aux capacités intellectuelles, aux appétences du public'. This justifies in some measure Lemer's method of argument, and of course allows Zola to remain, as he did for all left-wing critics of the period, the supreme novelist of the nineteenth century. It is also a straightforward contradiction of the much earlier themes of right-wing criticism, with which Lemer was familiar, that denied Balzac any value as a thinker and moralist.

Lemer's book was influential over younger left-wing critics in the 1890s. Robert Bernier, for example, claimed to have spoken of Balzac as a precursor of socialist ideals in 1890, before the publication of Lemer, but he respectfully quotes long anecdotes (on Hugo and Janin) from him in his published article on *Les Paysans*.[43] Bernier's conclusion is that Balzac's novel of peasant life shows a correct understanding of the interests of the rural proletariat as defined by Benoît Malon— editor of the review in which the article appeared. The author of the *Comédie humaine* was therefore if not a socialist at least a 'démocrate fortement accentué'. *Les Paysans* also provided the material for another, more specifically Marxist approach to Balzac by Charles Bonnier, and he too quotes Julien Lemer but not Karl Marx. All these critics treat the novels not as literature but as history and philosophy. The confusion of real life with the representation of life was not confined to critics of the ideological right.

Balzac's novels of the countryside (*Le Curé de village*, *Le Médecin de campagne*, and *Les Paysans*) are political novels to a large extent, and their meaning does require elucidation. The most sympathetic interpretation made of them in the 1890s came from a representative of Le Querdec's movement for social catholicism, which shared with Balzac himself a debt to the religious thinker Montalembert. Charles Calippe, who composed these articles, shows how Bénassis, in *Le Médecin de campagne*, fulfills the role of a priest in spreading social harmony by reducing pauperism. In *Les Paysans*, vice and irreligion are shown to be the result of poverty and discord, and thus in Balzac's universe, as in Le Querdec's theory, the work of a man like Bénassis is moral and religious as well as social and material.[44] Calippe's

[43] *La Revue socialiste*, May 1892.
[44] C. Calippe, 'Le Curé, d'après Balzac', *La Quinzaine*, 15 July 1896 (XI. 238–56).

presentation of Balzac as a major contributor to the ideas of catholic humanitarianism is not unreasonable, and contains a large element of truth. Likewise, Edmond Biré's almost scholarly work on Balzac's royalism, although argued from a clear political standpoint, elucidated the development of the novelist's actual opinions to a considerable extent. Not all the explicitly political approaches to Balzac were worthless, and not all the fashionably *fin de siècle* critics got lost like Barrière and Baumann in confusions of life and art.

The most impressive piece of Balzac criticism in the 1890s came from a minor symbolist poet and Baudelairean scholar, Gustave Kahn. The main point of his article is to show how the anonymous early novels, in particular *Jane la Pâle* and *Argow le Pirate*, were related to the *Comédie humaine*. Few previous critics had paid any attention at all to these works, and most that had either dismissed them as a bad start or used them as evidence of how hard Balzac had had to work to learn to write.[45] Kahn presents all that Balzac wrote as expressions of his protean personality, but develops a subtle idea of what the personality of a writer is. Balzac put his imagination of himself into his works, and that imagination was full of the archetypes of romantic literature. Thus de Marsay is Balzac in his Don Juan disguise, with thematic variations provided by La Palférine and Maxime de Trailles; Raphaël de Valentin is a mixture of Prometheus, Hamlet, and Balzac himself. 'Il se figure des Balzac, des Balzac riches, amoureux, puissants, Don Juanesques, et il écrit leur histoire en la compliquant un peu; il l'écrit parce qu'il y croit, et que ces différents Balzac lui sont apparus vrais une minute.'[46] The early novels, he says, are prefigurements of the *Comédie humaine*, but they differ from the later works in the depth of their associations. The pirate in *Argow* is a first version of Vautrin, but whereas the former has purely literary roots in Jean Valjean, the master criminal of the *Comédie humaine* is a version of the myth of Satan. His love for Lucien de Rubempré is therefore tragic, because by definition Satan cannot love.

Balzac's fictions move from the poetic archetypes of the romantic imagination to the details of the real world. Sometimes it is enough for Balzac to observe and to copy—his descriptions of provincial heroines and of the machinery of the law, for example, draw their literary value from their absolute veracity alone. Mostly, though, it is the movement

---

[45] This is the line taken by Sainte-Beuve in the original version of his review of *La Recherche de l'absolu*. See above, p. 69.

[46] G. Kahn, 'Notes sur Balzac', *La Revue Blanche*, May 1899.

from real to imaginary that gives the *Comédie humaine* its infinite suggestiveness. Balzac's genius lies in his ability to compound the qualities of observation and poetic exaggeration.[47] Kahn's argument is here very reminiscent of Taine, and it was no doubt through Baudelaire's writings that these views were transmitted to him. Like Taine, too, Kahn does not have much time for Balzac's political views on Church and Throne. These attitudes were but the product of envy, and the novelist was a snob—'si on peut être un snob avec du génie . . .'[48] That Balzac was a genius, Kahn does not doubt, but his qualities were very different from the 'sculpture verbale' of Chateaubriand and Flaubert, or the rigorousness of Stendhal. If the *Comédie humaine* possesses any truth, he concludes, it is the truth of a 'chimère à tête humaine': a hybrid of the real and the imagined. If it has beauty, then it is a particular and period-restricted beauty, rather than a general and universal quality: 'non pas une beauté absolue, mais une idiosyncratie absolue'.

Kahn's short article is then an original and suggestive use of a number of older themes of Balzac criticism, and would appear to owe nothing at all to Émile Faguet and the idea of classical realism. The three major academic critics of modern French literature in the 1890s—Faguet, Brunetière, and Lanson—actually acquired the reputation of not liking Balzac, and several of the pieces discussed in this chapter were specifically directed against Faguet, who had done more than anyone to create the critical atmosphere in which Balzac's institutionalization as a classic was possible. In fact, there was a certain justification for the belief that Balzac was still misunderstood and disliked in the Sorbonne and the Collège de France. In his *Histoire de la littérature française*, Gustave Lanson pillaged Faguet's article of 1887 for his chapter on Balzac, and like his source begins his consideration of the *Comédie humaine* with a list of the novels' faults. However, the vigour of his remarks on Balzac's lack of style, of restraint, of true feeling for nature, and on the tastelessness of his authorial interruptions and digressions make his ensuing praise seem insincere. He garbles Faguet's arguments on the novelist's place in the French tradition: 'En un sens, Balzac est de la tradition classique; il n'y a que l'homme qui l'intéresse . . . et il est exclusivement peintre des relations sociales et des natures humaines.' Of course, Lanson denies the truth of Balzac's association with 'le réalisme contemporain'—that is to say, Zola—but explains it by the romantic exuberance of his novels. This

---

[47] Ibid., p. 80.   [48] Ibid., p. 82.

is once again Faguet's argument compressed to absurdity. In conclusion, Balzac was at his best when describing the middle classes, 'où il semble que l'art réaliste doive toujours se confiner chez nous'.[49] The implication once again is that Zola was wrong to write 'realistically' about the urban proletariat (*L'Assommoir*), the industrial working classes (*Germinal*, etc.), and the peasantry (*La Terre*). The schematic nature and evident plagiarism of Lanson's chapter on Balzac, taken together with another article which he published twice,[50] suggest that the founder of literary history had no great taste for the *Comédie humaine*. Nor is there much evidence that Faguet himself actually enjoyed the novels, however much he liked scoring witty points at the expense of Taine,[51] and lesser contemporary critics. Brunetière's views were extremely variable, as has already been mentioned: in 1875, he declared in reply to Zola that 'Balzac n'est pas réaliste'; in 1880, 'Balzac n'a pas fondé notre roman actuel'; but in his *Manuel d'histoire de la littérature française* of 1898, he argued that Balzac had founded the modern novel by introducing the doctrines of realism, and thus destroying an already moribund romantic movement. There is no way of telling which of these views were sincerely held, or whether they represent a change in the critic's attitude. His two later contributions to Balzac criticism were both apotheoses of the novelist as the very incarnation of the novel, but both were written as political rather than literary acts (despite their avoidance of any explicitly political arguments) during and after the enormous furore of the centenary celebrations in 1899.

Every two or three years during the final twenty years of the last century, one or two newspapers would commemorate the anniversary of Balzac's death, or his birthday, with a special article or even a special issue.[52] The novelist's ninety-ninth birthday, in 1898, was greeted with more polemic than usual over his works, precipitated by the refusal of the Société des gens de lettres to accept the statue of Balzac that Rodin had made on their commission. The acrimony of the artistic debate prefigured the bitterness of the conflicts over the official celebration of Balzac's centenary the following year. There were

---

[49] Lanson, *Histoire de la littérature française* (Hachette, 1894), p. 991.

[50] In *La Revue bleue*, 4 May 1895, and as the introduction to *Pages choisies des grands écrivains. Balzac* (Colin et Lévy, 1895).

[51] 'De l'Influence de Balzac', *La Revue bleue*, 21 May 1898.

[52] See Appendix III under the following dates: 24 Aug. 1878, 20 Aug. 1881, Aug. 1883, 24 Aug. 1885, 10 and 25 Aug. 1887, 22 Aug. 1893, 9 May 1896.

two sets of competing organizers: the Société des gens de lettres, of course, who elected a very left-wing 'Balzac committee' to promote Balzacian events in Paris, but which in the end organized very little; and a provincial committee under the chairmanship of the deputy for Indre-et-Loire, Drake del Castillo, which set up a veritable festival of Balzac in Tours, the novelist's birthplace. The Ministry of the Interior took a close interest in these provincial happenings and delegated a senior official, Peytrand, to observe the work of the committee. Unfortunately, Drake del Castillo was not only the owner of the château of Saché but a man of the clerical, anti-Dreyfusard right, whilst the Tours municipal council was controlled by a socialist and republican majority. One of their number, a certain Maître Gorse, donated 500 francs of municipal funds to the Balzac committee, without consulting the council, and thereby provoked a local political storm that was widely reported in the Paris press and which accounts for the tenor of much of the criticism published in 1899.

It must be remembered that the official literary scene was dominated by an increasingly reactionary right wing in 1899, and that there were relatively few left-wing newspapers with large circulations or well-known contributors. Critics like Brunetière were not merely reactionary in politics, but xenophobic and anti-semitic. Brunetière himself was a committee member of the *Ligue de la Patrie française*, an organization that was shortly to become better known as *Action française*. In March 1899, he had addressed a meeting at Lille on 'Les Ennemis de l'âme française'—and these enemies were politicians, intellectuals, free-thinkers, internationalists, and individualists. It was a virulently anti-Dreyfusard and anti-semitic outpouring, and was presumably known to the councillors of Tours. Furthermore, the first event to celebrate Balzac's centenary had been the production of *Mercadet* by the *Comédie française*, and there was a political point to the choice of this play, rather than of *La Marâtre*. Balzac's play, wrote Jules Case, had a very contemporary interest. Humanity was divided into two classes, the hunters and the ploughmen, and Mercadet was of the first sort, an impatient adventurer attracted by struggle. 'Ploughmen' are meant to represent the honest French, 'hunters' the foreign, unscrupulous Jew, in Case's argument. Thus Mercadet gives a portrait of

le type qui caractérise le mieux ce siècle . . ., l'homme affranchi des morales, des préjugés, des traditions, n'attendant plus de secours que de lui-même et lâché dans une civilisation frappée de démembrement . . .[53]

[53] J. Case, in *La Nouvelle Revue*, 15 Feb. 1899.

Despite the stilted and boring costume production that the *Comédie française* gave Balzac's play, all right-wing newspapers gave it extremely laudatory reviews; and left-wing reviewers emphasized the extent to which it was not Balzac's work, but D'Ennery's. Émile Faguet, however, produced an entirely predictable essay in which *Mercadet* appears an immortal classic not because it attacked 'quelque manie transitoire de la Bourse' but ridiculed 'le fond même du caractère des hommes d'argent'.[54] The political tone of Balzac's centenary was set by the choice of *Mercadet* and by the play's critical reception: it was confirmed by the presence of Brunetière on Drake del Castillo's committee.

The socialist councillors of Tours decided that they were being involved in a reactionary political manifestation and withdrew the subsidy of 500 francs granted to the Balzac celebrations. The novelist, they realized, had indeed been a catholic and a monarchist, and so they dissociated themselves entirely from the commemoration of his centenary. They refused to allow the municipal theatre to be used by the *Comédie française* for a performance of *Mercadet*, which eventually took place under canvas; and bunting was removed from the streets. The greatest objection that the town council had was to the name of the speaker invited to address the assembled Balzacians: Ferdinand Brunetière. Drake del Castillo defended this choice to the *conseil général* of the *département*:

On prétend que nous pouvions en choisir un autre [conférencier]. En effet, on a proposé M. Lemaitre, mais nous l'avons écarté précisément parce qu'il est mêlé de trop près, à l'heure actuelle, à des affaires politiques. Il nous restait, selon quelques uns, M. Zola, malheureusement nous n'avons pas son adresse. (*Rires et applaudissements*.)[55]

No further arguments are needed to prove that the Balzac centenary celebrations in Tours were a political rather than a literary event. The local socialists had protected their honour by dissociating themselves from this affair but had also 'lost' Balzac to the right. In Paris, attempts were made by the left to recuperate the novelist's name.

Paul Adam, for example, condescendingly explained to his provincial colleagues that Balzac could hardly be blamed for not propagating the thought of Proudhon.

Sa tâche lui semblait différente . . . Composer la *Comédie humaine*, dénuder tant de mensonges dans les *Illusions perdues*, exposer les tares du capitalisme

---

[54] *Le Journal des débats*, 6 Feb. 1899.
[55] *Le Journal d'Indre-et-Loire*, 14 Apr. 1899.

en créant les figures de Nucingen et de du Tillet . . . n'est-ce point là la plus formidable attaque contre le régime bourgeois?[56]

The major item in the left's counter-attack was an article by Jean Mélia in the May 1899 issue of *La Revue socialiste*. Before that appeared, however, the socialist deputy Eugène Fournière had proposed a *projet de loi* in the National Assembly that Balzac's mortal remains should be transferred to the Panthéon to lie beside those of Hugo. The debate on this bill was adjourned and, so far as I know, never resurrected: Balzac remains to this day at Père Lachaise.

The speech Fournière made to the House was predictable and double-faced. In one paragraph he declared that 'Honoré de Balzac n'appartient à aucun parti. Il appartient à la France.' In the following lines, however, he makes a blatant appeal to left-wing sentiments by citing Béranger, in a story attributed by Lemer to Jules Janin:[57] 'car, je vous le dis en vérité, Balzac est un des hommes qui, pour me servir de l'expression de Béranger, ont le plus richement ensemencé les champs de l'avenir'.[58] The Paris committee for the Balzac centenary refused to have any dealings with the Tours committee or to attend the celebrations,[59] which for some reason took place on the 6th and 7th May 1899, and not on either Balzac's real birthday, the 20th, or on the 16th, the date erroneously given by Laure Surville, Théophile Gautier, and others. Rumours were bruited in the Paris press that the festivities would be broken up by a 'cabale socialiste',[60] and most of the major papers sent special correspondents to Tours to report on the events.

On the 6th, a gala was held, which included readings, 'causeries', and projections of slides. The next day, a banquet 'agrémenté par les mélodies d'un orchestre de femmes vêtues de rose' was followed by the performance of *Mercadet* 'dans un ancien cirque pompeusement baptisé Théâtre-français'[61] and by Brunetière's lecture. There were no riots to mar the celebrations.

Brunetière arrived late on the 7th and in ill health.[62] In his lecture, he steered clear of politics of any kind; he also steered clear of criticizing Balzac. Giving an eulogy of the *Comédie humaine* involved, for Brunetière, contradicting what he had said earlier on the subject, and contradicting things he was to write later. He began by saying that Taine's *Essai* of 1858 (was this an intentional misnomer?) had been as nearly

[56] *Le Journal*, 16 Apr. 1899.
[57] See above, p. 66
[58] *La Revue socialiste*, May 1899, p. 594n.
[59] Ibid., p. 595.
[60] See *Le Gaulois*, 8 May 1899.   [61] Ibid.
[62] *La Croix*, 9 May 1899.

definitive as anything could have been at that time: the following year, Brunetière commenced his lectures on Balzac with an onslaught on Taine's article copied from Droz. None the less, he pursued in 1899, Taine was out of date, and Balzac required a fresh examination. Two objections must first be dealt with: Balzac's style and his alleged immorality. Brunetière had previously exercised his sarcasm at the expense of Balzac's style[63], but in a eulogy he could only praise, and that is what he did. Balzac, he said, had the capacity to 'faire vivant', and, though he sometimes spoilt his effects by self-conscious overwriting, he succeeded more often than not in creating a subtle, living language, 'd'une corruption délicieuse'. His so-called immorality was but a function of his striving to 'faire vivant', to represent life in its totality: 'il n'est ni plus ni moins immoral que la vie elle-même'. Balzac's achievement had been to create the feeling of 'histoire réelle' in fiction, in the same way that Walter Scott had done. He had given an invaluable historical document to posterity in the *Comédie humaine*, and established the novel as the major form of literary expression in France in the nineteenth century.[64]

This anodyne lecture was warmly applauded by the audience and was favourably commented on by several Paris newspapers. The political quarrel over Balzac was by no means ended by this eminently apolitical lecture, however: but its focus shifted from Tours back to Paris.

Fournière's bid to give Balzac the honours of the Panthéon was opposed by the deputy Maréjouls on the grounds that the novelist had lacked a republican spirit, and the nation was now republican. Alexandre Hepp wrote a savage attack on such stupidity, maintaining not that Balzac was a republican, but that it didn't matter.[65] Some journalists were by this time expressing disgust at the time and ink wasted in futile polemics over Balzac's politics when, as Henry de Bruchard said, they should be reading the novels themselves.[66] This idea was taken up by Remy de Gourmont, who suggested that the money wasted on the 'fêtes vulgaires' should have been used to found a *Revue Balzacienne*, which would make the *Comédie humaine* 'un centre intellectuel . . . une archiconfrérie . . . dont le lien serait le goût des choses de l'esprit'.[67] These ideas did not have much impact on the

[63] See above, p. 139.
[64] Lecture reprinted in *Le Temps*, 8 May 1899.
[65] *Le Journal*, 8 May 1899.
[66] *La Presse*, 6 May 1989.
[67] *Le Mercure de France*, 1 June 1899.

journalists of *La Croix*, for example, who took the socialist initiative to move Balzac to the Panthéon as an opportunity to attack not the socialists but Balzac himself. Balzac's picture of society was false, distorted, and all the more dangerous because it appeared to be true, they claimed: 'Doué d'un merveilleux talent d'observation, il lui donnait libre cours. C'était un moyen de succès: tant pis pour la morale!'[68] Balzac was still on the Index and the ultra-catholic *La Croix* was duty bound to object to the celebration of the centenary of his birth. The reasons for these festivities, *La Croix* hinted, lay in some 'Zoliste' plot: 'Balzac est le précurseur, ou mieux, le chef d'école des Zolistes; moins grossier, moins repoussant peut-être, mais il est le chef d'école. Voilà la raison de l'apothéose!'[69] Branches of the extreme left (Maréjouls, the Tours Council) and of the extreme right, then, dissociated themselves from this apotheosis. Émile Faguet suggested that it was contradictory to celebrate the centenary of a man who had been a thorough pessimist about human nature: for, if Balzac had been right, and men were truly evil, then being evil we should have no gratitude; or if men were truly good, we should ignore Balzac because he had been wrong about human nature; 'Dans les deux cas, point d'apothéose. L'apothéose est un démenti.'[70] This witty and perverse paradox rests on an interpretation of Balzac as a pessimist—and the pessimistic readings that can be put upon Balzac's depiction of human folly and passion in the *Comédie humaine* were to become, in the following years, very much part of the Balzac praised and adopted by the *Action française*.

Jean Mélia's article in the *Revue socialiste* appears to have been written before Brunetière gave his speech at Tours, but amended after the 5th May to include details, in a footnote, of Fournière's proposition to the Chambre des députés. The *Revue socialiste*, in any case, appeared on the 15th of each month, so that the political onslaught on Brunetière appeared after he had given his eminently non-political lecture, and fell rather flat. Mélia is also rather out of date in his claim that Brunetière denigrated Balzac and that he is risible in stating that Balzac 'n'a pas fondé notre roman actuel'. The critic had changed his mind since he had made those statements. However, Mélia was probably correct in asserting that Brunetière had only been chosen to give the lecture 'en vue de l'accomplissement d'une manifestation réaction-

---

[68] *La Croix*, 10 May 1899.
[69] Ibid. See Saint-Gayrac, 'Les Deux Balzac', *La Vérité française*, 21 Feb. 1901, for a very similar view.
[70] *Le Gaulois*, 7 May 1899.

naire'.[71] Balzac, Mélia admits, was a monarchist in his opinions, and even had political ambitions. This can be explained by Balzac's extreme pessimism about human nature, which led him to the view that only an absolute authority could save mankind from destruction. However, Mélia accepts Hugo's view, quoted by Lemer,[72] that Balzac would have gone into opposition under the Second Empire. All his life, Balzac had been a poor man, toiling under immense economic pressures; he was really a 'déclassé dans le monde aristocratique et le parti royaliste où il avait cependant aspiré de briller'.[73] Balzac's work, Mélia continues, is full of evidence that shows the revolutionary nature of his criticism of French society, and that is why the left should claim Balzac as theirs when 'les réactionnaires voudront s'emparer de son nom'.

Balzac lifts the cloak of hypocrisy that hides the horrors of the modern capitalist world: sinister figures like Troubert, in *Le Curé de Tours*, characters of utter depravity, like Hulot, Marneffe, and Crevel in *La Cousine Bette*, reveal the full extent of evil in contemporary life. After reading the *Comédie humaine*, 'on se dit: C'est un monde qu'il faut balayer, c'est la société qu'il faut refaire.' In method too, Balzac belongs to the revolutionary left, according to Mélia. As a materialist and a 'scientist', Balzac produces 'caractères-types', or personifications of particular vices. His depiction of the environmental factors that create the 'caractères-types' is also scientifically accurate: 'C'est le cinématographe des pourritures et des laideurs de la société moderne.' The revolutionary content of the *Comédie humaine* was for Mélia as great as that of the beliefs of the anarchist terrorists Henry and Vaillant, who declared, before they were executed for a bomb-throwing incident, that society was rotten to the core and must be destroyed.

The *Comédie humaine* would not have been so accurate nor so savage had Balzac been a richer man: 'Les révolutionnaires ne l'oublient pas,— et si par une ironie quelconque ils remercient un Dieu en qui ils ne croient pas, ils le remercient pour avoir fait de Balzac un esclave de la créance.' The sources of Mélia's approach to Balzac are obvious, and for the most part acknowledged. Mélia's description of Balzac's 'scientific method' is adapted from Taine; his interpretation of *Le Curé de Tours* is similar to Lemer's; and *La Cousine Bette* was the perennial stand-by of all nineteenth-century left-wing criticism of Balzac. Mélia's

[71] J. Mélia, 'Balzac révolutionnaire', *La Revue socialiste*, 15 May 1899.
[72] In *Balzac, sa vie, son œuvre* (Sauvaître, 1892).
[73] Cf. Gustave Kahn on Balzac as a 'snob', quoted above on p. 175.

frequent invocations of 'authorities' on Balzac reveal his desire not to suggest that his own interpretation was a new one, but that it was the correct and respectable one. Mélia understood full well that this battle was not a conflict of intellects, but a conflict of interests between the right and the left. That interest would be destroyed if there were the slightest doubt, in the impression created by his article, as to the eminent respectability and classic status of Balzac. It was Balzac's prestige and propaganda value that the left wanted, not any new understanding of his works. Consequently, all the patron saints of the *fin de siècle* left are put through their paces in this article: Hugo, Taine, Henry and Vaillant, Paul Adam—and, in the last paragraphs, Émile Zola.

By the end of the century, the pattern of themes and arguments about the political significance of the *Comédie humaine* was clearly established. The left no longer argued about what Balzac's real personal opinions might have been, though Hugo's opinion on that was gratefully quoted by most left-wing critics; it was generally accepted that Balzac had held right-wing, monarchist, and catholic views. The left concentrated their interpretations on Balzac's critique of the bourgeois social system, on his depiction of reality and of the forces— economic, historical, and political—behind that system. Naturally enough, the left also took the view that Balzac was a realist and an observer, and that Zola was his literary and political heir. Right-wing interpretations, on the other hand, concentrated on Balzac's actual political opinions and on the differences between his imaginative idealism and Zola's vulgar materialism. The left had an immediate preference for *Le Curé de Tours, La Rabouilleuse, Illusions perdues,* and *La Cousine Bette;*[74] the right, for *Les Paysans, Le Médecin de campagne,* and *Le Curé de village.* The right emphasized Balzac's imagination, and minimized the role of observation in the *Comédie humaine.* All the interpretations of Balzac's volitional philosphy, political programmes, scientific, magnetic, and 'hypnotic' ideas were implicitly, if not explicity, right-wing. Gaston Malet, for example, wrote articles on Balzac and the supernatural as well as pieces on 'Balzac royaliste'.[75] Flat and Nordau, fascinated by Balzac's ideas on magnetism and willpower, were hostile to Zola in politics as in literature.

[74] Cf. Jean Mitrou in *La Petite République,* 22 Aug. 1900: 'Les penseurs libres et les affranchisseurs de races pourront toujours se revendiquer le Balzac des *Parents pauvres,* des *Illusions perdues* et de *Mercadet* . . .'
[75] In *La Gazette de France,* on 1 June 1898 and 9 and 11 May 1899.

Some critics, of course, cannot be fitted into this scheme: for example, Louis Dîmier, an extreme right-wing polemicist, none the less wrote in praise of Balzac's realism.[76] The most notable exception to this scheme was Ferdinand Brunetière. Although he held strong, reactionary views in politics, his view of Balzac was always one step behind—or ahead of—the right-wing fashions of the day. As Balzac's political and ideological message became more and more the centre of right-wing interpretations of the *Comédie humaine*, Brunetière saw fit to praise the novelist for exclusively non-political aspects of his work. His speech at Tours, the climax of a political quarrel of the first magnitude, contained not a mention of Balzac's politics, nor indeed of those themes associated with the right—mysticism, magnetism, hypnosis. His lectures on Balzac, published in 1900, enlarge and expand the ideas of the Tours speech, but again without touching even indirectly on politics or the ideological content of the *Comédie humaine*.[77]

The fiftieth anniversary of Balzac's death was commemorated in August 1900 by, among other things, a polemic over Balzac's politics that was almost the mirror image, on a smaller scale, of the quarrel of 1899. It was the left which in 1900 organized a 'manifestation' in honour of Balzac, and which published the first article claiming Balzac as its own. This article also was by Jean Mélia, and in it he repeated in a shortened form all the arguments he had put forward in 1899. He claimed notably that 'seuls les socialistes sont, à l'heure actuelle, en droit de réclamer Balzac comme un des leurs'.[78] Charles Maurras provided the *Gazette de France* with a reply to this 'theft' of Balzac: 'Dans ce vol, c'est nous qu'on vole . . . Défendons un bien royaliste.'[79] The left-wing claim that Balzac denounced a corrupt society, a corrupt bourgeoisie, clergy, and aristocracy. If that makes him a revolutionary, Maurras exclaims, then the *Gazette de France* would welcome a revolution to establish a 'Monarchie de salut public', which would destroy the Republic . . . as Balzac would have wished. The distinction between Balzac's private opinions and the meaning of the *Comédie humaine* which the socialists are forced to make, continues Maurras, does not

[76] L. Dîmier, *Les Maîtres de la contre-révolution au XIXe siècle* (Saint-Pères, 1907), pp. 115–35.

[77] *Revue des Cours et conférences*, 25 May and 14 June 1900.

[78] *La Petite République*, 19 Aug. 1900.

[79] *La Gazette de France*, 19 Aug. 1900.

exist. Balzac was a royalist in all things, a disciple of de Maistre and Bonald in the *Comédie humaine* as in his correspondence. For the two days following the appearance of Maurras's article, the *Gazette de France* carried quotations from *Le Médecin de campagne* in bold-type *entrefilets*, a form of space-filling propaganda which it used again in November and December 1902.[80] In 1903, *L'Action française* published suitable quotations from Balzac under the rubric: *Nos Maîtres*.[81] At the *Institut de L'Action française*, Louis Dîmier lectured on Balzac as one of the 'Maîtres de la contre-révolution'.[82]

The political squabble over Balzac in 1899 and 1900 resolved nothing: it accentuated, rather than diminished, the differences between the left and the right in their interpretations of the *Comédie humaine*, and each side acquired increased confidence in its own rightness. Few writers can ever have enjoyed the position of Balzac at the end of the last century and in the early years of this, acclaimed as a political master by two diametrically opposed political factions. One may be justified in thinking that it was the fundamental ambiguity of Balzac's work— which is fairly close to what critics of earlier periods meant by its 'immorality'—rather than its diversity or wealth which inspired so much critical activity. Attention was however focused principally not on the qualities of the novels as works of literature, but on their 'meaning' and on the details of the author's biography. The distortions and sterility introduced into Balzac criticism by a too exclusive concentration on matters external to the literary value of the works were not the doing of 'la critique universitaire'. The root cause of the low quality of criticism of *La Comédie humaine* in the 1890s, as throughout the nineteenth century, was political passion.

In August 1900, Marc Legrand conducted a survey under the title: 'Que restera-t-il de Balzac?' Seventeen writers, critics, and Balzacians replied to the question:

Quelles sont celles des œuvres de Balzac qui garderont le plus de lecteurs populaires et quelles sont celles qui, plus ignorées ou moins populaires, sont destinées à sortir de l'ombre, soit en raison de la direction du goût vers telle forme du roman, soit en raison des préoccupations mystiques ou sociales des esprits?[83]

The replies were not particularly prophetic, and reflect far more the

---

[80] Every day from 20 Nov. to 18 Dec. 1902.   [81] 15 Aug. 1903 and 1 Feb. 1904.
[82] Reprinted in L. Dîmier, op. cit.   [83] *La Revue d'Europe*, 1 Sept. 1900, p. 194.

situation of Balzac criticism in 1900 than any future changes in popularity or reputation. Édouard Martin-Videau, for example, found the
political polemics over the novelist's significance so explosive as to
prevent him answering the question: for him the subject was 'trop
périlleux'.[84] Jean Destrem also failed to answer the question, but for
reasons of a different order: 'Il ne restera rien de l'œuvre de Balzac.
Il ne restera rien de ceux qui écrivent en prose . . . Si vous n'êtes pas
l'auteur d'une œuvre unique, courte, ou d'un sonnet, vous êtes destiné
à périr . . . après votre décès!'[85] The question formulated by Legrand
implied that some of Balzac's novels were in fact popular in 1900.
This assumption was questioned by many of the respondents. Marcel
Barrière, for example, believed that 'Balzac n'a jamais eu . . . de lecteurs
populaires . . . La lecture de la *Comédie humaine* n'amuse pas: elle fait
penser . . . En principe, il faut avoir quarante ans pour lire Balzac.'[86]
Remy de Gourmont also thought that Balzac was probably not very
popular in 1900[87] and Pontsevrez confirmed this on the basis of his
experience as a public lecturer.[88] Only in the distant future, when
education will have improved the tastes of the masses, could Balzac
hope to become really popular, according to Gustave Toudouze.[89]

In the view of Henry Bordeaux, it was unimportant whether Balzac
was popular with the masses or not: 'L'humanité n'avance pas en tas,
mais par le fait d'une élite'[90] Of the few who actually answered the
question as put by Legrand, a large proportion thought that the novels
of the countryside—*Les Paysans*, *Le Médecin de campagne*, *Le Curé
de village*—would, or should, increase in popularity. There is a strong
and obvious political motivation to Barrès's claim that these were
Balzac's greatest work,[91] as there was to Barrière's hope that they should
become better known.[92] Henry Bordeaux, too, liked the novels for
their 'social content' and believed that they would be read increasingly.[93] Lovenjoul was probably taking account of political attitudes,
rather than propagating one, when he too agreed that *Les Paysans*
would increase in popularity.[94]

Only five of the seventeen respondents declined to make a choice
between the novels of the *Comédie humaine*.[95] Of these, only Victor-
Émile Michelet suggested that it was because the *Comédie humaine*

---

[84] *La Revue d'Europe*, 1 Sept. 1900, pp. 168–9.
[85] Ibid., pp. 166–7. [86] Ibid., p. 162. [87] Ibid., p. 178.
[88] Ibid., pp. 170–2. [89] Ibid., pp. 178–81.
[90] Ibid., pp. 165–6. [91] Ibid., p. 162. [92] Ibid., pp. 162–4.
[93] Ibid., p. 165. [94] Ibid., p. 173.
[95] Jules Claretie, Gabriel Ferry, Henry Mazel, V.-E. Michelet, Georges Ohnet.

should be read as a single work—and he quoted a conversation with Barbey d'Aurevilly to justify this view, far from current at the end of the last century.[96]

The most obvious contenders for popularity—*Eugénie Grandet* and *Le Père Goriot*—are mentioned a few times, by Barrière, Claretie, Poradowska, and Thiaudière: but they are obviously less attractive to the respondents than the novels of the countryside. The question put by Legrand was loaded in favour of the 'social' and 'mystical' novels, and it is no surprise that they figure frequently in the replies. It is also insignificant, since the seventeen respondents hardly represented a cross-section of opinion on Balzac in 1900. Not a single Naturalist writer, let alone a left-wing critic, is present; and Lovenjoul is the only Balzac scholar among them. As a conclusion to a half-century of Balzac criticism, Legrand's survey is indeed a paltry effort.

Balzac's statue by Falguière was finally inaugurated on 22 November 1902—nearly half a century after Dumas's first attempts to erect a monument to his former rival. Zola died in October 1902: had he survived another six weeks, he would, as president of the Societé des gens de lettres, have given the speech at the inauguration, and it would no doubt have been more vigorous than the one his successor, Abel Hermant, delivered. Hermant tried to poke fun at the notion of 'Balzac réactionnaire', pointing out that Taine had also been a hero of the reactionaries but had none the less held Balzac's politics in utter contempt.[97] This speech is evidence of Hermant's conviction that the left had 'lost' Balzac, and that the right-wing view, even if incorrect, was widely and definitively accepted.

In 1906, Ferdinand Brunetière published his last book, entitled *Honoré de Balzac*. In this book, Balzac becomes a hero of truly fabulous qualities: all that preceded him in the novel was but a preparation of the *Comédie humaine*, all that followed but a decadence. Balzac was not a novelist: he was the novel itself. Brunetière had of course made this point before, but with less enthusiasm, and with less documentation on the novel before Balzac. In 1906, he had André Le Breton's solid study to rely on in this respect.[98] As in his Tours speech, Brunetière justifies in his book many of the things he had previously criticized in Balzac: his style, of which all the faults are excused by his ability to make language 'live'; his depiction of high society, which Brunetière

---

[96] *La Revue d'Europe*, 1 Sept. 1900, pp. 169–70.
[97] Abel Hermant, *Discours* (Ollendorff, 1903), pp. 43–61.
[98] *Balzac, l'homme et l'œuvre* (Colin, 1905), pp. 52–111.

here claims is neither vulgar nor inaccurate; and his 'realism', which Balzac's utter truthfulness in description made a masterful method. His alleged immorality is swept aside as a function of his truthfulness to life. If these are reasons for admiring Balzac, Édouard Rod pointedly asked, why does Brunetière not admire Émile Zola even more?[99]

Brunetière professes a complete lack of interest in Balzac's political and religious significance: his concern, he said, was to characterize the literary excellence of the *Comédie humaine*. His arguments are not always strictly logical, as Rod again pointed out; but by concentrating on the literary aspects of Balzac's works, Brunetière created a volume which has itself many of the literary virtues—a polished style, a sense of taste, and a sureness of purpose. To these virtues of a past century, Brunetière added many of its faults: an insistence on systematizing not only literary history but the talents of individual writers, deficient documentation, and an indulgence in gross generalizations. Most of all, however, Brunetière, like so many of the nineteenth-century critics of Balzac, lacked what is now called a 'feel for literature': a perception of the hidden motifs and structures that make a novel more than a story.

The true apotheosis of Balzac was not the one denounced by Pontmartin in 1856, nor even the one Faguet dismissed in 1899, but the appearance of Brunetière's book. It is the culmination of more than fifty years of posthumous Balzac criticism: the total acceptance of the *Comédie humaine*, its faults excused, its virtues enlarged, by the most authoritative critic of the day.

[99] In *La Revue latine*, 25 May 1906.

Conclusions

THE first conclusion that can be drawn from this study of Balzac's reputation in the nineteenth century is that critics' ideologies, and more specifically their political attitudes, played a singularly important role in aligning them 'for' and 'against' Balzac. Furthermore, political associations, particularly in the last quarter of the century, account for the distribution of themes between different critics. For much of the earlier part of the period studied, political and religious arguments were expressed in terms of morality: under the Third Republic, the rhetoric of morality and immorality gives way to clearer expressions of political interest and interpretation. The questions that arise out of this conclusion are not easy to answer. Was Balzac's reputation typical in this respect? If it was not, for what reasons was the *Comédie humaine* subject to so much politically based polemic? The first question cannot be answered on the basis of the material presented in this book. However, it would not be surprising if the reputations of many of Balzac's contemporaries had been even more subject to political variation, given their greater direct involvement with political ideas and action— writers such as Sand, Sue, Hugo, Dumas could hardly have expected an ideologically neutral reception. On the other hand, it appears to have been the ambiguity of Balzac's novels—both in their moral values and their political direction—that allowed so much ideologically based discussion, rather than a clear political association, after the manner of Sand, Sue, and Hugo. Perhaps the accepted notion of great literature as containing an inexhaustible multiplicity of meanings is related to the way in which 'survivors' have been selected by the literary system of the last two centuries: for without his political and moral ambiguity, Balzac would have been a much less attractive subject for discussion and reference in newspapers that were for the most part politically committed in one direction or another.

The second point to be made is that the idea of beauty was not at all central to nineteenth-century Balzac criticism. Most critics were more intent on establishing whether the *Comédie humaine* was true, in what respects it was true, and what the sources of its truthfulness were. Balzac's declared intention of writing a history of manners was taken very seriously, not only by Zola, but also by Sainte-Beuve, Castille, and the *réalistes* themselves, who saw the *Comédie humaine* as failing to achieve its truthful and historical objective. Even by the end of the century, the criterion of beauty only enters criticism of Balzac in respect of his style. This feature is almost certainly not restricted to Balzac criticism, and underlines the distinction made between prose fiction and other kinds of literature.

There were four major public moments in the development of Balzac's reputation in the period studied: the funeral oration delivered by Hugo in August 1850; the publication of Taine's *Étude sur Balzac* in 1858; the pronouncements of Zola between 1878 and 1881; and Émile Faguet's first article on the *Comédie humaine* in 1887. The first of these events broadcast the idea of Balzac as a revolutionary; the second put forward several themes, the most important of which was the notion of Balzac as a visionary, imaginative writer; the third elaborated the doctrine of Balzac as a Naturalist; and the last expounded the view that Balzac was a classic. All four of these important articles were preceded by other, now forgotten pieces that opened up the themes of criticism they deal with. All four have been presented as expressions of attitudes that had already gained a certain degree of acceptance, and not as 'turning-points' or completely new departures. If a turning-point must be found, then it is in the decade of the 1870s that it must lie: the difference between the reverential tone of nearly all post-1880 criticism and the either deprecatory or crusading edge of nearly all pre-1869 criticism is very marked. A number of significant events help to account for this. Had Balzac lived his 'natural' life-span he would have died around 1870—as did so many of his own literary generation (Sainte-Beuve, Sand, Dumas, Janin, Gautier, Laure Surville, Chasles all died between 1869 and 1875). There was of course a change of regime and political climate in those years also; and the first edition of Balzac's complete works preceded the collapse of the Empire, as the first major publication of his letters followed the formal establishment of the Third Republic. Balzac's emergence as a classic followed the end of a generation, the end of a regime and the proper publication of his writings. These events, rather than any particular article, may be said to constitute the crucial turning-point in the story of his survival, and suggest a possible periodization which would not distort the known facts. From 1850 to 1869, Balzac was a novelist whose value was disputed, but claimed to be very great by a relatively small section of critics; from 1882 to 1900, Balzac was an undisputed master of the novel genre, but whose nature and intentions were hotly disputed by a wide variety of factions and schools. Between 1869 and 1882, Balzac underwent a whole series of transformations, not only at the hands of Émile Zola, and which cannot be condensed into a neat phrase or paragraph.

This rough periodization is also congruent with what has been found out about public demand for the *Comédie humaine*. The first period, 1850–69, is characterized by low demand for a wide variety of Balzac's novels; the third period, 1882–1900, shows demand steadily increasing from a low point to an enormous peak in the early years of this century. Between the two periods there is a marked trough in demand for all July Monarchy fiction, and out of which Balzac's contemporaries and competitors, Dumas, Sue, and Sand, did not rise. There may be no answer to the question: why Balzac?, other than the detailed narrative of this book on how Balzac survived.

Most of the developments in what have been called the themes of Balzac criticism can be shown to derive either from a *contradiction* (of some existing theme), or from an *analogy* (true or false), or from *new information*. The idea that Balzac was really a monarchist was put forward in 1850 as a contradiction of Victor Hugo's view that the novelist was a revolutionary; Brunetière's view of Balzac as a romantic (in 1885) was a contradiction of Zola. Zola's reinvention of the idea of 'Balzac révolutionnaire' in 1869 has been shown to be the result of an analogy between his own novel, *La Fortune des Rougon*, and its principal source, Balzac's *Pierrette*. Later changes in Zola's view of Balzac may be described more unkindly as examples of 'grafting' rather than analogy. From the 1870s on, and with the exception of Gustave Kahn, less and less attempt was made to judge Balzac on his own terms, and more and more critical arguments rely on analogies with contemporary practice and fashion—most notably with Paul Bourget's psychologism, with the pseudo-sciences of animal magnetism, hypnotism, and with the fundamentally different political interests of the anti-Dreyfusard right. The effect of new material has been studied in the debt Taine and Gautier owed to Laure Surville's biography of her brother; and in the change of attitude imposed by the publication of Balzac's *Correspondance* in 1876.

This book has not pierced all the mysteries surrounding the establishment of a high literary reputation like that of the *Comédie humaine*. Indeed, it has deepened the murky question of the ultimate reason why it occurred, by showing so many of the specific changes in Balzac's reputation to be dependent on incidental factors—on pure chance, in some cases. The selection of a small number of 'classics' from the vast overproduction of literary books may be a natural feature of the literary system, but the selection of specific survivors, such as Balzac, may be as much the result of chance as of any internal logic or necessity. Since we cannot separate our notion of literary excellence from the works on which that notion is based, it is impossible to avoid circularity if we argue that Balzac survived because he was a great writer. He is a great writer because he survived.

Chronological summary of events

MOST of the critical writing on Balzac in the last century was sparked off by identifiable events of different kinds, many of which were public and official, and others more literary. The following list gives an overview of the succession of events related to Balzac criticism. Over three-quarters of the items listed in the Bibliography (Appendix III) were generated by the events listed below. Entries in brackets concern the end of Balzac's literary generation.

1850   Performance of *Vautrin*.
        Death of Balzac.

1851   Performances of *Mercadet* and *La Peau de Chagrin*.
        Essay contest set by the Académie de Châlons-sur-Marne.

1853   Performance of *Le Lys dans la vallée*.
        A. Baschet appeals for Balzac's letters.

1854   Dumas's proposal for a Balzac monument quashed by Mme Ève de Balzac.

1856   (Death of A. Dutacq, Balzac's *exécuteur testamentaire*.) Essay contest on Balzac, set by the Société des gens de lettres ('Prix Véron').
        Publication of Laure Surville's biography of Balzac.
        Publication of Flaubert's *Madame Bovary*.

1857   (Death of Eugène Sue.)

1858   Publication of Taine's *Étude sur Balzac*.

1859   Performance of *Paméla Giraud* and *La Marâtre*.

1863   Performance of *Les Ressources de Quinola*.

1865   Vallès lectures on Balzac.

1868   Performance of *Les Treize* and *Mercadet*.

1869   (Death of Sainte-Beuve.)
        Publication of the definitive edition of the *Comédie humaine*.
        Zola writes *La Fortune des Rougon*.

1870   (Death of A. Dumas père.)

1872   (Death of T. Gautier.)

1874   (Deaths of Jules Janin and Philarète Chasles.)

1876 (Death of George Sand.)
Publication of Balzac's *Correspondance*.

1877 Publication of Zola's *L'Assommoir*.

1878 (–81) 'La Bataille naturaliste'.

1879 Publication of Lovenjoul's *Histoire des Œuvres de Balzac*.

1880 Zola proposes a Balzac monument.

1881 *Le Figaro* publishes a special supplement on the anniversary of Balzac's death.

1882 Death of Mme Ève de Balzac, auction of her estate.

1883 The Société des gens de lettres launches a fund for a Balzac monument.

1886 The Académie française sets the subject of its *prix d'éloquence* as: 'L'Œuvre d'Honoré de Balzac'.

1887 Publication of Faguet's *Étude sur Balzac*.
New appeal for Balzac statue.

1888 Performance of *Mercadet* (flops).

1889 *Eugénie Grandet* added to the *agrégation* reading list.

1890 Luxury edition of *Les Chouans*.

1893 Publication of Flat's *Essais sur Balzac*.
Rodin commissioned for the Balzac statue.

1894 Performance of *Les Chouans*.

1895 Publication of the first 'Pages choisies de Balzac'.

1898 Rodin's statue presented then refused.

1899 Performance of *Mercadet* at the Comédie française.
Celebration of Balzac's centenary at Tours.

1900 'Que restera-t-il de Balzac?'
Celebration of the 50th anniversary of Balzac's death in Paris.
Copyright on all but posthumous works lapses.

1902 Falguière's statue of Balzac unveiled.

Bibliography of Balzac criticism
1829–1849

THIS is simply a list of the critical articles referred to in the introductory sketch of Balzac's critical reception up to his death (Introduction, II, pp. 5–17), and is far from complete. It was compiled on the basis of the bibliographies of Weinberg, Royce, Barbéris (see the foreword to Appendix III for fuller details of these works).

The first appearance of a reprinted article carries a forward reference to its next publication after the abbreviation repr.; its subsequent appearances carry a date reference to its original publication after the symbol *.

1829

Apr. Anon., 'Le Dernier Chouan', Le Mercure de France au XIXe siècle, XXV. 138.

15 May Anon., 'Le Dernier Chouan', L'Universel.

1830

7 Feb. JANIN, Jules, 'La Physiologie du mariage', Le Journal des débats.

Mar. PETETIN, Anselme, 'Le Dernier Chouan', La Revue encyclopédique, XLV. 720–7.

29 Apr. Anon., 'Scènes de la vie privée', Le Sylphe.

8 May Anon., 'Scènes de la vie privée', Le Corsaire.

25 June Anon., 'Scènes de la vie privée', Le Globe.

1831

6 Aug. CHASLES, Philarète, 'La Peau de chagrin', Le Messager des chambres.

14 Aug. JANIN, Jules, 'La Peau de chagrin', L'Artiste, II. 18–21.

28 Aug. Anon., 'La Peau de chagrin', La Quotidienne.

8 Sept. Anon., 'La Peau de chagrin', Le National.

28 Oct. Anon., 'Romans et Contes philosophiques par M. de Balzac', Le Constitutionnel.

1 Nov. DESCHAMPS, Émile, 'M. de Balzac', RDM IV. 313–22. repr. La Revue étrangère (1832), II.

6 Nov. MONTALEMBERT, C.-R., 'La Peau de chagrin', L'Avenir.

1832

Saint-C., 'Nouveaux Contes philosophiques', *L'Artiste*, IV. 282–3.

Mar.   Charton, Édouard, '*Les Cent Contes drolatiques*', *La Revue encyclopédique*, LIII. 683–8.

29 June Anon., '*Scènes de la vie privée*', *La Quotidienne*.

1833

Feb.   Anon., '*Louis Lambert*, par M. de Balzac', *RDP* XLVII. 155.

Oct.   Desessarts, Alfred, '*Le Médecin de campagne*', *La France littéraire*, IX. 412–14.

1834

15 Nov. Sainte-Beuve, Charles-Augustin, 'Poètes et romanciers modernes de la France, XVI. M. de Balzac. *La Recherche de l'Absolu*', *RDM* IV. 440–58.
repr. 1836, 1846, 1855, 1869.

1835

Cherbuliez, Joël, '*Le Père Goriot*', *Le Bulletin littéraire et scientifique*, 3e année, p. 80.

15 Jan. Muret, Théodore, 'Monsieur de Balzac', *Le Voleur*.

23 Mar. I.C.T., 'Revue littéraire. *Le Père Goriot*, par M. de Balzac', *Le Constitutionnel*.

1 July   Robert, Clémence, '*Le Père Goriot*', *Le Journal des Femmes*.

15 July Anon., 'Quelques gens de lettres dans leur intérieur', *Le Mercure de France*, No. 6.

12 Dec. Guinot, Eugène, 'Études littéraires. Œuvres de M. de Balzac. *La Fleur-des-pois*', *Le Charivari*. (Second article on 22 Dec. 1835.)

1836

Sainte-Beuve, Charles-Augustin, *Critiques et Portraits littéraires* (Renduel), III. 56–89.
*15 Nov. 1834.

Feb.   Gonzalès, Emmanuel, 'Honoré de Balzac', *La Revue du théâtre* (= *Art et progrès*), II. 243– .

9 Feb.   Nettement, Alfred, 'Études littéraires. Les Modernes.—M. de Balzac', *La Gazette de France*. (Second article on 16 Feb. 1836.)
repr. *Une Étude impartiale sur Honoré de Balzac* (1836).

19 May   Anon., 'Littérature. *Jane la Pâle*', *Le Charivari*.

29 Oct.   Anon., 'Nouvelles Balzachinades', *Le Charivari*.

29 Oct.   CHAUDES-AIGUES, J.-G., 'M. de Balzac', *La Revue du XIXe siècle*, VI. 411–15.

1837

LECOMTE, Jules-François, *Lettres sur les écrivains français* (Brussels, 1837), pp. 19–24. Signed: Van Engelgom de Bruxelles.

23 June   Anon., 'Topographie littéraire', *Le Charivari*. Further articles on 26 June, 7 Aug. 1837.

20 Aug.   Anon., 'Le Sire de Balzac dans sa terre de Villerglé', *Le Charivari*.

1838

Oct.   CHERBULIEZ, Joël, '*La Femme supérieure* . . .', *La Revue critique des livres nouveaux*, p. 308.

15 Oct.   SAINTE-BEUVE, Charles-Augustin, 'Charles de Bernard', *RDM* XVI. 253–7.

21 Oct.   PICHOT, Amédée, '*La Maison Nucingen*', *RDP* LVIII. 226–9. Signed: Pickersghill.

1 Nov.   SAINTE-BEUVE, Charles-Augustin, 'H. de Balzac. Études de mœurs au XIXe siècle. *La Femme supérieure. La Maison Nucingen. La Torpille*', *RDM* XVI. 366–9. Unsigned.
repr. *Premiers Lundis* (Michel Lévy, 1875), II. 360–7.

1839

July   JANIN, Jules, '*Un Grand Homme de province à Paris*, par M. de Balzac', *RDP* VII. 145–78.

28 July   SECOND, Albéric, 'Le Dernier Livre de M. de Balzac', *Le Figaro*.

1 Sept.   SAINTE-BEUVE, Charles-Augustin, 'De la littérature industrielle', *RDM* XIX. 675–91.
repr. *Portraits contemporains* (Michel Lévy, 1870), II. 444–71.

Nov.   CHAUDES-AIGUES, J.-G., 'M. de Balzac. *Une Fille d'Ève*', *RDP* XI. 20–38.
repr. *Les Écrivains modernes de la France* (Gosselin, 1841), pp. 199–232.

1840

1 Mar.   SAINTE-BEUVE, Charles-Augustin, 'Dix Ans après en littérature', *RDM* XXI. 689–702.
repr. *Portraits contemporains* (Michel Lévy, 1870), II. 482–3.

16 Mar.   JANIN, Jules, 'Théâtre de la Porte Saint-Martin. *Vautrin*, de M.
          de Balzac', *Le Journal des débats*.

18 Mar.   NETTEMENT, Alfred, '*Vautrin*', *La Gazette de France*.

22 Mar.   GONZALÈS, Emmanuel, '*Vautrin*', *La Caricature*.

15 Sept. SAINTE-BEUVE, Charles-Augustin, 'M. Eugène Sue', *RDM*
          XXIII. 869–85.

1841

          CHAUDES-AIGUES, J.-G., *Les Écrivains modernes de la France*
          (Gosselin, 1841), pp. 199–232.
          *Nov. 1839.

25 Apr.   GIRAULT, Francis, 'Les Romanciers, Honoré de Balzac', *Le
          Bibliographe*.
          Further articles on 2 and 3 May, 1 July 1841.

May   CHAUDES-AIGUES, J.-G., '*Le Curé de village*', *RDP* XXIX.
          342–6.

Oct.   BERTHOUD, Samuel-Henry, 'Études littéraires. M. de Balzac',
          Le Musée des familles, IX. 31–2.

25 Nov.   BARTHÉLÉMY LANTA, A. de, '*Le Curé de village*', *L'Écho de la
          littérature et des beaux-arts*, II. cols. 560–4.

1842

15 Mar.   MOLÈNES, Paul Gaschon de, 'Revue littéraire. *Les Mémoires de
          deux jeunes mariées*', *RDM* XXIX. 979–86.

1 Apr.   MOLÈNES, Paul Gaschon de, '*Les Ressources de Quinola*', *RDM*
          XXX. 136–51.

1 Nov.   MOLÈNES, Paul Gaschon de, 'Simples Essais d'histoire littéraire',
          RDM XXXII. 390–411.

1843

          OZENNE, Louise-Laure, *Mélanges critiques et littéraires* (Didot,
          1843), p. 160.

          SAINT-MARC GIRARDIN, *Cours de littérature dramatique* (Char-
          pentier, 1843), I. 241–5.

13 Jan.   ASSELINE, Alfred, '*Un Ménage de garçon en province*', *RDP* XIII,
          supplément pp. 61–7.

6 May   CORMENIN, Louis de, 'Portraits littéraires.—M. de Balzac',
          L'Unité.

15 June   MOLÈNES, Paul Gaschon de, 'Revue littéraire', *RDM* II. 990–8.

1 Dec.   MOLÈNES, Paul Gaschon de, 'Les Derniers Romans de M. de

Balzac et de M. Frédéric Soulié', *RDM* IV. 810–29. (Signed: F. de Lagenevais.)

1844

CHASLES, Philarète, 'Balzac', *Dictionnaire de la conversation* (Garnier, 1844), supplément, II. 413–15. (Signed: V. Caralp.)

4 May ASSELINE, Alfred, '*Modeste Mignon*, par M. de Balzac', *RDP* I. 11–12.

1 June LIMAYRAC, Paulin, 'Simples Essais d'histoire littéraire, V. De l'Esprit de désordre en littérature', *RDM* II. 808–9.

25 July THOMAS, Alexandre, '*Un Début dans la vie*, par M. de Balzac', *RDP* I. 430–1.

29 Sept. ASSELINE, Alfred, 'Un Mot sur M. de Balzac, à propos de son nouveau roman, *Splendeurs et Misères des Courtisanes*', *L'Artiste*, II. 75.

28 Dec. THOMAS, Alexandre, '*Les Paysans*, par M. de Balzac', *RDP* II. 609–11.

1845

NETTEMENT, Alfred, *Études critiques sur le feuilleton-roman* (Perrodil, 1845), I. 36– .

1846

SAINTE-BEUVE, Charles-Augustin, *Portraits Contemporains* (Didier, 1846), I. 443–65.
*15 Nov. 1834.

15 Apr. BAUDELAIRE, Charles, 'Conseils aux jeunes littérateurs', *L'Esprit public*.
repr. *L'Art Romantique* (Conard, 1925), p. 274.

25 Aug. BAUDELAIRE, Charles, 'Comment on paye ses dettes quand on a du génie', *L'Écho des théâtres*.
repr. *Juvenilia* (Conard, 1939), I. 114–17.

4 Oct. CASTILLE, Charles-Hippolyte, 'M. H. de Balzac', *La Semaine*.
repr. *L'Abeille littéraire*, Feb. 1847.

18 Oct. NERVAL, Gérard de, [n.t.], *L'Artiste*.

24 Oct. BAUDELAIRE, Charles, 'Causerie', *Le Tintamarre*.
repr. *Juvenilia* (Conard, 1939), I. 127–8.

30 Nov. PELLETAN, Eugène, '*La Comédie humaine*, par M. de Balzac', *La Presse*.
repr. *Heures de travail* (Pagnerre, 1854), I. 98–107.

12 Dec.   WEILL, Alexandre, '*Les Parents pauvres*', *La Démocratie pacifique*. Second article on 27 Dec. 1846.

1847

CHAMPFLEURY, *Feu Miette. Fantaisies d'été* (Martinon, 1847), Dédicace.

SUE, Eugène, Letter to Alexandre Weill. Undated, c. 1847. Signed original, Lov. A.363, fo. 235–6.

ROUX, Gabriel, 'Avant-propos', in H. de Balzac, *Le Provincial à Paris* (Roux et Cassanet, 1847). (Signed: L'Éditeur.)

5 Jan.   WEILL, Alexandre, [n.t.], *La Démocratie pacifique*. Further article on 9 Jan. 1847.

25 Jan.   MARRON, Eugène, 'Critique littéraire. Année 1846', *La Revue indépendante*, VII. 237–54.

27 Jan.   AUBERT, Albert, 'Revue littéraire. Œuvres complètes de M. de Balzac', *Le Constitutionnel*.

1 Feb.   BABOU, Hippolyte, 'Petites lettres confidentielles à M. de Balzac par une femme du monde, un diplomate et un pédant', *La Revue nouvelle*, XIII. 91– . repr. *Lettres satiriques et critiques* (Poulet-Malassis et de Broise, 1860), pp. 75–117.

15 Apr.   LERMINIER, J.-L.-E., 'De la Peinture des mœurs contemporaines', *RDM*. XVIII. 193–216.

19 Apr.   HENNEQUIN, Victor, [n.t.], *La Démocratie pacifique*.

7 May   WEILL, Alexandre, [n.t.], *La Démocratie pacifique*.

1848

CHEVALET, Émile, 'De Balzac à Proudhon', MS. copy dated 1848–9 by Lovenjoul, Lov. A.361, fo. 8–17. Published in *L'Avenir Républicain* (Issoudun), 21 June 1894.

29 May   JANIN, Jules, 'Théâtre historique . . .', *Le Journal des débats*.

29 May   GAUTIER, Théophile, '*La Marâtre*', *La Presse*.

May   BAUDELAIRE, Charles, [n.t.], *Le Salut public*. repr. *Œuvres posthumes* (Conard, 1939), I. 207.

1849

9 Jan.   VACQUERIE, Auguste, [n.t.], *L'Évènement*.

8 Oct.   SAINTE-BEUVE, Charles-Augustin, 'Les *Confidences* par M. de Lamartine', *Le Constitutionnel*.

Bibliography of Balzac criticism
1850–1900

THIS is a comprehensive listing of all articles and books containing references to Balzac that were written or published in the second half of the last century. It is the result of a great deal of hard labour amidst the defective catalogues of the Bibliothèque nationale, and was compiled in the following manner. W. H. Royce's *Balzac Bibliography*[1] was used as a starting-point and collated with the bibliography of Bernard Weinberg's thesis[2]—which turned out to have remarkably few errors, unlike Royce. The reviews of Balzac's plays listed by D. Z. Milatchitch[3] were then added to the growing card index, as were the articles on Balzac listed in the bibliographies of Barbey d'Aurevilly's critical writings[4] and of Zola's journalism.[5] The indexes of the Goncourts' *Journal*, of the published correspondence of Taine, Baudelaire, Flaubert, Zola, Champfleury and others were combed, as was Delacroix's *Journal*. Further references were provided by works on Bourget[6] and by M. Raimond's thesis on *Balzac vu par les romanciers français de Zola à Proust*.[7] The list thus established was carefully checked against reality, using the resources of the British Museum, the Bibliothèque nationale, and the splendid collection of Second Empire newspapers in the Lovenjoul Library at Chantilly. The process of checking itself led to the discovery of a number of previously unlisted items and the correction of a number of inherited errors. A list of major Paris newspapers and literary reviews was then established, and these journals were examined as comprehensively as the Bibliothèque nationale's defective collections would permit. A very much wider spectrum that included very obscure papers was read for particular years when comment on Balzac might reasonably have been expected—August–September 1850, August 1851, the autumn of 1856, spring 1869, 1876, 1899, and 1900. The analytical indexes of the *Biblio-*

---

[1] Chicago, Syracuse University Press, 1929.

[2] *French Realism: The Critical Reaction 1830–1870* (London, O.U.P., 1937).

[3] *Le Théâtre de Honoré de Balzac* (Hachette, 1930).

[4] J. Petit & P. J. Yarrow, *Barbey d'Aurevilly journaliste et critique. Bibliographie* (*ALUB*, t. 28) (Les Belles Lettres, 1959).

[5] H. Mitterand & H. Suwala, *Émile Zola journaliste. Bibliographie . . . 1859–1881* (*ALUB*, t. 89) (Les Belles Lettres, 1968).

[6] L. J. Austin, *Paul Bourget, sa vie et son œuvre jusqu'en 1899* (Droz, 1940).

[7] Sorbonne Library, Paris, 1966.

graphie de la France were searched for volumes of criticism and literary history likely to contain mention of Balzac.

Provincial periodicals were not searched except those for 1899. The few provincial and foreign items included in this list, such as the Brussels items, are all derivative from other sources or the result of clues given in the Paris press. However, every item included in this bibliography has been read. A certain amount of unpublished manuscript material was found in the Lovenjoul library, Chantilly, which included an early Balzac bibliography by Henri Clouard.

Many of the items listed contain only two or three sentences on Balzac. It was not easy to decide when a reference to the *Comédie humaine* qualified for admission to Balzac criticism, but the general rule used was that if the author was of any importance, any reference to Balzac was to be counted; if he was not, then his remarks had to go beyond a mere phrase to be included. This left plenty of room for manœuvre and flexibility.

Important articles which were reprinted in whole or in part in the period are entered each time they appeared in this chronological listing. The first appearance of a reprinted article carries a forward reference to its next publication after the abbreviation repr.; its subsequent appearances carry a date reference to its original publication after the symbol *. Changes between the different versions are also indicated where relevant.

This bibliography will probably be superseded in due course by the Syracuse Balzac Bibliography. However, until such time as this long-awaited work does appear, the present listing will have to be considered the definitive bibliography of Balzac criticism between 1850 and 1900 despite its Parisian exclusivity and single-handed compilation.

Items are placed in this listing under the date on which they were published, except for letters, entries in diaries, and unpublished MSS., which are placed under the date which can be attributed to their composition, as are items which carry a specific date other than that of publication.

1850

SOUTERRE, André, *Hommage à la mémoire de Balzac*. Original MS. Lov. A.367. Undated: *c.* 1850.

16 Feb.   Anon., 'M. de Balzac retrouvé', *Le Journal pour rire*.

28 Feb.   MAZADE, Charles de, 'De la Démocratie en littérature' *RDM* V. 916.

22 Apr.   MATHAREL, Charles de, '*Vautrin*', *Le Siècle*.

24 Apr.   M., '*Vautrin*', *Le Foyer dramatique*.

25 Apr.   Anon., '*Vautrin*', *Le Messager des théâtres et des arts*.

25 Apr.   Anon., '*Vautrin*', *Le Pays*.

26 Apr.   G.D., 'Théâtres de Paris', *La Semaine*.

28 Apr. LUCAS, Hippolyte, '*Vautrin*', *Le Moniteur du Soir*.

29 Apr. DÉSARBRES, Nérée, 'Théâtres', *L'Ami du peuple*.

29 Apr. MATHAREL, Charles de, '*Vautrin*', *Le Siècle*.

29 Apr. THIERRY, Édouard, '*Vautrin*', *L'Assemblée nationale*.

29 Apr. Anon., 'Théâtre de la Gaîté', *Le Charivari*.

29 Apr. BUSONI, Philippe, '*Vautrin*', *Le Crédit*.

29 Apr. BANVILLE, Théodore de, '*Vautrin*', *Le Dix-Décembre*.

29 Apr. BRISSET, M.-J., '*Vautrin*', *La Gazette de France*.

29 Apr. JANIN, Jules, '*Vautrin* et M. de Balzac', *Le Journal des débats*.

29 Apr. ROMAGNY, Charles, '*Vautrin*', *La Liberté*.

29 Apr. MUSSET, Paul de, '*Vautrin*', *Le National*.

29 Apr. LECLERC, A., '*Vautrin*', *La République*.
         repr. *L'Estafette*, 30 Apr. 1850.

29 Apr. Y., '*Vautrin*', *L'Union*.

30 Apr. Anon., '*Vautrin*', *Le Corsaire*.

30 Apr. PONTMARTIN, Armand de, 'Revue', *RDM* VI. 574.

6 May   MEURICE, Paul, '*Vautrin*', *L'Évènement*.

7 May   MÉRAY, Antony, '*Vautrin*', *La Démocratie pacifique*.

4 July Anon., 'Nouvelles diverses', *Le Siècle*.

11 Aug. FIOUPIOU, Joseph, 'Revue de Paris', *Le Pouvoir*.

20 Aug. Anon., [n.t.], *L'Évènement*.
         Further articles in *L'Évènement* on 21, 22, 23, and 24 Aug. 1850.

20 Aug. Anon., [n.t.], *La Patrie*.
         Further articles in *La Patrie* on 21 and 22 Aug. 1850.

20 Aug. LERMINIER, J.-L.-E., Letter to la Comtesse Merlin (?). Damascéno Morgand, catalogue May 1956, no. 146.

21 Aug. HUGO, Victor, 'Funérailles de Balzac'.
         repr. *Actes et Paroles.—Avant l'Exil* (Imprimerie nationale, 1937).

21 Aug. JANIN, Jules, Conversation quoted by Julien Lemer in *Balzac, sa vie, son œuvre* (Sauvaître, 1892).

21 Aug. Anon., [n.t.], *Le Théâtre*.

21 Aug. Anon., [n.t.], *Le Charivari*.

21 Aug. Anon., [n.t.], *La Gazette de France*.

21 Aug. DELORD, Taxile, 'Mélanges, variétés', *Le Peuple de 1850*.

22 Aug.　Anon., [n.t.], *Le Siècle*.

22 Aug.　Anon., 'Les Obsèques de M. de Balzac', *Le Corsaire*.

23 Aug.　LECOMTE, Jules-François, 'Courrier de Paris.—Mort et funérailles de M. de Balzac', *L'Indépendance belge*.
Further article on 25 Aug. 1850.

23 Aug.　Anon., [n.t.], *La Gazette de France*.

24 Aug.　Anon., 'Notes sur Balzac', *Le Corsaire*.

24 Aug.　BARBEY D'AUREVILLY, Jules, 'Nécrologie. M. de Balzac', *La Mode*.
repr. *La Chronique des livres*, 10 and 25 Nov. 1904.
repr. *Les Cahiers aurevilliens*, no. 4.

24 Aug.　BUSONI, Philippe, 'Courrier de Paris', *L'Illustration*.

24 Aug.　CHASLES, Philarète, [n.t.], *Le Journal des débats*.

25 Aug.　FIOUPIOU, Joseph, 'Revue de Paris', *Le Pouvoir*.

25 Aug.　MÉRAY, Antony, [n.t.], *La Démocratie pacifique*.

25 Aug.　ACHARD, Amédée, [n.t.], *L'Assemblée nationale*.

26 Aug.　NERVAL, Gérard de, 'Théâtres', *La Presse*.

27 Aug.　FORGUES, Émile-Daurand, 'Honoré de Balzac', *Le National*.
(Signed: Old Nick.)

30 Aug.　FOREST, *Honoré de Balzac, poème*, original MS., Lov. A.363, fo. 67–8.

31 Aug.　FOREST, Letter to Escudier frères, original MS., Lov. A.363, fo. 66.

31 Aug.　BUSONI, Philippe, 'Balzac', *L'Illustration*.

31 Aug.　Anon., 'Honoré de Balzac', *Le Courrier de l'Europe*.

1 Sept.　AUBRYET, Xavier, 'Quelques mots sur Balzac', *L'Artiste*, V. 110.

1 Sept.　LECOMTE, Jules, 'Honoré de Balzac', *L'Artiste*, V. 117–19.

1 Sept.　LECOMTE, Jules, 'Courrier de Paris', *L'Indépendance belge*.
Further articles on 8, 16, 22, and 29 Sept. 1850.

1 Sept.　MAZADE, Charles de, 'Chronique', *RDM* VII. 912–17.

1 Sept.　MAINZER, E., 'Honoré de Balzac', *La Revue et Gazette musicale de Paris*.

1 Sept.　COHEN, Jacob, 'Honoré de Balzac', *La Semaine*.

2 Sept.　SAINTE-BEUVE, Charles-Augustin, 'Monsieur de Balzac', *Le Constitutionnel*.
repr. *Causeries du lundi* (Garnier, 1851), II. 346–62.
repr. *Causeries du lundi* (Garnier, 1858), II. 443–46.

2 Sept.　MATHAREL, Charles de, 'Revue des théâtres', *Le Siècle*.

5 Sept.   GUENOT, Georges, 'Honoré de Balzac', *Le Journal des femmes.*

11 Sept.   DESNOIRESTERRES, Gustave, 'M. de Balzac', *L'Ordre.*
Further articles on 12 and 13 Sept. 1850.
repr. *Le Psyché*, 15 Oct. 1850 (in part).
repr. *Honoré de Balzac* (Paul Permaint, 1851) (in full).

15 Sept.   P.B., 'Balzac et Fourier', *La Démocratie pacifique.*

6 Oct.   GUINOT, Eugène, 'Revue de Paris', *L'Ordre.*

7 Oct.   NERVAL, Gérard de, 'Théâtres', *La Presse.*
repr. *Le Messager des théâtres et des arts*, 20 Oct. 1850.

25 Oct.   CORNUT, Romain, 'Analyse critique des œuvres de Balzac', *Le Journal des faits.*
Series of articles continued regularly until 23 Dec. 1851.

14 Nov.   FLAUBERT, Gustave, Letter to Louis Bouilhet. *Correspondance* (Pléiade, 1973), I. 710.

17 Dec.   RICHARD, Gabriel, 'Études littéraires: La Comédie humaine', *Le Courrier de la Gironde.*
Second article on 18 Dec. 1850.
repr. *HOB* 480–7.

1851

DESNOIRESTERRES, Gustave, *Honoré de Balzac* (Paul Permaint, 1851).
*11 Sept. 1850.

BASCHET, Armand, *Variétés littéraires, H. de Balzac.—Étude variée. Généralités de la Comédie humaine*, avec notes historiques par Cham[p]fleury (Blosse, 1851).
repr. with alterations *Les Physionomies littéraires de ce temps Honoré de Balzac. Essai sur l'homme et sur l'œuvre*, avec notes historiques par Champfleury (Giraud et Dagneau, 1852).

JOLLY, Jules, *De l'Influence de la littérature et du théâtre sur l'esprit public et les mœurs pendant les vingt dernières années* (Amyot, 1851), pp. 36–40.

LACROIX, Paul, 'Notice biographique sur Balzac', in *Les Femmes de H. de Balzac* (Janet, 1851), pp. i-xii. (Signed: Le Bibliophile Jacob.)
This volume of extracts was compiled by Laure Surville.

ROVIGO, René de, and AUDEBRAND, Philibert, *Feuilles volantes*, pp. 31–6.

SAINTE-BEUVE, Charles-Augustin, *Causeries du Lundi* (Garnier, 1851), II. 346–62.
*2 Sept. 1850.

BAUDELAIRE, Charles, 'Du Vin et du haschisch', published in *Les Paradis artificiels* (Conard, 1928), p. 202.

21 Mar. Anon., 'Courrier de Paris', *L'Indépendance belge.*

Apr. CHAMPFLEURY, 'Sensations de voyage d'un essayiste', *L'Évènement.*

11 Apr. CHAMPFLEURY, Letter to his mother, published in J. Troubat, *Sainte-Beuve et Champfleury* (Société du Mercure de France, 1908), pp. 122–4.

14 June CHAMPFLEURY, 'M. de Balzac père de la critique future', *Le Messager de l'Assemblée.*

24 June VITU, Auguste, 'Portraits littéraires.—Monsieur de Balzac', *Le Messager de l'Assemblée.*
Further articles not published at request of Mme Ève de Balzac.

24 Aug. CELLIÉ, Eugène, 'Théâtre du Gymnase', *La Revue et Gazette des théâtres.*

25 Aug. THIERRY, Édouard, *'Mercadet le Faiseur'*, *L'Assemblée nationale.*

25 Aug. Anon., *'Mercadet'*, *Le Charivari.*

25 Aug. LIREUX, Auguste, *'Mercadet'*, *Le Constitutionnel,*

25 Aug. BRISSET, M.-J., 'Revue dramatique', *La Gazette de France.*

25 Aug. JANIN, Jules, 'La Semaine dramatique. *Mercadet'*, *Le Journal des débats.*
repr. *Critique dramatique* (Librairie des Bibliophiles, 1877).

25 Aug. LURINE, Louis, 'Théâtres.—*Mercadet'*, *Le Messager de l'Assemblée.*

25 Aug. MUSSET, Paul de, *'Mercadet'*, *Le National.*

25 Aug. PÈNE, Henri de, 'Revue dramatique.—*Mercadet'*, *L'Opinion publique.*

25 Aug. BUSONI, Philippe, *'Mercadet'*, *L'Ordre.*

25 Aug. PRÉMARAY, Jules de, 'Théâtres', *La Patrie.*

25 Aug. SAINT-VICTOR, Paul de, *'Mercadet'*, *Le Pays.*

25 Aug. MATHAREL, Charles de, *'Mercadet le Faiseur'*, *Le Siècle.*

25 Aug. MURET, Théodore, *'Mercadet'*, *L'Union.*
Second article on 1 Sept. 1851.

26 Aug. SAUVAGE, T., *'Mercadet'*, *Le Moniteur Universel.*

26 Aug. GAIFFE, Adolphe, *'Mercadet'*, *L'Évènement.*

27 Aug. DELORD, Taxile, 'Ne Touchez Pas à Mercadet', *Le Charivari.*

28 Aug. POMMEREUX, 'Paris', *La Revue et Gazette des théâtres.*

30 Aug.　BAUDELAIRE, Charles, Letter to Mme Aupick, in *Correspondance générale* (Conard, 1947), I. 141.

30 Aug.　BUSONI, Philippe, 'Courrier de Paris', *L'Illustration*.

30 Aug.　LEMER, Julien, '*Mercadet*', *La Sylphide*.

Sept.　FLAUBERT, Gustave, Letter to Louise Colet, in *Correspondance* (Conard, 1926) II. 316.

1 Sept.　GUINOT, Eugène, 'Le Prix d'un type', *Le Foyer dramatique*.

1 Sept.　GAUTIER, Théophile, '*Mercadet*', *La Presse*.

2 Sept.　LURINE, Louis, 'Mercadet et Philinte', *Le Messager de l'Assemblée*.

4 Sept.　JOUVIN, B., 'Chronique théâtrale', *La Chronique de Paris* (mensuel).

4 Sept.　CELLIÉ, Eugène, [n.t.], *La Revue et Gazette des théâtres*.

5 Sept.　GONZALÈS, Emmanuel, 'Dizaine dramatique', *La Mode*.

5 Sept.　FILLIAS, Achille, 'Théâtres de Paris', *La Semaine*, VI. 570–1.

7 Sept.　LEPOT-DELAHAYE, J., [on *La Peau de chagrin*], *La Revue et Gazette des théâtres*.

7 Sept.　LURINE, Louis, '*La Peau de chagrin*', *Le Messager de l'Assemblée*.

8 Sept.　JANIN, Jules, '*La Peau de chagrin*, mélodrame . . .', *Le Journal des débats*.

8 Sept.　GAUTIER, Théophile, '*La Peau de chagrin*', *La Presse*.

10 Sept.　CUVILLIER, J., 'Bulletin dramatique', *La Révolution littéraire*.

14 Sept.　MÉRAY, Antony, '*Mercadet*', *La Démocratie pacifique*.

14 Sept.　PLANCHE, Gustave, '*Mercadet*', *RDM* XI. 1135–8.

15 Sept.　LIREUX, Auguste, '*La Peau de chagrin*, mélodrame . . .', *Le Constitutionnel*.

15 Sept.　MATHAREL, Charles de, 'Revue des théâtres', *Le Siècle*.

19 Sept.　FILLIAS, Achille, 'Théâtres de Paris', *La Semaine*, VI. 601.

25 Sept.　GONZALÈS, Emmanuel, 'Dizaine dramatique', *La Mode*.

5 Oct.　CUVILLIER-FLEURY, A. A., 'Le Roman français en 1851', in *Études historiques et littéraires* (Michel Lévy, 1854), I. §xiv, 2e article.

23 Oct.　SAND, George, 'Notice' in *Le Compagnon du Tour de France* (Michel Lévy, 1885), p. 2.

30 Oct.　CORMENIN, Louis de, 'La Comédie sociale. Sur les types de Molière', *RDP* I. 88.

Nov.　CHERBULIEZ, Joël, '*Mercadet*', *La Revue critique des livres nouveaux*.

27 Nov. BAUDELAIRE, Charles, 'Les Drames et les romans honnêtes', *La Semaine théâtrale.*
  repr. *L'Art romantique* (Conard, 1925), pp. 285–7.

6 Dec. Anon., 'Préface' to 'Maximes et pensées de Balzac', *L'Illustration*, XVIII. 363.

1852

BASCHET, Armand, *Les Physionomies littéraires de ce temps. Honoré de Balzac. Essai sur l'homme et sur l'œuvre*, avec notes historiques par Champfleury (Giraud et Dagneau, 1852).
  *1851,

LOISNE, Charles Menche de, *Influence de la littérature française de 1830 à 1850 sur l'esprit public et les mœurs* (Garnier, 1852), pp. 35–259, 360–87.
  repr. Brussels, 1853.

PRAROND, Ernest, *De Quelques Écrivains nouveaux* (Michel Lévy, 1852), p. 1.

9 Jan. GUTTINGUER, A., '*Maximes et pensées* de H. de Balzac', *Le Corsaire.*

14 Feb. VIRMAÎTRE, 'Une Pensée de Balzac', *Le Corsaire.*

20 Feb. NERVAL, Gérard de, 'Particularités sur M. de Balzac', *La Sylphide.*
  repr. *Le Musée français*, Mar. 1859.

Mar. BAUDELAIRE, Charles, 'E. A. Poe, sa vie, ses ouvrages', *RDP.*
  repr. *Juvenilia* (Conard, 1939), I. 246.

14 Apr. CHAMPFLEURY, 'Physionomies littéraires: M. de Balzac, par Armand Baschet', *Le Pays.*

15 Apr. MOLÈNES, Paul Gaschon de, '*Pensées* de H. de Balzac', *Le Journal des débats.*

May DU CAMP, Maxime, [n.t.], *RDP.*

1 May Anon., [n.t.], *L'Artiste.*

15 May PLANCHE, Gustave, [n.t.], *RDM.*

18 June SECOND, Albéric, 'La Centième Représentation de *Mercadet*', *Le Constitutionnel.*
  repr. *À Quoi tient l'Amour* (Michel Lévy, 1856).
  repr. *Le Tiroir aux Souvenirs* (Dentu, 1886).
  repr. *HOB* 369–77.

Sept. CHERBULIEZ, Joël, '*Maximes et pensées* de H. de Balzac', *La Revue critique des livres nouveaux.*

26 Sept. WARENS, Henry de, 'Revue contemporaine', *Le Divan.*

11 Oct.   THIERRY, Édouard, '*Un Mari à la Campagne*, de Bayard et Wailly', *L'Assemblée nationale*.

29 Oct.   LERMINIER, J.-L.-E., [Review of Jolly (1851) and Loisne (1852)], *L'Assemblée nationale*.

Nov.   PONTMARTIN, Armand de, [On Champfleury], *La Revue contemporaine*.

1 Nov.   JOUVIN, B., 'Les Pieds d'argile: M. Sainte-Beuve', *La Chronique de France* (hebdomadaire).

Dec.   CHERBULIEZ, Joël, '*Le Théâtre de H. de Balzac*', *La Revue critique des livres nouveaux*.

9 Dec.   FLAUBERT, Gustave, Letter to Louise Colet, in *Correspondance* (Conard, 1927), III. 61.

17 Dec.   FLAUBERT, Gustave, Letter to Louise Colet, in *Correspondance* (Conard, 1927), III. 68.

26 Dec.   BOYER, Philoxène, and BANVILLE, Théodore de, *Le Feuilleton d'Aristophane*, comédie satirique (Michel Lévy, 1853).

1853

CLÉMENT DE RIS, Comte L., *Portraits à la plume* (Didier, 1853), pp. 291–333.

HIPPEAU, Célestin, 'Balzac (Honoré de)' in *Nouvelle Biographie universelle*, IV. cols. 328–30.

CASTILLE, Hippolyte, *Les Hommes et les mœurs en France sous le règne de Louis-Philippe* (Henneton, 1853), pp. 313–16, 320. Originally published in *RDP*.

TEXIER, Edmond, *Critiques et récits littéraires* (Michel Lévy, 1853), pp. 13, 20, 107–12.

LIMAYRAC, Paulin, 'Préface' in Stendhal, *De l'Amour* (Didier, 1853).

JANIN, Jules, *Histoire de la littérature dramatique* (Michel Lévy, 1853), IV. 176–7, V. 125–6, 350–1.

SIMON, Jules, 'Avertissement' in H. de Balzac, *Eugénie Grandet* (Hachette, 1853).
The only known copy of this article is in the Lovenjoul Library, Chantilly.

5 Feb.   DUFAÏ, Alexandre, '*Maximes et pensées*', *L'Athenaeum français*, II. 113–15.

15 Feb.   L'HÔTE, Édouard, 'De l'Influence de la littérature et du théâtre sur l'esprit public et les mœurs depuis 20 ans', *L'Artiste*, X. 27.

15 Feb.   LUCAS, Jules, 'Histoires en l'air', *La Chronique de France*.

Mar.   MAXIME, Théodore, 'Chronique théâtrale', *Le Causeur*.

Mar.   ULBACH, Louis, 'La Liquidation littéraire', *RDP* XVI. 377–401.
repr. *Écrivains et hommes de lettres* (Delahaye, 1857).

10 May   BARBEY D'AUREVILLY, Jules, '*Les Fantaisies de Claudine*', *Le Pays*.
repr. *Romanciers d'hier et d'avant-hier* (Lemerre, 1904), p. 27.

11 June   DELESSERT, Édouard, '*Traîté de la vie élégante*', *L'Athenaeum français*, II. 549.

14 June   LEVOL, F., '*Le Lys dans la vallée*', *La Revue et Gazette des théâtres*.

16 June   CARAGUEL, Clément, '*Le Lys dans la vallée*', *Le Charivari*.

18 June   FOURNIER, Édouard, '*Le Lys dans la vallée*', *Le Théâtre*.

19 June   MOURIEZ, Paul, 'Art dramatique', *L'Europe artiste*.

20 June   LIREUX, Auguste, '*Le Lys dans la vallée*', *Le Constitutionnel*.

22 June   BARBEY D'AUREVILLY, Jules, '*le Traîté de la vie élégante*, par H. de Balzac', *Le Pays*.
repr. *Romanciers d'hier et d'avant-hier* (Lemerre, 1904), p. 17– .

25 June   DESNOIRESTERRES, Gustave, 'Dizaine dramatique', *La Mode*.

28 June   FLAUBERT, Gustave, Letter to Louise Colet, in *Correspondance* (Conard, 1927), III. 225.

30 June   LARCHEY, Lorédan, 'Théâtres', *L'Abeille impériale*, I. 5.

1 July   MAXIME, Théodore, 'Chronique théâtrale', *Le Causeur*.

1 July   TEXIER, Edmond, 'Le Monde et le théâtre', *RDP*.

1 July   JOUVIN, B., 'Balzac à la Comédie française', *La Revue progressive*, I. 2.

13 July   BARBEY D'AUREVILLY, Jules, 'Stendhal et Balzac', *Le Pays*.
repr. *Romanciers d'hier et d'avant-hier* (Lemerre, 1904), pp. 1–16.

21 Aug.   WOESTYN, Eugène, '*La Théorie de la démarche*', *Paris*, II.

26 Sept.   FLAUBERT, Gustave, Letter to Louise Colet, in *Correspondance* (Conard, 1927), III. 353–4.

Oct.   SAND, George, 'Honoré de Balzac', preface to first issues of H. de Balzac, *Œuvres complètes illustrées* (Houssiaux, 1855).
repr. *Autour de la Table* (Michel Lévy, 1876), pp. 197–213.

6 Oct.   SORR, Angelo, 'Balzac, Prince Indien', *Paris*, III.

13 Oct.   WOESTYN, Eugène, [n.t.], *Paris*, III.

15 Oct.   LENOIR, Jules, 'Influence du matérialisme sur la littérature', *Le Monde artistique et littéraire*.

16 Oct.   JOUVIN, B., 'Les Statues de l'avenir: Balzac et Stendhal', *La Chronique de France*.

29 Oct.   PONTMARTIN, Armand de, [Review of Baschet (1852) and Clément de Ris (1853)], *L'Assemblée nationale*.
          repr. *Causeries littéraires* (Michel Lévy, 1854), pp. 292–303.

23 Nov.   BASCHET, Armand, 'Sur la Correspondance de Balzac', *Paris*, III.

26 Nov.   EGGIS, Étienne, 'Le *Théâtre* de Balzac', *Paris*, III.
          Second article on 1 Dec. 1853.

8 Dec.   BASCHET, Armand, 'Lettre à M. A. Dumas', *Le Mousquetaire*.

22 Dec.   DUTACQ, Armand, Letter to Mme Ève de Balzac, signed original, Lov. A.273, fo. 108.

29 Dec.   DUMAS, Alexandre, 'Buloz-y-en-a', *Le Mousquetaire*.

29 Dec.   HUGO, Victor, Letter to Alfred Busquet, signed original, Lov. A.363, fo. 82–3.

1854

PELLETAN, Eugène, *Heures de Travail* (Pagnerre, 1854), I. 98–107.
*30 Nov. 1846.

CUVILLIER-FLEURY, A. A., *Études historiques et littéraires* (Michel Lévy, 1854), I. §xiv, 2e article.
*5 Oct. 1851.

PONTMARTIN, Armand de, *Causeries littéraires* (Michel Lévy, 1854), pp. 292–303.
*29 Oct. 1853.

ALHOY, Maurice, TEXIER, Edmond, and DELORD, Taxile, *Mémoires de Bilboquet* (Librairie nouvelle, 1854).

CAYLA, J.-M., *Célébrités européennes*, IV.

LUCAS, Hippolyte, 'Pages oubliées.—Balzac moraliste', published in *Annales romantiques*, May–Aug. 1913.

MIRECOURT, Eugène de, *Les Contemporains: Balzac* (Rivoyre, 1854).

SAND, George, *Histoire de ma vie*.
repr. *Histoire de ma vie* (Calmann-Lévy, 1893), IV. 126–32, 135–8, 148, 183, 294–5.

STENDHAL, *Mémoires d'un touriste* (Michel Lévy, 1854), I. 57–8.

1 Jan. HENRIET, Frédéric, 'Une Édition revue . . . et corrigée', *La Chronique de France*.

1 Mar. CORMENIN, Louis de, 'Chronique de la Quinzaine', *RDP*.

7 Mar. DUTACQ, Armand, Letter to Mme Ève de Balzac, signed original, Lov. A.273, fo. 122–5.

10 Mar. WATRIPON, Antonio, 'Les Petits Malheurs littéraires du *Mousquetaire*', *Le Moustiquaire*.

11 Mar. WATRIPON, Antonio, 'Les Verts et les bleus', *Le Moustiquaire*.

12 Mar. WATRIPON, Antonio, 'L'École rocaille', *Le Moustiquaire*.

14 Mar. WATRIPON, Antonio, 'L'École réaliste', *Le Moustiquaire*.

15 Mar. DUMAS, Alexandre, 'Soulié.—Balzac', *Le Mousquetaire*.

17 Mar. BASCHET, Armand, 'Sur les Œuvres de M. de Balzac', *Le Mousquetaire*.

18 Mar. Anon., [On proposal for a Balzac monument], *Le Moustiquaire*.

31 Mar. LERMINIER, J.-L.-E., 'Lettre critique sur la littérature contemporaine', *La Revue contemporaine*, XII. 613.

2 Apr. ROUQUETTE, Jules, 'L'Esprit français', *Le Moustiquaire*.

5 May DUMAS, Alexandre, 'Monumens [sic] Soulié et Balzac', *Le Mousquetaire*.
(Contains a letter from Mme Ève de Balzac).

15 May BARBEY D'AUREVILLY, Jules, Letter to Trébutien, in *Lettres à Trébutien* (Bernouard, 1927), III. 64–5.

25 May BARBEY D'AUREVILLY, Jules, 'Avant-propos' to 'Pensées et maximes de Balzac', *Le Pays*.
repr. *Pensées et maximes de Balzac* (Lemerre, 1909), edited by Louise Read.

31 May NERVAL, Gérard de, Letter, in *Œuvres* (Pléiade, 1960), I. 1049.

2 July CUVILLIER-FLEURY, A. A., 'Conteurs français et flamands', *Le Journal des débats*.

6 July AUDEBRAND, Philibert, 'Petit Voyage à travers l'ancienne presse. Balzac et Lassailly', *Le Mousquetaire*.

25 Aug. BARBEY D'AUREVILLY, Jules, Letter to Trébutien, in *Lettres à Trébutien* (Bernouard, 1927), III. 103.

2 Sept. DELACROIX, Eugène, Entry on Balzac in *Le Journal d'Eugène Delacroix* (Plon, 1932), II. 251–2; further entry on 7 Sept. 1854, II. 255.

28 Oct. PONTMARTIN, Armand de, 'Causeries littéraires', *L'Assemblée nationale*.

8 Nov.　BAUDELAIRE, Charles, Letter to Hostein, in *Correspondance générale* (Conard, 1947), I. 308–11.

30 Nov.　FRANKLIN, Alfred, 'Honoré de Balzac', *L'Abeille impériale*.

1855

HOUSSAYE, Arsène, *Histoire du 41e fauteuil de l'Académie* (V. Lecou, 1854), pp. 348–52.

SAND, George, *Histoire de ma vie, 1854–5* (Calmann-Lévy, 1893), pp. 126–37, 294–5.

VIENNET, J. P. G., *Promenades philosophiques au cimetière de Père Lachaise*, 2e édition (Firmin Didot, 1855).

1 Jan.　LAURENT-PICHAT, 'Un Prix de 2.500 francs', *RDP*, p. 161.

14 Jan.　EGGIS, Étienne, 'Personnalités, *L'Artiste*.

28 Jan.　DUMAS, Alexandre, 'Causerie', *Le Mousquetaire*.

1 Feb.　PONTMARTIN, Armand de, 'Charles de Bernard', *RDM*.
　　　repr. *Nouvelles Causeries littéraires* (Michel Lévy, 1859), pp. 294–325.

Mar.　FONTAINE, F. de, '*Contes drolatiques* illustrés par Gustave Doré', *La Revue universelle des arts*.

4 Mar.　PÉTIGNY, Jules de, 'M. de Balzac', *La France centrale* (Blois).

26 Mar.　GONCOURT, Edmond et Jules de, Entry in *Le Journal des Goncourt* (Flammarion-Fasquelle, n.d.), I. 67.

31 Mar.　FORGUES, Émile-Daurand, 'Revue critique des ouvrages récents', *L'Athenaeum français*, IV. 253–5. (Signed: Old Nick.)

1 May　PLANCHE, Gustave, 'La Littérature française de 1830 à 1848', *RDM* II. 558–9.

26 May　BAUDELAIRE, Charles, 'Exposition universelle', *Le Pays*.
　　　repr. *Critique d'art* (A. Colin, 1965), I. 190.

28 May　DELORD, Taxile, 'Littérature', *Le Charivari*.

3 June　ULBACH, Louis, 'Du Roman moderne. Préface de *Suzanne Duchemin*', *L'Artiste*, IV. 60–4.
　　　repr. *RDP*, 1 and 15 Jan. 1856.
　　　repr. *Suzanne Duchemin* (Didier, 1855).

10 June　AUDEBRAND, Philibert, 'Les Buveurs de bière', *L'Artiste*.

29 Sept.　LUCAS, Jules, 'Critique dramatique', *La Chronique de France*, VI.

13 Oct.　GONCOURT, Edmond et Jules de, Entry in *Le Journal des Goncourt* (Flammarion-Fasquelle, n.d.), I. 90.

14 Oct.   FOURNEL, Victor, 'Su*z*anne Duchemin . . .', *L'Avenir*, I. 186–8.

15 Nov.   MAZADE, Charles de, 'Chronique de la quinzaine', *RDM* IV. 922.

1856

BARANDEGUY-DUPONT, *La Critique et les critiques au XIXe siècle* (Castel, 1856).

DESCOMBES, Charles-Maurice, *Histoire anecdotique du théâtre* (H. Plon, 1856), I. 417–18.

GONCOURT, Edmond et Jules de, *Une Voiture de masques* (E. Dentu, 1856).
   repr. *Les Nouvelles des Goncourt* (Charpentier, 1876).

GOZLAN, Léon, *Bal*z*ac en pantoufles* (Hetzel, Lévy et Blanchard, 1856).

JUDICIS DE MIRANDOL, Louis, *Le Monde de Bal*z*ac*, signed MS., Lov. A.249.

LURINE, Louis, *Société des gens de lettres. Discours* (Imprimerie de Brière, 1856).
   repr. *La Semaine*, 4 May 1856, pp. 273–83.
   repr. S. de Lovenjoul, *Une Page perdue de Bal*z*ac* (Ollendorff, 1903), pp. 279–327.

VACQUERIE, Auguste, *Profils et grimaces* (Michel Lévy, 1856).

27 Jan.   BANVILLE, Théodore de, 'Échos de Paris', *Le Figaro*.

1 Feb.   TAINE, Hippolyte, 'Charles Dickens, son talent et ses œuvres', *RDM* I. 636.

15 Feb.   LACROIX, Paul, '*Les Contes drolatiques* de Balzac', *L'Abeille impériale*, IV. no. 20.

15 Feb.   BARBEY D'AUREVILLY, Jules, '*Les Contes drolatiques*', *Le Pays*. Second article on 26 Feb. 1856.
   repr. *Romanciers d'hier et d'avant-hier* (Lemerre, 1904), pp. 28–41.

24 Feb.   MONSELET, Charles, 'Le Prince des critiques', *La Chronique de France*.

1 Mar.   Anon., 'Bulletin bibliographique. *Les Contes drolatiques*', *RDP* XXXI. 157–8.

5 Mar.   CAUVAIN, Henri, '*Les Contes drolatiques* . . .', *Le Constitutionnel*.

22 Mar.   BELLOY, A. de, [Review of *Les Contes drolatiques*], *L'Assemblée nationale*.

13 Apr.   MONSELET, Charles, 'Chronique littéraire', *La Chronique de Paris*.

26 Apr. BABOU, Hippolyte, 'Variétés, nouvelles', *L'Athenaeum français*, V. 17.

1 May MOUZAY, Comtesse de, 'Échos parisiens', *L'Abeille impériale*, V. 1.

1 May SURVILLE, Laure, 'Honoré de Balzac, d'après sa correspondance', *RDP*.
Further articles on 15 May and 1 June 1856.
repr. *Balzac, sa vie et ses œuvres d'après sa correspondance* (Librairie nouvelle, 1857).

1 May Anon., 'Bulletin bibliographique. *Le Cousin Pons*', *RDP* XXXI. 474.

1 May Anon., 'Bulletin bibliographique. *Le Père Goriot*', *RDP* XXXI. 473.

4 May LURINE, Louis, 'Discours sur Balzac', *La Semaine*, pp. 273–83. *1856.
repr. S. de Lovenjoul, *Une Page perdue de Balzac* (Ollendorff, 1903), pp. 279–327.

9 June MONTALEMBERT, C.-R., Remarks on *Les Paysans*, quoted in *Le Journal des Goncourt* (Flammarion-Fasquelle, n.d.), I. 101–2.

10 June BELLOY, A. de, 'Honoré de Balzac', *La Revue française*.
Second article on 17 June 1856.

14 June ASSELINEAU, Charles, [Review of Ch. Barbara, *Histoires émou-vantes*], *L'Athenaeum français*, V. 24.

10 July CHAMPFLEURY, 'Lettre à M. Louis Veuillot', *Le Figaro*. Also on 17 July 1856.

19 July PONTMARTIN, Armand de, [Review of Gozlan (1856)], *L'Assem-blée nationale*.

27 July LIMAYRAC, Paulin, [Review of Gozlan (1856) and of *Les Femmes de H. de Balzac* (1851)], *Le Constitutionnel*.

17 Aug. BATAILLE, Charles, 'Alexandre Dumas', *Diogène*.

24 Aug. ROLLAND, Amédée, 'H. de Balzac', *Diogène*.

14 Sept. JOUVIN, B., 'Comédie française', *Le Figaro*.

1 Nov. CHAMPFLEURY, 'La Jeunesse d'Honoré de Balzac', *La Gazette de Champfleury*.
repr. *Grandes Figures d'hier et d'aujourd'hui* (Poulet-Malassis et de Broise, 1861).

9 Nov. AUBRYET, Xavier, 'Revue parisienne. M. Champfleury', *L'Artiste*.

9 Nov. BUSQUET, Alfred, 'Le Jour des morts', *La Gazette de Paris*.

13 Nov. SIGNOURET, Raymond, 'La Tombe de Balzac', *Le Figaro*.

25 Nov.   PONTMARTIN, Armand de, 'Les Fétiches littéraires. I. M. de Balzac', *Le Correspondant*.
Second article on 25 Dec. 1856.
repr. *Causeries du samedi* (Michel Lévy, 1857), pp. 32–103.

1 Dec.   CHAMPFLEURY, *La Gazette de Champfleury*, no. 2, *passim*.

15 Dec.   DURANTY, 'Le Remarquable Article de M. de Pontmartin sur Balzac', *Le Réalisme*, no. 2.

15 Dec.   POITOU, Eugène, 'M. de Balzac. Étude morale et littéraire', *RDM* VI. 713–65.
repr. as a brochure.

1857

CHAMPFLEURY, *Le Réalisme* (Michel Lévy, 1857), pp. 1–14, 101–2, 201–2, 228.

GAUTIER, Théophile, 'Notice sur Baudelaire', in Charles Baudelaire, *Les Fleurs du Mal* (Poulet-Malassis et de Broise, 1857).

MONNIER, Henri, *Mémoires de M. Joseph Prudhomme* (Librairie nouvelle, 1857), II. 98–108.

MONSELET, Charles, *La Lorgnette littéraire*, dictionnaire des grands et petits auteurs de mon temps (Poulet-Malassis et de Broise, 1857).

POITOU, Eugène, *Du Roman et du théâtre contemporains et de leur influence sur les mœurs* (Durand, 1857), *passim*.

PONTMARTIN, Armand de, *Causeries du samedi* (Michel Lévy, 1857), pp. 32–103.
*25 Nov. 1856.

SURVILLE, Laure, *Balzac, sa vie et ses œuvres d'après sa correspondance* (Librairie nouvelle, 1857). Dated 1858, but appeared in Nov. 1857.
*1 May 1856.

ULBACH, Louis, *Écrivains et hommes de lettres* (Delahaye, 1857).
*Mar. 1853.

1 Jan.   BARBEY D'AUREVILLY, Jules, 'Honoré de Balzac', *Le Pays*.
repr. *Les Romanciers* (Amyot, 1865), pp. 1–14.

1 Jan.   BABOU, Hippolyte, 'La Vérité sur le cas de M. Champfleury', *La Revue française*, VII. 421–31.
repr. as a booklet (Poulet-Malassis et de Broise, 1857).

15 Jan.   THULIÉ, Henri, 'Du Roman.—La Description', *Le Réalisme*, no. 3.

15 Jan.   DESCHAMPS, Émile, 'Librairie et beaux-arts', *RDM* I. 26.

15 Feb.   THULIÉ, Henri, 'Champfleury', *Le Réalisme*, no. 4.

15 Feb.   ASSÉZAT, Jules, [Review of Gozlan (1856) and Surville (1856–7)], *Le Réalisme*, no. 4.

25 Mar.   CHAMPFLEURY, 'Quelques notes pour servir de préface', in *Le Réalisme* (Michel Lévy, 1857), pp. 1–21.

1 Apr.   LACROIX, Paul, 'Denon, Dorat et Balzac', *Le Bulletin du bouquiniste*.

28 Apr.   FIZELIÈRE, Albert de la, 'Curiosités', *Le Courrier de Paris*. repr. *Le Voleur*, 8 May 1857.

1 May   MAZADE, Charles de, 'Chronique', *RDM* III. 217–20.

7 June   LIMAYRAC, Paulin, 'Causerie littéraire', *Le Constitutionnel*.

26 June   AUBINEAU, Léon, 'D'un roman nouveau', *Univers, Union catholique*.

10 July   DONIS, J.-B., 'La Tradition littéraire et le roman moderne', *La Revue moderne*, no. 1.

11 July   ULBACH, Louis, [n.t.], *RDP*.

15 July   DU CAMP, Maxime, [Review of Pontmartin (1857)], *RDP*.

15 Aug.   Anon., [Review of Champfleury (1857)], *RDP*.

16 Aug.   WATRIPON, Antonio, 'De la Moralité en matière d'art et de littérature', *Présent*, I. 242–9.

Sept.   GONCOURT, Edmond et Jules de, Entry in *Le Journal des Goncourt* (Flammarion-Fasquelle, n.d.), I. 163.

1 Nov.   SARCEY, Francisque, 'La Première aux parisiennes. Lettres d'un provincial', *Le Figaro*. (Signed; Satané Binet.)

8 Nov.   AUDEBRAND, Philibert, 'Balzac journaliste', *La Gazette de Paris*. Second article on 15 Nov. 1857.

1858

ANCELOT, Mme L. V., *Les Salons de Paris* (Tardieu, 1858), p. 98.

Balzac, sa vie, son œuvre. Biographie par Théophile GAUTIER. Analyse critique par Hippolyte TAINE (Brussels, Dumont), *3 Feb. 1858 and 21 Mar. 1858.

GRANDEFFE, Arthur de, *La Pie bas-bleu* (Ledoyen, 1858), pp. 184–200.

MURET, Théodore, *A Travers Champs. Souvenirs d'un journaliste* (Garnier, 1858), I. 62–5.
*18 Mar. 1858 (in part).

SAINTE-BEUVE, Charles-Augustin, *Causeries du lundi* (Garnier, 1858), II. 443–63.
*2 Sept. 1850.

TAINE, Hippolyte, *Essais de critique et d'histoire* (L. Hachette, 1858), pp. 102–7, 195–201.

WERDET, Edmond, *Portrait intime de Balzac. Sa vie, son humeur et son caractère* (Dentu, 1858).

4 Jan.   DESCHANEL, Émile, [Review of Surville (1856–7)], *L'Indépendance belge.*

17 Jan.   CUVILLIER-FLEURY, A. A., [n.t.], *Le Journal des débats.*

21 Jan.   WEISS, Jean-Jacques, 'La Littérature contemporaine', in *Essais sur l'histoire de la littérature française* (Michel Lévy, 1865), pp. 82–4.

3 Feb.   TAINE, Hippolyte, 'Honoré de Balzac', *Le Journal des débats.*
Further articles on 4, 5, 23, and 25 Feb., and 3 Mar. 1858.
repr. *Balzac, sa vie, son œuvre* (Brussels, Dumont, 1858).
repr. *Nouveaux Essais de critique et d'histoire* (Hachette, 1864), as 'Étude sur Balzac'.

5 Feb.   FRÉMY, Arnould, 'Quelques mots sur Balzac', *Le Charivari.*

18 Mar.   MURET, Théodore, '*L'Union* et Honoré de Balzac', *Le Figaro.*
repr. *A Travers Champs, Souvenirs d'un journaliste* (Garnier, 1858).

21 Mar.   GAUTIER, Théophile, 'Honoré de Balzac', *L'Artiste.*
Further articles on 28 Mar., 2, 28, and 25 Apr., and 2 May 1858.
repr. *Le Moniteur universel*, 23 and 31 Mar., 9, 20, and 21 Apr., 4 and 5 May 1858.
repr. *Balzac, sa vie, son œuvre* (Brussels, Dumont, 1858).
repr. *Honoré de Balzac* (Poulet-Malassis et de Broise, 1859).
repr. *Portraits contemporains* (Charpentier, 1874), pp. 45–131.

24 Apr.   D'IVOI, Paul, 'Chronique parisienne', *Le Courrier de Paris.*

27 July   DELACROIX, Eugène, Entry in *Le Journal d'Eugène Delacroix* (Plon, 1932), III. 207

1 Sept.   BABOU, Hippolyte, 'Le Noviciat de Balzac. Lettre à Mme Surville', *La Revue française*, XIV. 236–44.
repr. *Lettres satiriques et critiques* (Poulet-Malassis et de Broise, 1860), pp. 55–74.

25 Sept.   SECOND, Albéric, 'Chronique', *L'Univers illustré.* (Signed: Gérôme.)

Oct.   GONCOURT, Edmond et Jules de, Entry in *Le Journal des Goncourt* (Flammarion-Fasquelle, n.d.), I. 198–9.

9 Oct. NETTEMENT, Francis, 'Les Excentricités de M. de Balzac', *La Semaine familiale*.
Second article on 16 Oct. 1858.

30 Oct. RÉVILLON, Tony, 'Personnalités littéraires et artistiques: Louis Ulbach', *Le Corsaire*.

23 Nov. LECOMTE, Jules, [Review of Werdet (1858)], *La Chronique parisienne*.

25 Nov. JANIN, Jules, 'Les et caetera du temps présent', *L'Indépendance belge*. (Signed: Éraste.)

1859

JANIN, Jules, *Critiques, portraits et caractères contemporains* (Hachette, 1859).

JANIN, Jules, *Variétés littéraires* (Hachette, 1859), pp. 106–15.
*20 Feb. 1843.

GAUTIER, Théophile, *Honoré de Balzac* (Poulet-Malassis et de Broise, 1859).
*21 Mar. 1858 (with changes).

SIRTÉMA DE GROVESTINS, Baron Charles, *Les Gloires du romantisme* (Dentu, 1859), II. 95–133.

DURANTY, 'Caractéristiques des œuvres de M. Champfleury', Preface to Champfleury, *Les Amis de la nature* (Poulet-Malassis, 1859).

LAMARTINE, Alphonse de, *Cours familier de littérature* (chez l'auteur, 1859), XVIII. 106–8 and 273–527.
repr. *Balzac et ses œuvres* (Michel Lévy, 1866).

VAPEREAU, Gustave, [on *La Marâtre*], in *L'Année littéraire*, II. 228–9.

BAUDELAIRE, Charles, *Théophile Gautier*. Précédé d'une lettre de Victor Hugo (Poulet-Malassis et de Broise, 1859).
*13 Mar. 1859.
repr. *L'Art romantique* (Conard, 1925), pp. 168–9.

Mar. NERVAL, Gérard de, 'Particularités sur M. de Balzac', *Le Musée français*.
*20 Feb. 1852.

5 Mar. MÉZIÈRES, Alfred, 'La Littérature anglaise', *Le Magasin de librairie*, III.

13 Mar. BAUDELAIRE, Charles, 'Galerie du XIXe siècle. Théophile Gautier', *L'Artiste*.
repr. *Théophile Gautier* (Poulet-Malassis et de Broise, 1859).

repr. *Œuvres complètes* (Michel Lévy, 1868), III. 176–7.

repr. *L'Art romantique* (Conard, 1925), pp. 168–9.

15 Mar. Anon., [On *La Belle Impéria*], *La Revue anecdotique*, VIII.

18 Mar. DURANTY, 'De l'État des lettres à cette époque', *Le Courrier de Paris*.

30 Apr. JOUVIN, B., '*La Seconde Jeunesse*, de Mario Uchard', *Le Figaro*.

26 June DENIS, Achille, [On *La Marâtre*], *La Revue et Gazette des théâtres*.
Further articles on 30 June and 3 July 1859.

July BABOU, Hippolyte, [Review of Gautier (1858–9)], *La Revue française*, pp. 506–7.

7 July DENIS, Achille, [On *Paméla Giraud*], *La Revue et Gazette des théâtres*.
Further article on 17 July 1859.

10 July SAINT-VICTOR, Paul de, [Review of *Paméla Giraud*], *La Presse*.

11 July FIORENTINO, Pier-Angelo, [Review of *Paméla Giraud*], *Le Constitutionnel*.

11 July CLAUDIN, Gustave, 'Théâtres', *Le Courrier de Paris*.

11 July TIENGOU, J.-M., [Review of *Paméla Giraud*], *La Gazette de France*.

11 July JANIN, Jules, [Review of *Paméla Giraud*], *Le Journal des débats*.

11 July GAUTIER, Théophile, [Review of *Paméla Giraud*], *Le Moniteur universel*.

11 July PRÉMARAY, Jules de, [Review of *Paméla Giraud*], *La Patrie*.

11 July BIÉVILLE, Éd. de, [Review of *Paméla Giraud*], *Le Siècle*.

11 July THIERRY, Édouard, [Review of *Paméla Giraud*], *Le Pays*.

11 July ESCANDE, A., [Review of *Paméla Giraud*], *L'Union*.

16 July JOUVIN, B., [Review of *Paméla Giraud*], *Le Figaro*.

4 Sept. DENIS, Achille, '*La Marâtre*', *La Revue et Gazette des théâtres*.

4 Sept. GAIFFE, Adolphe, '*La Marâtre*', *La Presse*.

5 Sept. CLAUDIN, Gustave, 'Théâtres', *Le Courrier de Paris*.

5 Sept. TIENGOU, J.-M., [Review of *La Marâtre*], *La Gazette de France*.

5 Sept. GAUTIER, Théophile, [Review of *La Marâtre*], *Le Moniteur universel*.

5 Sept. ESCANDE, A., [Review of *La Marâtre*], *L'Union*.

10 Sept. BUSONI, Philippe, [Review of a dramatization of *Le Bal de Sceaux*], *L'Illustration*.

12 Sept.   SARCEY, Francisque, [Review of *La Marâtre*], *L'Opinion nationale*.
           repr. *Quarante Ans de théâtre* (Bibliothèque des *Annales*, 1900).

12 Sept.   FIORENTINO, Pier-Angelo, [Review of *La Marâtre*], *Le Constitutionnel*.

12 Sept.   BIÉVILLE, Éd. de, [Review of *La Marâtre*], *Le Siècle*.

12 Sept.   FOURNIER, Édouard, [Review of *La Marâtre*], *La Patrie*.

17 Sept.   JOUVIN, B., 'Balzac dramaturge', *Le Figaro*.

1 Oct.   CARO, Elme-Marie, 'Le Roman contemporain. M. de Balzac, son œuvre et son influence', *La Revue européenne*.
           repr. *Poètes et romanciers* (Hachette, 1888).

3 Dec.   LECOMTE, Jules, 'Courrier de Paris', *Le Monde illustré*.

                              1860

           BABOU, Hippolyte, *Lettres satiriques et critiques* (Poulet-Malassis et de Broise, 1860), pp. 55–74, 75–117, etc.
           *Feb. 1847, and 1 Sept. 1858.

           SAINTE-BEUVE, Charles-Augustin, *Port-Royal* (Hachette, 1860). I. Appendice, 'Jugements divers sur *Port-Royal*'.

           SCHERER, Edmond, *Mélanges de critique religieuse* (Cherbuliez, 1860), p. 466.

Feb.   Anon., 'Aperçus littéraires', *Varia* (Michel Lévy, 1860), I. 191–5.

27 July   DELACROIX, Eugène, Entry in *Le Journal d'Eugène Delacroix* (Plon, 1932), III. 301–2.

25 Sept.   MOUY, Charles de, '*Honoré de Balzac*, par M. Théophile Gautier', *Le Magasin de librairie*, XII. 317–19.

6 Oct.   GEOGHEGAN, Edward, 'Causeries. De l'Influence de Balzac sur le mouvement littéraire actuel'.
           Source unknown; repr. in *HOB* 488–91.

20 Oct.   LECOMTE, Jules, 'Balzac à l'hôtel des Haricots', *Le Monde illustré*.

                              1861

           CHAMPFLEURY, *Grandes Figures d'hier et d'aujourd'hui* (Poulet-Malassis et de Broise, 1861), *passim*.
           *1 Nov. 1856, and 1 Dec. 1856.

May   VERNIER, Valéry, 'La Palférine', *La Revue du mois* (Lille).

June   LAURENT-PICHAT, 'Lucien de Rubempré', *La Revue du mois* (Lille).

31 Aug.   LECOMTE, Jules, 'Courrier de Paris', *Le Monde illustré*.

30 Sept. SAINTE-BEUVE, Charles-Augustin, 'M. Louis Veuillot', *Le Constitutionnel.*

14 Nov. MONSELET, Charles, '*Le Marquis de Villemer*, par George Sand', *Le Figaro.*

1 Dec. MONSELET, Charles, 'La Légende de Lassailly', *Le Boulevard*, numéro specimen.

1862

CLÉMENT DE RIS, Comte L., *Critiques d'art et de littérature* (Didier, 1862), pp. 306–8, 322–4.

PONTMARTIN, Armand de, *Les Jeudis de Madame Charbonneau* (Michel Lévy, 1862), pp. 135–6, 171–3, 265, 269.

NADAR, NOEL, LÉLIOUX, *Histoire de Murger* (1862), pp. 185, 235–6.

GOZLAN, Léon, *Balzac chez lui. Souvenirs des Jardies* (Michel Lévy, 1862).

19 Jan. ULBACH, Louis, 'A propos d'un article inédit de M. de Balzac', *La Réforme littéraire*, no. 1.

21 May GONCOURT, Edmond et Jules de, Entry in *Le Journal des Goncourt* (Flammarion-Fasquelle, n.d.), II. 28–9.

29 June DEPRET, Louis, 'La Gloire de Balzac', *Le Boulevard.*
Further articles on 6 and 13 July 1862.

July FLAUBERT, Gustave, Letter to Mme Roger des Genettes, in *Correspondance* (Conard, 1929), V. 36.

1 July MAZADE, Charles de, 'Les Romans nouveaux', *RDM* IV. 242–51.

4 Oct. SALLES, Eusèbe de, 'Balzac aux lanternes', *La Presse.*

9 Oct. VALLÈS, Jules, 'Les Victimes du livre', *Le Figaro.*
repr. *Les Réfractaires* (Achille Faure, 1865), pp. 143–6.

29 Oct. CLARETIE, Jules, [Review of Gozlan (1862)], *Le Boulevard.*

Nov. AVOND, Auguste, 'Le Roman moderne en France', *La Critique française*, IV. 321–8.

6 Nov. MONSELET, Charles, 'Lettre à Mme Balzac', *Le Figaro.*

1863

LUCAS, Hippolyte, *Histoire du Théâtre-français*, 2e édition (Brussels, A. Lacroix et Verboekhoven, 1863), III.

VAPEREAU, Gustave, '*Les Ressources de Quinola*', in *L'Année littéraire et dramatique*, VI. 235–8.

TAINE, Hippolyte, *Histoire de la littérature anglaise* (Hachette, 1863), I. vii; IV. 57, 126–9.

11 Jan. SALLES, Eusèbe de, 'Balzac dans le salon de Gérard', *Le Boulevard*. Second article on 25 Jan. 1863.

11 May GONCOURT, Edmond et Jules de, Entry in *Le Journal des Goncourt* (Flammarion-Fasquelle, n.d.), II. 90–1.

Aug. GASTINEAU, Benjamin, 'Détails sur Balzac', *La Loire illustrée* (Tours).
repr. *Les Génies de la Liberté* (A. Lacroix et Verboekhoven, 1865), pp. 119–36.

26 Sept. AUDEBRAND, Philibert, 'A propos des *Ressources de Quinola*', *Le Nain jaune*.

1 Oct. DELABORDE, Henri, 'La Lithographie en France', *RDM* V. 589.

12 Oct. SAINTE-BEUVE, Charles-Augustin, 'Gavarni', *Le Constitutionnel*.
repr. *Nouveaux Lundis* (Michel Lévy, 1866), VI. 160–1.

14 Oct. BARBEY D'AUREVILLY, Jules, 'Les Quarante Médaillons de l'Académie. XL. M. Sainte-Beuve', *Le Nain jaune*.

15 Oct. STIDMANN, Henri, '*Quinola*', *La Revue et Gazette des théâtres*.

15 Oct. JOUVIN, B., 'Balzac dramaturge', *Le Figaro*.

17 Oct. LANGEAU, Théodore, 'Théâtres', *Le Nain jaune*.

18 Oct. CERFBERR, Anatole, [Review of *Quinola*], *Le Théâtre*.

19 Oct. BÉCHARD, Frédéric, 'La Semaine dramatique', *La Gazette de France*.

19 Oct. ROQUEPLAN, Nestor, '*Les Ressources de Quinola*', *Le Constitutionnel*.

19 Oct. JANIN, Jules, 'La Semaine dramatique', *Le Journal des débats*.

19 Oct. GASPÉRINI, A. de, 'Revue théâtrale', *La Nation*.

19 Oct. SARCEY, Francisque, '*Les Ressources de Quinola*', *L'Opinion nationale*.

19 Oct. FOURNIER, Édouard, 'Théâtres', *La Patrie*.

19 Oct. SAINT-VALRY, G., 'Revue dramatique', *Le Pays*.

19 Oct. SAINT-VICTOR, Paul de, '*Les Ressources de Quinola*', *La Presse*.

19 Oct. BIÉVILLE, Éd. de, 'Revue des théâtres', *Le Siècle*.

19 Oct. TIENGOU, J.-M., '*Les Ressources de Quinola*', *L'Union*.

19 Oct. ULBACH, Louis, [n.t.], *Le Temps*.

21 Oct. DEULIN, Charles, 'Courrier des théâtres', *L'Esprit public*.

21 Oct. GAUTIER, Théophile, 'Revue dramatique', *Le Moniteur universel*.

24 Oct. BELLOY, A. de, '*Les Ressources de Quinola*', *L'Illustration*.

25 Oct. CHARVET, Paul, [Review of *Quinola*], *La Chronique théâtrale et littéraire*.

25 Oct. QUERCY, Louis de, 'Courrier de Paris', *Le Pays*.

28 Oct. LUCAS, Hippolyte, 'Bibliographie. La Canne de Balzac', *Le Siècle*.

31 Oct. CLAVEAU, A., '*Les Ressources de Quinola*', *La Revue contemporaine*.

  Nov. RACOT, Adolphe, 'Revue dramatique', *La Revue du progrès*, II, 206.

14 Nov. AUDEBRAND, Philibert, 'Où faut-il écrire?', *Le Nain jaune*. (Signed: E. de l'Isle-Adam.)

1864

DESCHANEL, Émile, *Physiologie des écrivains et des artistes* (Hachette, 1864), pp. 44, 45, 117, 118–19, 160, 171, 186–7, 236.

DUSOLIER, Alcide, *Nos Gens de lettres. Leur caractère et leurs œuvres* (A. Faure, 1864), pp. 17–19, 28–31, 257–8, 289–70.

NETTEMENT, Alfred, *Du Roman contemporain, ses vicissitudes, ses divers aspects, son influence* (Jacques Lecoffre, 1864).

15 Mar. SARCEY, Francisque, 'Les Livres de l'an 1863. *Salammbô*', *La Nouvelle Revue française*, I. 497–502.

11 May BARBEY D'AUREVILLY, Jules, 'Bibliographie. Shakespeare . . . et Balzac', *Le Pays*.
repr. *Portraits politiques et littéraires* (Lemerre, 1898), pp. 1–17.

30 May SAINTE-BEUVE, Charles-Augustin, 'Monsieur Taine', *Le Constitutionnel*.
repr. *Nouveaux Lundis* (Michel Lévy, 1867), VIII. 66–137.

15 June CHANCEL, Camille, 'La Genèse de la *Comédie humaine*', *La Nouvelle Revue de Paris*.
Further articles on 15 July and 15 Aug. 1864.

  Sept. COMBES, J.-E., 'Le Saint-Simonisme et son influence sur la littérature', *La Revue contemporaine*, XLVI. 193–221.

10 Oct. DOLLFUSS, Paul, 'Sur les Systèmes littéraires', *L'Artiste*, pp. 178–83.

24 Oct. GONCOURT, Edmond et Jules de, Entry in *Le Journal des Goncourt* (Flammarion-Fasquelle, n.d.), II. 183.

1865

BARBEY D'AUREVILLY, Jules, *Les Romanciers* (Amyot, 1865), pp. 1–14.
*1 Jan. 1857.

CLARETIE, Jules, *Pétrus Borel le Lycanthrope* (Pincebourde, 1865), contains P. Borel, 'La Maison de M. de Balzac' (1845).

GASTINEAU, Benjamin, *Les Génies de la Liberté* (A. Lacroix et Verboekhoven, 1865), pp. 119–36.
*Aug. 1863.

TAINE, Hippolyte, *Nouveaux Essais de critique et d'histoire* (Hachette, 1865), 'Étude sur Balzac'.
*3 Feb. 1858.

VALLÈS, Jules, *Les Réfractaires* (Achille Faure, 1865), pp. 112, 132, 143–6, 197–9. (Dated 1866.)
*9 Oct. 1862 (pp. 143–6 only).

VERMERSCH, Eugène, *Saltimbanques et pantins* (E. Sausset, 1865), pp. 6, 8, 10–11.

15 Jan.   VALLÈS, Jules, 'Balzac et ses œuvres', lecture given to the Cercle du Grand-Orient. Not reproduced.

17 Jan.   MALESPINE, [Review of Vallès's lecture], *L'Opinion nationale.*

17 Jan.   BELL, Gaston, [Review of Vallès's lecture], *La Presse.*

18 Jan.   PESSARD, Hector, [Review of Vallès's lecture], *Le Temps.*

29 Apr.   ZOLA, Émile, 'Revue littéraire', *Le Salut public* (Lyon).
repr. *Mes Haines* (A. Faure, 1866).

16 June   COMBES, Louis, 'Le Dieu Balzac et ses lévites', *L'Amateur d'autographes*, IV. 177–85 and 193–202.

17 Sept.   VALLÈS, Jules, 'Littérature anglaise. Le Roman', *Le Courrier du dimanche.*

1 Dec.   REYNALD, Hermile, '*Nouveaux Essais de critique et d'histoire* par M. H. Taine', *La Revue française*, XII. 629–30.

1866

BANVILLE, Théodore de, *Les Camées parisiennes*, 21e série (Pincebourde, 1866).
repr. *La Lanterne magique*, 1883.

FIORENTINO, Pier-Angelo, *Comédies et comédiens* (Michel Lévy, 1866), I. 167–82.

LAMARTINE, Alphonse de, *Balzac et ses œuvres* (Michel Lévy, 1866).
*1859.

LECOMTE, J.-Henry, *Frédérick-Lemaître* (chez l'auteur, 1866), pp. 45–6.

MONSELET, Charles, *Portraits après décès* (Achille Faure, 1866).

PAGÈS, Alphonse, *Balzac moraliste* (Michel Lévy, 1866).

ZOLA, Émile, *Mes Haines* (Achille Faure, 1866).
*29 Apr. 1865 ('Erckmann–Chatrian').

1 Jan.   GONCOURT, Edmond et Jules de, Entry in *Le Journal des Goncourt* (Flammarion-Fasquelle, n.d.), III. 7.

21 Mar. ZOLA, Émile, 'Correspondance littéraire', *Le Salut public* (Lyon). See also issue of 30 Mar. 1866.

28 Mar. VALLÈS, Jules, 'Les Livres', *La Liberté*.

31 Mar. DERAIMES, Maria, 'L'Influence du roman', *Le Nain jaune*.

2 Apr.   ZOLA, Émile, 'Livres d'aujourd'hui et de demain', *L'Événement*.

12 Apr. CLARETIE, Jules, 'Balzac', *Le Figaro*.

3 June   MARNICOUCHE, E., 'Lettre au rédacteur', *L'Événement*.

9 June   Anon., [On the *Dictionnaire des enseignes de Paris*], *La Petite Revue*.

11 June Anon., [On Balzac's bibliography], *La Petite Revue*.

1 Oct.   COLIGNY, Charles, 'Histoire littéraire', *La Revue du XIXe siècle*.

20 Oct. PERRAS, Alfred, 'De l'Influence du roman au point de vue de la morale', *La Revue gauloise*, pp. 211–19.

1867

WEILL, Alexandre, *Mes Batailles* (Dentu, 1867), pp. 187–90.

25 May   LEFRANÇAIS, G., 'Du Roman populaire', *Le Critique*.

29 May   ZOLA, Émile, Letter to A. Valabrègue, in *Correspondance* (Charpentier, 1908), II. 49.

3 Aug.   LUZARCHE, Robert, 'Un Livre immoral, S.V.P.', *Le Critique*.

1868

ASSELINEAU, Charles, '*Mercadet*', *Le Bulletin du bibliophile*, pp. 623–30.

BAUDELAIRE, Charles, *Œuvres complètes* (Michel Lévy, 1868), III. 176–7.

FÉVAL, Paul, *Rapport sur le progrès des lettres* (Imprimerie impériale, 1868), pp. 50–1.

VAPEREAU, Gustave, '*Mercadet*', *L'Année littéraire et dramatique*, XI. 89–90.

VIZENTINI, Albert, *Derrière la Toile* (A. Faure, 1868), pp. 101, 200, 203.

2 Jan.   LEROY, Louis, [Review of *Les Treize*, mélodrame], *Le Charivari*.

4 Jan.   LEMAIGRE, Louis, [Review of *Les Treize*, mélodrame], *Le Philosophe*.

12 Jan.   VALLÈS, Jules, 'Chronique parisienne', *La Situation*.

8 Feb.   ZOLA, Émile, 'Livres d'aujourd'hui et de demain', *Le Globe*.

29 Aug.   L'ESTRANGE, Roger, 'Balzac.—Les Femmes de Balzac à Venise', *Le Gaulois*.

1 Sept.   SAINTE-BEUVE, Charles-Augustin. 'Jean-Jacques Ampère', *Le Constitutionnel*.
           repr. *Nouveaux Lundis* (Michel Lévy, 1870), XIII. 264.

24 Oct.   WOLFF, A., '*Mercadet*', *Le Figaro*.

24 Oct.   LACOMBE, Leguevel de, '*Mercadet*', *L'Époque*.

24 Oct.   PÈNE, Henri de, 'La Reprise de *Mercadet*', *Le Gaulois*.

24 Oct.   FOURNIER, Édouard, '*Mercadet*', *La Patrie*.

24 Oct.   ARAGO, Étienne, '*Mercadet*', *L'Avenir national*.
           Second article on 26 Oct. 1868.
           repr. *Le Nain jaune*, 26 Oct. 1868.

25 Oct.   BIÉVILLE, Éd. de, '*Mercadet*', *Le Siècle*.

25 Oct.   LAGOGUÉE, Victor, '*Mercadet*', *La Revue et Gazette des théâtres*.

26 Oct.   ROQUEPLAN, Nestor, '*Mercadet*', *Le Constitutionnel*.

26 Oct.   CLARETIE, Jules, '*Mercadet*', *L'Opinion nationale*.

26 Oct.   SARCEY, Francisque, '*Mercadet*', *Le Temps*.

26 Oct.   JOUVIN, B., '*Mercadet*', *La Presse*.

26 Oct.   SAINT-VICTOR, Paul de, '*Mercadet*', *La Liberté*.

26 Oct.   BERNARD, D. L., '*Mercadet*', *L'Union*.

26 Oct.   GAUTIER, Théophile, '*Mercadet*', *Le Moniteur universel*.

29 Oct.   MORIN, Tony, '*Mercadet*', *La Libre Parole*.

31 Oct.   SECOND, Albéric, '*Mercadet*', *L'Univers illustré*. (Signed: Gérôme.)

15 Nov. ÉBELOT, Alfred, 'Théâtres', *RDM* LXXVIII. 503.

16 Nov. BÉCHARD, Frédéric, '*Mercadet*', *La Gazette de France*.

1869

CARO, Elme-Marie, *Études morales sur le temps présent*, 2e édition entièrement refondue (Hachette, 1869), p. 322.

SAINTE-BEUVE, Charles-Augustin, *Portraits contemporains* (Michel Lévy, 1869), II. 327–57.
*15 Nov. 1834 (with changes).

ZOLA, Émile, *Différences entre Balzac et moi*, original MS., BN N.a. fr. 10345. Published in *Œuvres complètes* (Bernouard, 1927), I. 356–7.

19 Jan. ZOLA, Émile, 'Les Livres d'aujourd'hui et de demain', *Le Gaulois*.

8 Feb. ZOLA, Émile, 'Les Livres d'aujourd'hui et de demain', *Le Gaulois*.

17 Mar. ZOLA, Émile, 'Les Livres d'aujourd'hui et de demain', *Le Gaulois*.

30 Mar. MONSELET, Charles, '*Vautrin*', *L'Étendard*.
Second article on 5 Apr. 1869.

3 Apr. LEROY, Louis, '*Vautrin*', *Le Gaulois*.

3 Apr. WOLFF, A., '*Vautrin*', *Le Figaro*.

4 Apr. PONTMARTIN, Armand de, 'Balzac', *La Gazette de France*.
repr. *Nouveaux Samedis* (Michel Lévy, 1876), pp. 74–89.

4 Apr. LISTENER, M., '*Vautrin*', *La Revue et Gazette des théâtres*.

4 Apr. NEULSORT, Léo de, 'Bulletin dramatique', *L'Époque*.

5 Apr. ROQUEPLAN, Nestor, '*Vautrin*', *Le Constitutionnel*.

5 Apr. SARCEY, Francisque, '*Vautrin*', *Le Temps*.

5 Apr. BIÉVILLE, Éd. de, '*Vautrin*', *Le Siècle*.

5 Apr. GAUTIER, Théophile, '*Vautrin*', *Le Journal officiel*.

5 Apr. SAINT-VICTOR, Paul de, '*Vautrin*', *La Liberté*.

5 Apr. ARAGO, Étienne, '*Vautrin*', *L'Avenir national*.

6 Apr. MOUSSELLE, Charles de la, 'Revue dramatique', *Le Pays*.

6 Apr. CLARETIE, Jules, 'Chronique théâtrale', *L'Opinion nationale*.

8 Apr. FRÉDÉRIX, Gustave, 'Balzac', *L'Indépendance belge*.

10 Apr. Anon., '*Vautrin*', *L'Illustration*.

2 June ZOLA, Émile, 'Livres d'aujourd'hui et de demain', *Le Gaulois*.

10 July BOULÉ, Alphonse, 'Une Préface à la *Comédie humaine*, contenant un ordre de lecture', *L'Illustration*.
Second article on 17 July 1869.
repr. as a pamphlet dated Arpajon, 1872; printed by Hennuyer, 1873.

23 July LUCAS, Hippolyte, 'Œuvres complètes de M. de Balzac', *Le Siècle*.

31 July ZOLA, Émile, 'Livres d'aujourd'hui et de demain', *Le Gaulois*.
repr. M. Kanes, *L'Atelier de Zola* (Geneva, Droz, 1963), pp. 140–2.

10 Oct. CUVILLIER-FLEURY, A. A., 'Œuvres complètes de H. de Balzac', *Le Journal des débats*.

31 Oct. ZOLA, Émile, 'Causerie', *La Tribune*.
repr. M. Kanes, *L'Atelier de Zola* (Geneva, Droz, 1963), pp. 202–6.

1870

SAINTE-BEUVE, Charles-Augustin, *Portraits contemporains* (Michel Lévy, 1870), II. 444–71.
*1 Sept. 1839.

24 Jan. BARBEY D'AUREVILLY, Jules, 'La Nouvelle Édition de Balzac', *Le Constitutionnel*.
repr. *Romanciers d'hier et d'avant-hier* (Lemerre, 1904), p. 54.

1 Mar. SCHERER, Edmond, 'Balzac', *Le Temps*.
repr. *Études sur la littérature contemporaine* (Michel Lévy, 1873), IV. 63–73.

13 May ZOLA, Émile, 'Les Livres. Balzac', *Le Rappel*.
repr. *Les Cahiers naturalistes*, no. 15 (1960), pp. 599–602.

1 Oct. ÉTIENNE, Louis, 'Les Hommes d'argent dans la comédie française', *RDM* LXXXIX. 513–25.
Second article on 15 Oct. 1870, pp. 698–718.

1871

KARR, Alphonse, *Les Guêpes*, nouvelle série (chez l'auteur, 1871), I. IV. 61–4.

10 July PONTMARTIN, Armand de, 'La Critique en 1871', *Le Correspondant*, XLVIII. 22–7.

18 Oct. FLAUBERT, Gustave, Letter to George Sand, in *Correspondance* (Conard, 1930), VI. 296.

1 Dec. ZOLA, Émile, 'Balzac', *La Cloche*.

5 Dec.   JANIN, Jules, 'Mémoires d'hier', *L'Indépendance belge*. (Signed: Éraste.)

21 Dec. AUDEBRAND, Philibert, 'L'Argent des gens de lettres', *Le Charivari*.

1872

MARX, Karl, *Le Capital* (Lachâtre, 1872), traduction de M. J. Roy.

BONNEFON, D., *Les Écrivains modernes de la France* (Sandoz et Fischbacher, 1872), pp. 394–7.

CARO, Marie-Elme, *Les Jours d'épreuve* (Hachette, 1872), pp. 238–41.

POTVIN, Charles, *De La Corruption littéraire en France. Étude de littérature comparée sur les lois naturelles de l'art* (Brussels, Muquardt).

15 Jan. JANIN, Jules, 'Mémoires d'hier', *L'Indépendance belge*. (Signed: Éraste.)

15 June ZOLA, Émile, 'Lettres parisiennes', *La Cloche*.

21 Aug. ZOLA, Émile, 'Lettres parisiennes', *La Cloche*.
         repr. *Mélanges, préfaces, discours* (Bernouard, 1929), pp. 97–101.

2 Oct.   ZOLA, Émile, 'Lettres parisiennes', *La Cloche*.

30 Oct. ZOLA, Émile, 'Lettres parisiennes', *La Cloche*.

23 Nov. CHAMPFLEURY, 'Balzac au collège', *Le Musée universel*.
         repr. *Balzac au collège* (Patay, 1878).

1873

SCHERER, Edmond, *Études sur la littérature contemporaine* (Michel Lévy, 1873), IV, 63–73.
*1 Mar. 1870.

3 May   CHAMPFLEURY, 'Balzac, sa méthode de travail', *Le Musée universel*.
         repr. *Balzac, sa méthode de travail* (Patay, 1879).

10 May   Anon., 'Mouvement littéraire', *La Renaissance artistique et littéraire*.

1874

GAUTIER, Théophile, *Portraits contemporains* (Charpentier, 1874), pp. 45–131.
*21 Mar. 1858.

24 Jan. CHAMPFLEURY, 'Balzac, sa méthode de travail, II', *Le Musée universel*.
      *repr. *Balzac, sa méthode de travail* (Patay, 1879).

4 Feb. GONCOURT, Edmond et Jules de, Entry in *Le Journal des Goncourt* (Flammarion-Fasquelle, n.d.), V. 86–7.

1875

CHAMPFLEURY, *Documents pour servir à la biographie de Balzac*, I. *Balzac propriétaire* (Patay, 1875).

CHASLES, Philarète, *La Psychologie sociale des nouveaux peuples* (Charpentier, 1875), pp. 132–61.

KARR, Alphonse, *Les Guêpes*, nouvelle série (chez l'auteur, 1875), IV. I. 222–4, 235–6, 311–12; III. 139–42; V. 381–4.

LECLERC, Ludovic, *Études dramatiques. III. Les Valets au théâtre* (Baur, 1875), pp. 88–94.

SAINTE-BEUVE, Charles-Augustin, *Premiers Lundis* (Michel Lévy, 1875), II. 360–7.
      *1 Nov. 1838.

1 Apr. BRUNETIÈRE, Ferdinand, 'Le Roman réaliste en 1875', *RDM* VIII. 700.
      repr. *Le Roman naturaliste* (Calmann-Lévy, 1883), pp. 1–28.

30 May GONCOURT, Edmond et Jules de, Entry in *Le Journal des Goncourt* (Flammarion-Fasquelle, n.d.), V. 152.

June MICHIELS, Alfred, Lecture on Dickens. Text not reproduced; see Royce, *A Balzac Bibliography* (Chicago, University Press, 1929), no. 945.

1876

SAND, George, *Autour de la Table* (Michel Lévy, 1876), pp. 197–213.
      *Oct. 1853.

CHASLES, Philarète, *Mémoires* (Charpentier, 1876), I. 303–8, 236, 274.

DUVAL, Georges, *Frédérick-Lemaître et son temps, 1800–76* (Tresse, 1876), pp. 204–8.

HUYSMANS, Joris-Karl, 'Zola et l'*Assommoir*', *L'Actualité* (Brussels).
      repr. *En Marge* (Crès, 1927), pp. 7–39.

PONTMARTIN, Armand de, *Nouveaux Samedis* (Michel Lévy, 1876), VII. 74–89.
      *4 Apr. 1869.

SAINTE-BEUVE, Charles-Augustin, *Chroniques parisiennes* (C. Lévy, 1876), pp. 72, 81–2, 113, 206–7, 227, 270–1.

TOPIN, Marius, *Les Romanciers contemporains* (Perrin, 1876), 2e série, pp. 37–49.
repr. *Les Romanciers contemporains* (Didier, 1881), pp. 39–43.

13 Mar. GONCOURT, Edmond et Jules de, Entry in *Le Journal des Goncourt* (Flammarion-Fasquelle, n.d.)

20 Apr. SAULIÈRE, Auguste, 'Les Romanciers nouveaux. I. Émile Zola', *La République des lettres*, IV. 157.

Oct. MAUPASSANT, Guy de, Letter to H. Roujon, in *Chroniques* . . . (Gründ, 1938), p. 216.

20 Oct. HOSTEIN, H., 'Souvenirs d'un directeur de théâtre', *Le Figaro*.
repr. *Historiettes et souvenirs d'un homme de théâtre* (E. Dentu, 1878).

23 Oct. MAUPASSANT, Guy de, 'Gustave Flaubert', *La République des lettres*.
repr. *Chroniques* . . . (Gründ, 1938), p. 3.

25 Oct. BÉRARD-VARAGNAC, Émile, 'Balzac', *Le Journal des débats*.
repr. *Portraits littéraires* (Calmann-Lévy, 1887), pp. 65–76.

31 Oct. BARBEY D'AUREVILLY, Jules, 'Les *Mémoires* de Philarète Chasles', *Le Constitutionnel*.
repr. *Mémoires historiques et littéraires* (Lemerre, 1893), p. 273.

5 Nov. LAUJOL, Henry, 'Les Abeilles', *La République des lettres*, II. 135.

12 Nov. FEUGÈRE, Gaston, 'Causerie littéraire. Honoré de Balzac d'après sa *Correspondance*', *Le Français*.
Second article on 19 Nov. 1876.

17 Nov. BIGOT, Charles, 'La *Correspondance* de Balzac', *Le Journal officiel*, pp. 8364–6.
Second article on 18 Nov. 1876, pp. 8406–8.

17 Nov. GONCOURT, Edmond et Jules de, Entry in *Le Journal des Goncourt* (Flammarion-Fasquelle, n.d.), V. 224.

22 Nov. MAUPASSANT, Guy de, 'Balzac d'après ses lettres', *La Nation*.
Signed: Guy de Valmont.)
repr. *Chroniques* . . . (Gründ, 1938), pp. 8–11.

23 Nov. CÉARD, Henri, '*Germinie Lacerteux*', *Les Droits de l'homme*.

27 Nov. BARBEY D'AUREVILLY, Jules, 'La *Correspondance* de Balzac', *Le Constitutionnel*.
repr. *Littérature épistolaire* (Lemerre, 1893), pp. 1–15.

28 Nov.   BERNARD, Daniel, 'La *Correspondance* d'Honoré de Balzac', *L'Union.*

9 Dec.   FLAUBERT, Gustave, Letter to his niece Caroline, in *Correspondance* (Conard, 1930), VII. 366.

10 Dec.   PONS, A.-J., 'Un Duel à la plume. Balzac et Sainte-Beuve', *Le Nain jaune.*

10 Dec.   FOURNEL, Victor, 'Les Œuvres et les hommes', *Le Correspondant*, LXIX. 901–6.

24 Dec.   BOURGET, Paul, 'Le Roman de la vie de Balzac', *La République des lettres*, III. 1–9.

31 Dec.   FLAUBERT, Gustave, Letters to Mme Roger des Genettes and Edmond de Goncourt, in *Correspondance* (Conard, 1930), VII. 384, 386.

? Dec.   GILLE, Philippe, [Review of Balzac's *Correspondance*], journal unknown.
          repr. *La Bataille littéraire* (Havard, 1889), I. 271–80.

1877

          CHASLES, Philarète, *Mémoires* (Charpentier, 1877), II. 206, 301–2.

          JANIN, Jules, *Critique dramatique* (Librairie des bibliophiles, 1877). *25 Aug. 1851.

1 Jan.   ZOLA, Émile, 'Balzac et sa *Correspondance*' (in Russian), *Viestnik Evropi* (St. Petersburg), p. 257.
          repr. *Les Romanciers naturalistes* (Charpentier, 1881).

6 Jan.   DERÔME, Léopold, 'La *Correspondance* de Balzac', *Le Soleil*. Further articles on 11, 16–17, and 28 Jan., 15 Feb., and 2 Mar. 1877.

7 Jan.   BANVILLE, Théodore de, 'Contes pour les femmes: le fin mot', *La République des lettres*, III. 68.

15 Jan.   Anon., 'Balzac plagiaire', *La Gazette anecdotique.*

21 Jan.   JOLY, Louis, 'La *Correspondance* de Balzac', *Le Moniteur universel*. Second article on 27 Jan. 1877.

8 Mar.   LESCLIDE, Richard, 'Balzac à l'Académie', *La Lune rousse*. repr. *HOB* 399–400.

10 Apr.   LEVALLOIS, Jules, 'Balzac et sa queue', *Le Correspondant*, LXXI. 112–42.

15 May   BERTHET, Élie, 'Silhouettes et anecdotes littéraires', *La Revue de France*, XXIII. 323–4.

11 June   ZOLA, Émile, 'Revue dramatique', *Le Bien Public*.
           repr. *Documents littéraires* (Charpentier, 1881).

   Aug.   FLAUBERT, Gustave, Letter to Mme Roger des Genettes, in
           Correspondance (Conard, 1930), VIII. 58.

1878

CHAMPFLEURY, *Documents pour servir à la biographie de Balzac*.
Balzac au Collège (Patay, 1878).
*23 Nov. 1872.

MONTIFAUD, Marc de, *Les Romantiques* (A. Reiff, 1878), pp. 74–
85.

ROYER, Alphonse, *Histoire universelle du théâtre* (Ollendorff,
1878), V. 150–60.

15 Mar.   Anon., 'Les Projets de Balzac', *La Gazette anecdotique*.

22 Apr.   ZOLA, Émile, Letter to Paul Bourget, in *Correspondance* (Char-
           pentier, 1908), II. 156.

1 May   Anon., [Review of Champfleury (1878)], *La Jeune-France*.

8 May   SIRAUDIN, Paul, 'Figaro Pic-nic. Balzac en robe de chambre',
           Le Figaro.

15 Aug.   BOURGET, Paul, 'La Genèse du roman contemporain', *La Vie
           littéraire*.

20 Aug.   ZOLA, Émile, 'Revue dramatique et littéraire', *Le Voltaire*.
           repr. *Le Roman expérimental* (Charpentier, 1880), p. 205.

24 Aug.   HUGO, Victor, 'Oraison funèbre de Balzac', *Le Figaro*.
           *21 Aug. 1850.

27 Aug.   ZOLA, Émile, 'Revue dramatique et littéraire' *Le Voltaire*.
           repr. *Le Roman expérimental* (Charpentier, 1880), p. 219.

1 Oct.   Anon., [Review of Zola, *Théâtre*], *La Jeune-France*.

13 Dec.   DURUY, Albert, 'La *Correspondance* de Balzac', *Le Moniteur
           universel*.

14 Dec.   MARX, Adrien, 'Paris l'hiver', *Le Figaro*.

22 Dec.   ZOLA, Émile, 'Le Roman contemporain', *Le Figaro*, supplément
           littéraire.
           repr. *Les Romanciers naturalistes* (Charpentier, 1881).

26 Dec.   VALLÈS, Jules, 'Notes d'un absent', *Le Voltaire*.

1879

GONCOURT, Edmond et Jules de, *Gavarni, l'homme et l'œuvre*
(Charpentier, 1879).

CHAMPFLEURY, *Documents pour servir à la biographie de Balzac.*
Balzac, sa méthode de travail (Patay, 1879).
*3 May 1873 and 3 Jan. 1874.

KARR, Alphonse, *Le Livre de bord* (Calmann-Lévy, 1879).

SPOELBERCH DE LOVENJOUL, Vicomte Charles, *Histoire des œuvres de Balzac* (Calmann-Lévy, 1879).
repr. 1886.

WERDET, Edmond, *Souvenirs de la vie littéraire* (Dentu, 1879), pp. 19–110.

Jan.   A.V., 'Balzac, sa vie, ses œuvres', *La Revue britannique.*

Jan.   ZOLA, Émile, 'Lettre de Paris, XLIV. La Scène dramatique contemporaine' (in Russian), *Viestnik Evropi* (St. Petersburg).
repr. *Le Roman expérimental* (Charpentier, 1880).

1 Jan.   Anon., [Review of Champfleury (1879)], *La Jeune-France.*

1 Jan.   MORNAND, Henri, 'Causerie littéraire', *La Plume.*

10 Jan.   SARCEY, Francisque, 'Une Coquille de Balzac', *Le Dix-neuviéme Siècle.*
Second article on 23 Jan. 1879.

31 Jan.   Anon., 'Orgueil littéraire de Balzac', *La Gazette anecdotique.*

1 Apr.   Anon., [Review of Huysmans, *Les Sœurs Vatard*], *La Jeune-France.*

4 Apr.   ZOLA, Émile, 'Études littéraires', *Le Voltaire.*
repr. *Documents littéraires* (Charpentier, 1881).

May   ZOLA, Émile, 'Deux Triomphes littéraires. V. Hugo et Renan' (in Russian), *Viestnik Evropi* (St. Petersburg).
repr. *Le Voltaire*, 17 May 1879.
repr. *Le Roman expérimental* (Charpentier, 1880).

1 May   ALIS, Harry, 'Le Naturalisme', *Revue moderne et naturaliste*, II. 8.

27 May   ZOLA, Émile, 'Revue dramatique et littéraire', *Le Voltaire.*
repr. *Le Roman expérimental* (Charpentier, 1880).

1 June   DAUDET, Alphonse, 'Mémoires d'un homme de lettres', *La Jeune-France*, pp. 57–60.
repr. *Trente Ans de Paris* (Marpon et Flammarion, 1888).

15 June   ENNIUS, 'Chronique littéraire', *La Plume.*

10 Aug.   PIERRE QUIROULE, 'L'Ambassade de Constantinople', *Figaro-Dimanche.*

26 Aug.   ZOLA, Émile, 'Revue dramatique et littéraire', *Le Voltaire.*
repr. *Le Roman expérimental* (Charpentier, 1880).

Sept.   Zola Émile, 'Lettre de Paris, LII' (in Russian), *Viestnik Evropi* (St. Petersburg).
repr. *Le Voltaire*, 16 and 18 Oct. 1879.
repr. *Le Roman expérimental* (Charpentier, 1880).

1 Dec.   Levallois, Jules, 'L'Œuvre de Balzac', *La Revue de France*, XXXVIII. 547–79.

1880

Anon., article Balzac, in *Encyclopédie populaire*, publiée sous la direction de M. Pierre Conil (Librairie Poussièlgue frères, 1880), p. 208.

Flaubert, Gustave, *Bouvard et Pécuchet* (Livre de Poche, 1959), p. 175.

Godefroy, Frédéric, *Histoire de la littérature française au XIXe siècle* (Gaume, 1880), pp. 231–7.

Spoelberch de Lovenjoul, Vicomte Charles, *Un Dernier Chapitre de l'histoire des œuvres de Balzac* (Dentu, 1880).
repr. *Histoire des Œuvres de Balzac*, 2e édition (Calmann-Lévy, 1886).

Zola, Émile, *Le Roman expérimental* (Charpentier, 1880), *passim*.
*20 and 27 Aug. 1878, Jan. and May 1879, 27 May, 26 Aug., and Sept. 1879, March 1880, 16 Mar., 8 and 23 June, and 26 July 1880.

15 Jan.   Anon., 'Balzac, casseur de vitres', *La Gazette anecdotique*.

20 Jan.   Theuriet, André, 'Lettre-préface', in Camille Fistié, *L'Amour au village* (Ollendorff, 1880).

23 Jan.   Zola, Émile, 'Revue dramatique et littéraire', *Le Voltaire*.

1 Feb.   Guillemot, Maurice, 'Émile Zola', *La Revue moderne et naturaliste*, III. 2.

Mar.   Zola, Émile, 'Lettre de Paris, LV. La rémunération du travail littéraire en France' (in Russian), *Viestnik Evropi* (St. Petersburg).
repr. *Le Roman expérimental* (Charpentier, 1880).

13 Mar.   Zola, Émile, 'Sainte-Beuve III', *Le Voltaire*.
repr. *Documents littéraires* (Charpentier, 1881).

16 Mar.   Zola, Émile, 'Revue dramatique et littéraire', *Le Voltaire*.
repr. *Le Roman expérimental* (Charpentier, 1880).

11 Apr.   Zola, Émile, 'Balzac', *Le Figaro*, supplément littéraire.
repr. *Les Romanciers naturalistes* (Charpentier, 1881).

1 May   GUILLEMOT, Maurice, 'Edmond de Goncourt', *La Revue moderne
           et naturaliste*, III. 5.

1 June   ALLENET, Alfred, 'Deux Morts vivants. Alfred de Musset et
           Gustave Flaubert', *La Jeune-France*, III. 68.

8 June   ZOLA, Émile, 'Revue dramatique et littéraire', *Le Voltaire*.
           repr. *Le Roman expérimental* (Charpentier, 1880).

15 June   BRUNETIÈRE, Ferdinand, 'Le Naturalisme français. Étude sur
           Flaubert', *RDM* XXXIX. 830.
           repr. *Le Roman naturaliste* (Calmann-Lévy, 1883), p. 139– .

23 June   ZOLA, Émile, 'Revue dramatique et littéraire', *Le Voltaire*.
           repr. *Le Roman expérimental* (Charpentier, 1880).

26 June   Anon., 'Causerie littéraire. Charles de Lovenjoul', *La Revue
           bleue*, XVIII. 1233–4.

26 July   ZOLA, Émile, 'L'Argent dans la littérature', *Le Voltaire*.
           repr. *Le Roman expérimental* (Charpentier, 1880).

27 July   ZOLA, Émile, 'Revue dramatique et littéraire', *Le Voltaire*.
           repr. *Les Romanciers naturalistes* (Charpentier, 1881).

3 Aug.   ZOLA, Émile, 'Revue dramatique et littéraire', *Le Voltaire*.
           repr. *Les Romanciers naturalistes* (Charpentier, 1881).

25 Aug.   DESCAURIET, Auguste, 'Le Dossier de Balzac imprimeur', *Le
           Figaro*.

17 Oct.   BRUMMEL, 'Tableaux mondains', *Le Voltaire*.

2 Dec.   GONCOURT, Edmond de, Entry in *Le Journal des Goncourt*
           (Flammarion-Fasquelle, n.d.), VI. 91–2.

6 Dec.   ZOLA, Émile, 'Une Statue pour Balzac', *Le Figaro*.
           repr. *Une Campagne* (Charpentier, 1882).

8 Dec.   CANIVET, Charles, 'Autre Statue', *Le Soleil*.

15 Dec.   PONS, A.-J., 'Balzac éditeur, imprimeur et fondeur de caractères',
           Le Livre, bibliographie ancienne, I. 274–9.

1881

TOPIN, Marius, *Les Romanciers contemporains* (Didier, 1881),
    pp. 39–43.
    *1876.

ZOLA, Émile, *Documents littéraires* (Charpentier, 1881).
    *11 June 1877, 4 Apr. 1879, and 13 Mar. 1880.

ZOLA, Émile, *Les Romanciers naturalistes* (Charpentier, 1881).
    *1 Jan. 1877, 22 Dec. 1878, 11 Apr., 27 July and 3 Aug. 1880,
    31 Mar. and 2 Apr. 1881.

31 Mar. ZOLA, Émile, 'Stendhal', *Le Globe*.
repr. *Les Romanciers naturalistes* (Charpentier, 1881).

1 Apr. CLARETIE, Jules, 'Souvenirs sur Balzac', *La Jeune-France*, III. 549–52.

2 Apr. ZOLA, Émile, 'Stendhal', *Le Globe*.
repr. *Les Romanciers naturalistes* (Charpentier, 1881).

24 Apr. CLARETIE, Jules, 'Balzac candidat', *Le Temps*.

15 May CHAMPFLEURY, 'Documents inédits pour servir à l'histoire de la vie et de l'œuvre de Balzac. Le Père de Balzac', *La Nouvelle Revue*, X. 396–400.

1 July Anon., [Review of H. Céard, *Une Belle Journée*], *La Jeune-France*, bulletin bibliographique.

15 Aug. LEMOYNE, André, 'Émile Zola. *Les Romanciers naturalistes*' *La Revue littéraire et artistique*.

20 Aug. *Le Figaro*, supplément littéraire. Special issue devoted to Balzac. Various articles (mainly anecdotal) reprinted; no new material.

15 Sept. BRUNETIÈRE, Ferdinand, 'Les Origines du roman naturaliste', *RDM* XLVII. 438–50.
repr. *Le Roman naturaliste* (Calmann-Lévy, 1883), pp. 243–69.

1882

ALBERT, Paul, *La Littérature français au XIXe siècle* (Hachette, 1882), pp. 245–73.

BANVILLE, Théodore de, *Mes Souvenirs* (Charpentier, 1882).
*21 Mar. 1882, pp. 277–87.

ZOLA, Émile, *Une Campagne, 1880–1881* (Charpentier, 1882), pp. 85–95.
*6 Dec. 1880.

16 Feb. Anon., 'Lettres inédites de Balzac et du maréchal Bugeaud', *Le Temps*.

6 Mar. LA FARE, 'La Veuve de Balzac', *Le Gaulois*.

10 Mar. CHAMPFLEURY, 'Croquis romantiques.—Le Bibliophile Jacob', *Le Livre*, bibliographie ancienne, III. 65–70.

21 Mar. BANVILLE, Théodore de, 'Sur Balzac', *Gil-Blas*.
repr. *Mes Souvenirs* (Charpentier, 1882), pp. 277–87.

31 Mar. Anon., 'Un Drame à la Balzac', *La Gazette anecdotique*.

13 Apr. CAZIN, Robert, 'Madame de Balzac', *L'Évènement*.

22 Apr. MAUPASSANT, Guy de, 'Les Amies de Balzac', *Le Gaulois*.

27 Apr. BOURGET, Paul, 'Les Manuscrits de Balzac', *Le Parlement*.

10 May   LACROIX, Paul, 'Simple Histoire de mes relations avec H. de Balzac', *Le Livre*, bibliographie ancienne, III. 151–61.
Second article on 10 June, III. 167–89.

10 June   Anon., [On Balzac's manuscripts], *Le Livre*, bibliographie ancienne, III. 192–3.

20 June   WALTER, Jehan, 'Les Papiers de Balzac', *Le Figaro*.

22 June   CÉARD, Henri, 'Balzac au pilon', *L'Express*.

22 June   SECOND, Albéric, 'Balzac à Angoulême', *Le Figaro*.
repr. *Le Tiroir au souvenirs* (Dentu, 1886), pp. 1–20.

23 June   CAZE, Robert, 'Exploits d'huissier', *Le Réveil*.

26 June   VALLÈS, Jules, 'Notes et croquis', *Le Réveil*.

1 July   SECOND, Albéric, 'Balzac à Paris', *Le Figaro*.
repr. *Le Tiroir aux souvenirs* (Dentu, 1886), pp. 21–36.

3 July   BONNIÈRES, Robert de, 'Les Papiers inédits de Balzac', *Le Figaro*, (Signed: Janus.)
repr. *Les Mémoires d'aujourd'hui* (Ollendorff, 1885), II. 131–44.

15 July   MICHIELS, Alfred, 'Les Continuateurs de Balzac. Les Frères Goncourt', *Le Constitutionnel*.

24 July   VALLÈS, Jules, 'La Révolution littéraire', *Le Réveil*.

20 Aug.   HAMM, Ernest, 'Balzac et Étex', *Le Gaulois*.

10 Sept. LACROIX, Paul, 'Simple Histoire de mes relations avec H. de Balzac', *Le Livre*, bibliographie ancienne, III. 270–87. (Third article.)

15 Sept. SECOND, Albéric, 'Les Morts oubliés. Louis Lurine', *Le Figaro*.
repr. *Le Tiroir aux souvenirs* (Dentu, 1886).

2 Nov.   MICHIELS, Alfred, 'Le Secret de Balzac', *Le Constitutionnel*.

6 Nov.   OHNET, Georges, 'Feuilleton théâtral', *Le Constitutionnel*.

1883

BARBIER, Auguste, *Souvenirs personnels et silhouettes contemporains* (Dentu, 1883), pp. 222–5.

BRUNETIÈRE, Ferdinand, *Le Roman naturaliste* (Calmann-Lévy, 1883), pp. 1–28, 136–95, 243–69.
*1 Apr. 1875, 15 June 1880, and 15 Sept. 1881.

DU CAMP, Maxime, *Souvenirs littéraires* (Hachette, 1883), II. 52 and *passim*.

WEILL, Alexandre, *Souvenirs intimes de Henri Heine* (Dentu, 1883), p. 119– .

4 Jan.   GEFFROY, Gustave, 'Aux Jardies', *La Justice.*
         repr. *Notes d'un journaliste* (Charpentier, 1887).

15 Jan.   MICHIELS, Alfred, 'Le Secret de Balzac', *Le Constitutionnel.*
         (Second article.)

6 Feb.   DELPIT, Albert, 'Notes sur Paris', *Paris.*

6 Feb.   DELPIT, Albert, 'Une Clef de la *Comédie humaine*', *Paris.*

10 Apr.   BOURGES, Élémir, '*Le Bonheur des dames*', *La Revue des chefs-d'œuvre*, I. xi.

21 June   DELPIT, Albert, 'Autour d'une statue', *Le Figaro.*

25 June   GEFFROY, Gustave, 'Une Statue à Balzac', *La Justice.*
         repr. *Notes d'un journaliste* (Charpentier, 1887), pp. 104–8.

27 June   LEROY, Albert, 'Balzac et *le Figaro*', *Le Réveil.*

27 June   MARCELLO, 'Chronique', *Le Télégraphe.*

Aug.   RACOT, Adolphe, 'Lettre de Paris. Balzac et le roman actuel', *La Revue générale* (Brussels), XXXVIII. 281–2.

11 Aug.   LA FORGE, Anatole de, 'Les Serviteurs de la démocratie: Balzac', *Le Siècle.*

20 Aug.   HOUSSAYE, Arsène, 'Les Dernières Heures de Balzac', *Le Figaro.*
         repr. *Les Confessions* (Dentu, 1888), IV. 255–61.

Sept.   PÉLADAN, Joséphin, 'J. Barbey d'Aurevilly, ses poésies inédites et ses livres perdus', *L'Artiste*, 53e année, II. 209–10.

10 Sept.   SAINT-HÉRAYE, B. H. G. de, 'La Littérature du choléra', *Le Livre*, bibliographie rétrospective, IV. 276–7.

3 Oct.   LEROY, Albert, 'La Statue de Balzac', *Le Réveil.*

25 Oct.   BOURGET, Paul, 'Études et portraits. L'Observation mondaine', *Le Parlement.*

5 Nov.   GEFFROY, Gustave, 'La Statue de Dumas', *La Justice.*
         repr. *Notes d'un journaliste* (Charpentier, 1887), pp. 111–17.

9 Nov.   DUVAL, Georges, 'Mon Carnet', *L'Évènement.*

10 Nov.   MONSELET, Charles, 'Les Oubliés et les dédaignés', *Le Livre*, bibliographie rétrospective, IV. 337–42.

22 Nov.   GONZALÈS, Emmanuel, 'Lettre au rédacteur, sur une statue de Balzac', *L'Évènement.*

23 Nov.   POIGNAND, Jules, 'Le Dieu Balzac', *Le Gaulois.* (Signed: Montjoyeux.)

26 Nov.   GEFFROY, Gustave, 'Balzac', *La Justice.*
         repr. *Notes d'un journaliste* (Charpentier, 1887), pp. 108–11.

29 Nov.   BOURGET, Paul, 'Études et portraits', *Le Parlement*.

1 Dec.   FOURNEL, Victor, 'La Chronique de Bernadille', *Le Moniteur universel*.

1 Dec.   DANCOURT, 'Lettre de Paris', *La Revue générale* (Brussels).

10 Dec.   THEURIET, André, 'Notes et impressions. La Statue de Balzac', *Le Parlement*.

10 Dec.   CHAMPFLEURY, 'Les Amis de Balzac', *Le Livre*, bibliographie rétrospective, IV. 377–8.

1884

DESPREZ, Louis, *L'Évolution naturaliste* (Tresse, 1884), pp. 1, 9–10, 23, 94–5, 194, 196, 257–8, 326, 355.

HEPP, Alexandre, *Paris-Patraque* (Dentu, 1884), pp. 9, 85–91, 156, 222–8, 236, 280–1.

HUYSMANS, Joris-Karl, *A Rebours* (Charpentier, 1884). Crès edition, 1922: pp. 184, 233.

THUREAU-DANGIN, Paul, *Histoire de la Monarchie de Juillet* (Plon, 1884), I. 319–30.

4 Jan.   CAZE, Robert, 'Balzac et ses amis', *Le Voltaire*. (Signed: Louis Durand.)
Second article on 10 Jan. 1884.

10 Jan.   DRUMONT, Édouard, 'Le Mouvement littéraire', *Le Livre*, bibliographie moderne, V. 1–5.

19 Jan.   MAUPASSANT, Guy de, 'Étude sur Flaubert', *La Revue bleue*.
Second article on 26 Jan. 1884.
repr. *Lettres de Flaubert à George Sand* (Charpentier, 1884).
repr. Flaubert, *Bouvard et Pécuchet* (Quantin, 1885).
repr. Maupassant, *Œuvres complètes* (Conard, 1930), XXX. 95–6.

20 Jan.   CAZE, Robert, 'Balzac et ses amis', *Le Voltaire*. (Third Article.) (Signed: Louis Durand.)

15 Apr.   AUDEBRAND, Philibert, 'Philarète Chasles', *La Nouvelle Revue*, XXVII. 776–815.

10 Aug.   PÈNE DU BOIS, Henri, [Review of E. E. Saltus, *Balzac*], *Le Livre*, bibliographie moderne, V. 492.

Sept.   CHRISTOPHE, Jules, 'Notes physiologiques sur Balzac', *La Revue indépendante*, I. 413–16.
Second article in Oct. 1884, pp. 502–17.

8 Sept.   LEPELLETIER, Edmond, 'Les Balzaciens', *L'Écho de Paris*.

1885

BONNIÈRES, Robert de, *Mémoires d'aujourd'hui* (Ollendorff, 1885), II. 131–44.
*3 July 1882.

GAUTIER, Théophile, *Portraits et souvenirs littéraires* (Charpentier, 1885).

HUYSMANS, Joris-Karl, *J.-K. Huysmans*, in *Les Hommes d'aujourd'hui*, 263rd fascicule. (Signed: A. Meunier.)
repr. *En Marge* (Crès, 1927), p. 59.

VALLÈS, Jules, *L'Insurgé* (Charpentier, 1885), chapter iv.

6 Apr. GONCOURT, Edmond de, Entry in *Le Journal des Goncourt* (Flammarion-Fasquelle, n.d.), VII. 26.

10 May CONTADES, Comte Georges de, 'L'Homme au camélia [Lautour-Mézeray]', *Le Livre*, bibliographie rétrospective, VI. 129–50.
repr. *Portraits et fantaisies* (Quantin, 1887), pp. 41, 54, 59, 60, 61.

6 June RACOT, Adolphe, 'Courrier de Paris', *La Gazette de France*. (Signed: Dancourt.)

10 Aug. RACOT, Adolphe, 'Le Critique maudit—Gustave Planche', *Le Livre*, bibliographie rétrospective, VI. 225–48.

24 Aug. SECOND, Albéric, 'Balzac à la campagne', *Le Figaro*.
repr. *Le Tiroir aux souvenirs* (Dentu, 1886), pp. 173–5.

10 Sept. DU PONTAVICE DE HEUSSY, Robert, 'Balzac en Bretagne', *Le Livre*, bibliographie rétrospective, VI. 255–77.
repr. *Balzac en Bretagne* (Rennes, chez l'auteur, 1885).

30 Sept. Anon., 'Balzac candidat', *La Gazette anecdotique*.

Oct. Anon., 'Chronique parisienne', *Bibliothèque universelle et revue suisse*, XXVIII. 178–80.

Nov. MAUPASSANT, Guy de, Remarks attributed to him by 'Mme X' in 'Guy de Maupassant intime. Notes d'une amie', *La Grande Revue*, LXXV (1912), p. 676.

15 Dec. Anon., 'Balzac à table', *La Gazette anecdotique*.

1886

GOZLAN, Léon, *Balzac intime. Balzac en pantoufles. Balzac chez lui*, nouvelle édition, avec une préface de Jules Claretie (Librairie illustrée, 1886).

HOUSSAYE, Arsène, *Les Confessions* (Dentu, 1886), II. vi.

PARDÓBAZAN, Emilia, *Le Naturalisme*, traduit de l'Espagnol par Albert Savine (Savine, 1886), *passim*.

DERÔME, Léopold, *Causeries d'un ami des livres*, Les Éditions originales des romantiques (E. Rouveyre, 1886), I. 56–62, 173–5, II. 283–7.

SECOND, Albéric, *Le Tiroir aux souvenirs* (Dentu, 1886), pp. 1–52, 173–5, 351.
*22 June, 1 July and 15 Sept. 1882, 24 Aug. 1885, and 18 June 1852.

SPOELBERCH DE LOVENJOUL, Vicomte Charles, *Histoire des Œuvres de Balzac*, 2e édition revue, corrigée et augmentée (Calmann-Lévy, 1886).
*1879, 1880.
repr. 1888.

Jan.   CERFBERR, Anatole, 'Histoire d'une historiographie', *La Jeune-France*, VIII. 349–53.

10 Jan.   Anon., 'Balzac poète', *Le Livre*, bibliographie moderne, VII. 35.

2 Feb.   BOURGET, Paul, 'Variétés. Un nouveau dictionnaire', *Le Journal des débats*.

6 Feb.   CORIVEAUD, A., 'Les Idées scientifiques de Balzac', *La Revue scientifique*, XI. 222.

15 Apr.   Anon., 'Balzac et le magnétisme', *La Gazette anecdotique*.

May   VOGÜÉ, Eugène Melchior de, 'Avant-propos', in *Le Roman russe* (Plon, 1886), pp. xxix–xxx.

15 June   PELLISSON, Maurice, 'Les Hommes, d'argent d'après quelques pièces contemporaines', *La Revue d'art dramatique*, II. 325–6.

10 Nov.   Anon., 'Balzac à l'Académie et *la Dernière Fée*', *Le Livre*, bibliographie moderne, VII. 602.

10 Dec.   DERÔME, Léopold, 'Une Œuvre anonyme de Balzac', *Le Livre*, bibliographie rétrospective, VII. 367–76.

1887

Anon., 'Comment travaillait Balzac', *La Revue rétrospective*, VI (1887), 74.

AUDEBRAND, Philibert, *Léon Gozlan. Scènes de la vie littéraire, 1828–65* (Librairie illustrée, 1887), pp. 193–228.

BÉRARD-VARAGNAC, Émile, *Portraits littéraires* (Calmann-Lévy, 1887), pp. 65–76.
*25 Oct. 1876.

CONTADES, Comte Georges de, *Portraits et fantaisies* (Quantin, 1887), pp. 41, 54, 59, 60, 61, 184.

FAGUET, Émile, *Études littéraires sur le XIXe siècle* (Lecène et Oudin, 1887), pp. 413–53.

FÉNÉON, Félix, *Jules Christophe et Anatole Cerfberr* (Les Hommes d'aujourd'hui, 1887).

GEFFROY, Gustave, *Notes d'un journaliste* (Charpentier, 1887), pp. 104–17, 123–5.
*4 Jan, 25 June, 5 and 26 Nov. 1883.

HOUSSAYE, Arsène, *Les Confessions* (Dentu, 1887) III. 117–21.

PONTMARTIN, Armand de, *Souvenirs d'un vieux critique* (Calmann-Lévy, 1887), VII. 201–16.

23 Jan. MONSELET, Charles, 'Un Souper offert par Balzac', *Le Figaro*, supplément littéraire.
repr. *Mes Souvenirs littéraires* (Librairie illustrée, 1888), pp. 1–12.

14 Feb. ULBACH, Louis, 'Un Scénario de Balzac', *Gil-Blas*.

21 Feb. COLOMBINE, 'Chronique', *Gil-Blas*.

15 Apr. Anon., 'Acte de naissance de Balzac', *La Gazette anecdotique*.

4 May TALMEYR, Maurice, 'Chronique. Le Style de Balzac', *Le National*.
repr. 'Balzac écrit-il?', *La Revue hebdomadaire*, 16 July 1898.

28 May CHAMPFLEURY, 'La Statue de Balzac', *Paris illustré*.

29 May FRANCE, Anatole, [Review of Cerfberr and Christophe, *Répertoire des personnages de la Comédie humaine*], *Le Temps*.
repr. *La Vie littéraire* (Calmann-Lévy 1888), II. 2–16.

1 June LECOMTE, J.-Henry, 'Frédérick-Lemaître', *Le Témoin*.
repr. *Un Comédien au XIXe siècle* (Chez l'auteur, 1888), II. 2–16.

12 June LEPELLETIER, Edmond, 'Balzac en feuilleton', *L'Écho de Paris*.

28 June BARRÈS, Maurice, 'La Contagion des Rastignac', *Le Voltaire*.

July WYZEWA, Théodore de, 'Chronique littéraire', *La Revue indépendante*, IX. 15.

2 July Anon., 'Les Dévots de Balzac', *Gil-Blas*.

10 July Anon., 'Les *Contes drolatiques* de Balzac en justice', *Le Livre*, bibliographie moderne, VIII. 384.

13 July BIRÉ, Edmond, 'Causeries littéraires', *L'Univers*.

10 Aug. UZANNE, Octave, 'Zigzags littéraires à travers l'œuvre de Balzac', *Le Livre*, bibliographie moderne, VIII. 393–407.
repr. *Les Zigzags d'un curieux* (Quantin, 1888).

25 Aug.	Anon., 'La Famille et les origines de Balzac', *Le Temps*.
10 Sept.	Anon., 'La Genèse de *Vautrin*', *Le Livre*, bibliographie moderne, VIII. 488.
27 Oct.	LEPELLETIER, Edmond, 'Balzac à la cour', *L'Écho de Paris*.
31 Oct.	Anon., 'Balzac poète', *La Gazette anecdotique*.

1888

CULLÈRE, Dr. A., *Les Frontières de la folie* (Baillière, 1888), pp. 351–3.

FAVRE, Dr. Henri, *La France en éveil. Balzac et le temps présent* (Marpon et Flammarion, 1888).

FERRY, Gabriel, *Balzac et ses amies* (Calmann-Lévy, 1888).

FRANCE, Anatole, *La Vie littéraire* (Calmann-Lévy, 1888), I. 141–55, 341, 348.

HOUSSAYE, Arsène, *Les Confessions* (Dentu, 1888), IV. 255–61.
*20 Aug. 1883.

LECOMTE, J.-Henry, *Un Comédien au XIXe siècle. Frédérick-Lemaître* (Chez l'auteur, 1888), II. 2–16.
*1 June 1887.

MONSELET, Charles, *Mes Souvenirs littéraires* (Librairie illustrée, 1888), pp. 1–12.
*23 Jan. 1887.

UZANNE, Octave, *Les Zigzags d'un curieux* (Quantin, 1888).
*10 Aug. 1887.

4 Apr.	MONTORGUEIL, G., 'Les Amies de Balzac', *Paris*.
7 Apr.	GAUCHER, Maxime, 'Causerie littéraire', *La Revue bleue*, XLI. 445.
16 Apr.	DORSEL, Robert, 'Le *Mercadet* de Balzac', *Le Moniteur universel*.
19 Apr.	ULBACH, Louis, 'Balzac et ses amies', *Le Petit Marseillais* (Marseille).
20 Apr.	Anon., 'Balzac et les femmes', *Le Temps*.
11 May	MICHELET, V.-Émile, 'Les Amies de Balzac', *Le Gaulois*.
11 May	FOURCAUD, Louis de, 'La Musique dans Balzac', *Universal Review* (London), pp. 111–32.
2 July	FOUQUIER, Henry, 'La Statue de Balzac', *Le Figaro*.
2 July	COLOMBINE, 'Chronique', *Gil-Blas*.
5 July	PESSARD, Hector, 'Au Bois sacré', *Gil-Blas*.
7 July	BANVILLE, Théodore de, 'Lire Balzac', *Le Figaro*.

8 July   PREIM, René, 'La Statue de Balzac', *Le Parisien.*

9 July   THEURIET, André, 'Chronique. La Statue de Balzac', *La République française.*

10 July   CASE, Jules, 'Chronique, La Statue de Balzac', *L'Estafette.*

15 July   BRUSSE, J.-Nicolas, 'Honoré de Balzac', *L'Indépendant littéraire*, II. 28–36.

1 Sept.   SOURIAU, Maurice, 'Balzac et son œuvre', *La Revue de l'enseignement secondaire et de l'enseignement supérieur.*
Further articles on 15 Sept. and 1 Oct. 1888.

1 Oct.   Anon., 'Balzac et les statuaires', *Le Temps.*

14 Nov.   Anon., 'Victor Hugo, Balzac et Mme Dorval', *Le Temps.*

15 Nov.   CABAT, Augustin, *Étude sur l'œuvre d'Honoré de Balzac*, prix d'éloquence de l'Académie française, décerné le 15 novembre 1888. Published 1889.

17 Nov.   BOUBÉE, Simon, 'Balzac et M. Augustin Cabat', *La Gazette de France.*

25 Nov.   BIRÉ, Edmond, 'Balzac et l'Académie française', *Le Correspondant*, CLIII. 675–88.
repr. *Études et portraits* (Lyon, 1894), pp. 155–80.
repr. *Honoré de Balzac* (Champion, 1897).

1889

CABAT, Augustin, *Étude sur l'œuvre d'Honoré de Balzac* (Didier, Perrin, 1889).

DRUMONT, Édouard, *La Fin d'un monde, étude psychologique et sociale* (Savine, 1889), pp. 270, 275, 287, 501.

GILLE, Philippe, *La Bataille littéraire* (Havard, 1889), I. 271–80.
*?Dec. 1876.

MORICE, Charles, *La Littérature de tout-à-l'heure* (Perrin, 1889), pp. 167, 190.

ROSNY, J.-H. aîné, 'M. Renan et la littérature contemporaine', *La Revue indépendante*, pp. 324, 475–6.

1 May   GONCOURT, Edmond de, Entry in *Le Journal des Goncourt* (Flammarion-Fasquelle, n.d.), VIII. 41–2.

Sept.   MAUPASSANT, Guy de, 'L'Évolution du roman au XIXe siècle', *La Revue de l'Exposition universelle de 1889*, II. 245–8.
repr. G. Délaissement, *Maupassant journaliste et chroniqueur* (Albin Michel, 1956).

25 Nov.   CÉARD, Henri, 'Chronique. La Statue de Balzac', *L'Évènement.*

1890

BANVILLE, Théodore de, *L'Âme de Paris* (Charpentier, 1890).

BARRIÈRE, Marcel, *L'Œuvre d'Honoré de Balzac. Étude littéraire et philosophique sur la Comédie humaine* (Calmann-Lévy, 1890).

HURET, Jules, *Enquête sur l'évolution littéraire* (Charpentier, 1890).

PELISSIER, Georges, *Le Mouvement Littéraire au XIXe siècle* (Hachette, 1890), pp. 249–56.

LUCAS, Hippolyte, *Portraits et souvenirs litteraires* (Plon, 1890), pp. 123–31.

ROSNY, J.-H., *Le Termite, roman de mœurs littéraires* (Savine, 1890), p. 25.

SIMON, Jules, 'Préface', in H. de Balzac, *Les Chouans* (Testard, 1890), illustré par Julien Le Blant.

BERNIER, Robert, 'L'Art et le socialisme', lecture given to *La Société du progrès social*. Not reproduced.

1 Mar. MICHELET, Victor-Émile, 'Les Jeunes Hommes de Balzac et la jeunesse actuelle', *La Revue de famille*, IV. 450–9.

1 Mar. FRANCE, Anatole, 'Études et portraits. Le Comte d'Orsay et Lady Blessington', *La Revue illustrée*, IX. 218–22.

23 Nov. GONCOURT, Edmond de, Entry in *Le Journal des Goncourt* (Flammarion-Fasquelle, n.d.), VIII. 146.

1891

AUGER, Hippolyte, *Mémoires*, publiées par P. Cottin (*La Revue rétrospective*, 1891), pp. 176, 246, 353, 361–3, 367–9, 642.

FRARY, Raoul, *Essais de critique* (A. Colin, 1891), pp. 275–300.

GIDEL, C.-A., *Histoire de la littérature française de 1815 jusqu'à nos jours* (Lemerre, 1891), II. 12–24.

UZANNE, Octave, 'Portaits curieux, inédits ou inconnus de Balzac', *Le Livre moderne*, IV. 128–35.

BONNIER, Charles, 'Les Lettres de soldat', *Zeitschrift für romanische Philologie*, IV (1891), 375–428.

Aug. FRANCE, Anatole, [Review of Marcel Schwob, *Un Cœur double*], *Le Temps*.
repr. *Le Livre moderne*, IV. 126.

10 Oct.   Anon., 'Nouvelles Pensées de Balzac', *Le Livre moderne*, IV.
           253–6.

30 Oct.   CÉARD, Henri, 'Le Père Goriot', *L'Évènement*.

15 Dec.   BRUNNE, Claire [i.e. Caroline Marbouty], 'Portrait de Balzac',
           La Gazette anecdotique.

1892

FRANCE, Anatole, *La Vie littéraire* (Calmann-Lévy, 1892), IV.
320.

LEMER, Julien, *Balzac, sa vie, son œuvre* (Sauvaître, 1892).

ROD, Édouard, *Stendhal* (Hachette, 1892), pp. 134–6.

SPOELBERCH DE LOVENJOUL, Vicomte Charles, 'Les Avatars
d'une œuvre de Balzac', *La Revue rétrospective*, 1892.
repr. *Un Roman d'amour* (Calmann-Lévy, 1896).

May   BERNIER, Robert, 'Balzac socialiste', *La Revue socialiste*, XV.
           590–601.

Dec.   BAZALGUETTE, Léon, [Review of Barbey d'Aurevilly, *Littérature
           épistolaire*], *Le Psyché*.

Dec.   AUDEBRAND, Philibert, 'Petites Comédies de paravent.—H. de
           Balzac épicier', *Matinées espagnoles—Nouvelle Revue inter-
           nationale*.

Dec.   RÉGNIER, H. de, 'Paul Adam', *La Revue blanche*.

1893

AUDEBRAND, Philibert, *Mémoires d'un passant* (Calmann-Lévy,
1893), pp. 71–95.

BARBEY D'AUREVILLY, Jules, *Mémoires historiques et littéraires*
(Lemerre, 1893), p. 273.
*31 Oct. 1876.

BARBEY D'AUREVILLY, Jules, *Littérature épistolaire* (Lemerre,
1893), pp. 1–15.
*27 Nov. 1876.

FLAT, Paul, *Essais sur Balzac* (Plon, 1893).

MORILLOT, Paul, *Le Roman en France depuis 1610 jusqu'à nos
jours* (Masson, 1893), pp. 464–70.

Mar.   FLAT, Paul, 'Les Artistes de Balzac', *L'Artiste*, V. 161–83.
           repr. *Essais sur Balzac* (Plon, 1893).

15 Mar.   FERRY, Gabriel, 'Balzac, auteur dramatique', *La Revue d'art
           dramatique*, XXIX, 351–6.

Apr.   SEMBAT, Marcel, 'L'Ame artiste et la critique littéraire. A propos des *Essais sur Balzac*, de Paul Flat', *L'Artiste*, V. 275–85.

19 Apr.   FOURCAUD, Louis de, '*Le Cousin Pons*', *Le Gaulois*.

1 July   NICOLAS, J., 'Le Cryptogramme de Balzac', *Le Figaro*.

1 July   MUHLFELD, Lucien, 'Maurice de Beaubourg', *La Revue blanche*, IX. 95.

22 Aug.   BRAISNE, Henri de, 'Un Anniversaire', *Le Gaulois*.

1894

BIRÉ, Edmond, *Études et portraits* (Lyon, 1894), pp. 155–80. *25 Nov. 1888.

FLAT, Paul, *Seconds Essais sur Balzac* (Plon, 1894).

LANSON, Gustave, *Histoire de la littérature française* (Hachette, 1894), pp. 15, 986–91, 1028, 1059–60.

SOREL, Albert, *Lectures historiques* (Plon, 1894), pp. 136, 141, 150–1.

16 Feb.   BARRÈS, Maurice, 'Enfin Balzac a vieilli', *Le Journal*.

1 Mar.   Anon., 'Balzac et Mme Hanska', *Le Temps*.

8 Mar.   RZEWUSKI, Stanislas, 'La Correspondance de Balzac', *Le Gaulois*.

Apr.   FLAT, Paul, 'Balzac féminin', *L'Artiste*, VII. 249–62.
repr. *Seconds Essais sur Balzac* (Plon, 1894).

9 Apr.   PARISIS, 'Balzac au théâtre', *Le Figaro*.

12 Apr.   DAUDET, Ernest, '*Les Chouans*', *Le Gaulois*.

13 Apr.   PESSARD, Hector, 'Les Premières', *Le Gaulois*.

13 Apr.   BOISEGUIN, 'Chronique. Balzac', *La République française*.

5 May   JANVRAIS, Théophile, 'Balzac au pays des Chouans', *Le Gaulois*.

June   BONNIER, Charles, 'Les Paysans de Balzac', *Ère nouvelle, revue du socialisme international*, pp. 139–47.

June   Anon., [Review of Flat (1894)], *L'Artiste*, VII. 430–2.

21 June   CHEVALET, Émile, 'De Balzac à Proudhon', *L'Avenir républicain* (Issoudun).

1 July   HUYSMANS, Joris-Karl, Letter to E. de Goncourt, in *Lettres inédites à Edmond de Goncourt* (Nizet, 1956), p. 120.

15 July   FERRY, Gabriel, 'Étude sur le théâtre de Balzac', *La Revue d'art dramatique*.

16 July   BIRÉ, Edmond, 'Le Vicomte de Lovenjoul', *La Gazette de France*.
Second article on 30 July 1894.

10 Nov.   CANIVET, Charles, 'Balzac et Maupassant', *Le Soleil.* (Signed: Jean de Nivelle.)

28 Nov.   BRISSON, Adolphe, 'Autour d'une Statue', *La République français.*

5 Dec.   GALDÉMAR, Ange, 'La Malechance de Balzac', *Le Gaulois.* (Signed: A.G.)

1895

DOCQUOIS, Georges, *Bêtes et gens de lettres* (Flammarion, 1895), pp. 1–25.

LANSON, Gustave, 'Balzac d'après sa correspondance', in *Pages choisies des grands écrivains. H. de Balzac* (Colin et Lévy, 1895), pp. i–xxiii.
*4 May 1895.

15 Mar.   DAUDET, Léon, 'Quinzaine littéraire: le désir exprimé par la littérature. Shakespeare et Balzac', *La Nouvelle Revue.*
repr. *Les Idées en marche* (Charpentier, 1896), pp. 37–43.
Cf. L. Daudet, *Alphonse Daudet* (Charpentier, 1898), pp. 208–13.

4 May   LANSON, Gustave, 'Balzac d'après sa correspondance', *La Revue bleue,* III. 546–51.
repr. *Pages choisies des grands écrivains. H. de Balzac* (Colin et Lévy, 1895), pp. i–xxiii.

9 May   DROZ, Gustave, 'Cours sur Taine', *Le Bulletin des cours et conférences,* I. 408–14.
Second article on 16 May 1895, pp. 416–23.

15 May   MUHLFELD, Lucien, 'La Vie littéraire', *La Revue blanche,* p. 435.

11 Sept.   SPOELBERCH DE LOVENJOUL, Vicomte Charles, 'Les Aventures de l'*École des ménages*', *Le Figaro.* Further articles on 12, 13, 14, and 16 Sept. 1895.
repr. *Autour de Balzac* (Calmann-Lévy, 1897).

1896

BAUMANN, Émile, *Le Symbolisme de la vie dans Balzac* (Verne, 1896).
Cf. *Mémoires* (1943), pp. 123, 128–9.

THEURIET, André, *Années de printemps* (Ollendorff, 1896).
repr. *Souvenirs des vertes saisons* (Ollendorff, 1904), p. 42.

DAUDET, Léon, *Les Idées en Marche* (Charpentier, 1896), pp. 37–43.
*15 Mar. 1895.

FOUQUET, Fernand, *À Travers la vie* (Lemerre, 1896), pp. 55–7.

GILBERT, Eugène, *Le Roman en France pendant le XIXe siècle* (Plon, 1896), pp. 132–49, 150–3.

SPOELBERCH DE LOVENJOUL, Vicomte Charles, *Études balzaciennes.—Un Roman d'Amour* (Calmann-Lévy, 1896).
*1892 (partly).

9 May FERZAC, C., 'La Crise de Balzac. La Journalophobie', *Le Gaulois*.

15 July CALIPPE, Charles, 'Le Curé, d'après Balzac', *La Quinzaine*, XI. 238–56.

15 July VASSELOT, Marquet de, 'A propos du monument de Balzac', *Matinées espagnoles—Nouvelle Revue internationale*.

15 Aug. FERRY, Gabriel, 'Les Interprètes de Balzac au théâtre, *La Revue bleue*, VI. 215–17.

12 Oct. BIRÉ, Edmond, 'Balzac et George Sand', *La Gazette de France*.

16 Oct. LEYRET, Henri, 'Balzac et la Russie', *Le Figaro*.

4 Nov. BRISSON, Adolphe, 'Promenades et visites. Le vicomte de Lovenjoul', *Le Temps*.
repr. *Portraits intimes* (A. Colin, 1901), III. 89–100.

19 Nov. MOCQUANT, Louis, 'Les Ancêtres de Balzac', *Le Gaulois*.

15 Dec. SPOELBERCH DE LOVENJOUL, Vicomte Charles, 'Notules sur H. de Balzac par un de ses amis', *Le Bulletin des bibliophiles*, pp. 601–10.

1897

BIRÉ, Edmond, *Honoré de Balzac* (Champion, 1897).
*25 Nov. 1888.

BIRÉ, Edmond, *Nouvelles Causeries littéraires* (Lyon, 1897).

FLEURY, Dr. Maurice de, *Introduction à la médecine de l'esprit* (Alcan, 1897), pp. 108–10, 159, 161, 220–1, 272–4.

MUHLFELD, Lucien, *Le Monde où l'on imprime* (Perrin, 1897), pp. 10, 144, 160, 294–5.

SPOELBERCH DE LOVENJOUL, Vicomte Charles, *Études balzaciennes. Autour de Honoré de Balzac* (Calmann-Lévy, 1897).
*11 Sept. 1895 (partly).

ZOLA, Émile, *Nouvelle Campagne, 1896–7* (Charpentier, 1897), pp. 103, 265.

Mar. Anon., 'Le *Balzac* de M. Edmond Biré', *La Revue du Bas-Poitou*.

29 June TESTE, Louis, 'Depuis Balzac . . .', *Le Gaulois*.

4 Aug. Curzon, H. de, 'Balzac et ses derniers historiens', *Le Moniteur universel.*

10 Oct. Royaumont, [n.t.], *Le Parisien de Paris.*

11 Dec. Galdémar, Ange, 'Un Précédent au cas de M. Zola.—Balzac dénonçant une prétendue erreur judiciaire', *Le Gaulois.*

15 Dec. Calippe, Charles, 'Balzac et la question agraire', *La Revue du clergé français*, XI. 97–108.

1898

Alexandre, Arsène. *Le Balzac de Rodin* (Floury, 1898).

Barbey d'Aurevilly, Jules, *Portraits politiques et littéraires* (Lemerre, 1898), pp. 1–17.
*11 May 1864.

Brunetière, Ferdinand, *Manuel d'histoire de la littérature française* (Delagrave, 1898), pp. 442–53.

Daudet, Léon, *Alphonse Daudet* (Charpentier, 1898), pp. 208–13. Cf. 15 Mar. 1895.

Fray-Fournier, A., *Balzac à Limoges* (H. Ducourtieux, 1898).

Lenient, Charles, *La Comédie en France au XIXe siècle* (Hachette, 1898), II. 224–67.

Maigron, Louis, *Le Roman historique à l'époque romantique* (Champion, 1898), *passim.*

Meunier, G., *Le Bilan littéraire du XIXe siècle* (E. Fasquelle, 1898).

Perrens, F.-T., *Histoire sommaire de la littérature française au XIXe siècle* (H.-L. May, 1898), pp. 107, 281, 293, 296, 302–311, 317, 318, 326, 347.

Rod, Édouard, *Nouvelles Études sur le XIXe siècle* (Perrin, 1898), pp. 23–7.

10 Jan. Pierre, Victor, 'La Messe de Samson', *Le Correspondant, CXC.* 113–18.

15 Mar. Le Blond, Maurice, 'Émile Zola devant les jeunes', *La Plume,* pp. 172 and 239–40.

19 Mar. Chincholle, Charles, 'La Statue de Balzac', *Le Figaro.*

20 Mar. Demaison, Maurice, 'La Statue de Balzac', *Le Journal des débats.*

2 May D., Ch., 'Le Balzac de Rodin', *Le Gaulois.*

7 May Tout-Paris, 'Balzac candidat à la députation', *Le Gaulois.*

11 May Un Domino, 'Écho de Paris', *Le Gaulois.*

12 May   CHINCHOLLE, Charles, 'La Vente de la statue de Balzac', *Le Figaro*.

13 May   CASE, JULES, 'Devant Balzac', *Le Gaulois*.

13 May   HALLAYS, André, 'La Statue de Balzac', *Le Journal des débats*.

16 May   F., 'Au jour le jour', *Le Soleil*.

21 May   FAGUET, Émile, 'De l'Influence de Balzac', *La Revue bleue*, IX. 642–9.
          repr. *Propos littéraires* (S.F.I.L., 1905).

23 May   Anon., 'La Famille du romancier Honoré de Balzac', *L'Eclair*.

29 May   *Le Parisien de Paris*, special Balzac number, containing the following articles:
          MAILLARD, L., 'Sur les marches de l'institut';
          SAULNIER, C., 'Des Extraits de la *Recherche de l'absolu*';
          MIREVOYRE, 'Un Logis de Balzac';
          MONIN, H., 'Les Portraits de Balzac par Louis Boulanger';
          ROYAUMONT, [On Balzac's house at Passy], *10 Oct. 1897;
          LAMARTINE, A. de, 'Portrait de Balzac', *1859.
          GERBAUD, J., 'Pères Goriot et pensions bourgeoises'.

1 June   MALET, Gaston, 'Le Merveilleux dans Balzac', *L'Écho du merveilleux* and *La Gazette de France*.

4 June   FERRY, Gabriel, 'Balzac et Victor Hugo aux Jardies', *La Revue bleue*, IX. 726–9.

15 June   JOUIN, Henry, 'Lettre ouverte à M. le Président de la Société des gens de lettres', *La Nouvelle Revue*, CXVIII. 589–94.

July   FERRY, Gabriel, 'Balzac après le 24 février 1848', *La Revue hebdomadaire*, pp. 235–68.

16 July   TALMEYR, Maurice, 'Balzac écrit-il?', *La Revue hebdomadaire*.
          *4 May 1887 (with changes).

Sept.   Anon., 'Récentes publications sur Balzac', *Polybiblion*, XXXIII. 279–80.

1899

CABANÈS, Dr. A., *Balzac ignoré* (Albin Michel, 1899).
*15 June 1899.

DAUDET, Alphonse, *Notes sur la vie* (Charpentier, 1899), pp. 24–5, 129, 139, 153.

SARCEY, Francisque, Preface, in H. de Balzac, *La Maison du chat-qui-pelote* (L. Carteret, 1899).

SPOELBERCH DE LOVENJOUL, Vicomte Charles, 'Avant-propos' in H. de Balzac, *Une Rue de Paris et son habitant* (Rouquette, 1899).

16 Jan. Biré, Edmond, 'D'un vieux livre imprimé par Balzac', *La Gazette de France*.

26 Jan. Adérer, Adolphe, 'Théâtres', *Le Temps*.

30 Jan. Rzewuski, Stanislas, 'Le Théâtre de Balzac à l'étranger', *Le Gaulois*.

30 Jan. Massiac, Théodore, 'Indiscrétions théâtrales', *Gil-Blas*.

31 Jan. Fouquier, H., 'Les Théâtres', *Le Figaro*.

31 Jan. Duquesnel, Félix, 'Les Premières', *Le Gaulois*.

31 Jan. Bernard-Derosne, Léon, 'Les Premières Represéntations', *Le Gaulois*.

31 Jan. Spoelberch de Lovenjoul, Vicomte Charles, 'Les Lectures de *Mercadet* à la Comédie française', *Le Temps*.
　　　　repr. *Une Page perdue d'Honoré de Balzac* (Ollendorff, 1903).

Feb. Anon., 'L'Édition originale de *Mercadet*', *La Revue biblio-iconographique*, VI. 97–8.

1 Feb. Anon., 'Chronique générale', *La Gazette de France*.

1 Feb. Muhlfeld, Lucien, 'Les Premières', *L'Écho de Paris*.

1 Feb. Gavault, Paul, '*Mercadet*', *Le Soir*.

1 Feb. Marrot, Paul, 'Les Premières', *La Lanterne*.

2 Feb. Massiac, Théodore, 'Le Père de Balzac', *Gil-Blas*.

2 Feb. Mendès, Catulle, 'Premières représentations', *Le Journal*.

5 Feb. Chevassu, Francis, 'Revue dramatique', *La Liberté*.

6 Feb. Faguet, Émile, 'La Semaine dramatique', *Le Journal des débats*.

6 Feb. Sarcey, Francisque, '*Mercadet*', *Le Temps*.

7 Feb. Croze, J.-M., '*Mercadet*', *La Presse*.

15 Feb. Lefèvre, G., '*Mercadet*', *La Revue des Revues*, XXVIII. 446–8.

15 Feb. Case, Jules, 'Critique dramatique', *La Nouvelle Revue*, CXVI. 745–7.

30 Mar. Pascal, Félicien de, 'Le Centenaire de Balzac', *Gil-Blas*.

Apr. Articles in Tours newspapers on the centenary celebrations and the political arguments over them:
　　　　Le Télégramme d'Indre-et-Loire, 2, 5, 6, 7, 8, and 9 Apr.
　　　　L'Écho d'Indre-et-Loire, 9 and 16 Apr.
　　　　Le Journal d'Indre-et-Loire, 12, 14, and 17 Apr.

6 Apr. L., 'Au Jour le jour. Balzac et les socialistes', *Le Journal des débats*.

16 Apr. Adam, Paul, 'Le Respect du contraire', *Le Journal*.

16 Apr. Anon., 'Balzac et les Tourangeaux', *Le Temps*.

22 Apr. Anon., 'Courrier de Paris. Balzac', *L'Illustration*, CXIII. 242.

May MÉLIA, Jean, 'Balzac révolutionnaire', *La Revue socialiste*, XXIX. 591–604.

4 May D'ALMÉRAS, Henri, 'Petite Gazette des lettres', *La Presse*.

4 May CHARLES, Étienne, 'Balzac au Panthéon', *La Liberté*.

4 May RZEWUSKI, Stanislas, 'Balzac jugé par son neveu', *Le Gaulois*.

4 May LEPELLETIER, Edmond, 'Tours et Vendôme', *L'Écho de Paris*.

4 May L.E., 'Quelques lettres de Balzac', *Le Temps*.

5 May SOUDAY, Paul, 'Les Jeunes Filles de Balzac', *La Revue pour les jeunes filles*, XVI. 449–60.

5 May FOURNIÈRE, Eugène, Speech in the Chambre des députés, in *La Revue socialiste*, XXIX. 594n.

6 May BRISSON, Adolphe, 'Promenades et visites. Un ami de Balzac', *Le Temps*.
  repr. *Portraits intimes* (A. Colin, 1903), V. 209–17.

6 May BRUCHARD, Henri de, 'Une Gloire monnayée', *La Presse*.

6 May CHARLES, Étienne, 'Les Opinions de Balzac', *La Liberté*.

6 May Anon., 'Le Tombeau de Balzac', *Le Gaulois*.

6 May NORMAND, Maurice, 'Une Collection balzacienne à Bruxelles', *L'Illustration*, CXIII. 294–7.

6 May Anon., 'Balzac et compagnie au Panthéon', *La Croix*.

7 May FAGUET, Émile, 'Une Apothéose', *Le Gaulois*.

7 May L'HEUREUX, Marcel, 'Courrier de Paris', *La Liberté*.

7 May DE BEAUREPAIRE-FROMENT, 'Balzac méridional', *La Presse*.

7 May RZEWUSKI, Stanislas, 'L'Esclave de M. de Balzac', *Le Gaulois*.

7 May GOZLAN, Léon, 'Balzac intime', *La Revue Mame*.
  *1886.

7 May MARROT, Paul, 'Balzac au Panthéon', *La Lanterne*.

8 May D'ALMÉRAS, Henri, 'Chez M. Maréjouls', *La Presse*.

8 May BRUNETIÈRE, Ferdinand, 'Conférence sur Balzac', *Le Temps*.
  repr. *Études critiques sur l'histoire de la littérature française* (Hachette, 1903), 7e série, appendice.

8 May HEPP, Alexandre, 'La Grande Politique', *Le Journal*.

8 May PRADIER, Marcel, 'Les Fêtes de Balzac', *Le Journal*.

8 May RAMEAU, Jean, 'Tout le monde au Panthéon', *Le Gaulois*.

8 May   P.R., 'Les Fêtes de Balzac à Tours', *Le Gaulois*.

8 May   Brisson, Adolphe, 'Promenades et visites. Les Ennemis de Balzac', *Le Temps*.
repr. *Portraits intimes* (A. Colin, 1903), V. 219–22.

9 May   L.C., 'Les Fêtes de Balzac à Tours', *Le Gaulois*.

9 May   Rzewuski, Stanislas, 'Le Mariage de Balzac', *Gil-Blas*.

9 May   Anon., 'Les Fêtes du centenaire de Balzac à Tours', *La Croix*.

9 May   Stiegler, Gaston, 'Les Fêtes de Balzac', *L'Écho de Paris*.

9 May   Brisson, Adolphe, 'Promenades et visites. Autour de Balzac', *Le Temps*.

9 May   Guerlin, Henri, 'Les Fêtes du centenaire de Balzac à Tours', *Le Journal des débats*.
Second article 10 May 1899.

9 May   Malet, Gaston, 'Balzac royaliste', *La Gazette de France*.
Second article on 11 May 1899.

10 May   F., 'Pour les romanciers', *Le Gaulois*.

10 May   Jollivet, Gaston, 'Balzac au Panthéon', *L'Éclair*.

10 May   Brisson, Adolphe, 'Promenades et visites. La Vallée du Lys', *Le Temps*.
repr. *Portraits intimes* (A. Colin, 1903), V. 222–8.

10 May   Le Paysan, 'Balzac', *La Croix*.

11 May   Foemina, 'Les Femmes de Balzac', *Le Gaulois*.

11 May   Nestor, 'Honoré de Balzac', *L'Écho de Paris*.

11 May   Saint-Blancard, 'Le Pèlerinage balzacien en Touraine', *Gil-Blas*.
Second article on 12 May 1899.

12 May   Vanor, Georges, 'Balzaciana', *Gil-Blas*.

12 May   Hallays, André, 'En flânant. La Sépulture de Balzac', *Le Journal des débats*.

13 May   Anon., 'Courrier de Paris', *L'Illustration*, CXIII. 306.

13 May   O'Monroy, Richard, '*La Comédie humaine*', *Gil-Blas*.

13 May   *Le Gaulois du dimanche*, special Balzac issue, containing;
Foucher, G., 'Acte de naissance de Balzac';
Surville, L., 'Les Débuts littéraires de Balzac', *1856–7;
Léger, A., 'Balzac jugé par ses statuaires';
Ferry, G., 'Balzac exploiteur de mines et exploité';
Séguy, G., 'Le Dernier Interprète survivant de Balzac';
Rzewuski, S., 'La Belle-fille de Balzac. Mme la Comtesse Anna Mniszech'.

15 May   KAHN, Gustave, 'Notes sur Balzac', *La Revue blanche*, XIX. 81–9.

15 May   *La Chronique médicale*, special Balzac issue, containing the fol-
          lowing extracts from A. Cabanès, *Balzac ignoré* (Albin Michel,
          1899;
          'La Manie ambulatoire de Balzac';
          'L'Hygiène de Balzac';
          'La Chasteté de Balzac';
          'La Mégalomanie de Balzac';
          'Les Médecins de la *Comédie humaine*';
          'Le Réalisme de Balzac'; and
          MICHAUT, Dr., 'Balzac et Dupuytren';
          CULLÈRE, Dr., 'L'Œuvre de Balzac en regard de la psy-
          chologie morbide'.

18 May   RÉGNIER, Henri de, 'Beaumarchais', Journal unknown.
          repr. *Figures et caractères* (Société du Mercure de France,
          1908), pp. 157–8.

20 May   *L'Art français*, special Balzac issue, containing:
          MARY, J., 'Lettre';
          JAVEL, F., 'Balzac critique d'art'.

20 May   PARSONS, Léon, 'Balzac et l'Académie', *La Revue bleue*, XI. 628–
          731.

21 May   LICHTENBERGER, André, 'L'*Orgon* de Balzac', *Le Journal des
          débats*.

21 May   SPOELBERCH DE LOVENJOUL, Vicomte Charles, '*Orgon*, comédie de
          H. de Balzac', *Le Figaro*.

21 May   GABILLARD, Paul, 'Une Pièce inédite de Balzac', *Le Gaulois du
          dimanche*.

27 May   PROVINS, Michel, 'Une Théorie inédite de Balzac', *Le Gaulois*.

27 May   GUILLEMOT, Maurice, 'Le Portrait de Balzac', *Gil-Blas*.

29 May   LARROUMET, Gustave, 'Balzac. *Mercadet*', *Le Temps*.
          repr. *Études de critique dramatique* (Hachette, 1906), I.

29 May   GOURMONT, Remy de, 'Épilogues. Balzac au Panthéon', *Le
          Mercure de France*, XXX. 750–6.

June   LOLIÉE, Frédéric, 'Balzac et le roman de sa vie', *Le Mois lit-
          téraire et pittoresque*.

10 June   LENÔTRE, G., 'Variétés. Pauvre Balzac!', *Le Monde illustré*.

15 June   DOUMIC, René, 'Amour de tête', Journal unknown.
          repr. *Études sur la littérature française* (Perrin, 1901), IV.
          78–98.

20 June   *Revue franco-allemande/Deutsch-französischer Rundschau*, special Balzac issue, containing articles in French and German by: Fèvre, H., Gramont, L. de, Fleury, E., Michelet, V.-E., Braisne, Henri de, Nordau, Dr. Max, Julllien, J., Lemonnier, C., Morel, E., Riotor, L., and Uzanne, Octave.

7 Aug.   Biré, Edmond, 'Causerie littéraire', *La Gazette de France*.

12 Aug.   Faguet, Émile, 'Les Amours de Balzac', *La Revue bleue*, XII. 201–4.

26 Aug.   Maurras, Charles, [Review of H. de Balzac, *Lettres à l'Étrangère*], *La Revue encyclopédique* (Larousse), IX. 668–9.

1 Sept.   Mélia, Jean, 'Stendhal et Balzac', *La Revue des Revues*, XXX. 497–505.

1 Nov.   Bordeaux, Henri, 'Balzac amoureux', *La Grande Revue*, IV. 450–73.

1900

Faguet, Émile, *Histoire de la littérature française* (Plon, Nourrit, 1900), II. 355–7.

5 Jan.   R.-A., 'Les Grands Hommes au Panthéon', *Le Temps*.

2 Mar.   Huret, Jules, 'L'Œuvre de Balzac et le domaine public', *Le Figaro*.
repr. *La Revue encyclopédique* (Larousse), 1900, p. 274.

14 Mar.   Prévost, Marcel, 'Le Roman français au XIXe siècle', *La Revue bleue*, XIII. 449–56.

24 May   Brunetière, Ferdinand, 'Balzac', *La Revue des cours et conférences*, VIII. 433–443.
Second article on 14 June 1900, pp. 577–89.

8 July   Bauer, Henry, 'Le Travail intellectuel', *La Petite République* (socialiste).

15 Aug.   Mélia, Jean, 'Balzac révolutionnaire', *La Petite République* (socialiste).

18 Aug.   Muhlfeld, Lucien, 'Le Trésor de Balzac', *Le Gaulois*.

18 Aug.   Spoelberch de Lovenjoul, Vicomte Charles, 'La Genèse d'un roman de Balzac.—*Les Paysans*', *La Revue bleue*.
Further articles on 25 Aug., 1 Sept., 1, 8, 15, and 22 Dec. 1900, and 30 Mar. 1901.
repr. *La Genèse d'un roman de Balzac* (Ollendorff, 1901).

19 Aug.   Mitrou, Jean, 'Les Lettres et les arts', *La Petite République* (socialiste).

19 Aug. FAGUET, Émile, 'Balzac, son génie littéraire', *La Renaissance politique et littéraire*.

19 Aug. MAURRAS, Charles, 'Balzac royaliste'. Révolutionnaires comme Balzac', *La Gazette de France*.

19 Aug. BIRÉ, Edmond, 'Balzac—ses opinions politiques et religieuses', *La Renaissance politique et littéraire*.

21 Aug. TALMEYR, Maurice, 'L'Heur de Balzac', *Le Gaulois*.

22 Aug. MITROU, Jean, 'Toquade de grand homme', *La Petite République* (socialiste).

24 Aug. UZANNE, Octave, 'Le Roman vécu et posthume de Balzac', *L'Écho de Paris*.

25 Aug. TALMEYR, Maurice, 'Billets de quinzaine. Le vrai Balzac', *La Revue hebdomadaire*, pp. 571–4.

26 Aug. DUPRAT, G., 'L'Exposition et Balzac', *La Renaissance politique et littéraire*.

1 Sept. 'Que Restera-t-il de Balzac?', questionnaire conducted by M. Legrand, answers from BARRÈS, M., BARRIÈRE, M., BORDEAUX, H., CLARETIE, J., DESTREM, J., FERRY, G., GOURMONT, R. de, MARTIN-VIDEAU, E., MAZEL, H., MICHELET, V.-E., OHNET, G., PONTSEVREZ, PORADOWSKA, M., SPOELBERCH DE LOVENJOUL, C., THIAUDIÈRE, TOUDOUZE, G., in *La Revue d'Europe*, IV. 161– .

9 Sept. COMMINES, 'Paris-Revue. Le nom de Balzac', *La Renaissance politique et littéraire*.

10 Sept. CHANTAVOINE, Henri, 'Le Roman français au XIXe siècle', *Le Correspondant*, CC. 945–9.

14 Sept. HALLAYS, André, 'Pèlerinages balzaciens', *Le Journal des débats*. repr. *En flânant* (Perrin, 1912), V. 33–47.

15 Nov. MÉRÉ, Charles, 'Le Classicisme de Balzac', *La Nouvelle Revue*, XXIV. 295–306.

Bibliography of secondary sources

This appendix gives the full details of all works referred to in the footnotes and not included in Appendices II and III.

AUSTIN, L. J., *Paul Bourget, sa vie et son œuvre jusqu'en 1889* (Paris, Droz, 1940).

BALDICK, R., *The Life and Times of Frédérick-Lemaître* (London, History Book Club, 1956).

BARBÉRIS, P., *Aux Sources de Balzac* (Paris, Aux Bibliophiles de l'originale, 1965).

——, 'L'Accueil critique aux premières grandes œuvres de Balzac', *AB* (1967), 51–72, and (1968), 165–95.

——, *Balzac, une mythologie réaliste* (Paris, Larousse, 1971).

BELLET, R., *Presse et journalisme sous le Second Empire* (Paris, Kiosque, 1967).

BELLOS, D., 'Du nouveau sur Balzac, écrivain révolutionnaire', *AB* (1969), 282–91.

——, 'The *Bibliographie de la France* and its sources', *The Library*, XXVIII (1973), 64–7.

——, 'French Printing Statistics in the XIXth century', *Proceedings of the VIIth Congress of the International Comparative Literature Association* (forthcoming).

——, 'Barbey d'Aurevilly et les *Pensées* de Balzac', *Cahiers Barbey d'Aurevilly* (forthcoming).

BILLY, A., *Sainte-Beuve, sa vie et son temps* (Paris, Flammarion, 1952).

——, 'Balzac, sa sœur et Sainte-Beuve', *Le Figaro littéraire*, 29 June 1950.

BLANCHARD, M., *Témoignages et jugements sur Balzac* (Paris, Champion, 1931).

BOOTH, C. Wayne, *The Rhetoric of Fiction* (Chicago, University Press, 1961).

BORY, J.-L., *Eugène Sue, roi du roman populaire* (Paris, Hachette, 1962).

BOURGET, P., 'Notes sur Balzac', *Minerva*, 15 Nov. 1902.

——, *Nouvelles Pages de critique et de doctrine* (Paris, Plon-Nourrit, 1922).

CABANIS, J., 'Balzac, Taine et la critique', *Le Figaro littéraire*, 7 Oct. 1965.

CARTER, A. E., *The Idea of Decadence in French Literature, 1830–1900* (Toronto, University Press, 1958).

——, *Baudelaire et la critique française, 1868–1917* (Columbia, University Press, 1963).

CASTEX, P.-G., 'Balzac et Baudelaire', *RSH* (1958), 139– .

——, 'Introduction', in H. de Balzac, *Eugénie Grandet* (Paris, Garnier, 1965).

CLARK, J., *La Pensée de Ferdinand Brunetière* (Paris, Nizet, 1954).

COURVILLE, G., 'A propos des *Maximes et Pensées* de Balzac', *Études balzaciennes*, VII (1959), 263–75.

CROUZET, M., *Un Méconnu du réalisme: Duranty* (Paris, Nizet, 1954).

CURTIUS, E.-R., *Balzac* (Paris, Grasset, 1933).

DÉLAISSEMENT, G., *Maupassant journaliste et chroniqueur* (Paris, Albin Michel, 1956).

DÎMIER, Louis, *Les Maîtres de la contre-révolution au XIXe* (Paris, Saint-Pères, 1907).

DONNARD, J.-H., *Les Réalités économiques et sociales dans la Comédie humaine* (Paris, A. Colin, 1961).

DUMESNIL, R., *Le Réalisme et le naturalisme* (Paris, Del Duca, 1965).

ESCARPIT, R., *Sociology of Literature* (London, Routledge, 1971).

——, *Le Littéraire et le social. Éléments pour une sociologie de la littérature* (Paris, Flammarion, 1970).

FAGUET, E., *Balzac* (Paris, Hachette, 1913).

FARGEAUD, M., 'Dans le sillage des grands Romantiques. S.-H. Berthoud', *AB* (1962), 213–43.

FAYOLLE, R., *La Critique littéraire* (Paris, A. Colin, 1964).

——, 'Défense de la socio-critique', *Le Monde*, 18 Sept. 1970.

——, *Sainte-Beuve et le XVIIIe siècle, ou comment les révolutions arrivent* (Paris, A. Colin, 1972).

FISCHER, E.-W., *Études sur Flaubert inédit* (Leipzig, J. Zeitler, 1908).

FORD, G. H., *Dickens and his readers, Aspects of novel-criticism since 1836* (New York, Norton, 1965).

FRYE, Northrop, *Anatomy of Criticism* (Princeton, University Press, 1957).

GEFFROY, G., 'Émile Zola', *International Quarterly*, New York, VI (1902), 370–1.

GEORGE, A. J., *Books by Balzac* (Chicago, Syracuse University Press, 1960).

GILLE, G., *Jules Vallès, 1832–1885* (Paris, Flammarion, 1941).

GRÉARD, O., *Prévost-Paradol* (Paris, Hachette, 1894).

GUISE, R., 'Un Grand Homme du roman à la scène, ou les illusions reparaissantes de Balzac', *AB* (1966), 171–216, (1967), 177–214, (1968), 337–68, and (1969), 247–80.

HATIN, E., *Bibliographie historique et critique de la presse périodique française* (Paris, F. Didot, 1866).

HEMMINGS, F. W. J., *Émile Zola*, 2nd edition (Oxford, Clarendon Press, 1970).

HERMANT, A., *Discours* (Paris, Ollendorff, 1903).

D'HEYLLI, G., *Dictionnaire des pseudonymes* (Paris, Dentu, 1889).

HUNT, H. J., *Le Socialisme et le romantisme en France* (Oxford, Clarendon Press, 1935).

HYTIER, J., 'Balzac et Sainte-Beuve', *Estudios franceses*, Mendoza, Argentina, VI (1950), 47–68.

IKNAYAN, M., *The Idea of the Novel in France. The Critical Reaction, 1815–1848* (Geneva, Droz, 1961).

JACKSON, J. F., 'Balzac and Sainte-Beuve', *PMLA*, XLV (1930), 918–38.

JOSZ, V., 'La Statue de Balzac', *L'Européen*, 25 Oct. 1902.

KANES, M., *L'Atelier de Zola* (Geneva, Droz, 1963).

——, 'Balzac, Zola, et la *Fortune des Rogron*', *French Studies*, XVIII (1964), 203— .

LAPP, J. C., 'Taine et Zola: autour d'une correspondance', *RSH* (1957), 319–26.

LE BRETON, A., *Balzac, l'homme et l'œuvre* (Paris, A. Colin, 1905).

LEVALLOIS, J., *Mémoires d'un critique* (Paris, Librairie illustrée, 1894).

LEVIN, A., *The Legacy of Philarète Chasles* (North Carolina, University Press, 1957).

LORANT, A., 'La Maison infortunée', *AB* (1961), 73–96.

——, *Les Parents pauvres. Étude historique et critique* (Geneva, Droz, 1967).

MAILLARD, F., *Histoire anecdotique et critique des 159 journaux parus en l'an de grâce 1856* (Paris, chez l'auteur, 1857).

MARTINO, P., *Le Roman réaliste sous le Second Empire* (Paris, Hachette, 1913).

MARX, K., and ENGELS, F., *Über Kunst und Literatur* (Berlin, Bruno Henschel Verlag, 1950).

MAUPASSANT, G. de, *Chroniques, études, correspondance*, ed. R. Dumesnil (Paris, Gründ, 1938).

MAUROIS, A., *Prométhée ou la vie de Balzac* (Paris, Hachette, 1965).

MÉLIA, J., *Stendhal et ses commentateurs* (Paris, Mercure de France, 1911).

MILATCHITCH, D., *Le Théâtre de Honoré de Balzac* (Paris, Hachette, 1930).

MITTERAND, H., and SUWALA, H., *Émile Zola journaliste. Bibliographie . . . 1859–81*, *ALUB*. LXXXIX (Paris, Les Belles Lettres, 1968).

MOREAU, P., *La Critique selon Sainte-Beuve* (Paris, S.E.D.E.S., 1964).

PETIT, J., and YARROW, P. J., *Barbey d'Aurevilly journaliste et critique. Bibliographie, ALUB*, XXVIII (Paris, Les Belles Lettres, 1959).

PICHOIS, C., ed. Charles Baudelaire, *La Fanfarlo* (Monaco, Éditions du Rocher, 1957).

——, *Philarète Chasles et la vie littéraire au temps du romantisme* (Paris, José Corti, 1965).

PICON, G., *Balzac par lui-même* (Paris, Le Seuil, 1956).

POMMIER, J., 'Balzac, écrivain révolutionnaire', *AB* (1967), 247–58.

PROUST, M., *Pastiches et mélanges* (Paris, N.R.F., 1921).

RAIMOND, M., *La Crise du roman du lendemain du naturalisme aux années vingt* (Paris, José Corti, 1967).

——, *Balzac vu par les romanciers français de Zola à Proust*, unpublished thesis (1966), Sorbonne Library, Paris.

ROBERT, G., 'Trois Textes inédits de Zola', *RSH* (1948), 181–207.

——, 'Le Réalisme devant la critique littéraire, 1851–61', *RSH* (1953), 5–26.

ROD, É., 'Honoré de Balzac', *La Revue latine*, 25 May 1906.

ROYCE, W. H., *A Balzac Bibliography* (Chicago, University Press, 1929).

SAINTE-BEUVE, Charles-Augustin, *Cahiers*, ed. R. Molho (Paris, Gallimard, 1973).

SAINT-GAYRAC, 'Les Deux Balzac', *La Vérité française*, 21 Feb. 1901.

SEALY, R. J., 'Montégut, Brunetière—and George Eliot', *MLR*, Jan. 1971.

TALMEYR, M., *Souvenirs de la Comédie humaine* (Paris, Perrin, 1927).

TOLLEY, B. R., *The Social role of art and literature according to the Saint-Simonians*, 1825–33, unpublished thesis (1967), Bodleian Library, Oxford.

TROUBAT, J., *Sainte-Beuve et Champfleury* (Paris, Mercure de France, 1908).

VIAL, André, 'Flaubert, émule et disciple émancipé de Balzac. *L'Éducation sentimentale*', *RHLF* XLVIII (1948), 233–63.

WEINBERG, B., *French Realism: the critical reaction 1830–1870* (New York and London, O.U.P., 1937).

WELLEK, R., *History of Western Criticism* (London, Cape, 1966), IV.

——, and WARREN, A., *Theory of Literature* (London, Penguin, 1963).

'Mme X', 'Guy de Maupassant intime. Notes d'une amie', *La Grande Revue*, 25 Oct. 1912.

ZELDIN, Theodore, *France, 1848–1945. Love, ambition, politics* (Oxford, Clarendon Press, 1973).

Subject Index

Bold numerals refer to principal passages.

Index of Names

Titles of works are given in *italics*; names of fictional characters in lower case; and names of historical persons in CAPITALS. **Bold** numerals refer to principal passages, and *italic* numerals to entries in the bibliographies.

DATE DUE